SECURWARE 2019

The Thirteenth International Conference on Emerging Security Information, Systems and Technologies

October 27 - 31, 2019

Nice, France

SECURWARE 2019 Editors

Stefan Rass, Universitaet Klagenfurt, Austria
George Yee, Carleton University, Canada

Printed from e-media with permission by:

Curran Associates, Inc.
57 Morehouse Lane
Red Hook, NY 12571

Some format issues inherent in the e-media version may also appear in this print version.

Printed with permission by Curran Associates, Inc. (2020)

International Academy, Research, and Industry Association (IARIA)
412 Derby Way
Wilmington, DE 19810

Phone: (408) 893-6407
Fax: (408) 527-6351

petre@iaria.org

Additional copies of this publication are available from:

Curran Associates, Inc.
57 Morehouse Lane
Red Hook, NY 12571 USA
Phone: 845-758-0400
Fax: 845-758-2633
Email: curran@proceedings.com
Web: www.proceedings.com

Table of Contents

SECURWARE 2019

Forward

The Thirteenth International Conference on Emerging Security Information, Systems and Technologies (SECURWARE 2019), held between October 27, 2019 and October 31, 2019 in Nice, France, continued a series of events covering related topics on theory and practice on security, cryptography, secure protocols, trust, privacy, confidentiality, vulnerability, intrusion detection and other areas related to low enforcement, security data mining, malware models, etc.

Security, defined for ensuring protected communication among terminals and user applications across public and private networks, is the core for guaranteeing confidentiality, privacy, and data protection. Security affects business and individuals, raises the business risk, and requires a corporate and individual culture. In the open business space offered by Internet, it is a need to improve defenses against hackers, disgruntled employees, and commercial rivals. There is a required balance between the effort and resources spent on security versus security achievements. Some vulnerability can be addressed using the rule of 80:20, meaning 80% of the vulnerabilities can be addressed for 20% of the costs. Other technical aspects are related to the communication speed versus complex and time consuming cryptography/security mechanisms and protocols.

Digital Ecosystem is defined as an open decentralized information infrastructure where different networked agents, such as enterprises (especially SMEs), intermediate actors, public bodies and end users, cooperate and compete enabling the creation of new complex structures. In digital ecosystems, the actors, their products and services can be seen as different organisms and species that are able to evolve and adapt dynamically to changing market conditions.

Digital Ecosystems lie at the intersection between different disciplines and fields: industry, business, social sciences, biology, and cutting edge ICT and its application driven research. They are supported by several underlying technologies such as semantic web and ontology-based knowledge sharing, self-organizing intelligent agents, peer-to-peer overlay networks, web services-based information platforms, and recommender systems.

To enable safe digital ecosystem functioning, security and trust mechanisms become essential components across all the technological layers. The aim is to bring together multidisciplinary research that ranges from technical aspects to socio-economic models.

We take here the opportunity to warmly thank all the members of the SECURWARE 2019 technical program committee, as well as all the reviewers. The creation of such a high quality conference program would not have been possible without their involvement. We also kindly thank all the authors who dedicated much of their time and effort to contribute to SECURWARE 2019. We truly believe that, thanks to all these efforts, the final conference program consisted of top quality contributions.

We also thank the members of the SECURWARE 2019 organizing committee for their help in handling the logistics and for their work that made this professional meeting a success.

We hope that SECURWARE 2019 was a successful international forum for the exchange of ideas and results between academia and industry and to promote further progress in the area of security information, systems and technologies. We also hope that Nice, France provided a pleasant environment during the conference and everyone saved some time to enjoy the charm of the city.

SECURWARE 2019 Chairs

SECURWARE Steering Committee

Yuichi Sei, The University of Electro-Communications, Japan
Carla Merkle Westphall, Federal University of Santa Catarina, Brazil
Hans-Joachim Hof, Technical University of Ingolstadt, Germany
Eric Renault, Institut Mines-Télécom - Télécom SudParis, France
Steffen Wendzel, Worms University of Applied Sciences, Germany
Aspen Olmsted, College of Charleston, USA
Calin Vladeanu, University Politehnica of Bucharest, Romania
George Yee, Carleton University & Aptusinnova Inc., Ottawa, Canada
Sokratis K. Katsikas, Norwegian University of Science & Technology (NTNU), Norway
Hector Marco Gisbert, University of the West of Scotland, United Kingdom

SECURWARE Research/Industry Chairs

Rainer Falk, Siemens AG, Germany
Mariusz Jakubowski, Microsoft Research, USA
Malek ben Salem, Accenture Labs, USA
Jiqiang Lu, Institute for Infocomm Research, Singapore
Heiko Roßnagel, Fraunhofer IAO, Germany
Scott Trent, Tokyo Software Development Laboratory - IBM, Japan
Robert Forster, Edgemount Solutions S.à r.l., Luxembourg
Peter Kieseberg, SBA Research, Austria
Tzachy Reinman, Cisco, Israel

SECURWARE 2019
Committee

SECURWARE Steering Committee

Yuichi Sei, The University of Electro-Communications, Japan
Carla Merkle Westphall, Federal University of Santa Catarina, Brazil
Hans-Joachim Hof, Technical University of Ingolstadt, Germany
Eric Renault, Institut Mines-Télécom - Télécom SudParis, France
Steffen Wendzel, Worms University of Applied Sciences, Germany
Aspen Olmsted, College of Charleston, USA
Calin Vladeanu, University Politehnica of Bucharest, Romania
George Yee, Carleton University & Aptusinnova Inc., Ottawa, Canada
Sokratis K. Katsikas, Norwegian University of Science & Technology (NTNU), Norway
Hector Marco Gisbert, University of the West of Scotland, United Kingdom

SECURWARE Research/Industry Chairs

Rainer Falk, Siemens AG, Germany
Mariusz Jakubowski, Microsoft Research, USA
Malek ben Salem, Accenture Labs, USA
Jiqiang Lu, Institute for Infocomm Research, Singapore
Heiko Roßnagel, Fraunhofer IAO, Germany
Scott Trent, Tokyo Software Development Laboratory - IBM, Japan
Robert Forster, Edgemount Solutions S.à r.l., Luxembourg
Peter Kieseberg, SBA Research, Austria
Tzachy Reinman, Cisco, Israel

SECURWARE 2019 Technical Program Committee

Nabil Abdoun, Université de Nantes, France
Habtamu Abie, Norwegian Computing Centre, Norway
Afrand Agah, West Chester University of Pennsylvania, USA
Rose-Mharie Åhlfeldt, University of Skövde, Sweden
Jose M. Alcaraz Calero, University of the West of Scotland, UK
Firkhan Ali Bin Hamid Ali, Universiti Tun Hussein Onn Malaysia, Malaysia
Basel Alomair, University of Washington-Seattle, USA / King Abdulaziz City for Science and Technology (KACST), Saudi Arabia
Eric Amankwa, Presbyterian University College, Ghana
Louise Axon, University of Oxford, UK
Ilija Basicevic, University of Novi Sad, Serbia
Carlos Becker Westphall, Federal University of Santa Catarina, Brazil
Francisco J. Bellido, University of Cordoba, Spain
Cătălin Bîrjoveanu, "Al.I.Cuza" University of Iasi, Romania
Wided Boubakri, ESSECT, Tunisia
Arslan Brömme, Vattenfall GmbH, Germany
Francesco Buccafurri, University Mediterranea of Reggio Calabria, Italy

Krzysztof Cabaj, Warsaw University of Technology, Poland
Cándido Caballero-Gil, University of La Laguna, Spain
Luca Calderoni, University of Bologna, Italy
Paolo Campegiani, Bit4id, Italy
Juan-Vicente Capella-Hernández, Universitat Politècnica de València, Spain
Aldar Chan, University of Hong Kong, Hong Kong
Tan Saw Chin, Multimedia University, Malaysia
Te-Shun Chou, East Carolina University, USA
Marijke Coetzee, Academy of Computer Science and Software Engineering | University of Johannesburg, South Africa
Gianpiero Costantino, Istituto di Informatica e Telematica | Consiglio Nazionale delle Ricerche, Pisa, Italy
Jun Dai, California State University, USA
Roberto Carbone, Security and Trust Research Unit - Fondazione Bruno Kessler, Italy
Jörg Daubert, Technische Universität Darmstadt, Germany
Ruairí de Fréin, Dublin Institute of Technology, Ireland
P.P. Deepthi, National Institute of Technology Calicut, Kerala, India
Michele Di Lecce, iInformatica S.r.l.s., Matera, Italy
Josep Domingo Ferrer, Universitat Rovira i Virgili, Spain
Changyu Dong, Newcastle University, UK
Safwan El Assad, University of Nantes/Polytech Nantes, France
Tewfiq El Maliki, University of Applied Sciences Geneva, Switzerland
Navid Emamdoost, University of Minnesota, USA
Rainer Falk, Siemens AG, Germany
Eduardo B. Fernandez, Florida Atlantic University, USA
Daniel Fischer, Technische Universität Ilmenau, Germany
Robert Forster, Edgemount Solutions S.à r.l., Luxembourg
Steven Furnell, University of Plymouth, UK
Amparo Fuster-Sabater, Institute of Physical and Information Technologies -CSIC, Madrid, Spain
François Gagnon, Cégep Sainte-Foy, Canada
Clemente Galdi, University of Napoli "Federico II", Italy
Michael Goldsmith, University of Oxford, UK
Stefanos Gritzalis, University of the Aegean, Greece
Vincent Grosso, CNRS/Université de Saint-Etienne, France
Bidyut Gupta, Southern Illinois University Carbondale, USA
Faisal Hameed, University of Oxford, UK
Jinguang Han, Nanjing University of Finance and Economics, China
Petr Hanáček, Brno University of Technology, Czech Republic
Daniel Harkins, Hewlett-Packard Enterprise, USA
Ragib Hasan, University of Alabama at Birmingham, USA
Dominik Herrmann, University of Bamberg, Germany
Hans-Joachim Hof, Technical University of Ingolstadt, Germany
Fu-Hau Hsu, National Central University, Taiwan
Abdullah Abu Hussein, St. Cloud State University, USA
Sergio Ilarri, University of Zaragoza, Spain
Roberto Interdonato, Uppsala University, Sweden
Vincenzo Iovino, University of Luxembourg, Luxembourg
Mariusz Jakubowski, Microsoft Research, USA
P. Prasad M. Jayaweera, University of Sri Jayewardenepura, Sri Lanka

Copyright Information

On the Compositionality of Dynamic Leakage and Its Application to the Quantification Problem

Bao Trung Chu, Kenji Hashimoto, Hiroyuki Seki
Nagoya University, Japan
Email: trungchubao@sqlab.jp, {k-hasimt, seki}@i.nagoya-u.ac.jp

***Abstract*—Quantitative Information Flow (QIF), as summed up by Smith (2019), is traditionally defined as the expected value of information leakage over all feasible program runs. The traditional QIF fails to identify vulnerable programs where only a limited number of runs leak large amount of information. As discussed in Bielova (2016), a good notion for dynamic leakage and an efficient way of computing the leakage are needed. To address this problem, the authors have already proposed two notions for dynamic leakage and a method of quantifying dynamic leakage based on model counting. Inspired by the work of Kawamoto et al. (2017), this paper proposes two efficient methods for computing dynamic leakage, a compositional method along with the sequential structure of a program and a parallel computation based on the disjoint value domain decomposition. For the former, we investigate both exact and approximated calculations. For implementation, we utilize Binary Decision Diagrams (BDDs) and deterministic Decomposable Negation Normal Forms (d-DNNFs) to represent Boolean formulas in model counting. Finally, we show experimental results on several examples.**

Keywords–Dynamic leakage; Composition; Quantitative Information Flow; BDD; d-DNNF.

I. Introduction

Since first coined by [15] in 1982, the noninterference property has become one of the main criteria for software security [1][5]. A program is said to satisfy noninterference if any change in confidential information does not affect a publicly observable output of that program. However, noninterference is so strict that it blocks many useful, yet practically safe systems and protocols, such as password checkers, anonymous voting protocols, recommendation systems and so forth. Quantitative Information Flow (QIF) was introduced to loosen the security criterion in the sense that, instead of seeking *if there is* a case that a confidential input affects a public output, computing *how large* that effect is. That is, if the QIF of a program is insignificant, the program is still judged as secure. Because of its flexibility, QIF has gained much attention in recent years. However, it has an inherent shortcoming, as shown in the example below.

Example 1.1: Consider the following program taken from [10].

if $source < 16$ then $output \leftarrow 8 + source$
else $output \leftarrow 8$

Assume $source$ to be a non-negative 32-bits integer which is uniformly distributed on that domain. Then, there are 16 possible values of $output$, ranging from 8 to 23. Observing any number between 9 and 23 as an output reveals everything about the confidential $source$, whilst observing 8 leaks small information; there are many possible values of $source$ $(0, 16, 17, 18, \ldots, 2^{32}-1)$, which produce 8 as the output. QIF is defined as the average of the leakage over all possible cases. So, it fails to capture the above situation because we cannot distinguish *vulnerable* and *secure* cases if we take the average. Hence, as argued in [4], a notion for dynamic leakage should reflect individual leakage caused by observing an output.

As illustrated in Figure 1, there are two different scenarios of quantifying dynamic leakage. We call the first scenario, which corresponds to diagram (A), ***Compute-on-Demand*** (*CoD*), and the second, which corresponds to diagram (B), ***Construct-in-Advance*** (*CiA*). A box surrounded by bold lines represents a heavy-weighted process, which requires extensive computing resources. The main difference between (A) and (B) is the relative position of the heavy-weighted process, i.e., in (A), the process is put after augmenting an observed output and then the process is run each time we need (on demand) to compute dynamic leakage, or, in (B) the process is put before augmenting an observed output (in advance) so that we run the process only once for one program. In *CoD*, the heavy-weighted process is a projected model counting, for which off-the-shelf tools, such as SharpCDCL [32], DSharp-p [27] and GPMC [28] can be used. In *CiA*, the heavy-weighted process is the one that generates BDD [22] or d-DNNF [13], which are data structures to represent Boolean formulas given in Conjunctive Normal Form (CNF). Generally, it takes time to generate BDD or d-DNNF but counting all solutions (models) by using them is easy. *CiA* takes full advantage of this characteristic. Consider again Example 1.1 above. The set of all feasible pairs of ($source$, $output$) is 2^{32}. Even for such a simple program, using BDD or d-DNNF to store all those pairs is quite daunting in terms of both memory space and speed. Therefore, for programs with simple structure but a large number of input and output pairs, *CoD* works better than *CiA*. On the other hand, *CiA* is preferable to *CoD* when quantifying dynamic leakage is required many times on the same program. However, *CoD* or *CiA* alone is not a solution to the problem of scalability.

In this paper, we introduce two compositional methods for computing dynamic leakage inspired by the work of Kawamoto et al. [16] on the compositionality of static leakage. One method is to utilize the sequential structure of a given program $P = P_1; P_2$. We first analyze P_2 and then compute the leakage of P by analyzing P_1 based on the result on P_2. For the sequential composition, besides the benign yet time-consuming exact counting based on Breadth-First-Search (BFS), we also investigate an approximated approach. For an upper bound of the count, we leverage the results on each sub-program by Max#SAT in [14]. For a lower bound of the count, we simply use Depth-First-Search (DFS) with timeout, i.e., DFS will stop when the execution time exceeds the predetermined timeout.

The other method we propose is based on the decomposi-

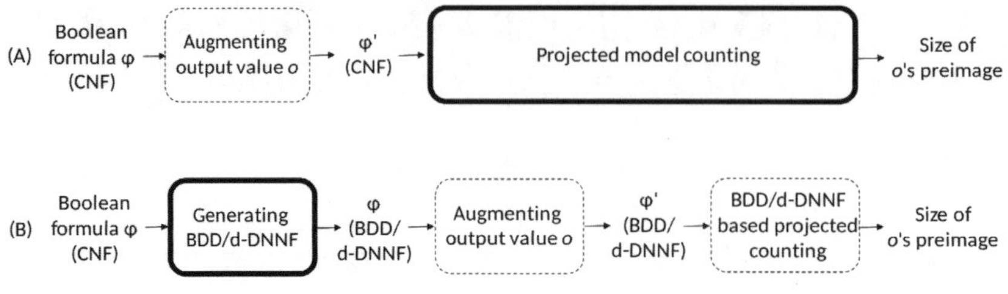

Figure 1. (A): Compute-on-Demand, (B): Construct-in-Advance.

tion of the value domain of a program. For example, we divide the input domain as $I = I_1 \cup I_2$ and the output domain as $O = O_1 \cup O_2$ of a program $P(I, O)$, compute the leakages of $P(I_i, O_j)$ for $i = 1, 2$ and $j = 1, 2$, then use them to compute the leakage of the whole program $P(I, O)$. This value domain based decomposition has two merits. First, it is flexible yet simple to adjust the components. Secondly, the exact dynamic leakage of the composed program can be simply derived by taking the sum of those of its components. Despite the fact that the number of components can be large, this approach is promising with parallel computing.

In summary, the contributions of this research are four-fold:

- We propose a compositional method for dynamic leakage computation based on the sequential structure inside a given program and the composability of the leakage of the whole program from those of subprograms.
- We propose another compositional method based on value domains, which is suitable for parallel computing.
- We propose an approximated approach where we upper bound the count using Max#SAT problem and lower bound the count by DFS with predetermined timeout.
- We prototype a tool that can do parallel computation based on value domain decomposition and both exact counting and approximated counting for the sequential composition. By using the tool, we investigate feasibility and advantages of the proposed compositional methods for computing dynamic leakage of several examples. The tool can be accessed freely via [26]. We also consider to develop a more capable open source analyzer based on this prototype in the future.

Related work *Definitions of QIF:* Smith [21] gives a comprehensive summary on entropy-based QIF, such as Shannon entropy, guessing entropy and min entropy and compares them in various scenarios. Clarkson et al. [11], on the other hand, include the attacker's belief into their model. Alvim et al. [3] introduce a gain function to generalize information leakage by separating the probability distribution and the impact of individual information. *Computational Complexity:* Yasuoka and Terauchi [24] prove complexity on computing QIF, including PP-hardness of precisely quantifying QIF for loop-free Boolean programs. Chadha and Ummels [8] show that the QIF bounding problem of recursive Boolean programs is EXPTIME-complete. *Precise Calculation:* In [17], Klebanov et al. reduce the QIF calculation to #SAT problem projected on a specific set of variables. On the other hand, Phan et al. [20] reduce the QIF calculation to #SMT problem to leverage existing Satisfiability Modulo Theory (SMT) solvers. Recently, Val et al. [23] reported a SAT-based method that can scale to programs of 10,000 lines of code. *Approximated Calculation:* Approximation is a reasonable alternative for scalability. Köpf and Rybalchenko [18] propose approximated QIF computation by sandwiching the precise QIF with lower and upper bounds using randomization and abstraction, respectively, with a provable confidence. LeakWatch, by Chothia et al. [9], also gives an approximation with provable confidence by executing a program multiple times. Its descendant, called HyLeak [7], combines the randomization strategy of its ancestor with precise analysis. Biondi et al. [6] utilize ApproxMC2, which provides approximation on the number of models of a Boolean formula in CNF by Markov Chain Monte Carlo method. *Composition of QIF:* Another attempt to the scalability is to break the system down into smaller fragments. In [16], Kawamoto et al. introduce two parallel compositions: with distinct inputs and with shared inputs, and give theoretical bounds on the leakage of the main program using those of the constituted sub-programs. Though our research was motivated by [16], we focus on a sequential structure of a target program and a decomposition of the value domain of the program while [16] uses a parallel structure of the target. *Dynamic Leakage:* Bielova [4] discusses the importance of dynamic leakage and argues that any well-known QIF notion is not appropriate as a notion for dynamic leakage. Recently, we proposed two notions for dynamic leakage, QIF_1 and QIF_2 and gave some results on computational complexity, as well as a quantifying method based on model counting [10].

The rest of the paper is organized as follows. We review the definition of dynamic leakage and describe our program model in Section 2. Section 3 is dedicated to a method for computing dynamic leakage based on the sequential composition and also proposes approximation methods. Section 4 proposes a parallel computation method based on value domain decomposition. Section 5 evaluates the proposed compositional methods including the comparison of *CiA* vs. *CoD* and exact vs. approximated computation based on the experimental results. Then, the paper is concluded in Section 6.

II. Preliminaries

A. Dynamic leakage

The standard notion for static QIF is defined as the mutual information between random variables S for secret input and O for observable output:

$$\text{QIF} = H(S) - H(S|O) \tag{1}$$

where $H(S)$ is the entropy of S and $H(S|O)$ is the expected value of $H(S|o)$, i.e., $H(S|O) = \sum_{o \in \mathcal{O}} p(o) H(S|o)$, and

$H(S|o)$ is the conditional entropy of S when observing an output o. Shannon entropy and min-entropy are often used as the definition of entropy, and in either case, $H(S) - H(S|O) \geq 0$ always holds by definition.

In [4], the author discusses the appropriateness of the existing measures for dynamic QIF and points out their drawbacks, especially, each of these measures may become negative. For example, if we adopt $H(S) - H(S|o)$ as a measure of dynamic QIF, the measure may become negative depending on an observed output value o.

Let P be a program with secret input variable S and observable output variable O. For notational convenience, we identify the names of program variables with the corresponding random variables. Throughout the paper, we assume that a program always terminates. The syntax and semantics of programs assumed in this paper will be given in the next section. Hereafter, let $\mathcal{S}$ and $\mathcal{O}$ denote the finite sets of input values and output values, respectively. For $s \in \mathcal{S}$ and $o \in \mathcal{O}$, let $p_{SO}(s, o)$, $p_{O|S}(o|s)$, $p_{S|O}(s|o)$, $p_S(s)$, $p_O(o)$ denote the joint probability of $s \in \mathcal{S}$ and $o \in \mathcal{O}$, the conditional probability of $o \in \mathcal{O}$ given $s \in \mathcal{S}$ (the likelihood), the conditional probability of $s \in \mathcal{S}$ given $o \in \mathcal{O}$ (the posterior probability), the marginal probability of $s \in \mathcal{S}$ (the prior probability) and the marginal probability of $o \in \mathcal{O}$, respectively. We often omit the subscripts as $p(s, o)$ and $p(o|s)$ if they are clear from the context. By definition, $p(s, o) = p(s|o)p(o) = p(o|s)p(s)$, $p(o) = \sum_{s \in \mathcal{S}} p(s, o)$, $p(s) = \sum_{o \in \mathcal{O}} p(s, o)$.

We assume that (the source code of) P and the prior probability $p(s)$ ($s \in \mathcal{S}$) are known to an attacker. For $o \in \mathcal{O}$, let $\text{pre}_P(o) = \{s \in \mathcal{S} \mid p(s|o) > 0\}$, which is called the preimage of o (by the program P).

Considering the discussions in the literature, we define new notions for dynamic QIF that satisfy the following requirements [10]:

(R1) Dynamic QIF should always be non-negative because an attacker obtains some information (although sometimes very small or even zero) when he observes an output of the program.

(R2) It is desirable that dynamic QIF is independent of a secret input $s \in \mathcal{S}$. Otherwise, the controller of the system may change the behavior for protection based on the estimated amount of the leakage that depends on s, which may be a side channel for an attacker.

(R3) The new notion should be compatible with the existing notions when we restrict ourselves to special cases, such as deterministic programs, uniformly distributed inputs, and taking the expected value.

The first notion is the self-information of the secret inputs consistent with an observed output $o \in \mathcal{O}$. Equivalently, the attacker can narrow down the possible secret inputs after observing o to the preimage of o by the program. We consider the self-information of $s \in \mathcal{S}$ after the observation as the logarithm of the probability of s divided by the sum of the probabilities of the inputs in the preimage of o (see the upper part of Figure 2, where bold lines indicate the mapping between $\mathcal{S}$ and $\mathcal{O}$ that are taken into consideration when defining $\text{QIF}_1/\text{QIF}_2$).

$$\text{QIF}_1^P(o) = -\log\Big(\sum_{s' \in \text{pre}_P(o)} p(s')\Big). \tag{2}$$

The second notion is the self-information of the joint events $s' \in \mathcal{S}$ and an observed output $o \in \mathcal{O}$ (see the lower part of Figure 2). This is equal to the self-information of o.

$$\begin{aligned}\text{QIF}_2^P(o) &= -\log\Big(\sum_{s' \in \mathcal{S}} p(s', o)\Big) = -\log p(o) \\ &= -\log p(s, o) + \log p(s|o).\end{aligned} \tag{3}$$

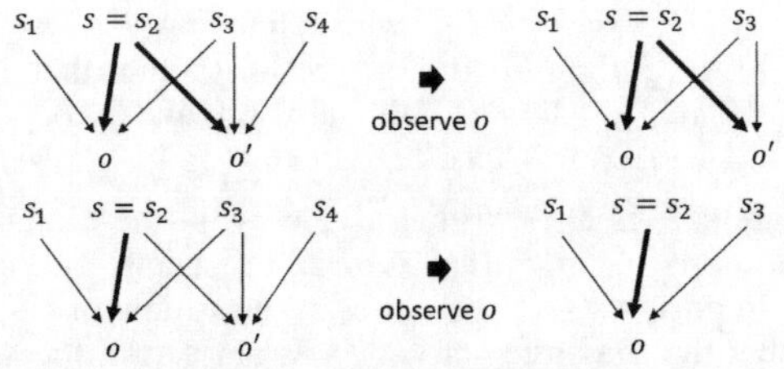

Figure 2. QIF_1 (the upper) and QIF_2 (the lower)

Both notions are defined by considering how much self-information values are reduced by observing an output. We propose these two notions because there is a trade-off between the easiness of calculation and the appropriateness [10].

Theorem 2.1 ([10]): If a program P is deterministic, for every $o \in \mathcal{O}$ and $s \in \mathcal{S}$,

$$\text{QIF}_1^P(o) = \text{QIF}_2^P(o) = -\log p(o).$$

If input values are uniformly distributed, $\text{QIF}_1^P(o) = \log \frac{|\mathcal{S}|}{|\text{pre}_P(o)|}$ for every $o \in \mathcal{O}$. □

B. Program model

We assume probabilistic programs where every variable stores a natural number and the syntactical constructs are assignment statement, conditional statement, probabilistic choice, while loop and concatenation:

$$\begin{aligned} b &::= \bot \mid \top \mid \neg b \mid b \vee b \mid e < e \\ e &::= X \mid n \mid e + e \\ c &::= \text{skip} \mid X \leftarrow e \mid \text{if } b \text{ then } c \text{ else } c \text{ end} \\ &\quad\ \mid c\ {}_r[]_{1-r}\ c \mid \text{while } b \text{ do } c \text{ end} \mid c; c \end{aligned}$$

where $<, X, n, +$ stand for a binary relation on natural numbers, a program variable, a constant natural number and a binary operation on natural numbers, respectively, and r is a constant rational number representing the branching probability for a choice command where $0 \leq r \leq 1$. In the above BNFs, objects derived from the syntactical categories b, e and c are called conditions, expressions and commands, respectively. A command $X \leftarrow e$ assigns the value of expression e to variable X. A command $c_1\ {}_r[]_{1-r}\ c_2$ means that the program chooses c_1 with probability r and c_2 with probability $1 - r$. Note that this is the only probabilistic command. The semantics of the other constructs are defined in the usual way.

A program P has the following syntax:

$$P \ ::= \ \text{in } \vec{S};\ \text{out } \vec{O};\ \text{local } \vec{Z}; c \mid P; P$$

where $\vec{S}, \vec{O}, \vec{Z}$ are sequences of variables which are disjoint from one another. A program is required to satisfy the following constraints on variables. We first define $In(P), Out(P), Local(P)$ for a program P as follows.

- If $P = \text{in } \vec{S}; \text{ out } \vec{O}; \text{ local } \vec{Z}; c$, we define $In(P) = \{V \mid V \text{ appears in } \vec{S}\}$, $Out(P) = \{V \mid V \text{ appears in } \vec{O}\}$ and $Local(P) = \{V \mid V \text{ appears in } \vec{Z}\}$. In this case, we say P is a simple program. We require that no varible in $In(P)$ appears on the left-hand side of an assignment command in P, i.e., no input variable is updated.
- If $P = P_1; P_2$, we define $In(P) = In(P_1)$, $Out(P) = Out(P_2)$ where we require that $In(P_2) = Out(P_1)$ holds. We also define $Local(P) = Local(P_1) \cup Local(P_2) \cup Out(P_1)$.

A program P is also written as $P(S, O)$ where S and O are enumerations of $In(P)$ and $Out(P)$, respectively. A program $P_1; P_2$ represents the sequential composition of P_1 and P_2. Note that the semantics of $P_1; P_2$ is defined in the same way as that of the concatenation of commands $c_1; c_2$ except that the input and output variables are not always shared by P_1 and P_2 in the sequential composition. If a program does not have a probabilistic choice, it is *deterministic*.

III. SEQUENTIAL COMPOSITION

This section proposes a method of computing both exact and approximated dynamic leakage by using sequential composition. For making the idea behind the proposed method understandable, we first assume the programs under analysis are deterministic with uniformly distributed input, so that the problem of quantifying dynamic leakage is reduced to model counting. Then, in the later part of this section, we will discuss the extensibility of the proposed method to probabilistic programs with input of an arbitrary distribution.

A. Exact calculation

For a program $P(S, O)$, an input value $s \in \mathcal{S}$ and a subset $\mathcal{S}'$ of input values, let

$$\begin{aligned} \text{post}_P(s) &= \{o \mid p(o|s) > 0\}, \\ \text{post}_P(\mathcal{S}') &= \bigcup_{s \in \mathcal{S}'} \text{post}_P(s). \end{aligned}$$

If P is deterministic and $\text{post}_P(s) = \{o\}$, we write $\text{post}_P(s) = o$.

Let $P = P_1; P_2$ be a program. We assume that $In(P_1), Out(P_1), In(P_2), Out(P_2)$ are all singleton sets for simplicity. This assumption does not lose generality; for example, if $In(P_1)$ contains more than one variables, we instead introduce a new input variable that stores the tuple consisting of a value of each variable in $In(P_1)$. Let $In(P) = In(P_1) = \{S\}$, $Out(P_1) = In(P_2) = \{T\}$, $Out(P) = Out(P_2) = \{O\}$, and let $\mathcal{S}, \mathcal{T}, \mathcal{O}$ be the corresponding sets of values, respectively. For a given $o \in \mathcal{O}$, $\text{pre}_P(o)$ and $p(o)$, which are needed to compute $\text{QIF}_1^P(o)$ and $\text{QIF}_2^P(o)$ (see (2) and (3)), can be represented in terms of those of P_1 and P_2 as follows.

$$\text{pre}_P(o) = \bigcup_{t \in (\text{pre}_{P_2}(o) \cap \text{post}_{P_1}(\mathcal{S}))} \text{pre}_{P_1}(t), \quad (4)$$

$$p(o) = \sum_{s \in \mathcal{S}, t \in \mathcal{T}} p(s) p_1(t|s) p_2(o|t). \quad (5)$$

```
Pre[2..n] ← empty
Stack ← empty
level ← n
acc_count ← 0
Push(Stack, o)
Pre[n] ← EnumeratePre(P_n, o)
while not Stack.empty and execution_time < timeout do
    if level = 1 then
        acc_count ← acc_count+ CntPre(P_1, Stack.top)
        level ← level + 1
        Pop(Stack)
    else
        v ← PickNotSelected(Pre[level])
        if v = AllSelected then
            level ← level + 1
            Pop(Stack)
        else
            Push(Stack, v)
            level ← level − 1
            if level > 1 then
                Pre[level] ← EnumeratePre(P_level, v)
return acc_count
```

Figure 3. LowerBound($P_1, \cdots, P_n, o$, timeout)

If $p(s)$ is given, we can compute (4) by enumerating $\text{pre}_{P_1}(t)$ for $t \in (\text{pre}_{P_2}(o) \cap \text{post}_{P_1}(\mathcal{S}))$ and also for (5). In practice, $\text{pre}_P(o)$ is computed by augmenting the information about an observed output value to the CNF that represents P, as illustrated in the flow of *CiA* and *CoD* in Figure 1. Then, the preimage can be either enumerated or counted, up to what is needed for the calculation. This approach can easily be generalized to the sequential composition of more than two programs, in which the enumeration is proceeded in a Breadth-First-Search fashion. However, in this approach, search space will often explode rapidly and lose the advantage of composition. Therefore, we come up with an approximation, which is explained in the next subsection, as an alternative.

B. Approximation

Let us assume that $P(S, O)$ is deterministic and S is uniformly distributed. In this subsection, we will derive both upper-bound and lower-bound of $|\text{pre}_P(o)|$, which provide lower-bound and upper-bound of $\text{QIF}_1^P(o) = \text{QIF}_2^P(o)$ respectively. In general, our method can be applied to the sequential composition of more than two sub-programs.

1) Lower bound: To infer a lower bound of $|\text{pre}_P(o)|$, we leverage Depth-First-Search (DFS) with a predefined timeout such that the algorithm will stop when the execution time exceeds the timeout and output the current result as the lower bound. The method is illustrated in Figure 3. For a program $P = P_1; P_2; \cdots; P_n$, an observable output o of the last subprogram P_n and a predetermined *timeout*, the algorithm in Figure 3 derives a lower bound of $|\text{pre}_P(o)|$ by those n subprograms.

In Figure 3, *CntPre(Q, o)* counts $|\text{pre}_Q(o)|$, *PickNotSelected(Pre[i])* selects an element of $Pre[i]$ that has not been traversed yet or returns *AllSelected* if there is no such element, and *EnumeratePre(P_i, v)* lists all elements in $\text{pre}_{P_i}(v)$. $Pre[i]$ stores $\text{pre}_{P_i}(o_i)$ for some o_i. For P_1, it is not necessary to store

```
1: Result ← CntPre(P_n, o)
2: for i ← 1 to n do
3:     Result ← Result * MaxCount(P_i)
4: return Result
```

Figure 4. UpperBound($P_1, \cdots, P_n, o$)

its preimage because we need only the size of the preimage. Lines 1 to 5 are for initialization. Line 6 enumerates $\text{pre}_{P_n}(o)$. Lines 7 to 21 constitute the main loop of the algorithm, which is stopped either when the counting is done or when time is up. When $level = 1$, lines 8 to 11 are executed and $CntPre$ will return $\text{pre}_{P_1}(Stack.top)$ in which $Stack.top$ is the input of P_2 that leads to output o of P_n, then back-propagate; lines 13 to 16 check if all elements in the preimage set of the current level is already considered and if so, back-propagate, otherwise push the next element onto the top of $Stack$ and go to the next level.

Theorem 3.1: In Figure 3, if $P_1, \cdots, P_n$ are deterministic, acc_count, which is returned at line 22, is a lower bound of the preimage size of o by $P_1, \cdots, P_n$. □

2) Upper bound: For an upper bound of $|\text{pre}_P(o)|$ we use Max#SAT problem [14], which is defined as follows.

Definition 3.1: Given a propositional formula $\varphi(X, Y, Z)$ over sets of variables X, Y and Z, the Max#SAT problem is to determine $max_X \#Y.\exists Z.\varphi(X, Y, Z)$.

If we consider a program Q, $In(Q)$, $Out(Q)$ and $Local(Q)$ as φ, Y, X and Z respectively, then, the solution X to the Max#SAT problem can be interpreted as the output value, which has the biggest size of its preimage set. In other words, $max_X \#Y.\exists Z.\varphi(X, Y, Z)$ is an upper bound of the size of pre_Q over all feasible outputs. Therefore, the product of those upper bounds of $|\text{pre}_{P_i}|$ over all i ($1 \leq i \leq n$) is obviously an upper bound of $|\text{pre}_P|$. The algorithm in Figure 4 computes this upper bound where $CntPre(P_n, o)$ returns the size of the preimage of o by P_n. Notice that, to avoid enumerating the preimages, which costs much computation time, we count only $|\text{pre}_{P_n}(o)|$. For $i = 1, ...n-1$, we compute $MaxCount(P_i)$ as an upper bound for pre_{P_i}, regardless of the corresponding output value. For prototyping, we used the tool developed by the authors of [14], which produces estimated bounds of Max#SAT with tunable confidence and precision. As explained in [14], the tool samples output values of k-fold self-composition of the original program. The greater k is, the more precise the estimation is, but also the more complicated the calculation of each sampling is. Note that $MaxCount(P_i)$ can be computed in advance only once. Though the precision is not always good in general, this approach provides a rather simple computation method. Also, note that the leakage is the logarithm of the model count.

Theorem 3.2: In Figure 4, if $P_1, \cdots, P_n$ are deterministic, then $Result$, which is returned at line 4, is an upper bound of the preimage size of o by $P_1, \cdots, P_n$. □

C. Extensibility to Probablistic Programs

When a program is probabilistic, a single input value may produce more than one output values. Therefore, when we count the preimage set of a specific output value, an input value may be counted multiple times, which results in an upper approximation. Though this does not invalidate our proposed algorithm, which computes an upper bound using Max#SAT, it could degrade the precision.

For the algorithms of exact counting and lower bounding, the following modifications will retain both their validity and precision as presented above when analyzing probabilistic programs. Notice that the algorithm in Figure 3 gives exact count when $timeout$ is sufficiently long.

- Maintain a list of distinct input values that produce the observed output value o'. In line 9 of Figure 3, instead of only counting models, enumerate all feasible input values, then update that list by adding the new input values. As the result, the final set is exactly the preimage set of o'.
- Provided the input distribution, i.e., the prior probability $p(s)$ of each input value s, QIF_1 can be calculated by taking the logarithm of the sum of $p(s)$ for s belonging to the preimage set, which is already computed by the above modification.
- Provided the channel matrix representing the conditional probability $p(o|s)$ of each output value o given an input value s, QIF_2 can be calculated by computing the probability $p(o')$ that the observed output value o' is produced.

IV. VALUE DOMAIN DECOMPOSITION

Another effective method for computing the dynamic leakage in a compositional way is to decompose the sets of input values and output values into several subsets, compute the leakage for the subprograms restricted to those subsets, and compose the results to obtain the leakage of the whole program. The difference between the parallel composition in [16] and the proposed method is that in the former case, a program under analysis itself is divided into two subprograms that run in parallel, and in the latter case, the computation of dynamic leakage is conducted in parallel by decomposing the sets of input and output values.

Let $P(S, O)$ be a program. Assume that the sets of input values and output values, $\mathcal{S}$ and $\mathcal{O}$, are decomposed into mutually disjoint subsets as

$$\mathcal{S} = \mathcal{S}_1 \uplus \cdots \uplus \mathcal{S}_k,$$
$$\mathcal{O} = \mathcal{O}_1 \uplus \cdots \uplus \mathcal{O}_l.$$

For $1 \leq i \leq k$ and $1 \leq j \leq l$, let P_{ij} be the program obtained from P by restricting the set of input values to $\mathcal{S}_i$ and the set of output values to $\mathcal{O}_j$ where if the output value o of P for an input value $s \in \mathcal{S}_i$ does not belong to $\mathcal{O}_j$, the output value of P_{ij} for input s is undefined. In practice, this disjoint decomposition can be done simply by augmenting the program under analysis with appropriate constraints on input and output.

By definition, for a given $o \in \mathcal{O}_j$,

$$\text{pre}_P(o) = \bigcup_{1 \leq i \leq k} \text{pre}_{P_{i,j}}(o). \quad (6)$$

By (2) and (3), we can compute QIF_1 and QIF_2 in a compositional way.

By Theorem 2.1, if P is deterministic and the prior probability of S is uniformly distributed, what we have to compute is $|\text{pre}_P(o)|$, which can be obtained by summing up each $|\text{pre}_{P_{i,j}}(o)|$ by (6):

$$|\text{pre}_P(o)| \quad = \quad \sum_{1 \leq i \leq k} |\text{pre}_{P_{i,j}}(o)|.$$

Otherwise, probabilistic programs with arbitrary input distribution can be handled in a manner similar to the one described in the last paragraph of the previous section.

V. Experiments

This section will investigate answers for the following questions: (1) How well does parallel computing based on the value domain decomposition improve the performance? (2) How well does sequential composition help improve the performance? (3) How well does approximation in the sequential composition work in terms of precision and speed? and (4) Is *CiA* always better than *CoD* or vice versa? We will examine those questions through a few examples: *Grade protocol* is for question (1), *Bit shuffle* and *Population count* are for (2) and (3), while (4) is considered based on both the former and the latter. The benchmarks and prototype are public in [26].

A. Setting up

The experiments were conducted on Intel(R) Xeon(R) CPU ES-1620 v3 @ 3.5GHz x 8 (4 cores x 2 threads), 32GB RAM, CentOS Linux 7. For parallel computation, we use OpenMP [12] library. At the very first phase, to transform C programs into CNFs, we leveraged the well-known CBMC [25]. For the construction of a BDD from a CNF and the model counting and enumeration of the constructed BDD, we use an off-the-shell tool PC2BDD [30]. We use PC2DDNNF [31] for the d-DNNF counterpart. Both of the tools are developed by one of the authors in another project. Besides, as the ordering of Boolean variables of a CNF greatly affects the BDD generation performance, we utilize FORCE [2] to optimize the ordering before transforming a CNF into a BDD. We use MaxCount [29] for estimating the answer of Max#SAT problem. We implemented a tool for algorithms in Figure 3 and Figure 4, as well as the exact count in sequential compositions in Java.

B. Grade protocol

This benchmark is taken from [19]. By this experiment, we investigated how well parallel computation improves the performance of counting models, hence of quantifying dynamic leakage, in value domain decomposition. This benchmark sums up (then takes the average of) the grades of a group of students without revealing the grade of each student. We used the benchmark with *4 students* and *5 grades*, and all variables are of 16 bits. For model counting, we suppose the observed output (the sum of students' grades) to be **1**, and hence the number of models is 4. GPMC [28], one of the fastest tools for quantifying dynamic leakage as shown in [10], was chosen as the representative tool for *CoD* approach. We manually decompose the original program into 4, 8 and 32 sub-programs by adding constraints on input and output of the program based on the value domain decomposition (the set of output values is divided into 2 and the set of input values is divided into 2, 4 or 16 disjoint subsets). Table I is divided into sub-divisions corresponding to specific tasks: BDD construction, d-DNNF construction and model counting based on different approaches. In each sub-division, the **bold number** represents the shortest execution time in each column (i.e., the same number of decomposed sub-programs, but different numbers of threads). '$-$' represents cases when the number of threads is greater than the number of sub-programs, which are obviously meaningless to do experiments.

TABLE I. TIME FOR CONSTRUCTING DATA STRUCTURE AND COUNTING MODEL.

		$n = 32$	$n = 8$	$n = 4$	$n = 1$
BDD Construction	$t = 32$	**218.53s**	–	–	–
	$t = 16$	$222.27s$	–	–	–
	$t = 8$	$237.54s$	**137.74s**	–	–
	$t = 4$	$254.88s$	$144.55s$	**155.90s**	–
	$t = 2$	$376.21s$	$233.34s$	$214.65s$	–
	$t = 1$	$736.74s$	$450.85s$	$391.99s$	**243.85s**
d-DNNF Construction	$t = 32$	$93.17s$	–	–	–
	$t = 16$	**91.49s**	–	–	–
	$t = 8$	$107.31s$	**123.48s**	–	–
	$t = 4$	$141.27s$	$147.79s$	**175.34s**	–
	$t = 2$	$215.92s$	$226.93s$	$247.45s$	–
	$t = 1$	$398.99s$	$391.67s$	$457.38s$	**304.88s**
Model Counting (*CiA* - BDD based)	$t = 32$	**0.21s**	–	–	–
	$t = 16$	$0.22s$	–	–	–
	$t = 8$	$0.25s$	**0.13s**	–	–
	$t = 4$	$0.30s$	$0.16s$	**0.16s**	–
	$t = 2$	$0.65s$	$0.31s$	$0.24s$	–
	$t = 1$	$0.86s$	$0.36s$	$0.31s$	**0.30s**
Model Counting (*CiA* - d-DNNF based)	$t = 32$	**0.05s**	–	–	–
	$t = 16$	**0.05s**	–	–	–
	$t = 8$	**0.05s**	**0.01s**	–	–
	$t = 4$	$0.07s$	**0.01s**	**0.01s**	–
	$t = 2$	$0.12s$	$0.02s$	$0.02s$	–
	$t = 1$	$0.18s$	$0.04s$	$0.03s$	**0.25s**
Model Counting (*CoD* - using GPMC)	$t = 1$	–	–	–	**44.69s**

In Table I, n: number of sub-programs decomposed from the original program; t: number of threads specified by *num_thread* compiling directive of OpenMP. Note that $n = 1$ means non-decomposition, $t = 1$ means a sequential execution and the number of physical CPUs is 8. From Table I, we can make the following inferences:

- As for the answer to question (1), parallel computing speeds up the calculation several times
  BDD Construction: **137.74s** vs. **243.85s**;
  d-DNNF Construction: **91.49s** vs. **304.88s**;
  Model Counting (CiA - BDD based): **0.13s** vs. **0.30s**.
  to tens times
  Model Counting (CiA - d-DNNF): **0.01s** vs. **0.25s**.
- In general, increasing the number of threads (up to the number of sub-programs) does improve the execution time in both the construction of BDD, d-DNNF and the model counting.
- When the number of sub-programs is close to the number of physical CPUs, which is eight, the execution time is among the best if not the best.

The performance with d-DNNF is better than that with BDD in this example, but this seems due to the implementation of the tools.

C. Bit shuffle and Population count

population_count is the 16-bit version of the benchmark of the same name given in [19]. In this experiment, the original program is decomposed into three sub-programs in such a way that each sub-program performs one bit operation of the original. Inspired by *population_count*, we created the benchmark *bit_shuffle*, which consists of two steps: firstly it counts the number of bit-ones in a given secret number (by *population_count*, actually we took the count modulo 6 to increase the preimage size by the first part), then it shuffles those bits to produce an output value. This original program is divided into two sub-programs corresponding to the above-mentioned two steps. Though *bit_shuffle* is probabilistic (i.e., the shuffling part), the algorithm in Figure 3 still works, because there is always only one possible input value (i.e., the number of bit-ones) for an output of the sub-program corresponding to the latter step.

Table II shows execution times of constructing BDD and d-DNNF for two sample programs. The last three columns: *non-decompose*, *decompose (serial)* and *decompose (parallel)* are execution time when computed for the original program, computed sequentially and parallelly for the decomposed sub-programs, respectively. **Bold numbers** are the best execution times in those three.

For model counting, we let an output value be 3 (the number of models is 13110) for *bit_shuffle* and 7 (the number of models is 11440) for *population_count*. Table III presents the execution times for model counting where the underlined numbers are the exact counts, the **bold execution times** are the best results among approaches for the exact count of each benchmark and the *italic data* are of approximated calculations. The execution times for the lower bounds are predetermined timeouts, which were designed to be 1/2, 1/5 and 1/10 of the time needed by the exact count, followed by the time by *CoD*. In *bit_shuffle* benchmark, lower bounds based on d-DNNF were not improved (all are zero) even when the timeout was increased. This happened because an intermediate result of counting for one d-DNNF is unknown until the counting completes while this benchmark contains only two sub-programs and the size of the preimage by the second sub-program is always one (i.e., the number of times to count d-DNNFs is only two, one for the first sub-program and one for the second one).

TABLE II. BDD AND d-DNNF CONSTRUCTION TIME FOR DIFFERENT APPROACHES.

		non-decompose	decompose (serial)	decompose (parallel)
BDD Construction	bit_shuffle	>1 hour	33.90s	**33.46s**
	population_count	0.48s	0.66s	**0.40s**
d-DNNF Construction	bit_shuffle	424.64s	50.28s	**48.39s**
	population_count	1.19s	0.71s	**0.69s**

TABLE III. MODEL COUNTING: EXECUTION TIME AND THE CHANGING OF APPROXIMATION PRECISION.

			bit_shuffle		population_count	
CoD using GPMC (non-decompose)			0.49s	13110	**0.09s**	11440
CiA-BDD based (decompose)	Exact count		1.47s	13110	10.98s	11440
	Approximation	Lower bound	*0.75s*	*6243*	*5.5s*	*5776*
			0.30s	*1918*	*2.2s*	*888*
			0.15s	*574*	*1.1s*	*312*
			0.49s	*3713*	*0.09s*	*0*
		Upper bound	0.02s	14025	0.07s	5898240
CiA-d-DNNF based (decompose)	Exact count		**0.27s**	13110	3.50s	11440
	Approximation	Lower bound	*0.13s*	*0*	*1.75s*	*4712*
			0.05s	*0*	*0.70s*	*1314*
			0.03s	*0*	*0.35s*	*52*
			0.49s	*13110*	*0.09s*	*0*
		Upper bound	0.07s	14025	0.13s	5898240

From the experimental results, we obtain the following observations.

- As for the answer of question (2), in case of *bit_shuffle*, sequential composition helps speed up the construction of BDD more than 100 times (**33.46s** vs. > 1 hour) and d-DNNF more than 8 times (**48.39s** vs. 424.64s). However, in case of *population_count*, the improvement is insignificant. For model counting, in both of the samples, sequential composition either helps just little or does not help.
- As for the answer of question (3), in case of upper bound for *bit_shuffle*, the precision is quite good. However, it was extremely low for *population_count*. For both of the samples, the calculation was very fast. For the lower bound, basically the precision gets better with longer timeout. In addition, because leakage is logarithm of model count, its upper bound and lower bound are much tighter than those of model count.

Note that, when we compare *CiA* with *CoD*, it is reasonable to ignore time of construction in *CiA*, because it happens only at the first time, then the result can be reused. For the question (4), in case of *grade protocol*, *CiA* shows a huge improvement over *CoD*, which is more than 4000 times (**0.01 s** vs. **44.69 s**). But in case of *population_count*, *CoD* is superior to *CiA* (**0.09 s** vs. 3.50 s). So, the answer is *NO*, i.e., sometimes *CiA* is better and the other time *CoD* is.

VI. Conclusion

In this paper, we focused on the efficient computation of dynamic leakage of a program and considered two approaches, *CoD* and *CiA*. Then, we proposed two compositional methods, namely, computation along with the sequential structure of the program and parallel computation based on value domain decomposition. In the first method, we also proposed approximations that give both lower bound and upper bound of model counting. Our experimental results showed that: (1) Parallel computation based on value domain decomposition works well generally; (2) Sequential composition sometimes helps significantly with construction of BDDs and d-DNNFs; (3) The precision of upper bounds depends on the way of decomposition while that of lower bound depends on the preset timeout; and (4) Both *CiA* and *CoD* are important because sometimes the former works better and the other times does the latter. All decomposition in the experiments were done manually. So, it is important to find a systematical way of deciding and guiding to a good decomposition. This is left as future work. One promising direction is to utilize static analysis, such as symbolic execution and program invariant. On the other hand, both BDD and d-DNNF have many applications other than computing dynamic leakage, but there is still a bottle neck at constructing them. The approach in this paper, *composition based on value domains*, can be a hint to speed up that process.

References

[1] P. S. Aldous, *"Noninterference in expressive low-level languages"*, http://www.cs.utah.edu/~peteya/papers/diss.pdf [retrieved: October, 2019], PhD thesis, The University of Utah, 2017.

[2] F. Aloul, I. Markov, and K. Sakallah, *"FORCE: a fast and easy-to-implement variable-ordering heuristic"*, Great Lakes Symposium on VLSI (GLSVLSI), 2003, pp. 116–119.

[3] M. S. Alvim, K. Chatzikokolakis, C. Palamidessi, and G. Smith, *"Measuring information leakage using generalized gain functions"*, 21st Computer Security Foundations Symposium (CSF), 2012, pp. 265–279.

[4] N. Bielova, *"Dynamic leakage - a need for a new quantitative information flow measure"*, ACM Workshop on Programming Languages and Analysis for Security (PLAS), 2016, pp. 83–88.

[5] N. Bielova and R. Rezk, *"A taxonomy of information flow monitors"*, 5th International Conference on Principles of Security and Trust (POST), 2016, pp. 46–67.

[6] F. Biondi et al., *"Scalable approximation of quantitative information flow in programs"*, Verification, Model Checking, and Abstract Interpretation (VMCAI), 2018, pp. 71–93.

[7] F. Biondi, Y. Kawamoto, A. Legay, and L. M. Traonouez, *"HyLeak: hybrid analysis tool for information leakage"*, Automated Technology for Verification and Analysis (ATVA), 2017, pp. 156–163.

[8] R. Chadha and M. Ummels, *"The complexity of quantitative information flow in recursive programs"*, Research Report LSV-2012-15, Laboratoire Spécification & Vérification, École Normale Supérieure de Cachan, 2012.

[9] T. Chothia, Y. Kawamoto, and C. Novakovic, *"LeakWatch: estimating information leakage from Java programs"*, 19th European Symposium on Research in Computer Security (ESORICS), 2014, pp. 219–236.

[10] B. T. Chu, K. Hashimoto, and H. Seki, *"Quantifying dynamic leakage: complexity analysis and model counting-based calculation"*, IEICE Transactions on Information and Systems, Vol. E102-D, No. 10, Oct. 2019 (to appear), pre-print version: https://arxiv.org/abs/1903.03802.

[11] M. R. Clarkson, A. C. Myers, and F. B. Schneider, *"Quantifying information flow with beliefs"*, 18th Computer Security Foundations Symposium (CSF), 2009, pp. 655–701.

[12] L. Dagum and R. Menon, *"OpenMP: an industry-standard API for shared-memory programming"*, IEEE Computational Science & Engineering, Volume 5 Issue 1, Jan 1998, pp. 46–55.

[13] A. Darwiche, *"On the tractability of counting theory models and its application to belief revision and truth maintenance"*, Jounal of Applied Non-Classical Logics 11(1-2), 2001, pp. 11–34.

[14] D. J. Fremont, M. N. Rabe, and S. A. Seshia, *"Maximum Model Counting"*, AAAI Conference on Artificial Intelligence, 2017, pp. 3885–3892.

[15] J. A. Goguen and J. Meseguer, *"Security policies and security models"*, IEEE Symposium on Security and Privacy (S&P), 1982, pp. 11–20.

[16] Y. Kawamoto, K. Chatzikokolakis, and C. Palamidessi, *"On the compositionality of quantitative information flow"*, Logical Methods in Computer Science, Vol. 13(3:11) 2017, pp. 1–31.

[17] V. Klebanov, N. Manthey, and C. Muise, *"SAT-based analysis and quantification of information flow in programs"*, Quantitative Evaluation of Systems (QEST), 2013, pp. 177-192.

[18] B. Köpf and A. Rybalchenko, *"Approximation and randomization for quantitative information flow analysis"*, 23rd Computer Security Foundations Symposium (CSF), 2010, pp. 3–14.

[19] Q. S. Phan, *"Model counting modulo theories"*, PhD thesis, Queen Mary University of London, 2015.

[20] Q. S. Phan and P. Malacaria, *"All-solution satisfiability modulo theories: applications, algorithms and benchmarks"*, 10th International Conference on Availability, Reliability and Security (ARES), 2015, pp. 100–109.

[21] G. Smith, *"On the foundations of quantitative information flow"*, 12th International Conference on Foundations of Software Science and Computational Structures (FOSSACS), 2009, pp. 288–302.

[22] F. Somenzi, *"Binary decision diagrams"*, http://www.ecs.umass.edu/ece/labs/vlsicad/ece667/reading/somenzi99bdd.pdf, 1999.

[23] C. G. Val, M. A. Enescu, S. Bayless, W. Aiello, and A. J. Hu, *"Precisely measuring quantitative information flow: 10k lines of code and beyond"*, IEEE European Symposium on Security and Privacy (EuroS&P), 2016, pp. 31–46.

[24] H. Yasuoka and T. Terauchi, *"On bounding problems of quantitative information flow"*, Journal of Computer Security (JCS), Vol. 19, 2011 November, pp. 1029–1082.

[25] C Bounded Model Checker, https://www.cprover.org/cbmc [retrieved: September, 2019].

[26] Dynamic Leakage Analyzer, https://bitbucket.org/trungchubao-nu/dla-composition/src/master/dla-composition/ [retrieved: September, 2019].

[27] DSharp-p, https://formal.iti.kit.edu/~klebanov/software/ [retrieved: September, 2019].

[28] GPMC, https://www.trs.css.i.nagoya-u.ac.jp/~k-hasimt/tools/gpmc.html [retrieved: September, 2019].

[29] MaxCount, https://github.com/dfremont/maxcount [retrieved: September, 2019].

[30] PC2BDD, https://git.trs.css.i.nagoya-u.ac.jp/t_isogai/cnf2bdd [retrieved: September, 2019].

[31] PC2DDNNF, https://git.trs.css.i.nagoya-u.ac.jp/k-hasimt/gpmc-dnnf [retrieved: September, 2019].

[32] SharpCDCL, http://tools.computational-logic.org/content/sharpCDCL.php [retrieved: September, 2019].

An Evaluation on Feasibility of a Communication Classifying System

Yuya Sato
Graduate School of Informatics
Nagoya University
Nagoya, Japan
Email: sato.yuya@f.mbox.nagoya-u.ac.jp

Hirokazu Hasegawa
Information Strategy Office
Nagoya University
Nagoya, Japan
Email: hasegawa@icts.nagoya-u.ac.jp

Hiroki Takakura
Center for Cybersecurity
Resarch and Development
National Institute of Informatics
Tokyo, Japan
Email: takakura@nii.ac.jp

***Abstract*—Recently, sophisticated cyber attacks targeting companies or governments have frequently occurred. With conventional measures, e.g., intrusion detection system or firewalls, we cannot protect our network completely because attackers act carefully to pass through such conventional measures. Against such situation, separated network is one of the effective countermeasures. It divides an organization's internal network into multiple segments and performs fine access control among separated segments. We have proposed an automated ACL (Access Control List) generation system to support constructing separated networks previously. However, this method focuses on the business continuity of the organization, and ACL will unconditionally permit communication of a section where traffic is observed. Therefore, we proposed a communication classifying system to judge the necessity of communication and its protocol by a two-step investigation. In the first step, the system judges the consistency of the observed communication by examining the reasons why conventional systems permitted the communication. In addition, the system judges the validity of the communication by checking the waiting state of its destination terminal in the second step. In this paper, we implement the communication classifying system we have proposed, and verify the feasibility of the system. In the experiment, we applied the implemented system to a prototype network consisting of nine clients and one file sharing server (SMB (Server Message Block) protocol). As a result, our system terminated most of the unintended communication between clients and server precisely.**

Keywords–Targeted Attacks; Network Separation; Access Control.

I. Introduction

Recently, cyber attacks targeting organizations such as specific companies or countries have frequently occurred. Such attacks are called targeted attacks, and unlike indiscriminate attacks aimed at spreading simple malware, attackers attack specific organizations with sophisticated groups which have abundant funds. Therefore, attackers prepare dedicated malware for targets, and it is difficult to prevent attacks by conventional measures, e.g., firewall and intrusion detection system. Because of the above situation, recently, the focus of countermeasures has been on the mitigation of damages such as information leakage and file destruction after intrusion of malwares [1].

One of the effective countermeasures against targeted attacks is the use of a separated network [2]. It divides the organization's internal network into multiple segments and performs fine access control among the divided segments. It can prevent unintended communication among segments caused by malware, e.g., lateral movement. In addition, when we detect malwares, it can minimize the harmful effect to business continuity because we can isolate only the infected segment. However, it needs various information about networks, human resources, business contents, and so on. So, we need a large amount of cost to construct and manage a separated network.

Therefore, we have previously proposed an automated ACL (Access Control List) generation system to support constructing a separated network [3]. We call this system as "AAGS (Automated ACL Generation System)" in this paper. It generates ACL based on user's access authority to directories or files. If a user has no access authority to directories or files in a file server, the communication between the user and the file server is prohibited. However, AAGS emphasizes business continuity so that it permits all communications observed in the network even if they are unnecessary. This method may cause overly permits of unnecessary communication.

To avoid the overly permission, we have proposed a communication classifying system [4]. We call this system as "CCS (Communication Classifying System)" in this paper. CCS judges the consistency of the communication occurring in the network by analyzing the reason it was permitted. In addition, CCS judges the validity of communication which lacks consistency by using stand-by states of destination terminals. These investigations make it possible to avoid overly permitted communication.

In this paper, to verify the feasibility of CCS, we implemented AAGS and applied it to prototype network. The network is constructed with real machines, and ACL, which overly permits communication, is applied. In the experiment, our proposal correctly judged most of the overly permitted communication as unnecessary. However, there are several misjudgements by the system, and we found several problems of the system that became our future works.

In the following, Section II describes the related works. In Section III, we will explain our proposed methods, AAGS and CCS. Section IV describes the architecture of CCS, and Section V describes its implementation. The experiments using the implemented system are described in Section VI. Finally, we summarize our work in Section VII.

II. Related Works

There are many researches for preventing malware activities in internal networks. Alessandro et al. have proposed a method for modeling communication patterns of malwares that perform lateral movement [5]. However, we need large cost to employ this method because it is necessary to install a communication analysis tool on all terminals. In the case of a separated network, the spread of infection can be suppressed without installing special tools on the terminal.

Methods to construct separated network have been widely studied. Watanabe et al. proposed a VLAN (Virtual Local

Area Network) configuration method [6]. In this method, they monitor traffic in the network, and generate a network design by using this monitoring information. When a certain amount of traffic exceeding threshold among terminals is observed, VLAN including these terminals is generated. Because it can summarize the terminals frequently communicating with each other, it is effective from the viewpoint of amount of traffic volume. However, when a VLAN including an infected terminal is generated, it cannot prevent malware activities in that VLAN. There are many other researches to support constructing VLAN [7][8][9]. However, it is difficult to construct fine access controls among VLANs.

In addition to the above researches, there are several products, e.g., "VLAN .Config" [10], for constructing VLAN automatically. By using such products, we can construct VLAN easily, however, it is difficult to generate ACL.

III. Our Previous Research

A. Automated ACL Generation System

To support constructing networks, we proposed an automated ACL generation system (AAGS) previously [3]. AAGS judges the necessity of communication sections based on access authority of a user to files or directories in servers. If a user has no access authority to all files in the server, AAGS decides that a communication section between the user and the server is unnecessary. The system gathers information of access authorities by analyzing the information in directory service server.

In addition, AAGS analyzes the mirrored packets of the internal network. Before applying the generated ACL, the system revises it by using mirrored packets. Even if a communication was judged as unnecessary previously, its new observation calls reevaluation and then, the communication is judged as necessary. Finally, based on the judgement, the system generates ACL to permit all of the necessary communication sections. It allows us to construct a separated network easily by applying the generated ACL.

B. Problems

Because of such idea, AAGS permits all communication observed in the network even if it is an unintentionally occurring one. In other words, the system may generate ACL which overly permits unnecessary communication sections. Furthermore, the ACL generated by the system is only based on source and destination IP addresses. Once the system judged the communication section to be allowed, all communication protocols on the section are permitted.

C. Communication Classifying System

In order to solve the problems of AAGS, we proposed a communication classifying system (CCS) [4] that improves ACL generated by AAGS. CCS investigates the consistency between the communication observed in the network and the reason why AAGS permitted such communication section. If a communication lacks consistency, CCS performs additional investigation. Because appropriate ports are listened at the destination terminals if the communication is rightful, the system performs a port scan to identify the listening port and then, compares the observed communication protocols and listening ports of destination terminals. These investigations make CCS possible to detect illegal communication. In order to permit only rightful communication, the system finally generates a new ACL including prohibition of unnecessary communication sections and protocols.

D. Assumption in CCS

We proposed CCS to complement our previous AAGS. CCS assumes that the network is roughly divided into several segments, and ACL generated by AAGS is applied to the network. The applied ACL is stored in database (ACL DB) by AAGS.

ACL DB that AAGS uses is extended by adding three new columns. First, we added "Permitted Reason" to register the reason why the communication is permitted, i.e., directory service information, or communication analysis, or both of them. AAGS uses the extended versions of DB so that the ACL describes permitted communication sections, e.g., source IP addresses, destination IP addresses, and Permitted Reason. The remaining two columns are "Destination Port" and "Status". However, AAGS ignores other these two columns as empty fields.

When CCS analyzes the communication section, it registers "analyzed" to Status field of such communication section. If there is only one record for the pair of source IP address and destination IP address, and such record's Status field is empty, it is the first time for the proposed system to analyze that communication section. If "analyzed" has been registered to Status filed of a communication section, CCS omits the analysis of the communication section.

In addition, we assume that protocols are accepted by an administrator by ways different from AAGS. For example, we proposed a Dynamic Access Control System permitting communication that is overly prohibited [11]. CCS assumes that "not_analyzed" is registered to Status filed of the communication section if any other systems or administrators permit such communication. If the Status field is "not_analyzed", CCS analyzes the communication protocols in such section.

In this paper, to simplify the discussion, we assume that all terminals are statically assigned IP addresses and such assignment information is managed in a directory service server. However, our method can be easily applied to environments that employ dynamically IP address assignment method, e.g., DHCP. We can control connected device's communication by identifying the user of the device with any authentication method, e.g., IEEE 802.1X. For example, we can assign the appropriate VLAN that the user should belong to, or update ACL based on the assigned IP address.

IV. Architecture of Communication Classifying System

Figure 1 shows the architecture of CCS. The system consists of five modules and the database extended in AAGS. The details of each modules are described below.

1) Traffic Collector: This module receives all mirrored packets generated in the internal network. This paper assumes that the collection period of mirrored packets for investigation is statically defined in advance, e.g., 1 day, 1 hour, and 10 minutes. After collecting mirrored packets, the module generates a list of packet information including sets of source IP address, destination IP address, and destination port from collected packet. The generated list of packet information is sent to the Consistency Judgement module.

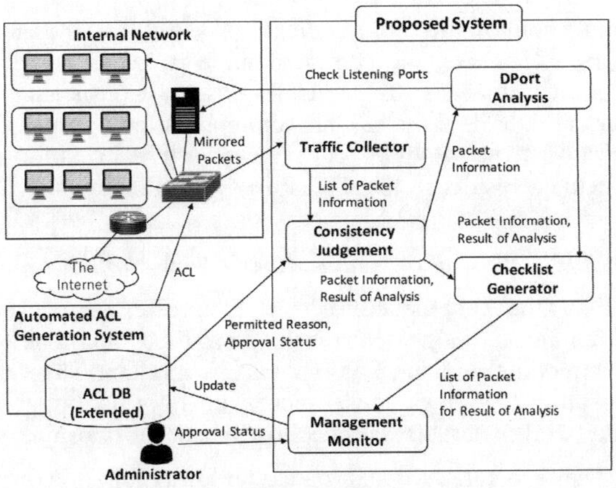

Figure 1. Architecture of Proposed System.

2) Consistency Judgment: First, when a list of packet information is received, this module searches records of ACL DB for each communication section by specifying each pair of source and destination IP addresses. When the status field is empty, the Consistency Judgment module analyzes all protocols captured in such communication section.

After extracting the subject of the communication for investigation, the Consistency Judgement module judges consistency of such communication. The module finds the permitted reason of such communication by checking ACL DB. As shown in Table I, there are six combinations of collected packet and communication reason. In the table, CA denotes communication analysis. Because AAGS checks the necessity of the file sharing communication by using a Directory Service Information (DSI), the Consistency Judgment module classifies the captured communication as SMB (Server Message Block) protocol or Other Protocols. In this paper, we assume that only SMB is used as file sharing communication protocol. SMB uses multiple ports and protocols, e.g., 139/tcp and 445/tcp. To simplify the discussion, we express these sets of all ports by using the term "SMB protocol".

TABLE I. COMBINATIONS OF PERMITTED REASON AND COLLECTED PACKET.

Collected Packet	Permitted Reason		
	DSI	DSI+CA	CA
SMB	1	2	3
Other Protocol	4	5	6

For the SMB protocol, combinations 1 and 2 of Table I have consistency. To permit these communication, the Consistency Judgement module sends this Packet Information to the Check List Generator module. On the other hand, in combination 3, communication lacks consistency, because communication of SMB protocol was observed even though there was no access authority by DSI. However, file sharing may be conducted among user's terminals directly without management by the directory service server. In order not to prohibit such communication, the Consistency Judgement module sends this Packet Information to the DPort Analysis module for additional investigation.

In case of any other protocols than SMB, only combination 4 lacks consistency. The Packet Information of such communication is sent to the Checklist Generator module to prohibit such communication. Combinations 5 and 6 have consistency, however, this module cannot determine sameness of the communication protocol collected by Traffic Collector and AAGS. The Packet Information of such communication is sent to the DPort Analysis module, which conducts a detailed investigation.

3) DPort Analysis: This module analyzes the normality of the communication. We assume that the destination terminal has to listen to the correct port of service for the communication. According to such assumption, the module judges normality of communication by using the current stand-by states of destination terminals. There are several ways to specify the listening ports of terminals, however, we adopt port-scanning against destination terminals in this paper.

Based on the result of port-scanning, when the destination port of a communication is listened on destination terminal, DPort Analysis judges that communication is necessary. On the other hand, the communication is judged as unnecessary if the destination port is blocked. Finally, these judgement results are sent to the Checklist Generator module with its packet information.

4) Checklist Generator: This module receives the packet information and judgement results from the Consistency Judgment module or DPort Analysis module. The Checklist Generator module combines these packet information and its analysis results, and generates a check list from these information for administrators. The generated check list of the packet information is sent to the Management Monitor module.

5) Management Monitor: Lists of the packet information and judgement results are sent from the Checklist Generator module to the Management Monitor module. This module presents to the administrators the combined received lists. Administrators check the list and authorize the permission or prohibition of the communication section. Finally, the module updates the ACL DB to register the authorized packet information as "analyzed" value in the status field. After updating the ACL DB, the ACL Applier in AAGS applies it to the network.

V. Implementation of Proposed System

This section describes the implementation of CSS. Figure 2 shows the basic structure of the modules and the data flow among modules. In this system, the Traffic Collector module, the Consistency Judgement module, and the DPort Analysis module run as batch processing written with Python. We adopt Node.js [12] as a Web server including the Checklist Generator module and the Management Monitor. In addition, we constructed an API server by using FastAPI [13] for smoothing data exchanges between each modules and the ACL DB.

In this paper, we implemented ACL DB and ACL Applier that are included in AAGS. We use MySQL [14] for ACL DB. By using the SDN (Software Designed Network) technique, we realized the ACL applier. We assume that Open vSwitch [15](OvS) is used as a network switch, and the SDN controller, e.g., Trema [16], instructs the OvS to control packets in the network.

In addition, all of these modules run on Docker [17], which manages applications using a container type virtual environment.

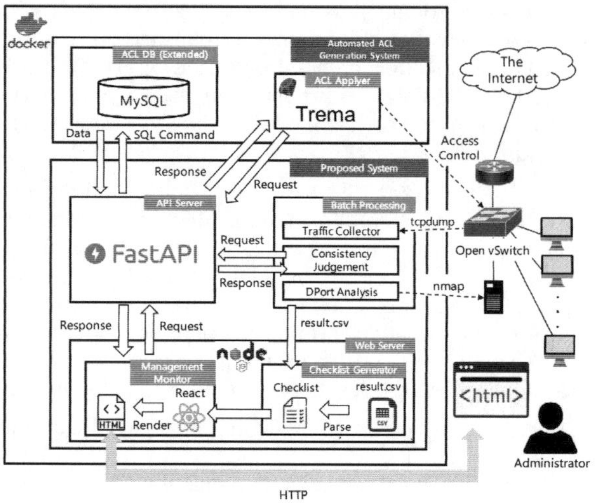

Figure 2. System Configuration Diagram.

A. *Traffic Collector*

This module receives mirrored packets and generates a list of packet information. We configure the OvS in advance to generate mirrors of all packets in the network and send them to the Traffic Collector. The Traffic Collector executes the `tcpdump` command and captures the mirrored packets sent from OvS for a collection period. As mentioned in Section IV, we set collection period as 10 minutes in this experiment.

The captured packets are saved as pcap files, and this module extracts sets of source IP address, destination IP address, and destination port for each packet from the pcap file by using dpkt [18], which is a module of Python. Finally, this module sends the extracted set as packet information to the Consistency Judgement module.

B. *Consistency Judgement*

After receiving the list of packet information, this module sends a request to the API server to search the record of communication section in the ACL DB corresponding to each packet information. In addition, this module checks the destination ports of each packet information and classifies them into SMB or other ports.

This module compares such destination ports and the result of the record search, and judges the consistency of the communication. When the module decides that the observed communication is necessary or not, it sends the packet information of that communication section with the judgement results to the Checklist Generator module. On the other hand, if the module determines that detailed analysis is necessary, it sends the packet information to the DPort Analysis module.

C. *DPort Analysis*

This module judges the normality of the communication that is included in packet information sent from Consistency Judgement module. To assess the listening ports of destination terminals, it uses the `nmap` command. At this time, we use the -S optional command of nmap to spoof the source IP address of the observed communication.

Based on the results of nmap, if the proper service port of packet information is listening at the destination terminal, the module judges this communication is rightful and it is necessary. Otherwise, the communication is judged unnecessary. After such analysis, the same way as the Consistency Judgement module determines that communication is necessary, the DPort Analysis module sends the packet information and its judgement results to the Checklist Generator module.

D. *Checklist Generator and Management Monitor*

The Checklist Generator module receives the packet information and its judgement results from the Consistency Judgement module and the DPort Analysis module. The Checklist Generator combines these pieces of information about the packet and generates the checklist of packet information.

The generated list of packet information is sent to the Management Monitor, and, based on this list, a html page is generated as interface for administrators by using React [19]. Figure 3 shows a sample of the generated Web page for administrators.

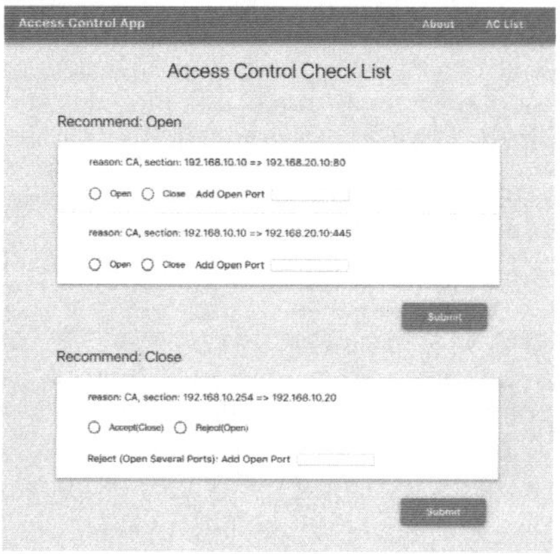

Figure 3. Sample of Management Monitor Web Page.

In this screen, there are two sections. The first section is "Recommend: Open". The communication sections displayed in this section is judged as necessary. If the administrator judges it as appropriate, he can authorize it by selecting "Open" button. However, only the displayed ports are judged necessary by the system, and all of other ports not displayed will be prohibited. When administrators want to permit several ports in addition to the system recommendation, they can insert such ports into "Add Open Port" form. Otherwise, they use the "Close" button to prohibit the displayed communication.

The other section is "Recommend: Close". The system judged communication displayed in this section is unnecessary. If the administrator selects "Accept (Close)" button, all communication in this section is prohibited. On the other hand, when the "Reject (Open)" is selected, the ACL permits all communication in this section. In addition, if the administrator wants to permit several ports in this section, he/she has to insert such ports into the "Add Open Port" form.

Finally, this module updates the ACL DB by using the API server after the "Submit" button is clicked. As mentioned in the next subsection V-E, the ACL DB stores only permitted communication sections. In case of that all analyzed communication is judged as still permitted, the system updated the status field of the flow_list table about such communication section as analyzed. If only several ports will be permitted, in addition to the above update, those ports are inserted into dst_port field.

On the other hand, if all protocols in the communication section are judged as unnecessary, the module updates the ACL DB to delete any record of such communication section in the section_list table.

E. ACL DB (Extended)

As described in Section IV, we extended ACL DB. ACL DB consists of two tables, "section_list" and "flow_list" shown in Table II. The section_list table consists of four columns: "id", "src_ip", "dst_ip", and reason. The src_ip and the dst_ip store the source IP address and destination IP address of the communication section permitted by AAGS. The reason column stores the permitted reason.

TABLE II. ACL DB (EXTENDED) TABLE SCHEMA.

Table Name	Column	Data Type	Example
section_list	id	Integer	3
	src_ip	String	192.168.10.10
	dst_ip	String	192.168.20.20
	reason	String	CA
flow_list	section_id	Integer	3
	dst_port	Integer	443
	status	String	analyzed

The flow_list table consists of three columns that are "section_id", "dst_port", and "status". The value of the section_id is corresponding to the id of section_list table. Permitted destination ports in the communication section are stored in the dst_port column. If the communication section is permitted with no analyzation by CCS, "not_analyzed" is stored in the status column. After analyzation by CCS, the value of status is updated to "analyzed".

F. ACL Applier

We use the SDN technique to implement the ACL Applier. The OvS (Open vSwitch) is operating as core switch in the network. We use Trema as OpenFlow controller to apply the contents of ACL DB to the network.

VI. Evaluation Experiment

In order to evaluate the effectiveness of CCS, we applied the implemented system to a prototype network. We verify that if CCS can generate a ACL which prohibits the communication sections overly permitted by AAGS.

A. Experimental Conditions

1) Network Structure: For the experiment, we prepared the prototype network shown in Figure 4. The internal network is divided into three client segments according to the departments of the organization in addition to server segment.

There are three Windows 10 PCs in each segment, and all of these PCs are assigned static IP addresses, e.g., 192.168.10.10. Otherwise, in the server segment, there is only one file server assigned 192.168.100.10.

We set Open vSwitch and each segment and router are connected to this switch. In addition, Trema is assigned 192.168.200.10 and connected to the Open vSwitch directory.

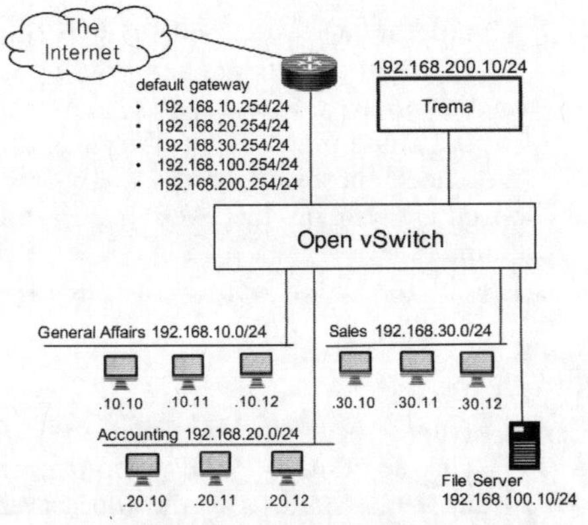

Figure 4. Proto Type Network Architecture.

2) Access Control: We assumed that AAGS generated the ACL, and we prepared the ACL shown in Table III. We configured Trema to permit only the communication listed in Table III in addition to the communications between the default gateway and all the terminals.

TABLE III. LIST OF COMMUNICATION SECTIONS PERMITTED BY PREVIOUS SYSTEM.

Source IP Address	Destination IP Address	Permitted Reason
192.168.10.10	192.168.100.10	DSI
192.168.20.10	192.168.100.10	DSI+CA
192.168.20.11	192.168.100.10	CA
192.168.30.11	192.168.100.10	CA

Although we did not prepare the directory service server in the network, the file server controls permission to files from users. In this experiment, we assume the terminals of 192.168.10.10 and 192.168.20.10 have access authority, and we insert "DSI" as Permitted Reason in the records of these communication sections.

In addition, we assume the presence of unintended communication between 192.168.20.10 and 192.168.100.10, and "CA" is added to Permitted Reason of that section. Similarly, communication sections from 192.168.20.11 and 192.168.30.11 to 192.168.100.10 are permitted because of unintended communication, and "CA" is registered as their Permitted Reason.

B. Experimental Method

The experiment was performed according to the following procedure.

- Step 1: Run the proposed system and start to collect mirrored packets in the network. In this experiment, we set the collection period to be 10 minutes.
- Step 2: In the collection period, terminals, i.e., 192.168.10.10 and 192.168.20.10, access the file server using the SMB protocol. In addition to these terminals, the terminal of 192.168.20.11 which has no access authority also tries SMB protocol communication with the file server. Otherwise, http protocol communication to the file server is conducted by terminals 192.168.20.10 and 192.168.30.11, although the file server does not provide http service. In addition, all nine client terminals access external sites on the Internet that are assuming activities of the organization.

Step 3: After 10 minutes, the collection period ends and the captured packets are analyzed by CCS. Based on the analysis result, the system generates the checklist and prepares the Web page.

Step 4: We check the result of the analysis by the proposed system on the Web page, and authorize them.

Step 5: Finally, the system applies the authorized ACL to the internal network.

C. Results of Experiment

The result of analysis by the proposed system is shown in Table IV. The legitimate SMB communication from 192.168.10.10 and 192.168.20.10 to the file server is judged as necessary correctly. In addition, the system judge the DNS protocol communication as necessary. However, it judges unintentional SMB communication between 192.168.20.11 and 192.168.100.10 as necessary.

TABLE IV. ANALYSIS RESULT BY OUR PROPOSED SYSTEM.

Internal Network Communication that Occurred			Result of
Source IP Address	Destination IP Address	Destination Port	Analysis
192.168.10.10	192.168.100.10	445	Open
192.168.20.10	192.168.100.10	445	Open
192.168.20.11	192.168.100.10	445	Open
192.168.10.12	192.168.10.254	53	Open
192.168.20.12	192.168.20.254	53	Open
192.168.30.10	192.168.30.254	53	Open
192.168.30.11	192.168.30.254	53	Open
192.168.30.12	192.168.30.254	53	Open
192.168.20.10	192.168.100.10	80	Close
192.168.30.11	192.168.100.10	80	Close
192.168.100.10	192.168.10.10	56591	Close
192.168.100.10	192.168.20.10	49977	Close
192.168.100.10	192.168.20.11	50253	Close
192.168.100.10	192.168.30.11	64131	Close
192.168.10.254	192.168.10.12	63489	Close
192.168.20.254	192.168.20.12	61236	Close
~	~	~	Close

Otherwise, the system judges several communication sections as unnecessary. It includes unintended http communication and high port number communication which seem to be returned packets.

D. Discussion

From the experimental result, we found that the proposed system correctly judged legitimate communication as necessary, i.e., SMB communication from 192.168.10.10 and 192.168.20.10 to 192.168.100.10. DNS concerned communication from clients to router is also judged as necessary correctly. In addition, unintended communication, i.e., http communication, is judged as unnecessary.

However, as the result of SMB communication between 192.168.20.11 and 192.168.100.10 shows, the proposed system misjudges the necessity of communication in the specific condition like this. This result shows the problem of CCS. In this case, the DPort Analysis module analyzed the stand-by state of 192.168.100.10 and judged it as necessary because 192.168.100.10 is a file server and it listened to SMB protocol ports for legitimate communication. So, the proposed system permits communication if the port of the destination terminal is opened although the communication is unintended.

Such problem is not only in the case of the SMB protocol, but it occurs in all services in which servers distinguish legitimate users by an authentication process. For example, if an unauthorized terminal attempts to access a Web server with login authentication, CCS allows this unintended communication because the HTTP and HTTPS protocols are listened in the Web server. Even when a service is provided to limited users in the same network, the proposed system makes a misjudgement and allows the communication.

If access controls are performed at terminals, this problem may not occur. To validate it, we conducted a further experiment. We set iptables at 192.168.100.10 to reject all communication not from 192.168.10.10 or 192.168.20.10, and ran CCS under that condition. In this further experiment, SMB communication between 192.168.20.11 and 192.168.100.10 is correctly judged as unnecessary.

Another solution is prohibiting access from users who have authentication process. By using authentication logs of each service, we can check whether the user has succeeded in authentication or not.

In addition to the above problem, the system displayed a lot of communication judgement between all client terminals and the router which is the default gateway of each segment. All these communications look like returned packets. We should not prohibit the returned packets, so these communications should be ignored by the system. However, if CCS simply permits all high port numbers communication, malware's communication using high port numbers is also permitted. Therefore, we need a method to distinguish whether high port communication is legitimate or not.

VII. Conclusion

In this paper, we implemented our proposed communication classifying system and applied it to a prototype network. In the experiment, the system judged necessity of most of the communication observed in the network correctly. As a result, it was confirmed that the feasibility of the proposed system, and most of the "overly permits of unnecessary communication" that was a problem in our previous proposal Automated ACL Generation System could be prohibited.

However, we found several problems from the experimental result. First, our proposed system judges unintended communication as necessary in a specific condition. When a communication occurs in the internal network and destination terminal provides service related to such communication, the CCS permits the communication unconditionally. In addition, the experimental result includes a lot of communication that is returned packets. To ignore such returned packets, we have to classify the communication as malware's activity or returned packet.

As future work, we have to propose methods to avoid misjudges and to classify the high destination port communication.

References

[1] P. Cichonski, T. Miller, T. Grance, and K. Scarfone, "Computer Security Incident Handling Guide," NIST Special Publication 800-61 Revision 2, 2012, NIST SP800-61 Rev.2.

[2] J. Information-technology Promotion Agency, "Design and Operational Guide to Protect against "Advanced Persistent Threats" Revised 2nd edition," 2011, URL: https://www.ipa.go.jp/files/000017299.pdf [accessed: 2019-09-03].

[3] H. Hasegawa, Y. Yamaguchi, H. Shimada, and H. Takakura, "An Automated ACL Generation System using Directory Service Information and Network Traffic Data (in japanese)," The IEICE Transactions on Information and Systems (Japanese Edition), vol. J100–D, no. 3, 2017, pp. 353–364.

[4] Y. Sato, H. Hasegawa, and H. Takakura, "Construction of Secure Internal Networks with Communication Classifying System," Proceedings of the 5th International Conference on Information Systems Security and Privacy, vol. 1, 2019, pp. 552–557.

[5] G. Alessandro, P. Giovanni, C. Alberto, and B. Giuseppe, "Advanced widespread behavioral probes against lateral movements," International Journal for Information Security Research, vol. 6, 2016, pp. 651–659.

[6] T. Watanabe, T. Kitazaki, T. Ideguchi, and Y. Murata, "A Proposal of Dinamic VLAN Configuration with Traffic Analyzation and Its Evaluation Using a Computer Simulation (in Japanese)," IPSJ Journal, vol. 46, no. 9, 2005, pp. 2196–2204.

[7] A. K. Nayak, A. Reimers, N. Feamster, and R. Clark, "Resonance: Dynamic Access Control for Enterprise Networks," Proceedings of the 1st ACM SIGCOMM 2009 Workshop on Research on Enterprise Networking, 2009, pp. 11–18.

[8] T. Miyamoto, T. Tamura, R. Suzuki, H. Hiraoka, H. Matsuo, and et al., "VLAN Management System on Large-scale Network (in Japanese)," Transactions of Information Processing Society of Japan, IPSJ Journal, vol. 41, no. 12, 2000, pp. 3234–3244.

[9] N. Gude, T. Koponen, J. Pettit, B. Pfaff, and M. Casado, "Nox: Towards an operating system for networks," ACM SIGCOMM Computer Communication Review, vol. 38, no. 3, 2008, pp. 105–110.

[10] "VLAN .Config," 2019, URL: http://www.iiga.jp/solution/config/vlan.html [accessed: 2019-09-03].

[11] S. Nakamura, H. Hasegawa, Y. Tateiwa, H. Takakura, Y. Kim, and et al., "A Proposal of Dynamic Access Control with SDN for Practical Network Separation," IEICE Technical Report, vol. 117, no. 299, 2017, pp. 65–69.

[12] "Node.js," 2019, URL: https://nodejs.org/ [accessed: 2019-09-03].

[13] "FastAPI," 2019, URL: https://fastapi.tiangolo.com [accessed: 2019-09-03].

[14] "MySQL," 2019, URL: https://www.mysql.com [accessed: 2019-09-03].

[15] "Open vSwitch," 2019, URL: https://www.openvswitch.org [accessed: 2019-09-03].

[16] "Trema," 2019, URL: https://trema.github.io/trema [accessed: 2019-09-03].

[17] "Docker," 2019, URL: https://www.docker.com [accessed: 2019-09-03].

[18] "dpkt," 2019, URL: https://dpkt.readthedocs.io/en/latest/ [accessed: 2019-09-03].

[19] "React," 2019, URL: https://reactjs.org [accessed: 2019-09-03].

Privacy Preserved Authentication: A Neural Network Approach

Ray R. Hashemi
Amar Rasheed
Jeffrey Young
Department of Computer Science
Georgia Southern University,
Savannah, GA, USA
e-mails: {rayhashemi, amarrasheed, alanyoung7}@gmail.com

Azita A. Bahrami
IT Consultation
Savannah, GA, USA
e-mail: Azita.G.Bahrami@gmail.com

***Abstract*—The anonymity of users during the authentication process for accessing computer-based Safety-Critical Systems (SCSs) is crucial for two reasons: (i) ever growing dependency of users on SCSs and (ii) Internet of Things (IoT), social media, and marketers put the privacy of users of SCS in jeopardy more than ever. The goal of this research effort is to introduce and develop a novel neural network-based system that is able to (a) employ Extracted Eelectro-Cardiogram (ECG) feature vectors of the user as biometric credentials for authentication, (b) preserve the privacy of users during the authentication process and (c) attest the authenticity of clients on a continuous basis during the time that the SCS serves the client. Such attestation is necessary to make sure the user, after initial successful authentication, has not been replaced by an entity with malicious intent. Ten datasets with the total of 246,690 synthesized ECG feature vectors were created to test the system. These vectors were generated out of borrowed real ECG feature vectors for 90 users. Each dataset had 2,169 legitimate users' credentials and 22,500 illegitimate ones. Our neural network-based system revealed the accuracy of (99.98%), precision of (100%), and sensitivity of (99.82%).**

Keywords-Anonymous Authentication; Encryption; Neural Network; Dynamic Authentication; Neural Network-based Authentication; Continuous Attesting Authenticity.

I. INTRODUCTION

The failure of Safety-Critical computer-based Systems (SCSs) may cause economic loss, loss of life, or both. These systems are at work in every segment of society including banking, state and federal elections, business, travel, service, military, manufacturing, insurance, hospitals, medicine, etc. There is a large class of SCSs with the following desired properties:

(a) Being accessed by a set of legitimate clients frequently,
(b) Preserving the clients' privacy during the authentication process,
(c) Attesting the authenticity of clients on a continuous basis during the time that the SCS serves the client.

The first property is innate in all SCSs because, in general, all SCSs are exposed to some degree of controlled access. The second property is crucial for two reasons: (i) ever growing dependency of users on SCSs and (ii) Internet of Things (IoT), social media, and marketers put the privacy of users of SCSs in jeopardy more than ever.

The second property also inherently proposes a major challenge. The challenge stems from the fact that the preservation of privacy and enforcement of security are at odds with each other. To support such oddity, the credentials by which a client seeks access to a SCS is transformed before being presented to the SCS. The intention is to make sure that the actual credentials can neither be seen by the SCS nor can the SCS get the actual credentials through the process of reverse engineering. Therefore, the transformation process totally takes place on the client side. In addition, every time that client wishes to access the SCS, the transformed version of the credentials must be different, although the client credentials remains the same. This is necessary to discourage any discovery attempt of the client credentials. At the SCS side, there is a depository of client credentials that are used for confirming the authenticity of the legitimate clients. Since the client credentials are transformed, each credential in the SCS depository also needs to be transformed. (Obviously, the transformation function used on the client side cannot be used on the SCS side.) The similarities between the transformed client's credentials and each one of the transformed credentials in the depository of the SCS are measured. The authentication is confirmed if the similarities are above a predefined threshold.

The third property is an antidote to laxation of the SCS after initial authentication. In other words, SCS requires a test of assurance that, during the period of service, the client has not been replaced by an entity with malicious intent. Although the credentials of the user are not changing during the service period, the transformation of the credentials has to change.

The goal of this research effort is to introduce and develop a novel neural network-based system that is able to (a) employ Extracted Electro-Cardiogram (ECG) feature vectors of a user as credentials for authentication, (b) preserve privacy and enforce the authentication process and (c) attest continuously the authenticity of clients who are using the SCS service. Since the transformation functions for transforming credentials on the client side and SCS side ought to be different, two new neural networks (one for the client side and one for the SCS side) are introduced.

One may ask why the ECG feature vectors are chosen for authentication. The answer is that ECG vectors are much less susceptible to compromise in comparison to the other biometric measures such as fingerprint, iris etc. [1].

The rest of the paper is organized as follows. The Previous Works are the subject of Section 2. The Methodology is presented in Section 3. The Empirical Results are discussed in Section 4. The Complexity Analysis of the system is the subject of Section 5. The Conclusions and Future Research are covered in Section 6.

II. PREVIOUS WORKS

Due to explosion of IoT and social media, privacy-preserved authentication has received tremendous attention over the last two decades. In general, four different paradigms are used: *hamming distance* paradigm, *oblivious* paradigm, *zero-knowledge proof* paradigm, *verifiable common secret encoding* paradigm, and *hybrid* paradigm. Secured weighted hamming distance and its modified versions are the nucleus of the hamming distance paradigm [2][3].

According to the oblivious paradigm, SCS has several strings of information and transfers one of the strings to the receiver and after that remains inattentive and or unconcerned (oblivious) about the transferred string of information [4][5].

According to the zero-knowledge proof paradigm, the client is able to prove his/her credentials to the SCS many times using polynomial authentication [6]-[8].

According to the verifiable common secret encoding paradigm, clients are arranged in groups and groups are dynamically formed by using a set of public keys ids. The privacy of the client is preserved through proving that it is an active member of a certain group [9][10].

According to the hybrid paradigm, a combination of more than one of the above mentioned paradigms are used [1] [11]-[13]. For example, a combination of hamming distance paradigm and oblivious paradigm are used frequently. We introduce and evaluate a novel privacy-preserved authentication paradigm—Neural Network-based paradigm.

III. METHODOLOGY

The methodology for meeting the three-prong goal of this research is explained in detail in this section. Let X be the binary vector of length N representing features for one biometric measurement of a user and also let Γ be a set of binary vectors on the SCS side that if the similarity of X with one of the elements in Γ is within an acceptable range then, X is valid. We separately explain steps taken in both client side and SCS side to provide access to SCS while preserving the privacy of users in the following two subsections. The reader needs to be reminded that providing access to SCS and preserving the privacy of users are the first two prongs of the goal for this study. The details of the last prong of the goal are the subject of the third sub-section.

A. *Actions on the Client Side*

We take X and divide it into equal size sections of $x_1, \ldots, x_n$. Let the number of bits in x_i be m. We build a *semi-feed forward neural network* with two layers of input and output. A feed forward neural net is unidirectional. That is, the difference between the output vector and target vector is not fed backward. Therefore, the weight matrix for the connections between the nodes of input layer and the nodes of output layer do not change. However, we call our neural network a semi-feed forward net because the weight matrix is updated after each input vector completes its journey through the net. We shortly introduce the updating process for the weight matrix.

The input layer has (m+1) nodes (the extra node is a bias node) and output layer has only m nodes. Sections x_i (for i = 1 to n) are used as input vectors to the net. The input for the bias node is always one, as shown in Figure 1.

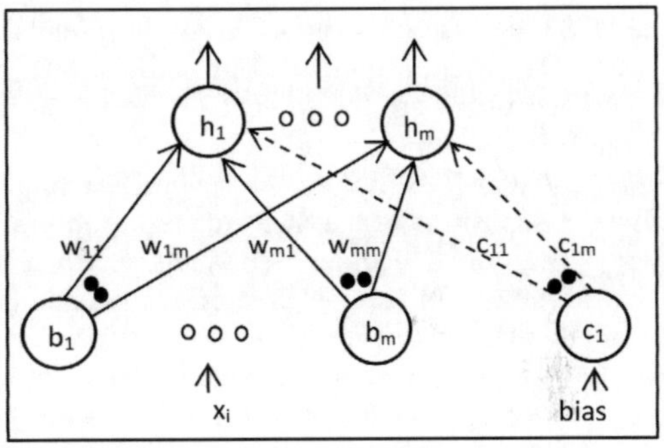

Figure 1. The client side feed forward neural network architecture

The initial weight matrix, W is:

$$W=\begin{bmatrix} a_{1,1} & e_{1,2} & \cdots & & e_{1,m} \\ e_{2,1} & a_{2,2} & e_{2,3} & \cdots & e_{2,m} \\ e_{3,1} & e_{3,2} & a_{3,3} & e_{3,4} \cdots & e_{3,m} \\ \vdots & & & & \\ e_{m,1} & e_{m,2} & e_{m,3} & \cdots & a_{m,m} \\ e_{m+1,1} & e_{m+1,2} & e_{m+1,3} & \cdots & e_{m+1,m} \end{bmatrix}$$

Elements $a_{i,i}$ of W are calculated using (1), where d is a random integer value >2.

$$a_{i,i} = 2^{k-i+1}, \; k \geq d*m+1 \qquad (1)$$

Elements $e_{i,j}$ of W are calculated using (2), where $c_{i,j}$ is a non-negative integer random number less than 2^m. (c_{ij} is randomly generated for each $e_{i,j}$.)

$$e_{i,j} = c_{i,j} * 2_m \quad (2)$$

The output of j-th node of the output layer for the input vector of I is calculated using (3), where $W_{*,j}$ means the j-th column of weight matrix W.

$$o_j = \sum_{j=1}^{m} IW_{*,j} \quad (3)$$

After an input vector completes the feed forward step, before the next input vector be fed to the net, all the e_{ij} elements of W are replaced by a new e_{ij} that is randomly generated using (2). This is an extra effort in preserving the privacy of the client.

The input vector of x_i generates an output vector that serves as a column of a new matrix. That is, using the neural net for input vectors of x_i (for i = 1 to n) generates a new matrix G such that the output for input vector x_i is the i-th column of matrix G. Therefore, G is a matrix of m rows and n columns. Matrix G is the one that leaves the client side as the transformation of X. SCS has neither the knowledge of input vectors nor weight matrix W and its updates.

B. *Actions on the SCS side*

The SCS receives only matrix G from the client side and the process of authentication is completed in two phases. Details of each phase are the subject of the following two subsections.

1) Phase I: Let Y be one of the several existing binary vectors in the depository of the SCS side representing a user. We shortly introduce another *semi-feed forward neural network* (different from the one used on the client side) that transforms Y. The differences between the transformed Y and transformed X are measured and if the difference is higher than an acceptable threshold then, X matches Y. The same process is repeated for every users' binary vectors until the authenticity of X is either validated or denied.

The vector Y is divided into equal size sections of $y_1, \ldots, y_n$ such that the number of bits in y_i is m. We convert y_i to a matrix of m by 1 and as a result Y is converted to a matrix, Z, of m rows and n columns.

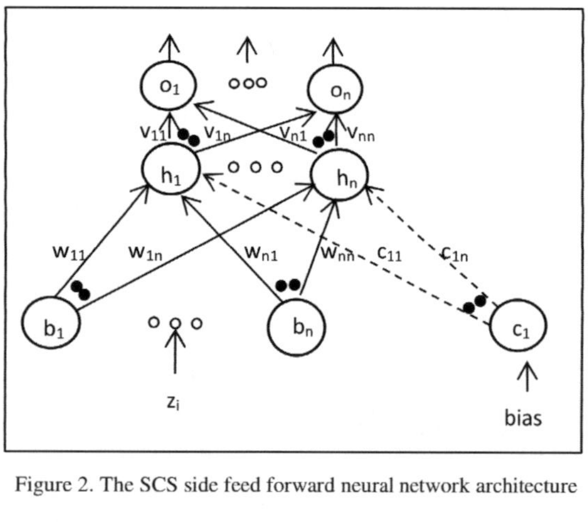

Figure 2. The SCS side feed forward neural network architecture

We introduce the *semi-feed forward neural network* for use in the SCS side that is different from the one introduced for the client side. The new neural net has three layers of input, hidden and output, as shown in Figure 2.

Two weight matrices are needed (one for connections between the nodes of input –hidden layers, W, and one for the connections between the nodes of hidden-output layers, V.) Creating and updating processes of the weight matrices are also different from the one for the client side. The input layer has (n+1) nodes (the extra node is a bias node), both the hidden layer and the output layer have n nodes. Each row of matrix Z along with an input of 1(for the bias node) serves as input to the feed forward neural network.

The initial weight matrix, W, has n+1 rows and n columns and it is built in two steps. During the first step, W = (2_{m-1})*W', where W' is an identity matrix of n X n. During the second step, the k-th row of G (k =1 for the initial weight matrix) is added to W to serve as the $(n+1)_{th}$ row of W. The value of k is increased by one for each incoming input vector.

$$W = \begin{bmatrix} a_1 & 0 & \cdots & & 0 \\ 0 & a_2 & 0 & \cdots & 0 \\ 0 & 0 & a_3 & 0 \cdots & 0 \\ & & \cdots & & \\ & & \cdots & & \\ 0 & 0 & 0 & \cdots & a_n \\ g_{k,1} & g_{k,2} & g_{k,3} & \cdots & g_{k,n} \end{bmatrix}$$

For the first input vector, the initial W is used. For the next input vector, W changes using (4) and (5).

$$new(w_{ij}) = old(w_{ij})/2 \quad (4)$$
(for i = 1 to m and j =1 to n)

$$new(w_{ij}) = g_{k,j} \quad (5)$$
(for i = m+1, j = 1 to n, and k = k+1)

The output of the j-th node of the hidden layer for the input vector of I is calculated using (1).

The weight matrix, V, for connections between nodes of the hidden layer and output layer has n rows and n columns. V is a binary matrix and it is randomly created such that every row and every column of V contains only one 1. Therefore, the total number of ones in V is equal to n. For each input vector, a new V is randomly generated. Let vector H be the output of the hidden layer nodes, the output of the j-th node in the output layer is calculated by (1). Using this neural net for all input vectors delivers a matrix of m rows and n columns, P.

2) Phase II: Let the largest element in matrix P be L bits long when it is converted into binary. We take the binary equivalence of p_{11}, first element in P, and padded with zeros (if needed) to make its length equal to L. We rotate the binary number to the left i=1 places and take the m+1 least significant bits as a value (q). The counter h is set using (6), where $r = q \bmod (2^m + 1)$.

$$h = (m_{r+1}) * \lfloor Cos(r) \rfloor \quad (6)$$

The above process is repeated for each remaining element, p_{ij}, in P using (7).

$$h = h + (m_{r+1}) * \lfloor Cos(r) \rfloor \quad (7)$$

The ultimate outcome of the second phase is h. Let N be the length of X and, thus, the length of Y. The threshold value $T= m(N - \beta)$. Let us explain what β is. In reality, X and Y are extracted feature vectors of a biometric of interest for a user. The extracted feature vectors are not always exactly the same and they may differ by negligible number of bits—β. The value for β is selected in such a way that the ratio of β/N is extremely small. If $h > T$ then, X and Y are matched.

C. *Attestation*

Our neural network-based system employs Extracted Electro-Cardiogram (ECG) feature vectors of users as credentials for authentication. An ECG shows the electrical signals of a human heart as a waveform and it is unique for each individual. The components of the ECG waveform are named P, Q, R, S, T, U, and V as illustrated in Figure 3.

The uniqueness of this waveform for each person makes it a vital biometric candidate for authentication. The physical characteristics of the ECG such as relationships among R, Q, and S peaks individually or collectively, duration and shape of P, T, and U waves and their relationships (that represent depolarization and repolarization phases of human heart) may be used as features of an ECG. To obtain such features: (i) several ECG waveforms of a person are recorded for a short period of time and (ii) recorded waveforms are analyzed using either fiducial points based approaches [14] [15] or pattern recognition based approaches [16][17], to conclude the features of ECG for the person. Such features are claimed to be independent of the heartrate [16].

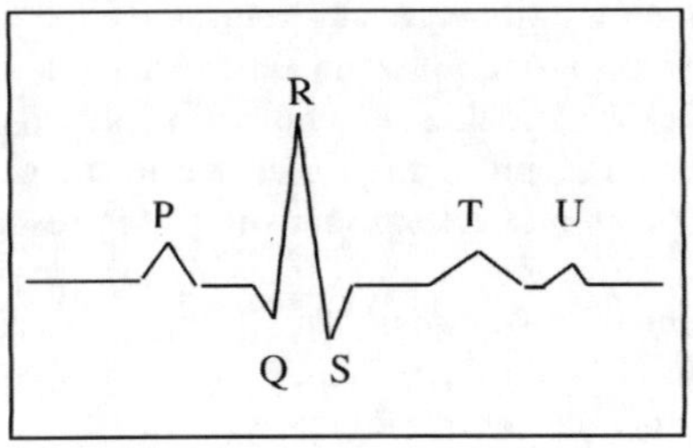

Figure 3. Components of ECG waveform

To complete attestation, a portable health device with sensors that are able to read constantly the ECG waveforms of a person may be used. Let us assume that the ECG of a person is read for t_1 units of time. These waveforms go to the process of ECG analysis for extraction of ECG features and the analysis process takes t_2 units of time. The authentication process using the neural network-based paradigm takes t_3 units of time. Thus, for the very first reading of ECG, it takes $t = t_1 + t_2 + t_3$ units of time that authentication be completed. However, ECG reading is done by a different device than the one in charge of all computations; therefore, the attestation is repeated every $t' = t_2 + t_3$ units of time, after the authentication is completed for the first reading of ECG.

IV. EMPIRICAL RESULTS

For a given authentication system, let us assume that out of U_1 number of users who have valid credentials only T_P of them were positively authenticated by the system and, therefore, F_N of them were rejected ($U_1 = T_P+F_N$.) Let us also assume that out of U_2 number of users who have invalid credentials only T_N of them were rejected by the system and, F_P of them were not ($U_2 = T_N+F_P$). The accuracy, precision, and sensitivity of the authentication for the system are calculated using (8), (9), and (10), respectively.

$$Accuracy = (T_P+T_N)/(U_1+U_2) \quad (8)$$
$$Precision = T_P/(T_P+F_P) \quad (9)$$
$$Sensitivity = T_P/U_1 \quad (10)$$

Bhutra et al. [1] reported extraction of a 240-bit long feature vector from a person's ECG that is recorded for 20 seconds and digitized at 500 Hz with 12-bit resolution over a nominal ±10 mV range. We assumed that the negligible number of bits is one ($\beta = 1$). To examine the behavior of our neural network-based authentication, the test dataset was borrowed from [1]. This dataset included feature vectors for 90 different eligible users and it was used as the depository of credentials on the SCS side.

For the client side, we repeated the following process for every one of the 90 feature vectors, FV_i. Out of the 240 bits in FV_i, randomly k ($2 \le k \le 10$) bits of the FV_i were chosen and corrupted (i.e., flipped) to generate a new FV_i. We generated 2500 new corrupted feature vectors out of each FV_i and thus, the total of 225,000 corrupted ones out of the original 90 feature vectors. (The reader needs to be reminded that the total possible corrupted vectors that can be created out of one FV_i using $2 \le k \le 10$, is more than 10^{17}. We just randomly generate 2500 of them.) Ten datasets of equal size were created randomly out of the corrupted feature vectors and named $D_1 \ldots D_{10}$ such that D_i contained 22,500 corrupted vectors (invalid credentials).

Following the same procedure for k =1, the total of 21,600 corrupted feature vectors generated using the original 90 vectors. The new corrupted vectors were treated as the original vectors with a negligible number of corrupted bits ($\beta = 1$). These vectors were randomly and equally added to the $D_1 \ldots D_{10}$ such that every vector appeared in only one of the datasets. (Each D_i was expanded by 2160 new vectors. In addition the original 90 vectors were randomly and equally divided among the ten datasets such that each vector appeared in only one dataset. As a result, each dataset D_i had the total of 24,669 vectors of which 22500 of them were invalid and 2169 vectors were valid. We measured the accuracy, precision, and sensitivity of our neural network-based authentication approach using the ten datasets and results are shown in Table I.

TABLE I: THE AVERAGES OF ACCURACY, PRECISION, AND SENSITIVITY MEASURES FOR OUR NEURAL NETWORK-BASED AUTHENTICATION APPROACH USING THE TEN DATASETS OF $D_1 \ldots D_{10}$.

Dataset	Accuracy	Precision	Sensitivity
D1	100	100	99.95
D2	99.99	100	99.91
D3	99.96	100	99.54
D4	100	100	99.95
D5	99.97	100	99.63
D6	100	100	99.95
D7	99.97	100	99.68
D8	99.98	100	99.72
D9	99.99	100	99.91
D10	99.99	100	99.91
Average	99.98%	100%	99.82%

We also examined whether the rejection or acceptance of a feature vector was dependent on the locations of those bits that are different between the two transformed vectors of X and Y. To explain further, let us assume that X and Y are both divided into 6 sections of (x1, x2, x3, x4, x5, and x6) and (y1, y2, y3, y4, y5, and y6) and each section is 3 bits long (thus, n = 6 and m = 3). Let us also assume that the number of bits that are different between X and Y is 6. These six bits may have several different distributions within X. For example, in one distribution, one bit is different in each corresponding section of x_i and y_i (for i =1 to 6). In another distribution, all the bits in x1and x2 (total of 6 bits) are different from the bits in y1 and y2, respectively. In a third distribution, two bits in each section of x1, x2, and x3, (total of 6 bits) are different from two bits in each section of y4, y5, and y6. Is the authentication influenced by distribution of the different bits between the vectors of X and Y?

To find the answer to the proposed question we selected randomly one of the 90 original feature vectors, Vector Y. We used m = 4 and n =60 to create 4-bit long 60 sections for Y. A new vector, X, was created. We assumed that the number of bits that are different between X and Y is B_i (for i = 3 to 30). The vector Y was considered as the true credentials and vector X was the one in which distributions of B_i flipped bits took place. For each B_i 200 different distributions of B_i flipped bits in Y were generated that collectively made a group of distributions for B_i—G_{B_i}. Each vector in the group is a new X vector and all X vectors in the group have the same number of B_i bits that are different from Y. The total number of distributions' groups was 27. We used every new X against the true credentials vector Y and findings showed that the authentication process is not influenced by the locations of B_i flipped bits.

V. COMPLEXITY ANALYSIS

On both the client side and the SCS side, the credentials are divided into n sections of m-bit long. The weight matrix W, on the client side has m +1 rows and m columns. Therefore, smaller m means smaller W. However, smaller m means larger n, which makes the weight matrices of W and V on the SCS side larger because they have n+1 rows and n columns. As a result, in choosing n and m one may pay attention to the size of the weight matrices. The Reader needs to be reminded that the size of m and the number of input records are moving in two different directions.

Let us assume that N = n and n >> m. The worst case is when the size of m becomes equal to the size of n and the size of the weight matrix is, therefore, N^2. The time complexity for the neural network on the client side, the neural network of phase I on the SCS side, and computation of phase II of SCS are $O(N^2)$, $O(2(N)^2)$, and $O(N^2)$, respectively. The total time complexity is $O(4N^2)$. Since N is a very small number so is the time complexity.

VI. CONCLUSIONS AND FUTURE RESEARCH

Two well-known paradigms of privacy based authentications are Zero Knowledge Proof (ZKP) and Verifiable Common Secrete Encoding (VCSE). In general, the former one uses a set of hardcoded parameters that are essential to its performance. The device that runs ZKP could be profiled by a *Side-Channel Attack* [18], which in turn could be used to disclose the set of parameters. The consequences of the parameters' disclosure are compromising the device and subsequently back engineering the authentication secrets. In contrast, our methodology (use of a neural network) creates a different set of weights every time it is used. This means that no matter how much profiling is done, no intrinsic data can be compromised.

VCSE uses public/private key encryption. It maintains anonymity by the use of a dummy list of keys, which is sent to the server. The server encrypts every key in the list using the same session key, concatenates each encrypted key with the same random number, r, and returns the list to the client. The client, in turn, decrypts and sends back r to be validated by the server. This makes the anonymity provided by VCSE considerable. The problem is that due to the overhead, the VCSE consumes a large amount of system resource, which results in a slow execution especially on devices with a small amount of resources. This is not the case with our neural network approach, which uses very little system resource to achieve anonymity.

In addition, our privacy preserving authentication approach also shows almost a perfect accuracy, precision, and sensitivity.

As future research, development of a neural network-based hybrid authentication system is in progress that will be tailored toward authentication at Boundaries of Cyber-Physical Systems.

REFERENCES

[1] G. Bhutra, A. Rasheed, and R. Mahapatra, "Privacy-Preserving ECG based Active Authentication (PPEA2) for IoT Devices", IEEE International Performance Computing and Communication Conferences (IPCCC 2018), Special Session on Networking in Cyber Physical Systems, pp. 1-8, 2018.

[2] R Kulkarni and A. Namboodiri, "Secure hamming distance based biometric authentication", Proceedings of 2013 International conference on Biometrics, pp. 1-6, 2013.

[3] M. Yasuda, "Secure Hamming distance computation for biometrics using ideal-lattice and ring-LWE homomorphic encryption", Online Information Security Journal: A Global Perspective, 26(2): 85-103, 2017.

[4] M. S. Kiraz, B. Schoenmakers, and J. Villegas, "Efficient committed oblivious transfer of bit strings", in Information Security, Lecture Notes in Computer Science, Springer, 4779:130–144, 2007.

[5] T. Tassa, "Generalized oblivious transfer by secret sharing", International Journal of Designs, Codes and Cryptography, Springer, 58(1):11–21, 2011.

[6] O. Goldreich and Y. Oren, "Definitions and Properties of Zero-Knowledge Proof Systems", Journal of Cryptology, Springer Verlag, 7:1-32, 1994.

[7] H. Wu, F. Bao, D. Ye, and R. Deng, "Cryptanalysis of Polynomial Authentication and Signature Scheme", Proceedings of the 5th Australasian Conference on Information Security and Privac0, Brisbane, Australia, 1841: 278-288, 2000.

[8] C. Rackoff and D. R. Simon, "Non-Interactive Zero-Knowledge Proof of Knowledge and Chosen Ciphertext Attack", Proceedings of the International Cryptology Conference, Springer Lecture Notes in Computer Science, 576: 433-444, 1991.

[9] T. Rabin and M. Ben-Or, "Verifiable secret sharing and multiparty protocols with honest majority", Proceedings of the twenty-first annual ACM symposium on Theory of computing, Seattle, Washington, pp. 73-85, 1989.

[10] C. Cachin, K. Kursawe, A. Lysyanskaya, and R. Strobl, "Asynchronous verifiable secret sharing and proactive cryptosystems", Proceedings of the 9th ACM conference on Computer and communications security, Washington Dc, pp. 88-97, 2002.

[11] M. S. Kiraz, Z. A. Genc, and S. Kardas, "Security and Efficiency Analysis of the Hamming Distance Computation Protocol Based On Oblivious Transfer", Security and Communication Networks, Wiley Online Library, 8(18):4123-4135, 2015.

[12] J. Bringer, H. Chabanne, and A. Patey, "Shade: Secure hamming Distance Computation from Oblivious Transfer", in Financial Cryptography and Data Security, Lecture Notes in Computer Science, Springer, 7862: 164–176, 2013.

[13] Y. Xi, K. Sha, W. Shi, L. Schwiebert, and T. Zhang, "Probabilistic Adaptive Anonymous Authentication in Vehicular Networks", Journal of Computer Science and Technology, 23(6):916-928, 2008.

[14] L. Biel, O. Pettersson, L. Philipson, and P. Wide "ECG analysis: a new approach in human identification", IEEE Transactions on Instrumentation and Measurement, 50(3): 808-812, 2001.

[15] S. Yazdani and J. Vesin, "Extraction of QRS Fiducial points from the ECG using adaptive mathematical morphology", Journal of Digital Signal Processing, Academic Press, 56:100-109, 2016.

[16] S. Israel, J. Irvine, A. Cheng, M. Wiederhold, and B. Wiederhold, "ECG to identify individuals." Pattern recognition, 38(1):133-142, 2005.

[17] K. N. Plataniotis, D. Hatzinakos, and J. K. M. Lee, "ECG biometric recognition without fiducial detection", Biometrics Symposium: Special Session on Research at the Biometric Consortium Conference, Baltimore, pp. 1-6, 2006.

[18] C. Carlet and E. Prouff, "Polynomial Evaluation and Side Channel Analysis", in the New Codebreakers, Lecture Notes in Computer Science, Springer, 9100: 315-341, 2016.

End-to-End Application Security over Intermediaries on the Example of Power System Communication

Steffen Fries, Rainer Falk
Corporate Technology
Siemens AG
Munich, Germany
e-mail: {steffen.fries|rainer.falk}@siemens.com

***Abstract*—Connecting client and server applications directly via a transport connection allows the application of existing security protocols directly, as known from classical Web applications. Typically, Transport Layer Security (TLS) is applied to protect the communication link end-to-end. This approach is utilized in substation automation to protect the Transmission Control Protocol (TCP)-based communication between a substation controller and a protection relay applying mutual authentication of the end-points. If a direct communication link is not available, communication is realized over an intermediary system. Providing end-to-end security over multiple communication hops, including mutual endpoint authentication (client and a target application service) as well as integrity and confidentiality of communicated data deserves specific attention, even if the communication hops with the intermediary are protected hop-by-hop by security protocols like TLS. In power system automation, this kind of communication involving an intermediary is used with publish subscribe protocols, e.g., when integrating Decentralized Energy Resources (DER) or when integrating into the German Smart Meter Gateway architecture. This paper investigates existing solutions and specifically analyses the end-to-end security approach defined for power system automation within the International Electrotechnical Commission (IEC) and motivates broader application in session-based communication scenarios.**

Keywords—security; device authentication; end-to-end security; multi-hop security; IEC 62351 Publish/Subscribe.

I. INTRODUCTION

Security in power system communication is getting more momentum, as energy supply is part of the critical infrastructure. For critical infrastructures, the European Network and Information System (NIS) Directive [1] requires security measures to be supported by the system operator. This directive has been ratified by the European member states. Germany, for instance, has passed the Information technology (IT) Security Act already in 2015 [2], which required the definition of domain-specific security standards that have to be implemented by operators of critical infrastructures. For the power system infrastructure, the domain specific security standard is provided by ISO 27019 [3] in conjunction with the IT security catalog of the German BNetzA [4]. Both documents target communication security in terms of authentication of communicating entities in addition to integrity and confidentiality protection of the data exchange, but without specifying specific technical means in terms of protocols to be used. Security requirements for critical infrastructures are also defined outside Europe, for instance in requirements specified by NIST Cybersecurity framework [5] and specifically for the power system infrastructure by the North American Energy Reliability Council in the NERC Critical Infrastructure Protection (CIP) standards [6]. These documents pose similar requirements, which relate most often to the processes of an operator and partly to supporting technology. Common to all of the requirement documents is that additional standards/specifications are necessary to address the implementation of such requirements in components and systems, while ensuring interoperability between different vendor's products.

One standard defining specific technical requirements is provided by the framework IEC 62443 [7], describing specifically in two distinct parts technical requirements for different security levels, which relate to the strength of the considered attacker. They also refer to security of communicated data.

Besides these technical requirements, different standards and draft standards exist, addressing communication security covering standard requirements for entity authentication, integrity protection and confidentiality protection. One example for such a standard protecting specifically TCP based communication is provided by the Transport Layer Security Protocol (TLS 1.2 [8], TLS 1.3 [9]).

As analyzed in [10], the necessity to support communication over multiple hops between two entities in power system automation has been emphasized by the support of Decentralized Energy Resources (DER). Integrating DER into the current energy distribution network requires to monitor and control these DER to a similar level as centralized energy generation in power plants to keep the stability of the power network. To cope with the fact that DER are typically operated within a private operator network protected by a firewall, the standard IEC 61850-8-2 [11] defines a communication approach based on the eXtensible Messaging and Presence Protocol – XMPP [12]. Here, both sides, the DER controller, as well as the control center, connect to an intermediate server node, which facilitates the communication between both entities. In this specific case, the standard IEC 62351-4 [13] ensures that the communication between the control center and the DER is secured in an end-to-end fashion. Meanwhile, this standard has been released and will be compared to other existing and meanwhile developed solutions.

The remaining part of the paper is structured as follows. Section II describes the communication overview and derives high level security requirements. These requirements are taken into consideration later in the description of the security approach taken for the integration of DER into the power system based on IEC 61850. Section III investigates a selection of existing approaches to provide end-to-end security (message-based and session-based methods). Section IV provides more insight into the actual design and application of the protocol defined in IEC 62351-4 to motivate broader application. Section V concludes the paper with an outlook.

II. Communication Architecture and Derivation of Security requirements

A. Communication architecture

For the discussion of end-to-end communication, the integration of DER resources into a power system control network is taken as example, see Figure 1. The lower part of the figure shows the distributed generators (photovoltaic and wind power) that are managed by the control function shown in the upper part. All entities are connected via a communication network in which the intermediary XMPP server in the middle provides the connectivity between the control center and the DER controller. The control function may be located at a Distribution Network Operator, a virtual power plant operator, or a smart energy market operator.

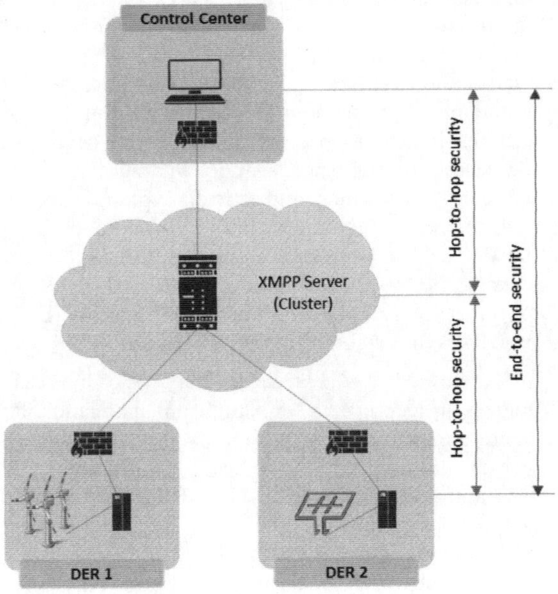

Figure 1. DER Integration based on IEC 61850 over XMPP

The data exchanged between the DER controller and the control center comprises different types of data:

- Customer data, which may be identification information, location data, consumption data or other information belonging to the DER owner.
- Control data, which may be either commands issued by the control center, or event and monitoring information from the DER controller.
- Market data, which may be tariff information provided from a marketplace via the control center or directly (not shown in Figure 1) to the DER controller.

In the context of utilizing IEC 61850 to connect DER to a control center, the communication between the DER controller and the XMPP server is secured using TLS as transport layer security protocol. The same holds for the connection between the control center and the XMPP server. Note that the XMPP server may belong to a different administrative domain and may therefore not be trusted to access the data exchanged between the DER controller and the control center. Hence, the communication relation between the DER controller and the control center is secured at application layer using IEC 62351-4, which will be analyzed in more detail in Section IV.

B. Derivation of Security Requirements

As stated in the introduction, there are different types of security requirements stemming, on one hand, from the obligation to comply with international and national regulations. On the other hand, security requirements are derived from the system architecture based on a risk-based approach. The international industrial security standard IEC 62443 [7] is a security requirements framework jointly developed by the International Electrotechnical Commission (IEC) and the International Society of Automation (ISA99) to address the need to design cybersecurity robustness and resilience into Industrial Automation and Control Systems (IACS). The standard covers both organizational and technical aspects of security over the life cycle of systems. It can be used in conjunction with ISO/IEC 27019 (the Information Security Management System (ISMS) profile for the energy domain based on ISO 27002) and with IEC 62351, providing specific security solutions. Here, the parts IEC 62443-3-3 (focus on system security requirements) and IEC 62443-4-2 (focus on component security requirements) can be used in the context of a risk-based approach, as they specify technical security requirements for four security levels, corresponding to different strengths of an attacker. For both views, system and component, foundational requirements groups have been defined. For each of the foundational requirements, several concrete technical Security Requirements (SR) and Requirement Enhancements (RE) to address a specific security level exist.

The overall approach applies to the systems and the communication connections are shown in Figure 1. In the context of this paper, the focus is placed on the communication relations only, to address the specific target of providing communication security over potentially untrusted nodes. The protection of the communication is addressed by different security requirements focusing on

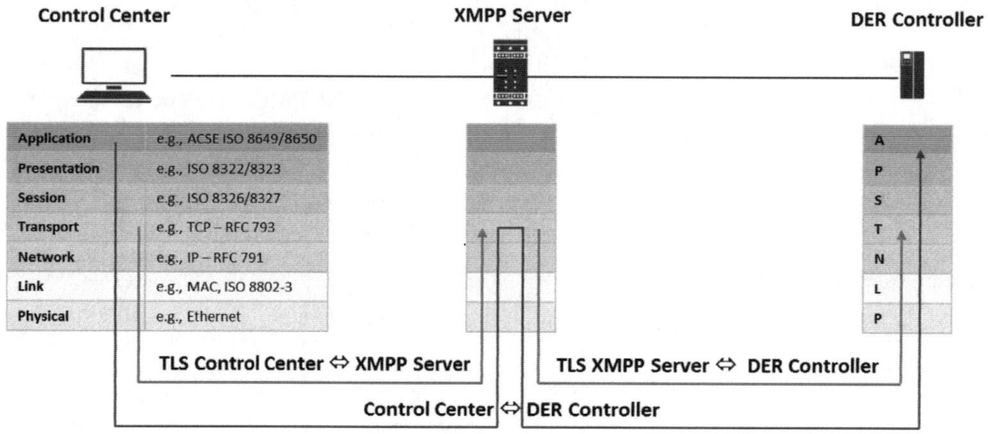

Figure 2. End-to-end-Security and hop-by-hop security according to IEC 62351-4

end-to-end security requirements and hop-to-hop security requirements. Note that the hop-to-hop security requirements contribute to the overall system security approach and may be used in conjunction with the end-to-end security. Figure 2 shows the data exchange between the control center and the DER controller via the XMPP server. The security requirements comprise specifically:

- End-to-end authentication between the DER controller and the control center to ensure identification and authentication of the communicating endpoints.
- End-to-end integrity protection to ensure that data in transit has not been tampered with (unauthorized modification) between the DER controller and the control center.
- End-to-end confidentiality protection to ensure that data in transit has not been accessed (read) in an unauthorized way by the XMPP server.

Hop-to-hop authentication between the XMPP client (DER controller, control center) and the XMPP server is used to identify and authenticate an intermediary system proxying the end-to-end communication between the DER controller and the control center.

III. Security Measures on Application Layer

This section investigates a selection of existing end-to-end security approaches, which can be used to provide authentication, integrity, and confidentiality. Note that XMPP enhancements to achieve end-to-end security between the clients connected via the XMPP server have already been discussed as part of [10] and are not further discussed here. The IETF drafts discussed in this respect are already outdated and have not been updated in the last two years. Therefore, they are not considered further. In the following examples of existing standards or standards in development supporting end-to-end security on application layer, are summarized. They are distinguished into message-based approaches and session-based approaches. Message-based approaches are independent of the actual communication session and can be applied to single messages. Session-based approaches are relying on a communication connection, which comprises at least an initialization phase and a data exchange phase. Both approaches have their merits, but also certain drawbacks.

A. *Message-based security*

The following examples target the protection of single messages and do not rely on an established communication connection:

- IETF RFC 3923 [14] describes end-to-end signing and object encryption utilizing S/MIME to protect the messages exchanged over XMPP connections. This approach is similar to using secure email. It provides end-to-end authentication based on a digital signature and confidentiality protection based on symmetric encryption. As this approach targets message-based communication, without a communication session it will result in a higher per message overhead, as the messages are protected using symmetric encryption, while the key for the symmetric encryption is encrypted with the recipient's public key. This approach has two drawbacks. It is performance intensive due to the use of asymmetric operations and it is bound to RSA as asymmetric algorithm. Newer algorithms like ECDSA based on elliptic curves may not be used.
- W3C defined XML security may also be used to address a secure data exchange on application layer. There are two different standards available, which are already utilized to provide security: XML Signatures [15] and XML Encryption [16]. Both can be used in conjunction, ideally on XML encoded data in so-called XML elements and support the given security requirements. XML encryption allows the encryption of any type of data with symmetric and asymmetric methods. XML signature on the other side applies asymmetric methods to achieve integrity protection and

non-repudiation. Note that there exist adequate standards for the binary data representation.

- The IETF working group for JavaScript Object Signing and Encryption (JOSE) defined two further standards, which can be used to protect messages encoded in JavaScript Object Notation (JSON). IETF RFC 7515 [17] specifies JSON Web Signatures, while IETF RFC 7516 [18] defines JSON Web Encryption. The combination of both documents is similar to XML documents developed by W3C for specific JSON encoding.
- A further IETF standard is provided with RFC 8152 [19] defining authentication, integrity protection, and confidentiality protection for Concise Binary Object Representation (CBOR), which enhanced the data model of JSON with a binary representation. This approach allows for enveloping and encryption of arbitrary message blocks.

B. *Session-based security*

The following examples target the protection of communication sessions for application data exchanges. For this, it is assumed that a communication session is established between two entities during which both participants can authenticate and negotiate a set of session keys for protecting further communication. This approach has the advantage for consecutive communication to result in less overhead for the bulk data handling as part of the communication session. This is due to the fact that the combination of symmetric encryption and an additional integrity protection or the direct application of authenticated encryption has a much better performance instead of invoking asymmetric cryptography on a per packet base.

- IETF draft on Application Layer TLS [20] leverages the existence of a TLS implementation on the communicating entities. The approach utilizes the option of TLS stacks to create and process TLS records based on access to the byte buffer. Based on this, the TLS packets may be transmitted over arbitrary transport connections. This approach has the advantage that the application layer security immediately benefits from new cipher suites and cryptographic algorithm support by the underlying TLS stack. In addition, several TLS stacks allow key material export using the approach defined in IETF RFC 5705 [21] to leverage the TLS key agreement and to utilize the negotiated key in the context of other protocols.
- Signal [22] is a protocol used in messaging systems, which allows to establish a secure session based on an authenticated triple Diffie Hellman key agreement in which EdDSA signatures are employed for integrity protection during the key establishment phase. The negotiated key material is applied to protect the integrity and confidentiality of the established session based on the Double Ratchet algorithm. Note that peer authentication is not directly supported by signal.
- Off-the-Record (OTR [23]) is a further protocol used in messenger applications to ensure integrity and confidentiality. In versions 2 and 3 of the protocol, peer authentication is also supported. Here, shared keys are utilized to achieve the authentication.
- Application Layer Transport Security (ALTS [24]) has been developed by Google in 2017 and is utilized to secure Remote Procedure Calls (RPC). The protocol is defined in a similar way as TLS, consisting of a handshake protocol and a record protocol. It allows for mutual authentication and session integrity and confidentiality. Authentication is bound to an entity rather than an instance (e.g., hostname) as the approach targets mainly cloud environments. Note that there are tradeoffs to TLS described in the specification [24], which relate to privacy concerns for the handshake messages and perfect forward secrecy. Note that these properties are supported out of the box in TLS 1.3, but not in TLS 1.2 and below.

IV. End-to-End Security Design in IEC 62351-4

As described in Section II.B, the security requirements for providing an application layer end-to-end security supporting DER integration can be summarized as:

- Mutual peer authentication between the DER controller and the control center. As existing security measures described in the context of IEC 62351 always rely on authentication using X.509 certificates, being intended for authentication, too.
- Session key management between the communicating peers supporting initial key agreement providing perfect forward secrecy as well as key update.
- Integrity protection of exchanged data to ensure that data in transit has not been tampered with.
- Optionally, confidentiality protection to ensure that an intermediary cannot access the content of the data exchange.

Note that it should be possible to use either distinct algorithms for integrity and confidentiality or a combined approach (authenticated encryption).

The standard IEC 62351-4 was updated in 2018 and specifies a transport security profile and an application security profile. The application security targets the provisioning of end-to-end security, as outlined by the requirements above. The following description depicts the protocol.

A. *Precondition*

The involved endpoints are expected to possess a certificate and corresponding private key as well as a root certificate trusted by both sides (e.g., bound to the operator) and a common set of Diffie Hellman base parameter.

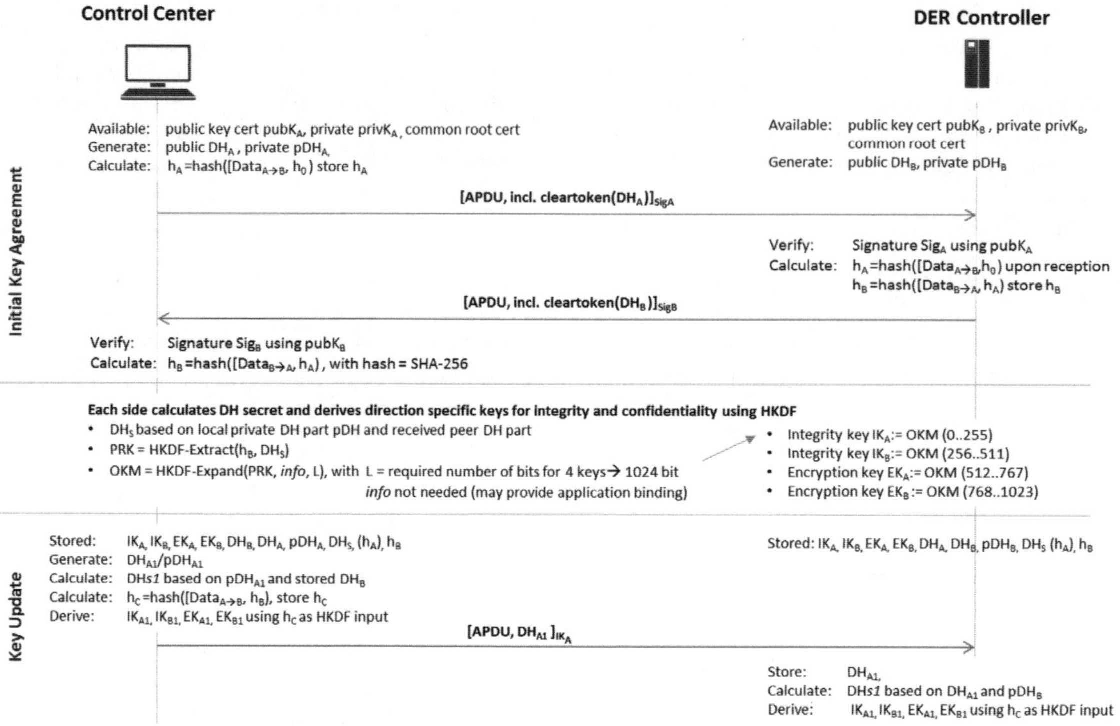

Figure 3. End-to-end-Security and hop-by-hop security according to IEC 62351-4

Additionally, a protocol is assumed that supports session initiation. In the specific example, this is provided by the Manufacturing Message Specification (MMS [25]) using the *MMS Initiate* and *MMS Initate Response* messages.

B. Session Handling

The session handling can be distinguished into the initial key agreement during the session initialization and a key update phase. Both sequences are shown in Figure 3. At the beginning of the session, both sides generate a Diffie Hellman key pair to be used in the key agreement resulting in an ephemeral Diffie-Hellman secret. All data necessary for the establishment of the security association between both peers are kept in a data structure called clear token (as the data s transmitted n clear, but integrity protected). From each of the handshake messages a fingerprint is taken using a hash function. The hash is calculated over the concatenation of the current message and the hash of the previous message (the first message uses "0" for the previous message). This fingerprint is used to ensure the right order of messages and to provide additional randomness to the messages. This "running" hash was inspired by the TLS handshake [8]. Upon reception of the initiation message, the receiver verifies the signature, calculates the fingerprint and generates the response message, from which again the fingerprint is taken. After providing the signed response to the imitator, both sides can calculate the Diffie-Hellman secret and utilize it together with the running hash over the response message as input for the hash based key derivation function HKDF. This will generate different keys per direction for integrity protection and confidentiality protection, resulting in four keys. The keys are applied according to the security association.

The key update can be done using a single message. Figure 3 shows the key update triggered by the control center. As in the initial step, the control center generates a fresh Diffie Hellman key pair and utilizes the already received and stored Diffie-Hellman key from the DER controller to immediately to calculate a new Diffie-Hellman secret and the resulting set of updated session keys. Once this message is received by the DER controller, it can calculate the updated set of keys.

C. Packet construction

Figure 4 shows the packet construction and how the different parts of the messages are protected. Note that during the initial handshake, the clear token is only integrity protected. As stated before, the clear token carries all cryptographic parameter necessary to establish the security association.

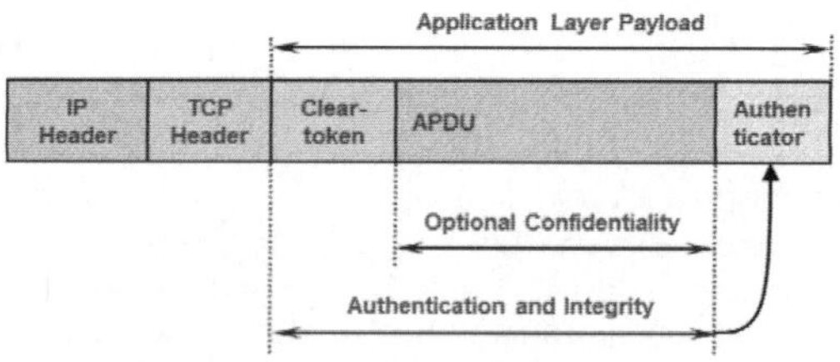

Figure 4. Application of IEC 62351-4 end-to-end security

V. CONCLUSIONS

The lean approach taken in IEC 62351-4 as described in Section IV establishes an end-to-end security session between two communicating peers with mutual entity authentication resulting in session keys being applied for end-to-end message integrity and confidentiality.

Two points should be obeyed when applying the discussed approach. First, the initial key agreement results in an ephemeral set of session keys, as both sides are expected to generate fresh Diffie Hellman parameters. The key update performed in a single message initiated by either peer results in a semi-static Diffie Hellman key agreement. Depending on the security requirements, the receiver may initiate another key update to ensure the freshness of his Diffie Hellman parameters. The second point relates to potential privacy requirements. The initial key agreement utilizes a clear-text token, which is only integrity protected. Thus, all information contained in the token is potentially readable by an intermediary. As the clear token also contains certificate information, it may allow to identify the communication end points.

This paper described an approach of handling end-to-end security over intermediate nodes from a system point of view, by investigating existing security requirements and existing solutions. The paper focused on the description of the end-to-end security approach defined in IEC 62351-4 from a general perspective protecting higher layer session-based communication in an end-to-end fashion, to motivate the re-use of this lean approach in other scenarios or protocol frameworks in industrial communication. As an outlook to this, it is intended to apply the described approach also to other publish-subscribe protocols utilized in automation scenarios like MQTT or AMQP.

REFERENCES

[1] European Commission, "The Directive on security of network and information systems (NIS Directive 2016/1148)", https://eur-lex.europa.eu/eli/dir/2016/1148/oj, [retrieved: June 2019].

[2] German IT Security Act, official web site (German) https://www.bsi.bund.de/DE/Themen/Industrie_KRITIS/KRITIS/IT-SiG/it_sig_node.html, [retrieved: June 2019]

[3] ISO 27019: Information technology - Security techniques - Information security controls for the energy utility industry, https://www.iso.org/standard/68091.html, [retrieved: June 2019].

[4] IT Security Catalog, https://www.bundesnetzagentur.de/SharedDocs/Downloads/DE/Sachgebiete/Energie/Unternehmen_Institutionen/Versorgungssicherheit/IT_Sicherheit/IT_Sicherheitskatalog_2018.pdf, [retrieved: June 2019].

[5] NIST Framework for Improving Critical Infrastructure Cybersecurity, https://nvlpubs.nist.gov/nistpubs/CSWP/NIST.CSWP.04162018.pdf, [retrieved: June 2019].

[6] NERC CIP Set of Standards, https://www.nerc.com/pa/Stand/pages/cipstandards.aspx, [retrieved: June 2019].

[7] IEC 62443, "Industrial Automation and Control System Security" (formerly ISA99), available from: https://www.isa.org/isa99/, [retrieved: June 2019].

[8] T. Dierks and E. Rescorla, "Transport Layer Security Protocol version 1.2", RFC 5246, August 2008, https://tools.ietf.org/html/rfc5246, [retrieved: June 2019].

[9] E. Rescorla, "Transport Layer Security Protocol version 1.3", RFC 8446, August 2018, https://tools.ietf.org/html/rfc8446, [retrieved: June 2019].

[10] S. Fries, R. Falk, H. Dawidczak, and T. Dufaure, "Decentralized Energy in the Smart Energy Grid and Smart Market – How to master reliable and secure control Secure Integration of DER into Smart Energy Grid and Smart Market," International Journal of Advances in intelligent Systems, vol. 9 no 1&2, 2016, ISSN: 1942-2679, page 65-75, https://www.thinkmind.org/download.php?articleid=intsys_v9_n12_2016_6, [retrieved: June 2019].

[11] ISO 61850-x: Communication networks and systems for power utility automation, https://www.iec.ch/search/?q=61850, [retrieved: June 2019].

[12] P. Saint-Andre, "Extensible Messaging and Presence Protocol (XMPP): Core," RFC 6120, https://tools.ietf.org/html/rfc6120 [retrieved: June 2019].

[13] IEC 62351-x Power systems management and associated information exchange – Data and communication security, https://www.iec.ch/search/?q=62351 [retrieved: June 2019].

[14] P. Saint-Andre, "End-to-End Signing and Object Encryption for the Extensible Messaging and Presence Protocol (XMPP)," RFC 3923, https://tools.ietf.org/html/rfc3923 [retrieved: June 2019].

[15] W3C: XML Signature Syntax and Processing Version 2.0, June 2015, https://www.w3.org/TR/xmldsig-core2/, [retrieved: June 2019].

[16] W3C: XML Encryption Syntax and Processing Version 1.1, April 2013, https://www.w3.org/TR/xmlenc-core1/, [retrieved: June 2019].

[17] M. Jones, J. Bradley, and N. Sakimura, "JSON Web Signature (JWS)," RFC 7515, https://tools.ietf.org/html/rfc7515, [retrieved: June 2019].

[18] M. Jones and J. Hildebrand, "JSON Web Encryption (JWE)," RFC 7516, https://tools.ietf.org/html/rfc7516, [retrieved: June 2019].

[19] J. Schaad, "CBOR Object Signing and Encryption (COSE)," RFC 8152, https://tools.ietf.org/html/rfc8152, [retrieved: June 2019].

[20] O. Friel, R. Barnes, M. Pritikin, H. Tschofenig, and M. Baugher, "Application layer TLS," IETF Draft, https://tools.ietf.org/html/draft-friel-tls-atls-02, [retrieved: June 2019].

[21] E. Rescorla, Key Material Exportes fro Transport Layer Security, " RFC 5705, https://tools.ietf.org/html/rfc5705, [retrieved: June 2019].

[22] Signal protocol, https://signal.org/docs/, [retrieved: June 2019].

[23] Off-the-record Protocol Description version 3, https://otr.cypherpunks.ca/Protocol-v3-4.1.1.html, [retrieved: June 2019].

[24] Application Layer Transport Security, https://cloud.google.com/security/encryption-in-transit/application-layer-transport-security/, [retrieved: June 2019].

[25] Manufacturing Message Specification, ISO 9506, https://www.iso.org/standard/37080.html, [retrieved: June 2019].

Reducing the Attack Surface for Private Data

George O. M. Yee
Computer Research Lab, Aptusinnova Inc., Ottawa, Canada
Dept. of Systems and Computer Engineering, Carleton University, Ottawa, Canada
e-mail: george@aptusinnova.com, gmyee@sce.carleton.ca

Abstract—**Breaches of private data have been occurring at an alarming rate, to the embarrassment and expense of companies that hold the data. It would appear that in each breach, the attack surface for the data has been sufficiently large to attract attackers. Reducing this attack surface is a way to lessen the likelihood of breaches. This paper presents methods for reducing the attack surface of private data held in the online computer systems of organizations. The methods are applied to a software system's architecture early in the design process, as an approach for designing-in security. This work defines the attack surface for the data, and then uses this definition to obtain a formula for calculating the attack surface. The definition further leads to identifying methods that can be used to reduce the attack surface. Reducing the attack surface may not prevent breaches, but it will make them less likely to occur.**

Keywords-privacy; private data; breaches; attack surface identification; attack surface reduction.

I. Introduction

Breaches of private data held by companies and other types of organizations have been occurring at an alarming rate. Consider the following sampling of recent breaches [1]:

- August 21 – September 5, 2018: British Airways, 380,000 customers affected; card payment information stolen; the airline's website and app were hacked.
- January 1, 2016 – December 22, 2017: Orbitz, 880,000 customers affected; payment card information and personal data (billing addresses, phone numbers, emails) stolen; the company's website was hacked.
- May 1, 2015 – July 4, 2018: SingHealth, 1.5 million users affected; names and addresses in the Singapore government's health database, and some histories of dispensed medicine were stolen; also, the prime minister of Singapore was specifically targeted; hackers orchestrated a deliberate, well-planned attack.
- August 20, 2018: T-Mobile, about 2 million users affected; a group of hackers accessed T-Mobile servers through an application programming interface and stole encrypted passwords and personal data, including account numbers, billing information, and email addresses.

Apparently, the attack surface for the data that was breached, or the number of ways that the data could be accessed and stolen, was sufficiently large and attractive to the attackers.

Given the rate of recent data breaches, it is clear that more needs to be done to reduce the probability of a data breach occurring. The objective of this work is to derive methods for reducing the attack surface of private data held in online (i.e., connected to the Internet) computer systems of organizations. The methods are obtained from consideration of the definition of the attack surface, which in turn is based on how an attack happens. This definition also leads to a straightforward formula for calculating the size of the attack surface, which can be used to verify that use of the methods does indeed reduce the attack surface. The methods focus on reducing the attack surface by altering the system architecture, rather than the deployment of add-on security appliances, such as firewalls and intrusion detection systems. The methods are meant to be applied at the early stages of design within a software development cycle, as part of the Design for Security toolset.

This paper is organized as follows. Section II explains private data, attacks, attack surface, and how to calculate the size of the attack surface. Section III derives methods for reducing the attack surface based on its definition. Section IV illustrates the methods using an application example. Section V describes related work, and Section VI presents conclusions and future work.

II. Private Data, Attacks, and Attack Surface

A. *Private Data, Attacks, and Attack Surface*

Private Data (PD), also known as personal data, is data about an individual, can identify that individual, and is owned by that individual [2]. For example, an individual's driver license number, passport number, or credit card number can each be used to identify the individual and are therefore considered as private data. The individual's privacy then refers to his/her ability to control the collection (what personal data and collected by which party), purpose of collection, retention, and disclosure of that data, as stated in the individual's privacy preferences [2].

DEFINITION 1: An *attack* is any action carried out against an organization's computer system that, if successful, results in the system being compromised.

This work focuses on attacks that compromise the PD held in the online systems of organizations. The attacker who launches an attack may be internal (inside attacker) or external (outside attacker) to the organization. This work applies to both types of attackers. An internal attacker usually has easier access to the targets of his/her attack and he/she may hide his/her attacks in the guise of normal duty.

Salter et al. [3] give an interesting insight into what enables a successful attack: "Any successful attack has three steps: One, diagnose the system to identify some attack. Two, gain the necessary access. And three, execute the attack. To protect a system, only one of these three steps needs to be blocked." Thus, an attack surface must contain a target that the attacker deems worthy of attack (suit his/her purpose for the attack) and that target must be accessible to the attacker. For this work, the target that is potentially worthy of attack is the PD that is accessible to attackers. In a computer system, this PD is either moving (travelling from one location to another), at rest (stored), or being used (by some process). This leads to the following definition of attack surface:

DEFINITION 2: The *attack surface* for private data contained in an online computer system is the set of all locations in the system that contain attacker accessible PD in the clear, where the PD is moving, at rest, or being processed.

Figure 1 shows an example attack surface.

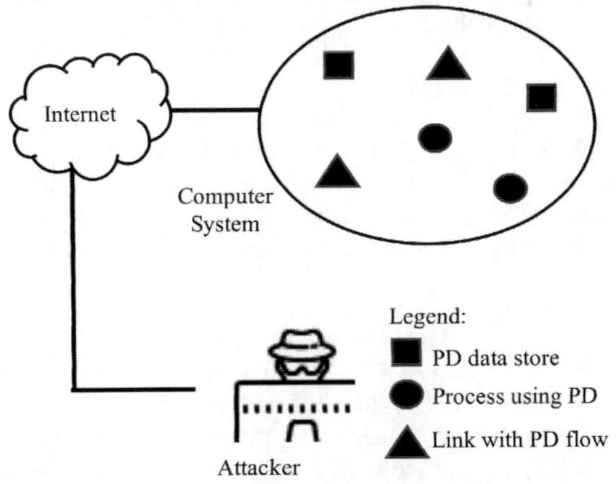

Figure 1. Example attack surface consisting of the set of all 6 attacker accessible locations in the system that contain PD in the clear.

In Definition 2, "attacker accessible PD" means that the attacker is able to exfiltrate the PD using some agent of attack, such as malware against stored PD and PD being processed, or a man-in-the-middle attack against a link containing moving PD.

An alternative definition of attack surface for PD contained in a computer system is the set of ways the attacker has to exfiltrate the PD. However, given the complexity of computer systems and the fact that the tools available to the attacker to use in his/her attacks are unknown to us, it is next to impossible to determine this set. On the other hand, locations that contain attacker accessible PD are easier to identify. Since an exfiltration must be from a location that contains PD, the set of such exfiltrations depends on the set of such locations. The larger the set of locations, the larger the set of exfiltrations. The smaller the set of locations, the smaller the set of exfiltrations. Therefore, Definition 2 in a sense includes this alternative definition, but in addition, is more easily applied.

As mentioned above, in the first step of a successful attack, the attacker diagnoses the system to identify the attack [3]. A smaller attack surface will make this step more difficult for the attacker. Therefore, a smaller attack surface corresponds to higher security, which is why we wish to reduce the attack surface. Definition 2 also gives rise to this conclusion: a smaller attack surface means a smaller number of locations that contain PD, which in turn means fewer opportunities for exfiltration of the PD, or in other words, higher security.

Definition 2 is consistent with the intuitive understanding of an attack surface, which is "the set of ways in which an adversary can enter the system and potentially cause damage" [4]. Each "way" corresponds to a location in Definition 2 that in turn corresponds to methods for exfiltrating PD from the location.

B. Calculating the Size of the Attack Surface

It would be useful to have a numerical value for the size of the attack surface, since then we could a) compare attack surfaces at different stages of development to see if the system's security is getting better or worse, b) compare attack surfaces of different systems when choosing a system for purchase, and c) easily see if actions taken to reduce the attack surface have indeed reduced it.

As mentioned above, private data held in a computer system can be in the following three states: moving, at rest, or being processed. These states correspond respectively, within a computer system, to PD that is moving along a link, PD that is stored in a data store, and PD that is being processed. Thus, the locations in Definition 2 refer to links, datastores, and processes that contain attacker accessible PD. Definition 2 then leads naturally to the following formula for calculating the size of the attack surface for private data.

Let N be the size of the attack surface for PD. Let m, n, and k be the number of links, data stores, and processes, respectively, that contain attacker accessible PD in the clear. Then

$$N = m + n + k \tag{1}$$

Equation (1) says that the size N of the attack surface is found by adding up the number of attacker accessible locations in the system that contain PD, namely: the number m of links, the number n of data stores, and the number k of processes, all of which contain attacker accessible PD. This equation follows directly from Definition 2, by simply replacing "attack surface" with "size of the attack surface" and "set" with "size of the set" in that definition. Applying this equation to Figure 1 gives an attack surface of size N = m + n + k = 2 + 2 + 2 = 6.

III. Reducing the Attack Surface

A. Methods for Redusing the Attack Surface

Equation (1) implies that the attack surface will decrease if and only if any or all of the quantities m, n, or k decrease. Therefore, the attack surface may be reduced by the following methods, where each method decreases m, n, or k:

a) Make a PD location useless to the attacker.
b) Combine two or more PD locations into a single PD location.
c) Deny the attacker access to a PD location.
d) Remove a PD location from the system.

The following explains these methods in greater detail and describes how they may be carried out.

a) Make a *PD Location Useless to the Attacker*

As mentioned above, in the first step of a successful attack, the attacker diagnoses the system to identify an attack, or in our case, the PD target for the attack. In this diagnosis, it is reasonable to assume that the attacker will ignore any target that he/she finds useless for his/her purposes. Such targets may be removed from the attack surface. Some ways to make a PD target useless to an attacker are:

- Obfuscate (e.g., encrypt) the PD at the location. The attacker will not want to exfiltrate PD that cannot be read. The computer system will need to able to de-obfuscate the data securely for its own purposes.
- Anonymize the PD at the location. Again, the attacker will not want PD that cannot be linked to individuals, since it is this linking that adds value to the data, e.g., for advertising purposes. The computer system will need to be able to de-anonymize the data securely for its own purposes.

To illustrate, obfuscating one data store and one process in Figure 1 results in Figure 2, where the obfuscated data store and the obfuscated process have been removed from the attack surface. It can be seen that the attack surface in Figure 2 is reduced (size 4) relative to the attack surface of Figure 1 (size 6).

b) Combine Two or More PD Locations into a Single PD Location

This method will decrease the number of PD locations and reduce the size of the attack surface per (1). Additional data links may need to be implemented in the system's design to carry PD that was previously carried by links to/from the locations that were combined. In addition, changes to the software logic may be needed for data stores or processes that were combined to accomplish reading or storing the data in the combined location (for combined data stores), or new processing of data in the combined location. (for combined processes). To illustrate, combining two data stores into one data store and combining two processes into one process in Figure 1 also results in the reduced attack surface shown in Figure 2.

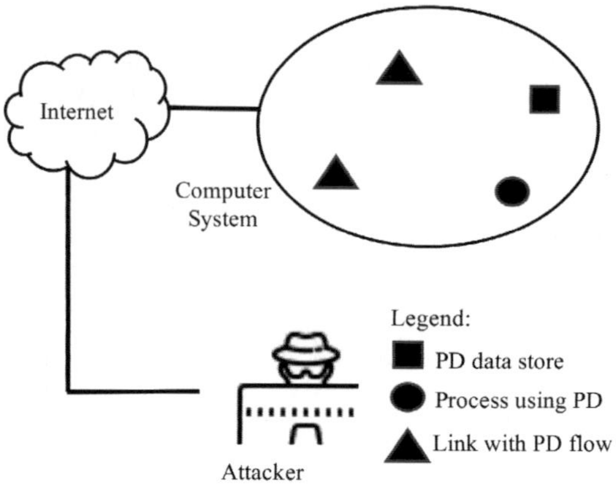

Figure 2. Resulting reduced attack surface of size 4 after obfuscating or combining locations in Figure 1.

c) Deny the Attacker Access to a PD Location

It may be possible to have some PD locations offline, thus denying the attacker access to these locations. For example, this may be possible for certain self-contained processing, such as analytics, that can be done using PD that is offline. In this case, all data stores, processes, and data links involved solely in such offline processing may be removed from the attack surface of the system to which these locations originally belonged, and re-constituted into an offline system. It may be necessary to update the offline PD data stores periodically using data from the system that is online. This update will need to be done in a secure fashion, perhaps by transferring the data manually using disks, after making sure that no malware can infect the offline system via this transfer. Although the destination locations are offline, it may still be possible for transferred malware to exfiltrate the offline data, e.g., hiding the data in the disks that are used for transfer and then transmitting the data once the disks are on the online part of the system.

d) Remove a PD Location from the System

Another way to reduce the attack surface is to remove a PD location from the system by deciding that the PD in the location is no longer required. For example, a company that stores the credit card information of its customers for their convenience may decide to stop storing this information, and instead, ask the customer for their credit card information every time the customer goes through checkout. This is in general a good decision, to avoid storing PD that may get compromised, at the cost of a little inconvenience. In this case, the associated credit card PD datastore would no longer be needed, and would be removed from the attack surface. Another example is the removal of a process that periodically sends customers the status of their order. The process uses PD consisting of the customer's name and email address to send the status. Suppose that this process is no longer necessary because the customer can now use a new Web interface to check order status. Removal of this process from the system removes it from the attack surface. Interestingly, removal of a PD location can also result in removing other PD locations that are connected to the location that is removed. For example, the removal of a PD data store or a process that uses PD can result in also removing connected PD locations, such as the links that carry PD, or a PD data store that the removed process was exclusively using. Thus, removing a PD location not only removes that location from the attack surface but can also lead to removing other PD locations further reducing the attack surface.

B. Applying the Methods

Since the above methods operate on attacker accessible PD locations, it is recommended that they be applied in the second phase of two phases, where the attacker accessible PD locations are identified in the first phase. These phases are carried out on an architectural representation of the online system, such as a Data Flow Diagram (DFD) [5] (see the application example in Section IV). The phases are as follows.

- Phase 1: Identify PD locations by tracing the flow of private data in the online computer system, looking for where PD enters the system, where PD flows (links), where it is stored (data stores), and where it is used (processes). Identifying the PD locations by tracing the flow of PD in the system implies that there are paths to the PD that an attacker can use to exfiltrate the PD. We therefore conclude that all PD locations found in this manner in an online system are attacker accessible PD locations. Given the ingenuity of attackers (the exfiltration could even be aided by an insider of the organization that owns the computer system, through social engineering), this conclusion is valid.
- Phase 2: Apply the above methods to the attacker accessible PD locations found in Phase 1, where possible, while considering the potential negative effects on the following aspects of the system:
  - Performance
  - Reliability and dependability
  - Ease of maintenance
  - Implementation cost

  For example, encryption or anonymization incurs extra overhead, combining data stores may introduce a performance bottleneck since the newly combined data store will now need to additionally support data accesses that were originally shared among the data stores that were combined. Combining PD locations in general may reduce modularity and lead to extra effort needed to maintain the system. A general guiding rule is to look for opportunities to apply the methods where the potential negative effects mentioned above are minimal. It may be more efficient to consider method a) last, since the other methods can add/delete links that are candidates for method a).

Carrying out the above phases clearly requires knowledge of the computer system in terms of identifying the PD locations. Some basic knowledge of security would also be advantageous. These skills should be found within the software development team responsible for developing the system, perhaps with a little security training if needed.

IV. Application Example

This section illustrates how to apply the methods for reducing the attack surface for private data using an example computer system for an online seller of merchandise (e.g., Amazon.com). Suppose this system is at the beginning stages of development and that the development team has produced a DFD showing how both private and non-private data will flow, be stored, and used in the system. This DFD is shown in Figure 3.

The system in Figure 3 allows the customer to enter his/her "name", "address", "email", "item selected" for purchase, and "credit card info" for payment. These comprise the PD for this example. Five processes cooperate to provide the functionality for the system. One datastore stores the customers' private data; another datastore contains inventory data, i.e., what items are in stock. The system is an online system since it is for an online seller. The PD locations will be found by tracing the flow of PD in the system (described below). Thus, all PD locations in the system are attacker accessible PD locations, as noted above in the description of Phase 1.

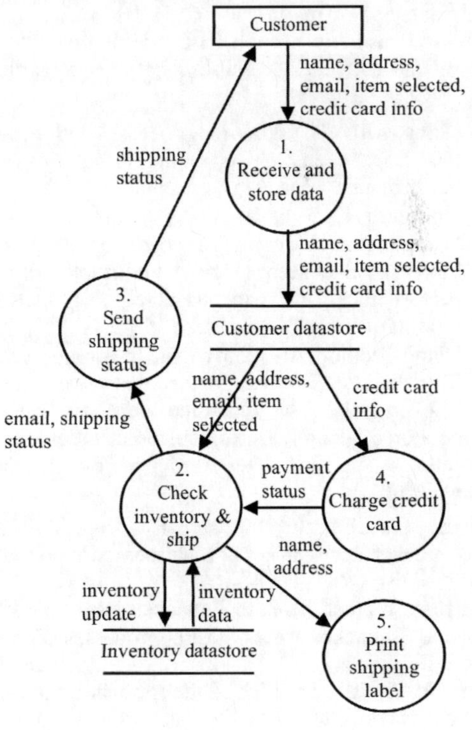

Figure 3. DFD for online seller system, showing how data flows, are stored, and used.

Applying Phase 1 in Section III B, we trace the flow of private data from the point where the data enters the system at process 1. From there, the PD passes through process 1 and is stored in the customer datastore. After this datastore, the PD is split up with the "credit card info" going to process 4 to be used, and the "name", "address", "email", and "item selected" going to process 2, where the "item selected" datum is used, and "name" and "address" are passed to process 5 to print the shipping label, whereas "email" is passed to process 3 to send the customer the shipping status. Thus, we can identify the PD locations as links, datastores, and processes through which the PD passes, is stored, and used. These attacker accessible PD locations are shown in Table I.

TABLE I. ATTACKER ACCESSIBLE PD LOCATIONS IN FIGURE 3

	Links	Datastores	Processes
1	link into process 1	customer datastore	process 1
2	link out of process 1		process 2
3	link from customer datastore to process 2		process 3
4	link from customer datastore to process 4		process 4
5	link into process 5		process 5
6	link into process 3		

Table I shows that there are 6 attacker accessible PD link locations, 1 attacker accessible PD datastore, and 5 attacker accessible PD processes. For Figure 3, prior to the application of the above methods, (1) gives the size N of the attack surface for private data as $N = m + n + k = 6 + 1 + 5 = 12$.

Applying Phase 2 in Section III B, we first use the above methods on the attacker accessible locations in Table I, as follows:

- Using method b), combine process 3 with process 2; this was seen to have negligible impact on performance and an acceptable reduction in modularity.
- Using method b), combine process 5 with process 2; this was also seen to have negligible impact on performance and an acceptable reduction in modularity.
- Using method d), remove the customer datastore from the system; it was decided that storing customer PD was not needed (customer purchase history can be stored securely on the customer's device by the seller's app and later retrieved by the seller's website).

These changes result in the DFD shown in Figure 4. Table II gives the attacker accessible PD locations corresponding to Figure 4.

Table II shows that there are 3 attacker accessible PD link locations and 3 attacker accessible PD processes. For Figure 4, (1) gives the size N of the attack surface for private data as $N = m + n + k = 3 + 0 + 3 = 6$. Thus, the application of methods b) and d) have reduced the attack surface from 12 to 6.

We can further reduce the attack surface as follows:

- Using method a), obfuscate (encrypt) the links in Table II; the impact on performance due to the extra over head is deemed acceptable.
- Using method a), obfuscate (encrypt) the PD in the processes shown in Table II; here, the impact on performance and the cost involved for extra code to handle encryption/decryption were considered unacceptable, and this reduction step was not done.

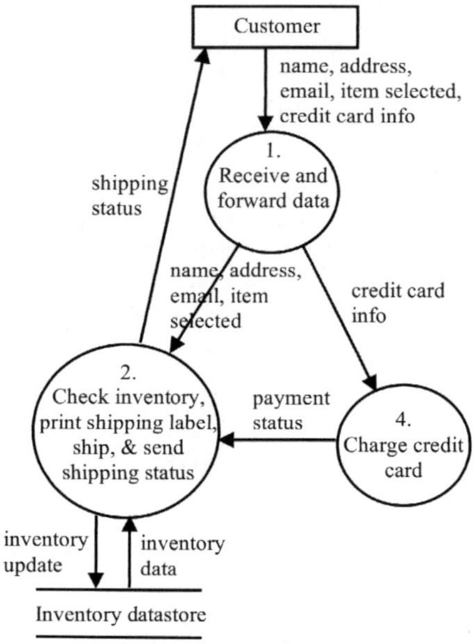

Figure 4. DFD for online seller system after combining processes and removing the customer data store.

TABLE II. ATTACKER ACCESSIBLE PD LOCATIONS IN FIGURE 4

	Links	Datastores	Processes
1	link into process 1		process 1
2	link from process 1 to process 2		process 2
3	link from process 1 to process 4		process 4

Table III shows the remaining attacker accessible PD locations after applying method a) to the links in Table II. The new attack surface is of size $N = m + n + k = 0 + 0 + 3 = 3$. The application of the methods in Section III has improved the security of private data in the system by reducing the size of the attack surface from 12 to 3.

Comparing Figure 4 to Figure 3, reducing the attack surface requires the following architectural changes to the system: a) reducing the number of processes from 5 to 3 by eliminating processes 3 and 5, b) changing the functionality of processes 1 and 2, and c) eliminating the customer database. As noted above, the implications of these changes were accepted by the development team.

TABLE III. REMAINING ATTACKER ACCESSIBLE PD LOCATIONS IN FIGURE 4 AFTER OBFUSCATING THE LINKS IN TABLE II

	Links	Datastores	Processes
1			process 1
2			process 2
3			process 4

The size of the attack surface obtained by applying the above methods depends on which methods were applied and the order in which they were applied. In particular, it may depend on the available opportunities for applying method b). For example, by using only method a) (obfuscation) on the locations in Table I and assuming that it is not advisable to apply method a) to the processes due to unacceptable impacts on performance and costs, we obtain an attack surface of size 5 (for the remaining 5 processes since the obfuscated links and datastore would have been removed from the attack surface), which is larger than the attack surface of size 3 obtained above by opportunistically first applying method b). This is the rationale for the comment made in the description of Phase 2 above, that it may be more efficient to consider applying method a) last.

V. RELATED WORK

Most closely related to this work is this author's previous work on reducing the attack surface [6]. However, this previous work differs from the current work in at least the following ways: a) the previous work deals with sensitive data (including private data) whereas the current work focuses on private data, b) the previous work proposes a graphical model with which to identify the attack surface whereas the current work does not require any such model, c) the previous work reduces the attack surface by requiring the developer to learn and modify the graphical model whereas the current work has no such requirement.

Some of the following related works deal with attack surface identification and reduction at the code or binary levels, whereas this work deals with it at the architectural level. A few of these works reduce the attack surface by removing unnecessary code or features similar to the removal of PD locations in this work. A. Kurmus et al. [7] look at reducing the attack surface of commodity OS kernels by identifying code that is not used and removing it or preventing it from executing. T. Kroes et al. [8] investigate reducing the attack surface through dynamic binary lifting, removal of unnecessary features, and recompilation. R. Ando [9] presents work on attack surface reduction through call graph enumeration in which attackable call graphs are removed. S. N. Bukhari et al. [10] propose reducing the attack surface corresponding to cross-site scripting by employing secure coding practices. G.V. Neville-Neil [11] writes that "the best way to reduce the attack surface of a piece of software is to remove any unnecessary code". M. Sherman [12] looks at attack surface identification only and investigates attack surfaces for mobile devices. This author claims that mobile devices exhibit attack surfaces in capabilities, such as communication, computation, and sensors, that are generally not considered in current secure coding recommendations.

Some works propose to increase security through attack surface expansion rather than attack surface reduction. For cloud services, T. Al-Salah et al. [13] propose three attack surface expansion approaches that use decoy virtual machines co-existing with the real virtual machines in the same physical host. They claim that simulation shows that adding the decoy virtual machines can significantly reduce the attackers' success rate. For enterprise networks, K. Sun and S. Jajodia [14] propose a new mechanism that expands the attack surface, so that attackers have difficulty in identifying the real attack surface from the much larger expanded attack surface. Note that these works do not contradict reducing the attack surface to improve security, since the real attack surface is not expanded. The attack surface only appears to be expanded due to the addition of decoys.

VI. CONCLUSIONS AND FUTURE WORK

This work has presented methods for reducing the attack surface for private data held within an online computer system. The methods are intended to be applied at the architectural level early in the development cycle prior to coding, as part of the Design for Security toolset.

Applying the methods does not require developers to learn a new model or a new coding language. Apart from the methods themselves, which are straightforward, a minimal level of security knowledge is needed, in order to understand the concept of attack surface, the purpose of the methods, and how they work. Knowledge of the computer system is the major requirement, but developers already have this knowledge. Although the methods themselves are straightforward, applying them can be challenging in terms of their impact on performance, ease of maintenance, and so on, as mentioned above.

Future work includes refining the methods from developer feedback, obtained perhaps through workshops and trials. Other future work consists of investigating new methods for reducing the attack surface and looking at tools that could indicate a method's impact on such aspects as performance, reliability, ease of maintenance, and implementation costs.

REFERENCES

[1] Business Insider, "The 21 Scariest Data Breaches of 2018," [retrieved: Sept., 2019] https://www.businessinsider.com/data-hacks-breaches-biggest-of-2018-2018-12

[2] G. Yee, "Visualization and Prioritization of Privacy Risks in Software Systems," International Journal on Advances in Security, issn 1942-2636, vol. 10, no. 1&2, pp. 14-25, 2017, [retrieved: Sept., 2019] http://www.iariajournals.org/security/

[3] C. Salter, O. Sami Saydjari, B. Schneier, and J. Wallner, "Towards a Secure System Engineering Methodology," Proceedings of New Security Paradigms Workshop, Sept. 1998, pp. 2-10.

[4] P. K. Manadhata and J. M. Wing, "An Attack Surface Metric," IEEE Transactions on Software Engineering, vol. 37, no. 3, pp. 371-386, May/June, 2011.

[5] T. DeMarco, Structured Analysis and System Specification, Prentice Hall, May, 1979.

[6] G. Yee, "Modeling and Reducing the Attack Surface in Software Systems," Proceedings, 11th Workshop on Modelling in Software Engineering (MiSE'2019), May 2019, pp. 55-62.

[7] A. Kurmus, A. Sorniotti, and R. Kapitza, "Attack Surface Reduction for Commodity OS Kernels: Trimmed Garden Plants May Attract Less Bugs," Proceedings of the Fourth

European Workshop on System Security (EUROSEC '11), April 2011, article no. 6 (no page number available).

[8] T. Kroes et al., "BinRec: Attack Surface Reduction Through Dynamic Binary Recovery," Proceedings of the 2018 Workshop on Forming an Ecosystem Around Software Transformation (FEAST '18), October 2018, pp. 8-13.

[9] R. Ando, "Automated Reduction of Attack Surface Using Call Graph Enumeration," Proceedings of the 2018 2nd International Conference on Management Engineering, Software Engineering and Service Sciences (ICMSS 2018), January 2018, pp. 118-121.

[10] S. N. Bukhari, M. A. Dar, and U. Iqbal, "Reducing Attack Surface Corresponding to Type 1 Cross-Site Scripting Attacks Using Secure Development Life Cycle Practices," Proceedings of the 4th International Conference on Advances in Electrical, Electronics, Information, Communication and Bio-Informatics (AEEICB-18), February 2018, pp. 1-4.

[11] G. V. Neville-Neil, "Reducing the Attack Surface," Communications of the ACM, vol. 61, issue 2, pp. 27-28, February 2018.

[12] M. Sherman, "Attack Surfaces for Mobile Devices," Proceedings of the 2nd International Workshop on Software Development Lifecycle for Mobile (DeMobile 2014), November 2014, pp. 5-8.

[13] T. Al-Salah, L. Hong, and S. Shetty, "Attack Surface Expansion Using Decoys to Protect Virtualized Infrastructure," Proceedings of the 2017 IEEE International Conference on Edge Computing (EDGE), June 2017, pp. 216-219.

[14] K. Sun and S. Jajodia, "Protecting Enterprise Networks through Attack Surface Expansion," Proceedings of the 2014 Workshop on Cyber Security Analytics, Intelligence and Automation (SafeConfig '14), November 2014, pp. 29-32.

Implementation of MQTT/CoAP Honeypots and Analysis of Observed Data

Hajime Shimada

Information Technology Center, Nagoya University
Nagoya-shi, Japan
Email: shimada@itc.nagoya-u.ac.jp

Katsutaka Ito

Meitetsucom Co., LTD
Nagoya-shi, Japan,
Email: itokatu@net.itc.nagoya-u.ac.jp

Hirokazu Hasegawa

Information Strategy Office, Nagoya University
Nagoya-shi, Japan
Email: hasegawa@icts.nagoya-u.ac.jp

Yukiko Yamaguchi

Information Technology Center, Nagoya University
Nagoya-shi, Japan
Email: yamaguchi@itc.nagoya-u.ac.jp

***Abstract*—Recently, there are many systems that utilize Internet of Things (IoT) effectively. Those systems often use simple IoT-aimed protocols, such as Message Queue Telemetry Transport (MQTT) or Constrained Application Protocol (CoAP). However, recent cyber-attacks have been targeting IoT systems (e.g., the "Mirai" malware) so we are concerned that malicious persons could also exploit IoT-aimed protocols in cyber-attacks. Thus, we proposed MQTT/CoAP honeypots to observe possible cyber-attack or scouting activities related to cyber-attack. To imitate real IoT systems, the proposed honeypots hold imitated sensing data which is updated periodically. Also, to avoid ill use by attackers, the proposed honeypot accepts update requests from the Internet, but the updated value is only visible to the same request source IP (Internet Protocol) address. The proposed honeypots were deployed in December 2016 (MQTT) and August 2017 (CoAP) and requests were observed from the Internet continuously. We observed several mysterious requests to both MQTT and CoAP honeypots. We observed that the MQTT honeypot received some non-MQTT protocol based requests to 1883/tcp and some of them are wrongly interpreted as MQTT protocol. We determined that an effective MQTT server must be robustly implemented to handle there types of requests.**

Keywords–Honeypot; Internet of Things; MQTT; CoAP.

I. INTRODUCTION

In recent years, there are many systems that utilize Internet of Things (IoT) effectively. Many of those systems use common protocol to transfer data, such as HTTP (Hyper-Text Transfer Protocol), however, such protocols were developed for transferring comparatively rich content that include a large amount of overhead even when sending small amounts of data. In some cases, the size of the protocol header becomes larger than the size of the sending data. As a result, some systems use simple IoT-aimed protocols, such as Message Queue Telemetry Transport (MQTT) and Constrained Application Protocol (CoAP) to reduce overhead [1][2].

However, recent cyber-attacks have been targeting IoT systems so we are concerned that malicious persons could also exploit IoT-aimed protocols in cyber-attacks. The use of those protocols is comparatively small, so there may exist many insecure servers which use those protocols. A number of services gather the opened ports and services of a server and list them via a Web service for security notice (e.g., Shodan [3]). However, such services can also be used by an attacker to explore servers, including the servers using IoT-aimed protocols.

In this paper, we report on the results of our previously proposed MQTT/CoAP honeypots to observe possible cyber-attacks or scouting activities related to cyber-attacks. To imitate real IoT systems, the proposed honeypots hold fake sensing data that are updated periodically. To avoid ill use by attackers, the proposed honeypot accepts update requests from the Internet but the updated value is only visible to the same IP (Internet Protocol) address that sent the updating request. This function can avoid ill use for a malware's Command and Control server. Also, we set the data transfer limit per hour to prevent DoS (Denial of Service) attacks (registering attack destinations as subscribers).

The MQTT version of the proposed honeypot was deployed in December 2016, and we presented our initial report at a domestic meeting in March 2017 [4]. We deployed our CoAP version in August 2017 and continuously observed requests from the Internet. Unfortunately, we lost data recorded after November 15, 2017 due to both system failure and careless backup treatment. So, the data that we could analyze are from December 1, 2016 to October 30, 2017 from the MQTT honeypot and from August 1, 2017 to October 30, 2017 from the CoAP honeypot. The analyzed results show that requests for MQTT were several times larger than those of CoAP in a month, but many of them came from security companies. We observed mysterious requests originating from 3 different countries with the same payload in around 2000 second intervals without following the standards of the protocol. We considered these requests to be attempts for unauthorized access or to attack the server.

The rest of the paper is organized as follows. Section II introduces related works about honeypots for IoT systems. Section III introduces the characteristics of IoT-aimed protocols that we cover in our proposed honeypot. We introduce our proposal and implementations in Section IV. Section V shows gathered accesses with the proposed honeypot and analysis results. Finally, we conclude and introduce future works in Section VI.

II. Related Works

Some honeypots implement IoT-aimed protocols as a part of their functions. A honeypot named Dionaea[5][6] has a MQTT module as a third party implementation. A generic low-interaction honeypot named glutton [7] also has a MQTT module. However, these honeypots only gather requests arrived to opened ports and cannot imitate a real IoT system.

Some studies have focused on honeypots that mimic IoT devices. Some of those honeypots gather information from attacks via telnet (23/tcp). Pa et al. proposed IoTPot[8][9] which analyze attacks by emulating telnet connection of various IoT devices. They detected 106 distinct types of malware from 5 malware families. Their observations were only limited to telnet so that our research differs in that we cover multiple IoT-aimed protocols. Wang et al. proposed ThingPot [10] which emulates multiple protocol servers including several IoT-aimed protocols, such as MQTT, CoAP, and Advanced Message Queuing Protocol (AMQP). But their emulation is limited to the server level and not the system level so that attackers can easily determine that it is a honeypot by checking the topics in the honeypot. Luo et al. proposed IoTCandyJar [11] which emulates multiple protocol servers including several IoT-aimed protocols, similar to ThingPot.

In this paper, we introduce a proposal of IoT honeypot system that imitates real IoT systems by registering fake sensing values periodically. We operated the systems over a long period to gather data on MQTT and CoAP connections, which were treated as being in the "minor connection category" in prior studies.

III. Introduction of IoT-Aimed Protocols

A. MQTT: Message Queue Telemetry Protocol

Message Queue Telemetry Transport (MQTT) [12] is a broker-based publish/subscribe-type messaging protocol. It can use both 1883/tcp and 1883/udp for implementation, but TCP is widely used. A fixed header of MQTT is only 2 bytes so that it is suitable for IoT devices and networks with limitations on processor and network performance.

An outline of MQTT usage is shown in Figure 1. The MQTT server is called a broker and clients are separated into publishers and subscribers. A subscriber sends a request to the broker by indicating the topic, and the broker sends the topic to all subscribers when a publisher sends a corresponding topic to the broker. Topics in a MQTT system are organized with a hierarchical structure similar to a directory in a file system (e.g., /8F/room806/temperature). The subscriber can use the wildcard "+" to represent a hierarchy to indicate multiple topics (e.g., /7F/+/humidity). The wildcard "#" can be used to represent all lower hierarchies to indicate multiple topics (e.g., /6F/#) or by itself to obtain all topics. The published message is discarded after distribution to the subscriber in the MQTT basic configuration. However, the MQTT has a retaining function that keeps the latest published topic in the broker and sends it to a new subscriber if they request the topic.

MQTT has 3 levels of QoS (Quality of Service) which are described as at most once, at least once, and exactly once, respectively. The QoS is present on both the publisher's and the subscriber's sides, and they are only valid between publisher/subscriber and broker.

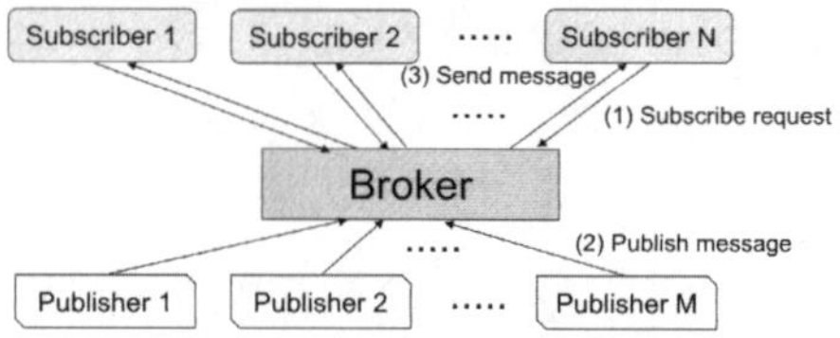

Figure 1. Outline of MQTT usage

TABLE I. METHODS OF CoAP AND CORRESPONDING RESPONSES

	Response from server	
Method	Resource exists	Resource does not exists
GET	2.05 Content	4.04 Not Found
PUT	2.04 Changed	4.04 Not Found
POST	2.04 Content	4.03 Created
DELETE	2.02 Deleted	4.04 Not Found

B. CoAP: Constrained Application Protocol

Constrained Application Protocol (CoAP) [13] is a simplified HTTP protocol based on UDP. Similar to MQTT, CoAP prepares a server to share messages between clients. Table I shows usable methods for CoAP clients and corresponding responses from the server. The client can manipulate resources by using both a URI (Uniform Resource Identifier) and method.

The client can obtain all resources with a "GET /.well-known/core" request. By adding the "observe" option to the GET method, the server automatically sends any updated data.

IV. Proposal of Honeypots

A. Concept of Implementation

Both MQTT and CoAP utilizes the server layer to gather data. So, a server with a fixed IP address becomes the target of a cyber-attack.

Figure 2 shows the concept of a honeypot implementation. The honeypot imitates a server using IoT-aimed protocols and accepts arbitrary requests from the Internet. To capture all requests received by the server, including out of standard requests (e.g., requests with other protocols), we capture whole packets that come to the honeypot at the layer 4 (TCP/UDP) level and send them to the analyzer module. To imitate a real IoT system, we prepare a fake data registration module that periodically registers fake IoT sensor node data (e.g., temperature, barometric pressure, CO_2 cardinality) to the honeypot.

The honeypot system also has to consider ill use of the honeypot by smart attackers. Possible malicious usages of the honeypot server and countermeasures are listed below.

a) Exploit honeypot process vulnerability to occupy server: By exploiting vulnerabilities in a server's processes and utilizing privilege escalation methods, an attacker can sometimes occupy servers. To limit the occupation range and stop the occupied server easily, we executed the honeypot on a Virtual Machine (VM) that can easily be stopped from a VM host. The packet capture module is placed on another VM host to achieve continuous capture even if the honeypot VM has been occupied by the attacker.

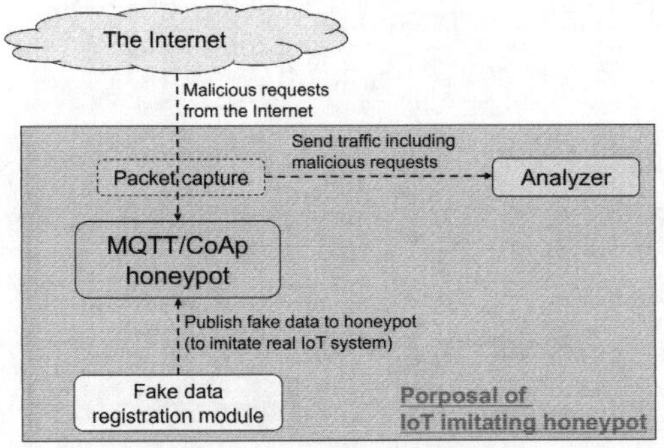

Figure 2. Concept of Implementation

b) Utilize as Command and Control server of malware: Command and Control server is the core server of a Botnet or Remote Administration Trojan type malware in which an attacker can use versatile servers for it even social networking services (e.g., Twitter, Slack). To avoid this type of ill use, we add a limitation to the server that an updated value is only visible from an IP address that sent the update request.

c) DoS attack to other host: Both MQTT and CoAP have a "distribute newly registered data to subscribers" mode which an attacker can use for DoS attacks by registering attack destinations as subscribers. To avoid this type of ill use, we modified the server source code to not distribute newly registered data even if those options have been enabled. Furthermore, we limit the outbound traffic rate at the VM host side.

d) Malicious message to IoT clients: There is possibility that some attacker may exploit other clients (fake data publisher module) by registering some malicious data to the honeypot. We implemented a fake data publisher module as an independent VM and only execute registration actions to the broker VM (no read action).

B. Detailed implementation of MQTT Honeypot

Figure 3 shows a detailed implementation of the MQTT honeypot. As discussed in Section IV-A, we separated the honeypot VM and fake data publisher VM. Furthermore, captured traffic is sent to the other host, to avoid suffering from VM host aiming attacks. Thus, we utilized 3 network domains, such as an Internet connection domain (133.x.x.x/26), fake data publisher connection domain (192.168.10.0/24), and analysis host connection domain (192.168.5.0/24).

We utilized mosquitto [14] which is a famous open source MQTT broker implementation, with the modifications described in Section IV-A. The fake data publisher and analyzer were implemented as a Python script with the paho-mqtt [15] module. We used tcpdump for the packet capture module.

The fake data publisher module publishes data to imitate a sensor network for a building energy management system. The topic format is organized as "/floor_number/ room_number/sensing_data." The floor number has 5 variations as represented by the "8F" notation. The room number has 17 variations as represented by the "708" notation. The sensing data has 3 variations, such as temperature, humidity, and pressure. An example topic is represented by the

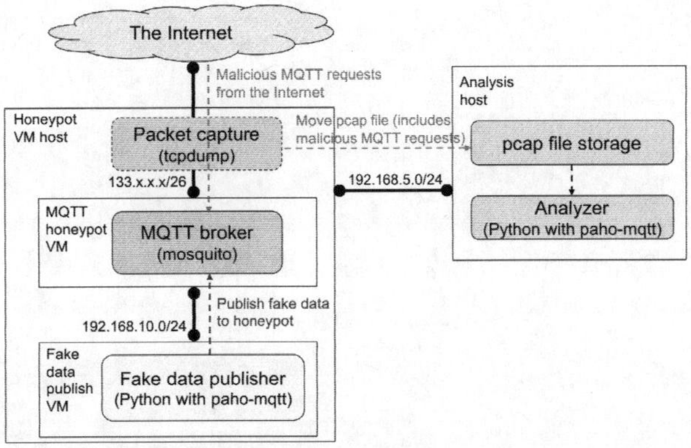

Figure 3. Detailed implementation of MQTT honeypot

TABLE II. HONEYPOT HOSTS

Host name	Type	Deployment day
IBmonitor.net....	MQTT	December 1, 2016
freezermonitor.net....	CoAP	August 1, 2017
co2monitor.net....	CoAP	August 1, 2017
furnacemonitor.net....	CoAP	August 1, 2017

"/8F/708/temperature" notation. All published data are registered with a retaining notification so that the attacker can see the fake data anytime.

C. Detailed implementation of CoAP Honeypot

The implementation of the CoAP honeypot is very similar to that of the MQTT honeypot so that the basic organization is identical to the one shown in Figure 3. We implemented "one topic to one CoAP server" so that the number of honeypot VMs and fake date register VMs are multiplied from those shown in Figure 3. This enable us to increase the number of honeypots to capture requests from different IP addresses. Note that either "multiple topic to one server" or "one topic to one server" can be selected from both the MQTT and CoAP honeypot. Instead of using the paho-mqtt module, as shown in Figure 3, we utilized Python with the aiocoap [16] module in the CoAP server, fake data registration client, and analyzer.

V. Analysis

A. Honeypot Setup

We created 1 MQTT honeypot and 3 CoAP honeypots, as shown in Table II. The MQTT honeypot utilized topics of the MQTT server to aggregate several fake sensor results into one MQTT server. Detailed topics on the MQTT server are shown in Section IV-B. We placed one topic on each CoAP server so that we prepared 3 CoAP servers. We added the word "monitor" to a part of the hostname, as shown in Table II. These hostnames emphasises that the hosts are monitor servers of an IoT system. The hostnames are registered to DNS before the observation term.

We deployed the MQTT and CoAP honeypots on different dates. This is why the deployment days differ. Unfortunately, due to both honeypot VM host failure and careless initialization of the backup host, we lost data after November 15, 2017 so that the following analysis was performed with data up until October 30, 2017.

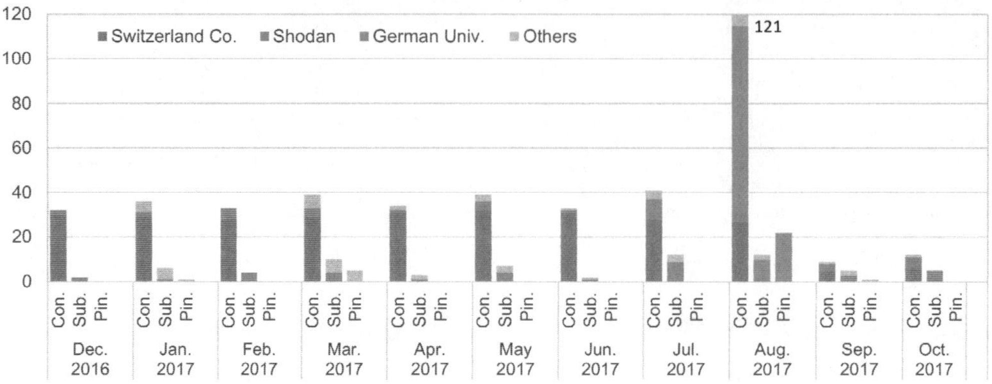

Figure 4. Number of MQTT requests per month

TABLE III. MQTT ACCESS SOURCES AT TCP SYN LEVEL (MORE THAN 3 TIMES)

Rank	IP address block or domain	Num of access	Organization
1	185.35.63.0/24	274	Security research team of Switzerland company
2	185.35.6.0/24	264	Security research team of Switzerland company
3	census.shodan.io	79	Shodan
4	134.147.202.0/24	76	Security research team of German university
5	members.linode.com	43	Hosting service A
6	zare.com	27	Hosting service B
7	180.149.126.0/24	20	Mongolian ISP A
8	180.149.125.0/24	15	Mongolian ISP B
9	research-scanner-dfn86.syssec.rub.de	12	Security research team of German university
10	150.100.253.0/24	10	Academic Network
11	188.166.165.0/24	6	Cloud service A
12	106.75.81.0/24	4	Cloud service B
13	182.86.142.0/24	3	Chinese ISP A
13	vmobile.jp	3	Japanese ISP A

B. Analysis of MQTT

We analyzed gathered MQTT requests minutely with net-mqtt-trace version 1.14 and Wireshark version 2.4.1.

1) Number of Requests: Figure 4 shows the number of the MQTT requests per month. The vertical axis shows the number of requests and the horizontal axis shows the months and types of request, such as MQTT connect requests (Con.), MQTT subscribe requests (Sub.), and MQTT ping requests (Pin.), respectively. The four layers per bar graph show a breakdown of the top 3 access sources shown in Section V-B2 and others. As shown in Figure 4, the request counts increased largely in August 2017. This is a result of a sudden large amount of requests from a German university, which is also described in Section V-B2. However, those request counts suddenly decreases in September 2017 including from other sources. This is possibly as result of the honeypots suddenly being omitted from Shodan's search result.

2) Source of Accesses: Table III shows slightly anonymized access sources attempting to access the MQTT honeypots at the TCP (Transmission Control Protocol) level more than 3 times. We counted TCP SYN packets from the Internet so that the counts listed in Table III include non-MQTT requests (e.g., send data of other protocols after the TCP handshake has been established). Thus, the sum of requests is a larger number than that shown in Figure 4. As shown at ranks 1, 2, 3, 4, and 9, security companies, services, and researchers frequently accessed the honeypot. We also plotted a breakdown of the top 3 access sources in Figure 4. As shown in the figure, the German university frequently accessed in August 2017, but did not access them at any other time. A Switzerland company sent continuous MQTT connect requests, but finished in September 2017 when the honeypots were omitted from Shodan. Shodan sent both continuous connect and subscribe requests.

However, as shown from lower ranks, tens of accesses came from ISPs (Internet Service Provider), hosting services, and cloud services. We also received mysterious accesses to the CoAP honeypots from ISPs (see Section V-C) so that those accesses may contain accesses from persons interested in exploiting MQTT or having a remotely dominated PC or server. There are 7 sources that accessed the honeypots twice and 28 sources that accessed them only once. Most of them were ISPs and so on, which indicates that a number of them were possible malicious sources.

3) Notable Accesses in MQTT: Below, we present the notable accesses to MQTT including minor visitors. As described below, a MQTT server that is exposed to the Internet receives non-MQTT requests to the 1883/tcp port and some of them were wrongly interpreted as MQTT requests. An effective MQTT server must be robustly implemented to handle these types of requests.

a) HTTP request after TCP establishment: We observed sent HTTP requests (starts from "GET HTTP/1.x...") after TCP establishment 7 times. 3 of them came from the vmobile.jp domain and the remaining 4 came from members.linode.com domain. In this case, character "G (0x47)" of "GET" word is treated as "MQTT Publish Ack Flag (0x47)" on the MQTT server so that we wrongly interpreted it as a mysterious MQTT connection.

b) SOAP request with MQTT Publish flag: We observed the following SOAP (Simple Object Access Protocol) request with the MQTT publish flag from the members.linode.com domain 3 times and from Cloud service A once. In this case, the character "<(0x3c)" of the "<soap:" notation is treated as "MQTT Publish Message Flag (0x3c)" on the MQTT server. This request also causes "crash at decode module in Publish.pm" error under the net-mqtt-trace program based analysis. Similar problems are likely to occur on the server side if the MQTT server has the same vulnerability.

```
<soap:Envelope
xmlns:xsd="http://www.w3.org/2001/XMLSchema"
xmlns:xsi="http://www.w3.org/2001/XMLSchema-instance"
xmlns:soap="http://schemas.xmlsoap.org/soap/envelope/">
<soap:Header>
<operationID>00000001-00000001</operationID>
</soap:Header><soap:Body>
<RetrieveServiceContent xmlns="urn:internalvim25">
<_this xsi:type="ManagedObjectReference"
type="ServiceInstance">ServiceInstance</_this>
</RetrieveServiceContent>
</soap:Body></soap:Envelope>
```

c) Multiple different protocol based requests recorded simultaneously: We observed the arrival of multiple different TCP-based protocol requests to 1883/tcp port from same IP address (zare.com) in the same day. The requests consisted of at least the following requests.

- HTTP protocols that started with "GET HTTP/1.0" or"GET /nice ports,/Tri\nity.txt.bak HTTP/1.0".
- SMB protocol that started with "PC NETWORK PROGRAM 1.0...".
- SIP protocol that started with "OPTIONS sip:nm SIP/2.0 Via: SIP/2.0/TCP nm;branch=foo...".
- Possible streaming protocol that started with "MMSNSPlayer/9.0.0.2980;...".
- Mysterious protocol that started with "dobjectClass0".
- Mysterious protocol that started with "(CONNECT_DATA=(COMMAND=version))".
- Mysterious protocol that started with "random1random2random3random4/".

d) Simultaneous requests from 2 domains: We observed that several domain pairs sent simultaneous requests. The detail of the requests is as follows. First, a part of the domain pair executes a TCP level observation that only sends SYN (does not reply to ACK even if the honeypot sends SYN/ACK) or sends SYN and RST (sends RST after SYN/ACK has arrived). Then, around 2000 seconds later, the other domain of the domain pair establishes a TCP connection and sends a MQTT connection request. Below, we present the pair of request sources. Source 3) achieved short intervals between requests, such as 7 or 8 seconds.

1) 185.35.62.0/24 and 185.35.63.0/24: 257 times
2) Mongolian ISP A and Mongolian ISP B: 13 times
3) amazonaws.com and 71.6.216.0/24: 2 times
4) 106.75.5.0/24 and sendclould.org: 1 time
5) 112.193.170.0/24 and 125.76.61.0/24: 1 time
6) 163data.com.cn and 175.152.30.0/24: 1 time

e) UDP MQTT request: Although MQTT permits UDP (User Datagram Protocol) requests, we recorded very few of them. We received 2 UDP MQTT requests from Chinese ISP A domain. The content of both requests are the same 41 bytes but we could not understand their purpose. The requested IP address also sent a TCP request on the same day.

TABLE IV. NUMBER OF CoAP REQUESTS PER MONTH

Month	Number of requests
August 2017	42
September 2017	45
October 2017	51

```
30:27:02:01:00:04:06:70:75:62:6c:69:63:a0:1a:02:02:
6f:0c:02:01:00:02:01:00:30:0e:30:0c:06:08:2b:06:01:
02:01:01:01:00:05:00)
```

f) QoS of MQTT: MQTT has 3 levels of QoS which are described as at most once, at least once, and exactly once, respectively. In observation, all connections and MQTT ping requests came with at most once and all subscribe requests came at least one.

g) Read topics of MQTT: We observed read-all requests which are the simplest request, 70 times. However, we also observed some cross topic type requests indicating that some access source recognized a topic and sent requests about corresponding topic. The number of cross topic type requests for /humidity, /pressure, and /temperature were 6, 19, and 7, respectively. Such a MQTT interaction based analysis is cannot obtain prior works listed in Section II.

C. Analysis of CoAP

We analyzed gathered CoAP requests minutely with Wireshark version 2.4.1.

1) Number of Requests: Table IV shows the number of requests to the 3 CoAP honeypots. The number of requests are the aggregated result of the 3 CoAP honeypots because the number of requests were limited. Thus, the average number of requests to one honeypot becomes one-third of the recorded value. The number of requests are also limited because the observation term was only 3 months.

2) Source of Accesses and Request Pattern: Table V shows slightly shaded all access sources to CoAP honeypots. They are separated into 3 large amount ones and 3 small amount ones. In large amount ones, Shodan is also seen in MQTT honeypot, but the left 2 access source were not seen in MQTT honeypot.

Table VI shows the request patterns in CoAP request packets from the analysis result of Wireshark. The large amount access sources have the same characteristics to the observed data on the MQTT honeypot, in which attempts were made to read data on the server. However, the last row of Table VI shows quite strange requests. We could not analyze the content of those requests, and their sizes were 542 bytes, which is comparatively larger than that of the frequent requests shown in large amount accesses.

Figure 5 shows the detail of the requests categorized as "Unknown 127" by Wireshark. There are three requests from different IP addresses to different CoAP honeypots. These 3 source IP addresses are also listed as rank 4, 5 and 6 in Table V. As shown in Table V, the IP addresses are existing ISPs of different countries so that this series of requests are quite dubious. We estimated that those accesses were attempting to exploit vulnerabilities of some devices.

TABLE V. ALL CoAP ACCESS SOURCES

Rank	IP address block or domain	Num of access	Request size (bytes)	Organization
1	customer.tdc.net	93	63	Danish Telecommunication
2	census.shodan.io	30	65	Shodan
3	185.121.173.0/24	9	60	In & Datacenter service
4	jogjaringan.net.id	2	542	Indonesian ISP
5	115.78.226.0/24	2	542	Vietnamese ISP
6	78.164.12.0/24	2	542	Turkish ISP

TABLE VI. REQUEST PATTERN OF CoAP

Request	Source domain
CON, GET, /.well-known/core	Danish Telecommunication
CON, GET, End of Block #0, /.well-known/core	Shodan
CON, GET, /	In & Datacenter service
Unknown 127	3 ISPs

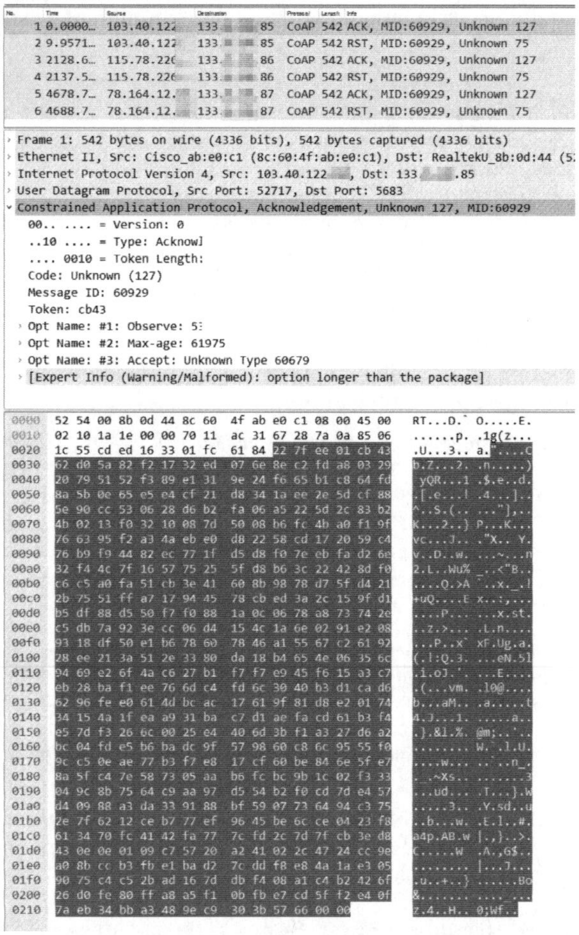

Figure 5. Mysterious CoAP requests from 3 different country ISPs to the 3 CoAP honeypots on the same day

VI. CONCLUSION

We introduced how to create and operate honeypots that observe IoT-aimed protocols in this paper. We also presented the analysis result of 11 months of MQTT honeypot observations and 3 months of CoAP honeypot observations. The observation results show that MQTT seems to get greater interest than CoAP on the basis of access count. However, we also observed mysterious CoAP requests so that we believe that we have to take care for both protocols. Furthermore, we observed that the honeypot received some non-MQTT protocol based requests to 1883/tcp and some of them are wrongly interpreted as the MQTT protocol, which indicates that an effective MQTT server must be robustly implemented to handle these types of requests.

For future works, we first have to restart the observation and continue them for the long term because we lost more than a year's worth of data, as explained in Section I. Second, there are many other IoT-aimed protocols (e.g., Advanced Message Queuing Protocol that uses 5672/TCP) so that we are planning to implement them as honeypots.

ACKNOWLEDGMENT

This work was partially supported by JSPS KAKENHI Grant Numbers 16K00071 and 19H04108.

REFERENCES

[1] D. H. Kim, J. B. Park, J. H. Shin, and J. D. Kim, "Design and Implementation of Object Tracking System Based on LoRa," *ICOIN 2017*, pp. 463–467, Jan. 2017.

[2] J. Joshi et al. "Performance Enhancement and IoT Based Monitoring for Smart Home," *ICOIN 2017*, pp. 468–473, Jan. 2017.

[3] https://shodan.io/ (Accessed on Sep. 10, 2019)

[4] K. Ito, H. Hasegawa, Y. Yamaguchi, and H. Shimada, "Primary Discussion about a Honeypot System for IoT Aied Protocols (in Japanese)," *IEICE Tech. Rep.*, Vol. 116, No. 522, pp. 103–108, Mar. 2017.

[5] "DinoTools/dionaea: Home of the dionaea honeypot" https://github.com/DinoTools/dionaea/ (Accessed on Sep. 10, 2019)

[6] "ysmal/dionaea: MQTT module" https://github.com/ysmal/dionaea/tree/master/modules/python/dionaea/mqtt/ (Accessed on Sep. 10, 2019)

[7] "mushorg/glutton: Generic Low Interaction Honeypot" https://github.com/mushorg/glutton/ (Accessed on Sep. 10, 2019)

[8] Y. M. P. Pa, S. Suzuki, K. Yoshioka, and T. Matsumoto, "IoTPOT: Analysing the Rise of IoT Compromises," *WOOT 15*, Aug. 2015.

[9] Y. M. P. Pa, S. Suzuki, K. Yoshioka, T. Matsumoto, T. Kasama, and C. Rossow, "IoTPOT: A Novel Honeypot for Revealing Current IoT Threats," *Journal of Information Processing*, Vol. 24, No. 3, pp. 522–533, Mar. 2016.

[10] M. Wang, J. Santillan, and F. Kuipers, "ThingPot: an interactive Internet-of-Things honeypot," arXiv: 1807.04114, pp. 1-8, Jul. 2018.

[11] T. Luo, Z. Xu, X. Jin, Y. Jia, and X. Ouyang, "IoTCandyJar: Towards an Intelligent-Interaction Honeypot for IoT Devices," Black Hat 2017, pp. 1-11, Aug. 2017.

[12] OASIS. "MQTT V3.1.1 OASIS Standard," Oct. 2014.

[13] IETF. "The Constrained Application Protocol (CoAP)," RFC7252, Jun. 2014.

[14] "Eclipse Mosquitto^{TM} - An open source MQTT broker," https://mosquitto.org/ (Accessed on Sep. 10, 2019)

[15] "Eclipse Paho - MQTT and MQTT-SN software," https://www.eclipse.org/paho/ (Accessed on Sep. 10, 2019)

[16] "chrysn/aiocoap: The Python CoAP lirary," https://github.com/chrysn/aiocoap/ (Accessed on Sep. 10, 2019)

VAULT: A Privacy Approach towards High-Utility Time Series Data

Christoph Stach

Institute for Parallel and Distributed Systems
University of Stuttgart
Universitätsstraße 38, 70569 Stuttgart, Germany
Email: Christoph.Stach@ipvs.uni-stuttgart.de

***Abstract*—While the *Internet of Things* (*IoT*) is a key driver for *Smart Services* that greatly facilitate our everyday life, it also poses a serious threat to privacy. Smart Services collect and analyze a vast amount of (partly private) data and thus gain valuable insights concerning their users. To prevent this, users have to balance service quality (i. e., reveal a lot of private data) and privacy (i. e., waive many features). Current IoT privacy approaches do not reflect this discrepancy properly and are often too restrictive as a consequence. For this reason, we introduce *VAULT*, a new approach for the protection of private data. VAULT is tailored to *time series data* as used by the IoT. It achieves a good tradeoff between service quality and privacy. For this purpose, VAULT applies five different privacy techniques. Our implementation of VAULT adopts a Privacy by Design approach.**

Keywords–Privacy; Time Series; Projection; Selection; Aggregation; Interpolation; Smoothing; Information Emphasization; Noise.

I. Introduction

The ever-increasing popularity of the *Internet of Things* (*IoT*) is both, a blessing and a curse. On the one hand, sensors built into everyday objects enable to monitor entities (e. g., a machine or a person) permanently and very precisely. Since the gathered data are always tagged with a time stamp, the data of different sources can be combined to obtain a comprehensive chronological profile of the monitored entity. Subsequent analyses can provide even more profound knowledge about the entity. The IoT is therefore an enabler for *Smart Services* from a wide variety of domains, including *Smart Homes*, *Smart Cars*, and *Smart Health*. Such services are a great benefit for the users as they facilitate their daily life [1].

On the other hand, these great capabilities of such services pose a great danger at the same time. In particular, if the monitored entity is a natural person, his or her privacy is at risk. Users are often not even aware of the coherences between gathered data and insights derivable them. However, Smart Services not only have access to the data of a single user but to the data of a vast number of users. This even enables them to learn from the behavior of these users and to predict future behavior patterns of different users [2].

For this reason, the *General Data Protection Regulation* of the EU (*GDPR*, see [3]) tries to provide guidance to meet the interests of both, service providers (in terms of data quality) and users (in terms of privacy requirements) [4]. Nevertheless, the user is faced with the difficult task of balancing service quality and privacy. The more data a user shares with a service, the better is its service quality, as it is thereby able to perform more precise analyses and thus establish a more profound knowledge base. Its users, however, are fully exposed in the process. Whereas, if a user conceals all data that could reveal private information, his or her privacy is protected effectively—yet, the service is practically useless as a result [5].

Today's privacy approaches for the IoT contribute little to solve this dilemma, as they suffer from three critical flaws. *a)* Users are often overwhelmed by these approaches, as the coherences between gathered data and derivable knowledge are not comprehensible. That is, if the user grants a service access to two seemingly harmless data sources, the combination of these two sources might provide new insights. *b)* These privacy approaches completely ignore service quality. They focus solely on concealing certain, possibly private data, and as a result the service quality is often considerably, yet unnecessarily impaired. *c)* These privacy approaches are only applicable to certain application scenarios and analysis methods. As a result, users need a variety of different privacy solutions to make all of their Smart Services privacy-aware.

To this end, we make the following three contributions: **(1)** We introduce a privacy **a**pproach towards high-**u**ti**l**ity **t**ime series data, called *VAULT*. VAULT is a concept for the protection of personal data, which achieves a good compromise between service quality and privacy and optimizes both of these aspects. Furthermore, specifying privacy requirements is still very simple for the user. **(2)** We present five different privacy techniques that are applied in VAULT. These techniques are tailored to the analysis methods applied to time series data as Smart Services mainly handle such data. **(3)** We describe an implementation of VAULT based on *InfluxDB* [6]. Yet, VAULT is completely independent from its data source, i. e., InfluxDB can be replaced by any data source providing time series data.

The remainder of this paper is as follows: In Section II, we introduce a sample use case from the *Ambient Assisted Living* (*AAL*) domain. Using this example, we identify requirements a privacy system has to meet in order to be effective for Smart Services. Section III discusses whether the related work meets these requirements. We introduce our concept for VAULT and the applied privacy techniques in Section IV. An implementation of this concept is given in Section V. In Section VI, we assess VAULT according to our identified requirements. Finally, Section VII concludes this paper.

II. Running Example

An application field, in which the IoT facilitates the users' daily routines by having access to highly sensitive data, is the healthcare domain. Sensors enable patients to monitor themselves permanently, while their physicians and other parties involved obtain the processed data tailored to their requirements. In the following, we illustrate this using an AAL use case.

Due to an aging population, the *World Health Organization* has introduced the paradigm of *active ageing* to enable elderly people to remain involved in social life. A key aspect in this respect is, that they are not pulled from their familiar surroundings (e. g., by accommodating them in a care facility) and that there is no loss of autonomy. AAL achieves this via sensors acting as permanently present but invisible caregivers [7].

An AAL platform offers wide-ranging monitoring services. Special metering devices are capable to monitor medical data continuously (e. g., blood glucose or weight). Physicians are informed about them and are then able to adjust the medication remotely. For some of these health parameters, they require the chronological progression with high accuracy (e. g., blood glucose), while for others an approximate progression is sufficient and single values are negligible (e. g., weight). It is also possible to check remotely, whether the required medication has been taken. Yet, this information is not required to be transferred permanently. It is sufficient to inform physicians if the medicine is not taken several times in a row. Fall detection is realized via wearables. This enables to alert a caregiver immediately if a senior has fallen and needs help. For this purpose, the data from the gyroscope, the accelerometer, and the position sensor are analyzed. In addition, the location where the fall occurred has to be determined, e. g., if the "fall" occurred in bed, it may have been a false alarm and the senior just went to sleep. Although location data has to be analyzed for this purpose, the caregiver must not be allowed to access this data. However, relatives with guardianship should be informed of the senior's whereabouts (e. g., if s/he is suffering from dementia and wander around confused and disoriented) [8].

This example illustrates that Smart Services gather a variety of private data. The GDPR must thus be observed in such use cases [9]. For instance, it requires *data minimization* [Art. 5(1)(c)]. Caregivers only have to be informed when a senior has fallen, whereas permanent access to the his or her location is not required for them. Yet, relatives need access to this data, if they are the senior's guardian. This is regulated by the *purpose limitation* [Art. 5(1)(b)]. Service providers have to ensure the *accuracy* of the processed data [Art. 5(1)(d)]. To make this feasible, privacy measures must not arbitrarily manipulate sensor data. Especially when particularly sensitive data, such as health data, is involved, the data subject must give *explicit consent* to their processing [Art. 9(2)(a)]. A solution with respect to these legal obligations is given in Article 25: Technical measures are postulated to ensure privacy compliance, i. e., Smart Services monitor and regulate themselves by default (*Privacy by Design*). To be effective, such a technical privacy solution has to meet the following five requirements:

- R_1 **Individual Privacy Enhancement.** Each user has different privacy requirements. While some people have no concerns about sharing their location data, others consider this kind of data as highly sensitive. Thus, every user has to be able to decide individually what information s/he wants to reveal, i. e., make available to a service.
- R_2 **Utility Preservation.** However, not only privacy requirements need to be considered. Users also have to decide which services they want to use and what data the respective service requires in order to operate. Only if the service receives these data in a sufficient accuracy and quantity, the user receives the expected service quality.
- R_3 **Privacy and Data Quality Harmonization.** Privacy and service quality, however, are by no means independent objectives. Enhancing privacy significantly impairs service quality and vice versa. A privacy system therefore has to consider both aspects equally to achieve *Pareto optimality*.
- R_4 **Privacy Method Adaption.** To make this possible, a privacy system has to be able to adapt its privacy methods to the service quality requested by a user. That is, the privacy system has to select a method which matches a service's specific data quality and quantity requirements.
- R_5 **Dynamic Policy Application.** The application of the privacy requirements has to be dynamic, i. e., before a service gets access to data, its properties must be checked (e. g., a relative only gets access to a senior's location if s/he is his or her guardian at the time of the request).

III. RELATED WORK

In the following, we review current privacy approaches for the IoT and assess them with regard to our running example.

Access Control: The most basic approach to ensure privacy is access control. In *role-based access control*, each involved party is assigned to a specific role (e. g., physician). A party can be assigned to several roles at the same time. Access rights to certain data sources are granted to these roles instead of individual users. Although this approach sounds promising at first as there are few roles (compared to the number of parties), and thus the number of access rights which have to be specified is reduced, it is not flexible enough for the IoT due to its fixed pre-defined roles [10]. Assigning access rights to certain attributes is significantly more dynamic. *Attribute-based access control* validates any kind of attribute at runtime (e. g., attributes that describe the party requesting data access or that party's current context). Data access is only granted if these attributes meet the data subject's authorization requirements [11]. This way, it is possible to model that relatives only have access to a senior's location data if they currently have the guardianship.

Nevertheless, pure access control approaches are far too restrictive and thus severely limit service quality. The user can only make a binary decision—either s/he grants or denies access to a data source. A fine adjustment, however, is not possible (e. g., reduce accuracy of the data or add mock data).

Attribute-based Privacy: To address this problem, a filter can be integrated into a data source. So, particular attributes of the data provided by that source can be filtered out, if they reveal private information. This enables users to specify, e. g., that their medical metering device still provides access to their blood glucose level, but not the blood oxygen level. Each filter can optionally be linked to a *spatiotemporal context* to specify when it should be active [12]. Such a filter can also be tailored to the respective data source. Instead of fully filtering out certain attributes, they can be replaced by mocked but realistic data, in terms of, e. g., value range and distribution [13].

A fundamental problem of these approaches is that they do not take chronological aspects inherent in this kind of data into account. Often, isolated data values do not pose a privacy threat. Only a sequence of single values results in a privacy-relevant pattern (e. g., a sequence of singular gyroscope and acceleration data results in an activity pattern). Yet, users have to filter all data of the concerning attribute in these approaches to ensure that such patterns are concealed. As a result, services depending on this type of data become non-functional.

Pattern-based Privacy: The intent of pattern-based privacy approaches is to conceal complex private information from a Smart Service without unnecessarily restricting its service quality. For this purpose, *Complex Event Processing* (*CEP*) is used. In CEP, no individual sensor values are considered, but higher-order events represented by a sequence of values within a given time window [14]. For instance, the event "senior leaves home" is a sequence of location data representing a motion vector heading away from the house. That way, users specify *private patterns* that must not be revealed and *public patterns* that are critical in terms of service quality. CEP is able to recognize these patterns and then private patterns are concealed by chronologically reordering some of the sensor values. A utility metric identifies the best permutation in terms of maximizing both, privacy and service quality [15].

Pattern-based privacy approaches are therefore particularly effective for maximizing service quality. They can also conceal patterns of any complexity consisting of sequences of individual values. However, such an approach is ineffective with respect to the principle of data minimization. By reordering, all individual values are still sent to the Smart Service. As it is known what kind of information is required by the service (via the public patterns), data could be pre-processed accordingly (e. g., by aggregating or tampering it) without affecting its service quality. For instance, to detect the pattern "senior leaves home", a Boolean statement whether this event occurred is sufficient—the whereabouts prior to this event are not required. Yet, this is not considered by pattern-based privacy approaches.

Statistical Privacy: Differential privacy is applicable to the IoT, e. g., in the context of *Smart Grids* [16]. There, data remains on each user's *Smart Meter*, while energy suppliers only receive aggregated data. It is ensured that no information about an individual user can be derived from the statistical analysis of this data. Yet, this kind of anonymization is only useful when information about a large group of users is required. It is not applicable to a use case like AAL, as in such a scenario sensor data must be evaluated for each user individually.

IV. VAULT CONCEPT

Our review of related work shows that none of these approaches is by itself effective in ensuring both, privacy and service quality. So, we combine and extend these concepts to provide a privacy concept that is tailored to IoT time series data, called VAULT. Figure 1 shows its concept and workflow.

To ensure service quality, a service has to define its quality requirements **(1)**. These include, e. g., which data a service requires and with what accuracy these data are required. Thus, the quality requirements correspond to the basic idea of the public pattern. In addition, a service description is mandatory that identifies the service, e. g., the service name, its execution environment, or the service owner **(1)**. This description is used to authenticate to VAULT. Like attribute-based access control, permissions in VAULT are not linked to a specific service, but to a set of its attributes. For instance, different permissions may apply to the same service depending on the country where it is hosted. The data subjects specify which permissions are assigned **(2)**. To this end, s/he provides a high-level description of his or her privacy requirements in natural language. Similar to the privacy patterns, s/he only has to describe which knowledge

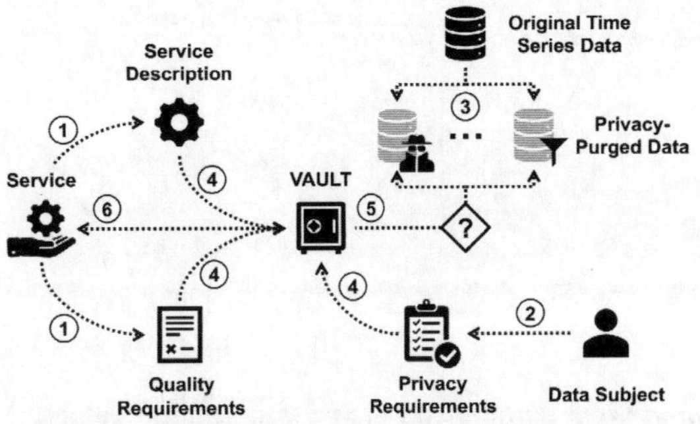

Figure 1. Concept of and Workflow for Data Access via VAULT.

must not be disclosed. A model in VAULT indicates from which data this knowledge can be derived (e. g., *ACCESSORS* [17] can be used to model these correlations). Based on this model, machine learning can automatically derive permissions from these privacy requirements [18]. As VAULT provides different privacy techniques depending on the respective service (i. e., in accordance with its quality and privacy requirements), the time series data has to be initially prepared accordingly **(3)**. **(1)** to **(3)** are independent tasks and can be carried out in any order.

If a service requests data access, VAULT first checks its service description (i. e., attributes of the service) and which permissions (i. e., privacy requirements) are linked to it. They are then consolidated with its quality requirements **(4)**. Based on these two requirement specifications, an appropriate VAULT privacy technique is selected **(5)**. Subsequently, the request is executed, and the results are sent back to the service **(6)**.

VAULT relies on existing techniques, which are already used for processing and analyzing time series data, to ensure privacy. As a result, the impact on service quality should be negligible. We discuss the following five privacy techniques:

Projection, Selection, and Aggregation: The most basic privacy technique used in VAULT is the application of relational algebra operators. A *projection* constrains the number of attributes whereas a *selection* filters out certain tuples of a data source entirely. As the data sources we consider in VAULT provide time series data, a selection operator is therefore synonymous with specifying a specific time frame. An *aggregation* can be used to consolidate the analyzed data (e. g., via set operators such as *average* or *sum*). Smart Services use these operators anyway to select the data that is relevant to them and thus reduce the huge amount of available data. VAULT is therefore able to restrict the available data according to the quality requirements of a service via theses operators in order to ensure privacy. For instance, a service gets only access to certain sensor values, certain days, or summarized data.

Data Interpolation: When dealing with sensor data, one has to reckon that sensors occasionally deliver no or incorrect values due to technical problems. To ensure that the data are still processed correctly, strategies must be implemented to deal with these missing and incorrect readings. For this purpose, these incorrect readings have to be substituted with artificial, yet realistic data. On the one hand, *interpolation techniques* can be used to smooth the temporal progression of the values, assuming that the sensor signal describes a continuous function [19]. On the other hand, it is possible to use machine learning to make

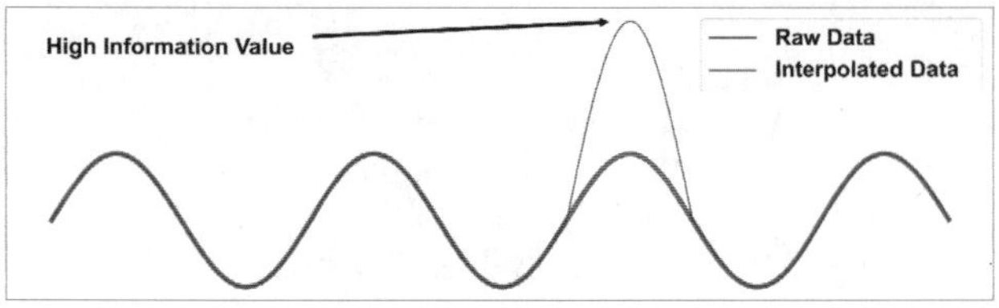

Figure 2. Application of a Spline Interpolation to Time Series Data.

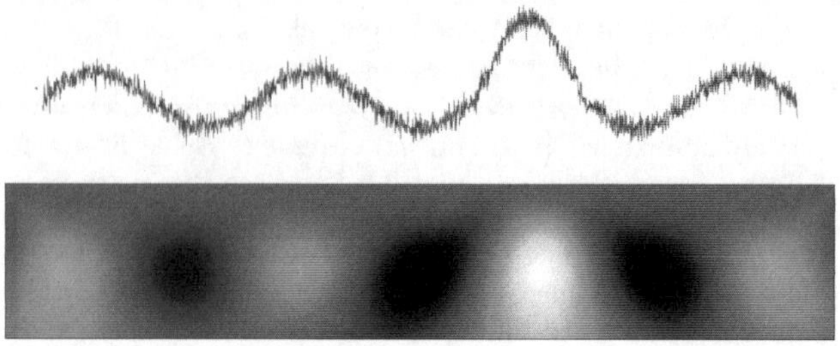

Figure 4. Time-Frequency Representation of Noisy Time Series Data.

predictions regarding the progression of the values. Missing values or outliers (in terms of values exceeding or falling below a threshold) can then be substituted with these predictions. We use these data cleansing techniques in VAULT to ensure privacy. In certain situations, outliers have a particularly high information value and are therefore considered as particularly sensitive data. Figure 2 shows the time course of a senior's whereabouts indicated as the distance to his or her home (blue line). S/he walks the same distance every day. One day, however, s/he changes this routine, which is a decisive information. For instance, if a service only needs to monitor that a senior takes a walk every day, VAULT first uses outlier detection to identify data points with high information value, deletes them, and then fills the resulting gap via *spline interpolation* (red line).

Data Smoothing: While data interpolation is well-suited for eliminating a few isolated outliers, sensor data can also be noisy as a total. Analyzing noisy data is often difficult and leads to poor results. So, the noise component is removed from the data by means of *filters*. Especially if the examined data contains some periodicity, which is often the case with AAL data due to regular daily routines, *Fourier transforms* are well-suited for noise reduction. This creates a band filter effect, i. e., certain interference frequencies can be attenuated [20]. Figure 3 shows the effect of a *Discrete Cosine Transform* on a noisy signal (blue line). The output is a smoothed signal (red line). However, this data cleansing method can also be used to protect private data. The transform removes details from the time series data and less information is shared with requesting services. Nevertheless, the actual data progression is still available to them with great accuracy.

Information Emphasization: Using wavelet transform, noise can even be filtered out to such an extent that only data with a high information value remains in the signal (e. g., peaks or turning points). For this purpose, the data progression is compared with a basic function, the so-called *wavelet*. This *window function* defines the weighting of each signal value in subsequent analyses. The *Continuous Wavelet Transform* constantly varies the parameters of this *mother wavelet* to obtain a band of *daughter wavelets*. This facilitates a particularly selective filtering and compression of the data [20]. In Figure 4, the noisy sensor signal (upper half of the figure) is converted into a *time-frequency representation* (lower half of the figure) using the *Mexican Hat Wavelet* as mother wavelet. Relevant data segments are exposed in this representation (light and dark zones). For instance, if the signal represents blood glucose levels, these zones indicate hypoglycemia or hyperglycemia, respectively. The information about the occurrence of these events is sufficient to generate appropriate recommendations concerning medication and treatment schedule. The exact glucose values need not be disclosed to a caregiver for this purpose. This increases privacy as no details in the data are available to third parties.

Adding Noise: A completely different privacy approach is adding noise to a signal on purpose. In Figure 5, *Gaussian noise* is added to formerly noise-free sensor data (blue line). That is, the noise in the resulting data is *Gaussian-distributed* (red line). So, actual values are concealed in a set of corrupted values. Although the general data progression is still noticeable, details and characteristics of the data are hidden by the noise. For instance, activity patterns are thus still recognizable despite the noise, whereas characteristics on how a senior performs that activity are concealed. While this initially sounds like a deterioration in data quality, it can even have a positive effect on certain data analyses. For instance, noise can cause *chaotic dynamics* within data. Therefore, if *deterministic chaos* is to be expected in a data set (e. g., data on the course of a disease), but it is not noticeable as too little data are available, adding noise can be useful in this regard to improve analysis results [21].

V. VAULT IMPLEMENTATION

There are three implementation strategies for the realization of the VAULT concept, which are shown in Figure 6.

Query pre-processing rewrites queries before execution and adds further constraints to eliminate private information from the result set. This is well-suited for simple privacy techniques such as projection or selection. Yet, these query adaptations become complex for more advanced privacy techniques. Then,

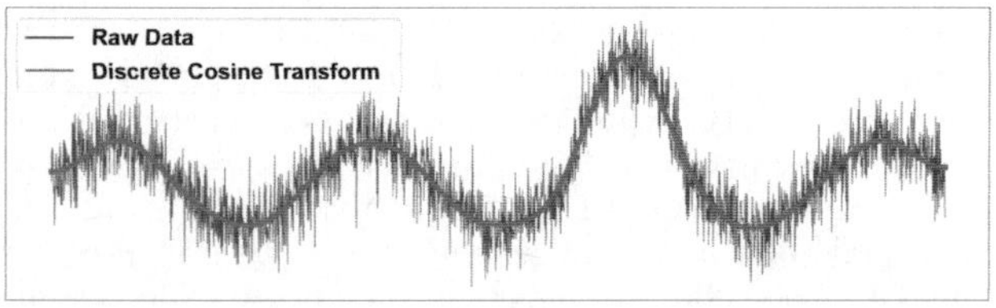

Figure 3. Application of a Fourier Transform to Time Series Data.

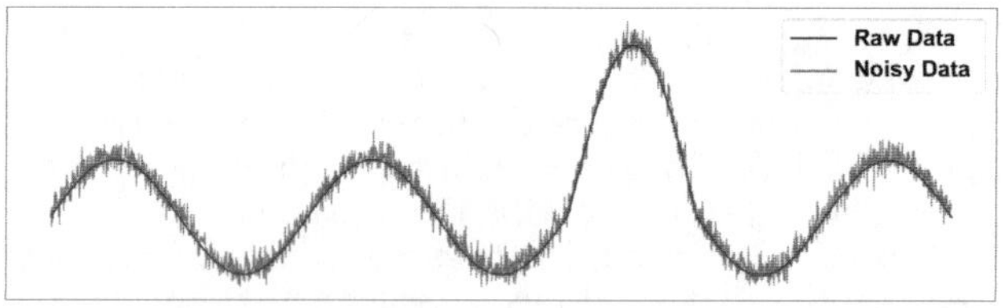

Figure 5. Adding Gaussian Noise to Time Series Data.

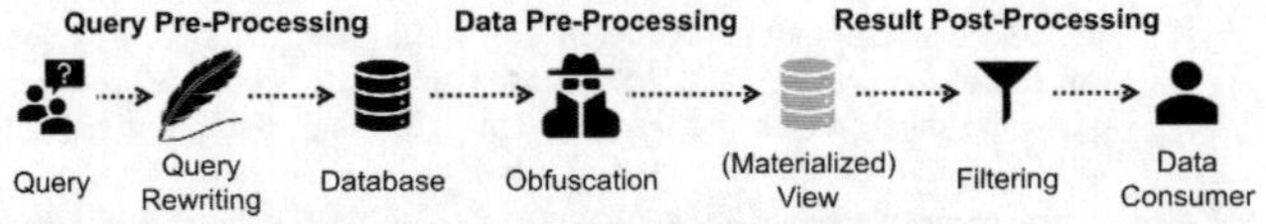

Figure 6. Implementation Strategies for the Privacy Techniques in VAULT.

errors are likely to occur when automatically rewriting queries. These errors compromise privacy as well as service quality.

Result post-processing enables a thorough control of a query's result set. That way, it can be filtered before forwarding it to the data consumer. However, a query can add hidden information to its result set. For instance, if the weight must not be revealed, a data consumer could query all data entries where the weight is x kg (without including the weight itself in the result set). Then, s/he repeats the query and increases x successively. Thus, s/he knows the weight for each entry implicitly, although it never explicitly appeared in the result set. Result post-processing is not able to detect and prevent this.

Due to the shortcomings of those strategies, we use *data pre-processing* in VAULT. This strategy pre-processes all data by removing or obscuring private data. Queries are not executed on the original data, but on this purged data. However, this data pre-processing increases the runtime. Yet, as Smart Services often use recurring queries, which are known due to their service descriptions, the runtime can be improved by using materialized views to persist the pre-processed data in advance.

Figure 7 shows how we realized the VAULT concept following the data pre-processing strategy. VAULT introduces a database abstraction layer to strictly isolate services from data sources. From a service's perspective, it therefore seems that it directly interacts with a data source and it is not aware of the privacy techniques applied to the data [22], [23].

Before using a service for the first time, it must define its quality requirements and the user must specify the privacy requirements. As this needs to be done only once (unless requirements change), these steps are not shown in Figure 7.

A registered service authenticates to VAULT with its attributes **(a)**. To prevent a service from getting too many permissions by falsifying its attributes, Gritti, Önen, and Molva [24] introduce a process for verifying these attributes. This approach takes into account that the privacy of the service has to be ensured as well, as the attributes might contain private information about the service provider. This approach is therefore a valuable supplement to the authentication process of a data provisioning platform, such as VAULT [25]. If a service is authorized to use VAULT, its queries are temporarily stored in a query buffer **(b)**. VAULT checks in the access policy which quality requirements this service has, and which permissions are granted to its attributes **(c)**. Then, a utility metric is used to search for privacy techniques that maximize both, privacy and service quality **(d)**. Basically, it compares how much information relevant to the service is concealed and how much private data is disclosed when a particular privacy technique is applied. Additionally, the user can determine via a weight, whether his or her focus is more on privacy or service quality [26]. We implemented each of the privacy techniques presented in Section IV as Python scripts. These scripts are

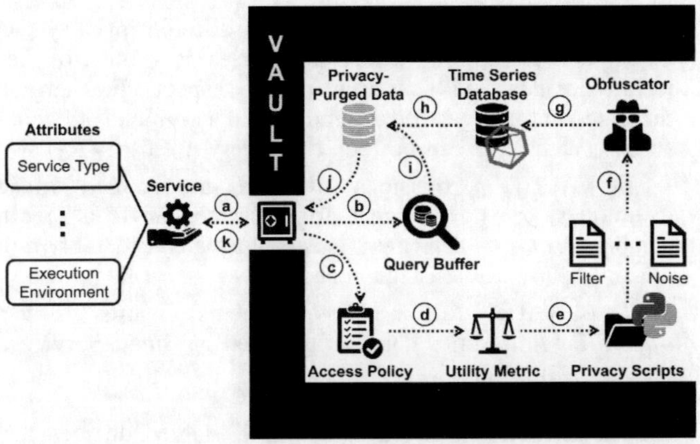

Figure 7. Implementation of and Query Processing in VAULT.

made available to VAULT in an archive. Further scripts and thus privacy techniques can be added to the archive to extend the functionality of VAULT. The utility metric selects the most suitable scripts and forwards them to the *Obfuscator* **(e)**. The Obfuscator merges the scripts and adjusts them according to the service **(f)**. It then applies the resulting script to the affected time series data **(g)**. In our prototype, we use InfluxDB. However, due to the database abstraction any other time series database can be used as well. The privacy-purged data are made available in materialized views **(h)** and the queries stored in the query buffer are executed on them **(i)**. Then, the database abstraction layer—which, in analogy to the result post-processing strategy, performs a final audit **(j)**—returns the results to the service **(k)**.

Without any loss of generality, a time series database is used in VAULT. Yet, VAULT can also be applied to a stream processing system for time series data, such as *Kapacitor* [6].

VI. Assessment

Having presented VAULT's concept and implementation, we now need to evaluate whether it meets the requirements towards a privacy system for Smart Services (see Section II).

In VAULT, each user is able to specify his or her individual privacy requirements. Since this is done in natural language and the mapping to actual data sources can be realized automatically, the configuration is also user-friendly. That way, users are enabled to specify their privacy requirements very precisely and VAULT fulfills these requirements as good as possible ($\mathbf{R_1}$).

VAULT also preserves the utility of a service when it is compatible with the privacy requirements. This is made possible by the specification of the service's quality requirements. This ensures that the service receives usable data in terms of quantity and quality. That is not the case with approaches working only with data suppression or mock data, which have a sustainably negative impact on these two parameters ($\mathbf{R_2}$).

The utility metric applied in VAULT balances privacy and quality requirements against each other and determines the best configuration. It aims to maximize both, the amount of concealed private data as well as the amount of revealed information, which is relevant to the service. As it might not be possible to maximize both of these values at the same time, at least Pareto optimality is achieved. The user can also weight, which of these objectives should be preferred by VAULT ($\mathbf{R_3}$).

To this end, VAULT provides five different privacy techniques that are tailored to IoT time series data. Each of these techniques deals with different privacy aspects. Furthermore, these techniques can be extended and combined so that a suitable technique can be found for every use case ($\mathbf{R_4}$).

In VAULT, permissions (and thus the applied privacy techniques) are not assigned to a service, but to a specific combination of its attributes. This enables a considerably more dynamic permission assignment ($\mathbf{R_5}$).

Thus, VAULT fulfills all requirements towards a privacy system for time series data as processed by Smart Services.

VII. CONCLUSION

The tremendous progress that IoT-enabled devices have made in recent years in terms of computing power, transmission speed, and sensor technology provides the technical foundation for a wide range of IoT applications. Such Smart Services affect all aspects of our daily lives (e. g., Smart Homes, Smart Cars, and Smart Health). In order to enjoy the benefits of these services, however, users have to disclose a lot of data, some of which revealing highly sensitive information. However, current privacy approaches are not adapted to the specific characteristics of time series data as processed by Smart Services, making them unnecessarily restrictive. As a result, users have to disclose too much private information in order to prevent that the service quality deteriorates too much.

In this paper, we therefore introduce VAULT, a new privacy concept for time series data. If data are queried by a service, VAULT considers besides privacy requirements also quality requirements of this service towards the data. This includes, among other things, what data is required, what accuracy this data must have, and how the data is pre-processed by the service. VAULT then selects a privacy technology fitting to this pre-processing. For instance, projection, selection, and information emphasization are suitable for data reduction, whereas data interpolation and data smoothing can be used as noise filters or for outlier suppression. Thus, VAULT can find a good ratio between privacy and service quality. In our prototype, five privacy techniques are implemented as Python scripts. However, these scripts can be combined, and more scripts can be added if needed. As a result, the service quality can be increased for any type of service and the privacy can be enhanced. VAULT can be applied to time series databases (e. g., InfluxDB) as well as stream processing systems for time series data (e. g., Kapacitor). That is, VAULT meets the request of the GDPR for a manageable Privacy by Design solution for the IoT.

As part of future work, the performance of the VAULT prototype has to be evaluated thoroughly in terms of processing time and data throughput.

ACKNOWLEDGMENT

This paper is part of the PATRON research project, which is financed by the Baden-Württemberg Stiftung gGmbH.

REFERENCES

[1] M. S. Jalali, J. P. Kaiser, M. Siegel, and S. Madnick, "The Internet of Things Promises New Benefits and Risks: A Systematic Analysis of Adoption Dynamics of IoT Products," *IEEE Security Privacy*, vol. 17, no. 2, pp. 39–48, 2019.

[2] Q. Pan, "Privacy in the New Age of IoT," in *Women Securing the Future with TIPPSS for IoT*, F. D. Hudson, Ed. Springer, 2019, pp. 37–52.

[3] European Parliament and Council of the European Union, "Regulation on the protection of natural persons with regard to the processing of personal data and on the free movement of such data, and repealing directive 95/46/EC," Legislative acts L119, 2016.

[4] S. Wachter, "Normative Challenges of Identification in the Internet of Things: Privacy, Profiling, Discrimination, and the GDPR," *Computer Law & Security Review*, vol. 34, no. 3, pp. 436–449, 2018.

[5] K. M. Ramokapane, A. C. Mazeli, and A. Rashid, "Skip, Skip, Skip, Accept!!!: A Study on the Usability of Smartphone Manufacturer Provided Default Features and User Privacy," *Proceedings on Privacy Enhancing Technologies*, vol. 2019, no. 2, pp. 209–227, 2019.

[6] InfluxData Inc. (2019). InfluxDB: Purpose-Built Open Source Time Series Database, [Online]. Available: https://www.influxdata.com.

[7] A. Dohr, R. Modre-Osprian, M. Drobics, D. Hayn, and G. Schreier, "The Internet of Things for Ambient Assisted Living," in *ITNG '10*, 2010, pp. 804–809.

[8] E. Borelli *et al.*, "HABITAT: An IoT Solution for Independent Elderly," *Sensors*, vol. 19, no. 5, pp. 1–23, 2019.

[9] E. Thorstensen, "Privacy and Future Consent in Smart Homes as Assisted Living Technologies," in *ITAP '18*, 2018, pp. 415–433.

[10] Y. Ning, Y. Zhu, R.-c. Wand, R. Malekian, and L. Qiao-min, "An Efficient Authentication and Access Control Scheme for Perception Layer of Internet of Things," *Applied Mathematics & Information Sciences*, vol. 8, no. 4, pp. 1617–1624, 2014.

[11] M. Hüffmeyer and U. Schreier, "Analysis of an Access Control System for RESTful Services," in *ICWE '16*, 2016, pp. 373–380.

[12] K. Olejnik *et al.*, "SmarPer: Context-Aware and Automatic Runtime-Permissions for Mobile Devices," in *SP '17*, 2017, pp. 1058–1076.

[13] S. Alpers *et al.*, "PRIVACY-AVARE: An approach to manage and distribute privacy settings," in *ICCC '17*, 2017, pp. 1460–1468.

[14] G. Cugola and A. Margara, "Processing Flows of Information: From Data Stream to Complex Event Processing," *ACM Computing Surveys*, vol. 44, no. 3, 15:1–15:62, 2012.

[15] S. M. Palanisamy, F. Dürr, M. A. Tariq, and K. Rothermel, "Preserving Privacy and Quality of Service in Complex Event Processing Through Event Reordering," in *DEBS '18*, 2018, pp. 40–51.

[16] K. Birman, M. Jelasity, R. Kleinberg, and E. Tremel, "Building a Secure and Privacy-Preserving Smart Grid," *ACM SIGOPS Operating Systems Review*, vol. 49, no. 1, pp. 131–136, 2015.

[17] C. Stach and B. Mitschang, "ACCESSORS: A Data-Centric Permission Model for the Internet of Things," in *ICISSP '18*, 2018, pp. 30–40.

[18] C. Stach and F. Steimle, "Recommender-based Privacy Requirements Elicitation – EPICUREAN: An Approach to Simplify Privacy Settings in IoT Applications with Respect to the GDPR," in *SAC '19*, 2019, pp. 1500–1507.

[19] M. Pourahmadi, "Estimation and Interpolation of Missing Values of a Stationary Time Series," *Journal of Time Series Analysis*, vol. 10, no. 2, pp. 149–169, 1989.

[20] T. Sakamoto *et al.*, "A crop phenology detection method using time-series MODIS data," *Remote Sensing of Environment*, vol. 96, no. 3, pp. 366–374, 2005.

[21] L. Billings and I. B. Schwartz, "Exciting chaos with noise: Unexpected dynamics in epidemic outbreaks," *Journal of Mathematical Biology*, vol. 44, no. 1, pp. 31–48, 2002.

[22] C. Stach and B. Mitschang, "The Secure Data Container: An Approach to Harmonize Data Sharing with Information Security," in *MDM '16*, 2016, pp. 292–297.

[23] ——, "CURATOR—A Secure Shared Object Store: Design, Implementation, and Evaluation of a Manageable, Secure, and Performant Data Exchange Mechanism for Smart Devices," in *SAC '18*, 2018, pp. 533–540.

[24] C. Gritti, M. Önen, and R. Molva, "Privacy-preserving delegatable authentication in the Internet of Things," in *SAC '19*, 2019, pp. 861–869.

[25] C. Stach, F. Steimle, C. Gritti, and B. Mitschang, "PSSST! The Privacy System for Smart Service Platforms: An Enabler for Confidable Smart Environments," in *IoTBDS '19*, 2019, pp. 57–68.

[26] C. Stach, F. Dürr, K. Mindermann, S. M. Palanisamy, and S. Wagner, "How a Pattern-based Privacy System Contributes to Improve Context Recognition," in *CoMoRea '18*, 2018, pp. 238–243.

Towards Empirically Assessing Behavior Stimulation Approaches for Android Malware

Aleieldin Salem, Michael Hesse, Jona Neumeier, and Alexander Pretschner

Technische Universität München
Garching bei München, Germany
Email: {salem, hessem, neumeiej, pretschn}@in.tum.de

***Abstract*—Android malware authors have increasingly relied on techniques to hinder dynamic analysis of their apps by hiding their malicious payloads or by scheduling their execution based on complex conditions. Consequently, researchers devise different approaches to bypass such conditions and stimulate the malicious behaviors embedded within the Android malware. Despite the availability of different behavior stimulation approaches and dynamic analysis tools that implement them, they are seldom empirically evaluated to assess their applicability and effectiveness. In this paper, we survey the literature to identify different behavior stimulation approaches and assess the performance of three tools implementing them against four datasets of synthetic and real-world malware. Using the obtained results, we highlight significant limitations of such analysis tools, including their instability and their inability to stimulate scheduled behaviors even in automatically generated synthetic malware. Those limitations enable simple approaches based on the random manipulation of an app's User Interface (UI) to outperform more sophisticated behavior stimulation approaches. We aspire that our results instigate the adoption of more rigorous evaluation methods that ensure the stability of newly-devised analysis tools across different platforms and their effectiveness against real-world Android malware.**

***Keywords*–Android Security; Application Analysis; Malware Detection.**

I. INTRODUCTION

Android malware authors utilize different techniques to hinder static analysis of their apps, such as anti-debugging techniques [1], code obfuscation and encryption [2], dynamic code loading [3], and triggering and scheduling [4] [5]. However, more recently, malware authors have increasingly relied on evasion techniques to hinder dynamic analysis as well [1]. For example, Wei et al. found that the majority of malicious apps they gathered and analyzed utilized *schedulers* to delay the execution of their payloads [5]. Consequently, researchers have devised different approaches to identify suspicious segments within Android apps and stimulate (i.e., execute) them, such as in [6]–[10]. We refer to these approaches as *behavior stimulation* approaches. Stimulating suspicious behaviors helps detection methods understand the true intentions of an app, and classify it correctly as malicious or benign [11].

In describing their stimulation approaches, and the dynamic analysis tools that implement them, researchers tend to focus on distancing their work from the previous work by, for example, enumerating the new features offered by their tools or the limitations of prior work their new tools tackle. Furthermore, approaches are usually evaluated using either a few samples [7] [9] [10] or mainly using synthetic malware datasets [6], to allow for a more in-depth description of the concepts upon which the approaches are built.

Unfortunately, this renders it difficult for other researchers to assess the applicability and effectiveness of the current behavior stimulation approaches against Android malware found in the wild. In particular, the answers to the following questions are unknown to researchers: **(Q1)** How well can the current behavior stimulation tools stimulate scheduled malicious behaviors embedded in (synthetic) Android malware? **(Q2)** How difficult is it to trigger malicious behaviors dwelling in Android malware found in the wild (e.g., app marketplaces)? And **(Q3)** What are the limitations that face some of the current analysis tools and their behavior stimulation approaches?

To answer such questions, we conducted preliminary experiments performed on (1) synthetic malicious apps that implement schedulers, and (2) random samples drawn from real-world Android malware datasets (i.e., *Piggybacking* [12] and *AMD* [5]). In those experiments, we compared the performance of three tools that represent different behavior stimulation approaches according to three criteria, viz. the time taken to analyze an app, whether a tool undermines the stability of an app (e.g., causes it to crash), and whether a tool managed to unveil the malicious code segments embedded within an app.

The results we obtained from our preliminary experiments suggest the following. Firstly, we found that a noticeable number of the behavior stimulation tools we surveyed are (a) poorly documented, which makes it difficult to set them up and configure them, and (b) did not deliver the functionalities described in their papers. Secondly, none of the tools we used during our experiments managed to stimulate malicious behaviors guarded by primitive schedulers (i.e., time-based triggers), embedded in synthetic malware generated by the repackaging tool, `Repackman` [4]. Thirdly, our results imply that Android malware authors implement their instances in a manner that exhibits some of their malicious behaviors without schedulers, especially malicious apps belonging to the less subtle types of `Adware` and `Riskware`. This enables primitive tools (e.g., the ones that interact with an app's UI), to outperform more sophisticated counterparts in terms of the aforementioned three criteria.

In summary, our contributions are:

- We survey the literature to identify the existing and available Android malware dynamic analysis tools that implement behavior stimulation approaches and categorize them according to such approaches (Section II).
- The conducted experiments revealed that the tools used during evaluation–including those mainly designed to bypass schedulers–were unable to stimulate malicious behaviors protected by simple time-based

triggers. We found that maintaining the stability of test apps is more important than the complexity of a tool's stimulation approach as it increases its chances to stimulate malicious behaviors in malware (Sections III and IV).

- We share with the research community the results of our experiments to verify, reproduce, and improve upon our findings.

II. Stimulation Approaches

We surveyed the literature in pursuit of dynamic analysis tools that (a) implement any behavior stimulation approach, and (b) are designed to analyze Android malware or, at least, accommodate for malicious apps. Tools such as `TriggerScope` [13], for instance, which identifies logic-based triggers embedded within an Android app, but does not include modules to stimulate behaviors within the app were ruled out. Using such criteria, we so far managed to identify 11 dynamic analysis tools with behavior stimulation modules, as seen in Table I. Those tools implemented three approaches to behavior stimulation that we refer to as *random UI manipulation*, *forcing execution*, and *environment adaptation*.

In addition to investigating the stimulation approach adopted by different analysis tools, we studied the techniques they use to target suspicious code segments within an app (*Code Targeting*), the mechanisms they utilize to execute the identified targets (*Code Triggering*), whether they require any modifications to the apps under test or the systems on which they are analyzed (*Invasiveness*), the programming language level they operate on (*Operation Level*), and whether they provide any documentation or source code to the research community (*Availability+Maintainability*). In the following sections, we briefly explain those strategies and techniques and how different tools utilize them.

A. Random UI Manipulation

The random manipulation of an app's user interface is the most primitive of stimulation approaches. Tools adopting this approach usually do not implement any strategies to target code segments within apps. Instead, the majority of such tools randomly interact with the graphical user interface elements of apps (e.g., `Button` or `TextField`), and their background components (e.g., `Service` or `BroadcastReceiver`), to instigate (suspicious) runtime behaviors. Consequently, random UI manipulation tools usually do not implement any automatic strategies to trigger specific segments of code. Such responsibility is delegated to the user in the form of scripts that define sequences of interactions with app components (e.g., start `Activity` A, then tap `Button` B, then broadcast `Intent` I) [16] [17].

The lack of code targeting and triggering strategies implies that random UI manipulation tools are, by and large, non-invasive. That is, apart from injecting logging statements into an app, such tools do not require any modifications to the app under test or the test environment to function. Furthermore, random UI manipulation tools tend to solely operate on apps' (graphical) components, without the need to explore or analyze the apps' codebases.

B. Forcing Execution

In Android apps, some code segments are implemented to execute only if some conditions are satisfied. For example, updates usually require devices to be connected to the internet via WiFi and the devices to be plugged in for charging. Forcing execution tools are designed to bypass any conditions that prevent the code of interest from executing, effectively forcing it to execute. We identified two main methods to force the execution of code segments. The tools `GroddDroid` [10] and `Harvester` [18] *replace* any conditional statements leading to the target code with unconditional ones, whereas `Droid-AntiRM` [19] and `ARES` [6] *alter* the boolean expressions of such conditional statements to values that lead to the execution of the target code. The majority of forcing execution tools maintain lists that define the Android Application Programming Interface (API) calls they should pursue in an app's code and attempt to execute. The API methods in those lists are known to be often utilized by malware (e.g., `sentTextMessage`) [7] [10].

Forcing execution tools usually operate on a low-level representation of an app's code (e.g., `DEX` bytecode), and utilize different techniques including slicing [18] and control-/data-flow analysis [10] [19], to find paths between entry points in the code (e.g., the app's main activity), and the target API calls. Modifying the apps' code implies app-level invasiveness. Moreover, some tools, such as `ARES`, require the modification of the test environment as well to generate trace logs that might reveal previously unforeseen execution paths.

After modification, the paths to target code should be unobstructed with any (boolean) conditions, and the target code should execute after simple, random interaction of the apps UI (e.g., using tools like `Monkey`). Some forcing execution tools embed a controller activity into the modified app, which calls the functions along the path leading to the target code [18].

C. Environment Adaptation

Environment adaptation attempts to trigger the target code without modifying an app's control flow or structure. To do that, tools adopting this approach alter the environment surrounding the app to steer its execution towards the targeted code. For example, if the target code needs access to the device's Global Positioning System (GPS) module to execute, the analysis tool would switch on the location services and grant the app any necessary permissions.

Environment adaption analysis tools rely on user-defined target code usually in the format of API calls to identify target code. Once identified, a path from an app's entry point to the target code is calculated, and variables along this path are included in constraints generated using symbolic execution [7]–[9]. The symbolic variables in such constraints depict values read from files, statuses returned after querying system modules, or variables inside the app's code.

During runtime, environment adaptation tools make sure that the symbolic variables in those constraints have values that steer an app towards the target code. Instead of altering the environment itself to influence the symbolic variables, current environment adaptation tools intercept the values returned from the system or queried resource, and replace them with the values required to execute the target code.

TABLE I. A SUMMARY OF THE IDENTIFIED ANDROID MALWARE DYNAMIC ANALYSIS TOOLS THAT IMPLEMENT A BEHAVIOR STIMULATION APPROACH. THE TOOLS WE UTILIZED DURING OUR EXPERIMENTS ARE HIGHLIGHTED IN RED.

Tool	Stimluation Approach			Code Targeting			Code Triggering		Invasiveness			Operation Level			Availability+ Maintainability			
	Random UI	Force Execn	Env Adaptn	None	Auto	Manual	Random UI	Guided	No	App	System	User Interface	Native Code	DEX Bytecode	User Manual	Source Code	Executable(s)	Last Commit
SmartDroid [14]	✓			✓			✓		✓			✓						
CopperDroid [15]	✓				✓		✓	✓			✓		✓	✓				
Droidbot [16]	✓			✓			✓	✓	✓			✓			✓	✓	✓	Apr'19
Droidmate-2 [17]	✓			✓			✓	✓		✓		✓			✓	✓	✓	Jun'19
GroddDroid [10]		✓				✓	✓	✓		✓				✓	✓	✓	✓	
Harvester [18]		✓				✓		✓		✓				✓	✓			
Droid-AntiRM [19]		✓				✓	✓			✓				✓				
ARES [6]		✓			✓		✓			✓	✓			✓	✓	✓	✓	Apr'18
IntelliDroid [9]			✓			✓		✓			✓			✓	✓	✓	✓	Dec'16
FuzzDroid [7]			✓			✓		✓		✓		✓		✓		✓	✓	Feb'17
Malton [8]			✓		✓	✓		✓	✓				✓					

To calculate the aforementioned constraints, the analysis tools usually operate on a low-level representation of the apps' code, such as DEX bytecode [7] [9] or on native code executed on Android Runtime (ART) layer [8]. In terms of invasiveness, Malton does not modify the apps or their testing environments, IntelliDroid needs a modified version of the Android operating system to include a service that feeds the app during execution with the values required to satisfy the constraints, and FuzzDroid injects logging statements into the apps for a similar purpose along with tracking the execution paths.

III. Experiments

*a) **Tools**:* Out of the 11 tools we identified so far, only six offered their source code or executables to the research community, which we attempted to install, configure, and test. Unfortunately, half of the remaining tools (i.e., three tools), either (a) were incomplete and needed a further extension before being used, or (b) did not deliver the functionality described in their respective papers. For example, the tool FuzzDroid needed to be extended to accommodate for different types of sensitive API calls apart from Short Message Service (SMS)-related ones. Furthermore, after obtaining the source code of the tool ARES, following the instructions available on its website to compile a customized version of the Android kernel, setting up and running it against the *EvaDroid* dataset, we could not reproduce the results reported in its paper [6], primarily because the tool did not manage to trigger the payloads in such apps. Consequently, we ran our experiments using the three remaining tools, namely Droidbot, GroddDroid, and IntelliDroid, which fortunately respectively represent the stimulation approaches of *random UI manipulation*, *forcing execution*, and *environment adaptation*.

*b) **Datasets**:* We ran the aforementioned three tools against four datasets of synthetic and real Android malicious apps. The first dataset we considered is *EvaDroid* [6], which comprises 24 manually-developed, synthetic malicious apps that implement different types of schedulers (e.g., time-based, virtualization fingerprinters, battery status checkers, etc.). The second dataset, referred to as *Repackman*, comprises 30 synthetic malicious apps automatically generated using the Repackman tool [4] by grafting trigger-protected malicious payloads into benign apps from the Google Play store. The third dataset is a random sample of 30 malicious apps drawn from the *Piggybacking* dataset, which includes real-world Android repackaged malware [12]. The distribution of malware types in this dataset is Adware (63%), Riskware (17%), Trojan (16.1%), and Spyware (3%). Lastly, we drew a random sample of 130 malicious apps out of 24,553 from the *AMD* dataset including different families and types of Android malware (e.g., Adware (57.7%), Trojan (27.78%), and Ransomware (8.74%)) [5].

A. Results

Table II summarizes the results obtained from our experiments. For each dataset, we calculated the **a**verage **t**ime taken (in seconds) by each tool to analyze an app (AT), the percentage of **a**pps that were successfully **a**nalyzed (AA), and whether the malicious **p**ayloads embedded within the apps were **t**riggered (PT) and found in the logs of the successfully analyzed apps. The time taken by Droidbot to analyze apps seems constant across different datasets because we allowed the tool to run for five minutes per app.

We defined an analysis to be successful if a tool that monitors the API calls issued by an app during runtime, Droidmon [20], managed to generate a log for an app. Droidmon monitors a defined list of API calls that (a) interact with sensitive system resources (e.g., user contacts), or (b) are known to be widely-adopted by malicious apps (e.g., sending and receiving SMS messages). We made sure to synchronize the lists of API calls targeted by GroddDroid and IntelliDroid and monitored by Droidmon itself. This means that stimulation tools, for example, GroddDroid, would attempt to target and execute the same API calls that are monitored and logged by Droidmon. Such synchronization is the only modification we made to the analysis tools. To automate the process of analysis, we wrote scripts that iterate over the apps in a dataset, launches the analysis tool, and downloads any logs generated by Droidmon from the virtual device on which the analysis was performed. We manually examined the generated Droidmon logs of each analyzed app to inspect whether any of its malicious payload(s) have exhib-

TABLE II. A SUMMARY OF THE RESULTS OBTAINED FROM OUR EXPERIMENTS.

Dataset	EvaDroid			Repackman			Piggybacking			AMD		
	AT	AA	PT	AT	AA	PT	AT	AA	PT	AT	AA	PT
Droidbot	305.6	100%	17%	304.45	100%	0%	305.89	96.67%	86.20%	306.34	76.15%	54.54%
GroddDroid	104.45	100%	37%	1434.2	40%	0%	2629.22	66.33%	68.42%	209.26	57.69%	46.67%
IntelliDroid	N/A	100%	33%	N/A	43%	0%	N/A	46.67%	71.42%	N/A	79.23%	42.67%

ited. For the synthetic malware datasets, the inspection was straightforward, especially since the malicious payloads were merely logging messages or `Toast` messages that indicate the execution of the targeted code (e.g., *Evil Payload Triggered!!*). We made sure that the analysis tools and `Droidmon` do indeed target and monitor such logging statements, respectively. As for apps in the *Piggybacking* and *AMD* datasets, we relied on the information available on `VirusTotal` [21] or provided by the dataset authors about the apps' behaviors.

IV. Discussion

In this section, we attempt to answer the research questions **(Q1)**, **(Q2)**, and **(Q3)** that we postulated in Section I.

Q1

How well can the current behavior stimulation tools stimulate scheduled malicious behaviors embedded in (synthetic) Android malware?

On the *EvaDroid* dataset, despite managing to outperform their simpler counterpart, `Droidbot`, the more sophisticated analysis tools `GroddDroid` and `IntelliDroid` performed mediocrely on such dataset, given the simplicity of its apps and the schedulers they utilize. Moreover, we noticed that some of the tools managed to analyze and trigger the payloads in apps that other tools did not manage to either successfully analyze or to reveal their payloads. For example, `GroddDroid` managed to uniquely trigger the payloads in the apps *accelH* and *network1*, whereas `IntelliDroid` triggered the payloads in *adbPortDetector*, *installedApps*, *qemuFingerprinting*, and *uptime*. Collectively, the three tools successfully analyzed and triggered the payloads in 13 (54%) out of 24 apps in the *EvaDroid* dataset, which continues to be a less than expected percentage.

The performance of all tools worsened on the *Repackman* dataset. While this can be expected from simple approaches as `Droidbot`'s, this result is indeed not expected from `GroddDroid` and `IntelliDroid`. One possible reason of failing to trigger such payloads is the inability of the `GroddDroid` and `IntelliDroid` to successfully analyze around 60% of the apps in the dataset, which might be a result of runtime errors rather than technical shortcomings. Upon futher investigation, we found that apps tested using `GroddDroid` did not generate any `Droidmon` logs as they encountered various types of runtime exceptions, mostly related to calling methods in classes that are yet to be loaded (e.g., `java.lang.NullPointerException` and `android.os.DeadObjectException`). A possible reason behind this behavior could be `GroddDroid`'s technique of skipping over specific code segments and conditions in order to execute the targeted code. As for `IntelliDroid`, unlike `GroddDroid`, we did not find any evidence of crashes in the system logs we downloaded from the virtual devices. In other words, failure to target and/or trigger any payloads in the apps might be due to some deficiencies in the tool's approach. We consider the failure of both tools to trigger such payloads as a significant source of concern, given the ability to generate hundreds of malicious apps using such automated method and the simplicity of the triggers injected into those apps.

The tools' performances on the *AMD* dataset are indeed more balanced, yet raise other concerns. The majority of malicious apps in this dataset makes use of schedulers that delay the execution of the apps' malicious payloads [5]. So, we expected `Droidbot` to be outperformed by the other tools in terms of triggering scheduled malicious payloads. However, as implied by the **(PT)**, **Droidbot** slightly outperformed **GroddDroid** and `IntelliDroid`. Similar to the *EvaDroid* dataset, we found that the three tools complemented one another in terms of apps they uniquely managed to trigger their payloads. Between the three tools, the payloads of 122 (93.84%) out of 130 apps were successfully triggered. We investigated the apps that tools uniquely analyzed and triggered in pursuit of patterns that might indicate the strengths of some of the tools.

On the one hand, `Droidbot` managed to uniquely trigger the payloads in three apps that belong to different malware types (i.e., `Ransomware`, `Trojan`, and `Adware`). The other tools could not identify any code to target within such apps. On the other hand, `GroddDroid` and `IntelliDroid` managed to trigger malicious payloads in 19 apps that `Droidbot` did not manage to trigger. We found the payloads in ten of those apps were uniquely triggered by `IntelliDroid`, whereas six were uniquely triggered by `GroddDroid`.

In pursuit of any differences between the apps successfully analyzed by each tool, we consulted `VirusTotal` and retrieved the labels given by different scanners to each app, the last time an app was modified (i.e., roughly its development date), and the Android Software Development Kit (SDK) versions an app supports according to its `AndroidManifest.xml` file. Firstly, the VirusTotal labels did not reveal any patterns vis-à-vis the malware families or types that each tool excels at analyzing. In other words, we could not find any evidence that suggests, for example, that `GroddDroid` can uniquely trigger payloads embedded in `Trojans` or the `DroidKungFu` malware family. The tools also shared the average year in which a malicious app was last modified and presumably developed viz., 2013, and the average minimum SDK supported by the apps they uniquely triggered their payloads (i.e., API level 6).

The results we observed imply, we argue, that the success of a tool to trigger the payloads in any given malicious app hinges on the app itself (e.g., its functionalities, utilized permissions, used libraries, etc.). Furthermore, the poor performance of older tools such as `GroddDroid` and `IntelliDroid` on apps in the *Repackman* dataset, which are newer than those in other datasets, implies that such tools do not generalize to newer apps with newer technologies (e.g., runtime permissions), or are meant to run on newer versions of Android. Consequently, as discussed earlier, the analysis of any given app should be carried out collectively using different analysis tools to increase the likelihood of successful analysis and payload triggering.

Q2

How difficult is it to trigger malicious behaviors dwelling in Android malware found in the wild (e.g., app marketplaces)?

To answer (**Q2**), we use the performance of `Droidbot` on the *Piggybacking* and *AMD* datasets as an indication of the difficulty to trigger the malicious payloads in an app. If `Droidbot`'s simple random UI manipulation stimulation approach stimulates any malicious behaviors in an app, we infer that complex schedulers did not protect such malicious behaviors and, hence, were easy to stimulate. The decent performance of `Droidbot`'s simple random UI manipulation implies that authors of Android malware in the *Piggybacking* dataset did not graft the legitimate apps they repackaged with sophisticated schedulers. We found that the majority of the malicious apps in the *Piggybacking* dataset comprise `Adware`, which usually focuses on the monetary gain rather than stealth and sophistication [12]. That is to say, the authors of `Adware` would rather trigger their malicious or *potentially unwanted* payloads as soon as possible to maximize their profit than hide the true intentions of their apps, especially since displaying more advertisements or implicitly rerouting their revenues does not bother device users or interrupt their usage as much as other more notorious breeds of malware (e.g., `Ransomware`). In this context, albeit unexpected, the performance of `Droidbot` is not necessarily surprising. `Droidbot`'s performance is not replicated in case of the *AMD* dataset, which implies the use of more sophisticated schedulers and triggers. Nevertheless, given the simplicity of its approach, the tool managed to trigger the malicious payloads embedded within more than 50% of the dataset's apps. Similar to the *Piggybacking* dataset, the majority of malware types in *AMD* is `Adware`, which may have facilitated the tool's task.

So, we argue that using stimulation approaches as simple as random UI manipulation, a subset of the malicious behaviors found in some real-world Android malware types (e.g., `Adware`) or indications of their presence (e.g., fingerprinting the device), might be revealed. Otherwise, the existence of (complex) schedulers in apps noticeably hinders the performance of all tools.

Q3

What are the limitations that face some of the current analysis tools and their behavior stimulation approaches?

In addressing (**Q3**), we identified the following limitations facing the analysis tools we examined so far. Firstly, apart from `Droidbot`, the utilized tools were either too slow in targeting code and devising strategies to trigger it or required manual operation, such as `IntelliDroid` (hence the **N/A** in Table II). Secondly, the approaches adopted by `GroddDroid` and `IntelliDroid`, seemed to have undermined the stability of the apps, which hindered their successful analysis. Being a pre-requisite for payload triggering, we believe that this has negatively affected the ability of such tools to trigger payloads. Lastly, we noticed that all tools could only analyze apps compatible with the Android versions that the tools target. That is to say, the tools seem to be limited to the environments within which they were implemented and evaluated. With the lack of maintainability, the analysis tools we examined cease to cope with the frequently changing structures and behaviors of Android (malicious) apps, rendering them obsolete within a few years.

V. Limitations and Future Work

*a) **Dataset Size**:* As discussed in Section III, one of the main criteria in evaluating the performance of a behavior stimulation approach is its ability to trigger malicious behaviors embedded within the apps. To make sure that payloads have indeed triggered, especially in real-world malware, we manually inspected the `Droidmon` logs generated by the dynamic analysis tool. Using the entire corpus of the *Piggybacking* and *AMD* datasets and the logs generated from their apps by each of the **three** analysis tools means manually analyzing around 77,859 logs. So, we randomly selected apps from those datasets for our experiments, in order to have a sample that, we argue, represents the entire population of apps, their trends, triggers, and payloads.

*b) **Subset of Tools**:* The second limitation is the utilization of a subset of dynamic analysis tools we identified in Section II: out of 11 analysis tools, we ran our experiments using three tools. In order not to mistakenly claim that a particular tool is incapable of stimulating malicious behaviors during our preliminary experiments, we only considered tools that we could set up correctly, and that exhibit the behaviors described in their corresponding papers.

*c) **Future Work**:* Our future work is planned to address the aforementioned two limitations. Firstly, we wish to increase the sizes of the datasets we use during our experiments. The challenge, however, is to devise a method to semi-automatically investigate the logs generated for different apps, and decide upon whether the payloads residing in the apps have triggered. Secondly, we wish to continue surveying the literature for more dynamic analysis tools in pursuit of different approaches to behavior stimulation. Along with the tools we already identified, we wish to re-run our experiments on larger datasets of Android malware. As for tools we did not manage to set up or execute, we wish to investigate the reasons behind their unexpected behaviors after consulting their developers.

VI. Related Work

In [22], Sadeghi et al. perform a large scale study on the approaches and techniques used to assess the security of Android apps in general. Among the plethora of tools discussed in this study, dynamic analysis tools that implement behavior stimulation approaches (e.g., `GroddDroid`), are discussed. However, the study does not consider behavior stimulation as a technique to distinguish between tools and, hence, does not discuss it. Tam et al., in [1], do consider behavior stimulation approaches in surveying the literature for static and dynamic tools and discuss those specifically built to analyze Android malware (e.g., CopperDroid). Richter [23] surveys different Android malware analysis tools and attempts to compare them concerning their weaknesses and limitations. In other words, without conducting any experiments, Richter studies the features and approaches offered and adopted by different tools (e.g., Harvester), and speculates the challenges that might face them. Lastly, Hoffmann et al. survey the literature for different analysis tools used to analyze Android (malicious) apps [2]. They focus, however, on the resilience of such analysis tools against obfuscation.

There are two main differences between our work and the aforementioned related work. Firstly, we focus on the approaches adopted by some dynamic analysis tools to increase the chance of stimulating malicious behaviors in Android apps. The majority of research efforts that survey dynamic analysis tools tend to ignore such approaches. Those that do consider it, such as [1], do not delve into comparing them. Secondly, to the best of our knowledge, there are no approaches that attempt to empirically compare the performance of different analysis tools against Android malware, even using small or sample datasets, which we do in this paper.

VII. Conclusion

Despite the existence of different behavior stimulation approaches, the research community does not possess any empirical studies on any scale that assess their applicability or effectiveness against (synthetic) Android malware. To address this gap, we surveyed the literature, identified three behavior stimulation approaches adopted by dynamic analysis tools, and assessed the performance of three tools representing them against four datasets of synthetic and real-world Android malware.

The results of our preliminary experiments suggest that, despite competing with more sophisticated behavior stimulation approaches, a simple approach based on the random manipulation of an app's UI can help reveal (subsets of) the malicious behaviors it contains. This proved to be the case with certain families of malware (e.g., Adware and Ransomware), whose authors usually do not implement complex schedulers to protect their malicious payloads. More importantly, our experiments revealed that all the utilized tools did not manage to trigger any time-scheduled payloads in synthetic malware generated by the automatic repackaging tool Repackman. Lastly, without maintaining a tool's code and adapting it to newer versions of Android, dynamic analysis tools seem to be suited to analyze a particular set of malicious apps viz., ones that were implemented for the same Android API version.

References

[1] K. Tam, A. Feizollah, N. B. Anuar, R. Salleh, and L. Cavallaro, "The evolution of android malware and android analysis techniques," ACM Computing Surveys (CSUR), vol. 49, no. 4, 2017, p. 76.

[2] J. Hoffmann, T. Rytilahti, D. Maiorca, M. Winandy, G. Giacinto, and T. Holz, "Evaluating analysis tools for android apps: Status quo and robustness against obfuscation," in Proceedings of the Sixth ACM Conference on Data and Application Security and Privacy. ACM, 2016, pp. 139–141.

[3] Y. Zhauniarovich, M. Ahmad, O. Gadyatskaya, B. Crispo, and F. Massacci, "StaDynA: Addressing the Problem of Dynamic Code Updates in the Security Analysis of Android Applications," in Proceedings of the 5th ACM Conference on Data and Application Security and Privacy, ser. CODASPY '15. ACM, 2015, pp. 37–48.

[4] A. Salem, F. F. Paulus, and A. Pretschner, "Repackman: A tool for automatic repackaging of android apps," in Proceedings of the 1st International Workshop on Advances in Mobile App Analysis. ACM, 2018, pp. 25–28.

[5] F. Wei, Y. Li, S. Roy, X. Ou, and W. Zhou, "Deep ground truth analysis of current android malware," in International Conference on Detection of Intrusions and Malware, and Vulnerability Assessment. Springer, 2017, pp. 252–276.

[6] L. Bello and M. Pistoia, "Ares: triggering payload of evasive android malware," in Proceedings of the 5th International Conference on Mobile Software Engineering and Systems. ACM, 2018, pp. 2–12.

[7] S. Rasthofer, S. Arzt, S. Triller, and M. Pradel, "Making malory behave maliciously: Targeted fuzzing of android execution environments," in Proceedings of the 39th International Conference on Software Engineering. IEEE Press, 2017, pp. 300–311.

[8] L. Xue, Y. Zhou, T. Chen, X. Luo, and G. Gu, "Malton: Towards on-device non-invasive mobile malware analysis for art," 2017, pp. 289–306.

[9] M. Y. Wong and D. Lie, "Intellidroid: A targeted input generator for the dynamic analysis of android malware." in NDSS, vol. 16, 2016, pp. 21–24.

[10] A. Abraham, R. Andriatsimandefitra, A. Brunelat, J.-F. Lalande, and V. V. T. Tong, "Grodddroid: a gorilla for triggering malicious behaviors," in 2015 10th international conference on malicious and unwanted software (MALWARE). IEEE, 2015, pp. 119–127.

[11] A. Salem, T. Schmidt, and A. Pretschner, "Idea: Automatic localization of malicious behaviors in android malware with hidden markov models," in International Symposium on Engineering Secure Software and Systems. Springer, 2018, pp. 108–115.

[12] L. Li, D. Li, T. F. Bissyandé, J. Klein, Y. Le Traon, D. Lo, and L. Cavallaro, "Understanding android app piggybacking: A systematic study of malicious code grafting," IEEE Transactions on Information Forensics and Security, vol. 12, no. 6, 2017, pp. 1269–1284.

[13] Y. Fratantonio, A. Bianchi, W. Robertson, E. Kirda, C. Kruegel, and G. Vigna, "Triggerscope: Towards detecting logic bombs in android applications," in Security and Privacy (SP), 2016 IEEE Symposium on. IEEE, 2016, pp. 377–396.

[14] C. Zheng, S. Zhu, S. Dai, G. Gu, X. Gong, X. Han, and W. Zou, "Smartdroid: an automatic system for revealing ui-based trigger conditions in android applications," in Proceedings of the second ACM workshop on Security and privacy in smartphones and mobile devices. ACM, 2012, pp. 93–104.

[15] K. Tam, S. J. Khan, A. Fattori, and L. Cavallaro, "Copperdroid: Automatic reconstruction of android malware behaviors," in Proc. of the Symposium on Network and Distributed System Security (NDSS), 2015.

[16] Y. Li, Z. Yang, Y. Guo, and X. Chen, "Droidbot: a lightweight ui-guided test input generator for android," in Software Engineering Companion (ICSE-C), 2017 IEEE/ACM 39th International Conference on. IEEE, 2017, pp. 23–26.

[17] N. P. Borges Jr, J. Hotzkow, and A. Zeller, "Droidmate-2: a platform for android test generation," in Proceedings of the 33rd ACM/IEEE International Conference on Automated Software Engineering. ACM, 2018, pp. 916–919.

[18] S. Rasthofer, S. Arzt, M. Miltenberger, and E. Bodden, "Harvesting runtime values in android applications that feature anti-analysis techniques." in NDSS, 2016.

[19] X. Wang, S. Zhu, D. Zhou, and Y. Yang, "Droid-antirm: Taming control flow anti-analysis to support automated dynamic analysis of android malware," in Proceedings of the 33rd Annual Computer Security Applications Conference. ACM, 2017, pp. 350–361.

[20] Droidmon. Droidmon - dalvik monitoring framework for cuckoodroid. [Online]. Available: https://goo.gl/HPtdtG

[21] VirusTotal. Virustotal. [Online]. Available: https://goo.gl/s7GSrn

[22] A. Sadeghi, H. Bagheri, J. Garcia, and S. Malek, "A taxonomy and qualitative comparison of program analysis techniques for security assessment of android software," IEEE Transactions on Software Engineering, vol. 43, no. 6, 2017, pp. 492–530.

[23] L. Richter, "Common weaknesses of android malware analysis frameworks," Ayeks. de, 2015, pp. 1–10.

Amplifying Side Channel Leakage by Hardware Modification of Xilinx Zynq-7 FPGA Evaluation Boards

Nadir Khan[1], Sven Nitzsche[1], Raffaela Frank[1], Lars Bauer[2], Jörg Henkel[2], Jürgen Becker[1, 3]
[1]FZI Research Center for Information Technology Karlsruhe, Germany
[2]Chair for Embedded Systems, Karlsruhe Institute of Technology, Karlsruhe, Germany
[3]Institute for Information Processing Technologies, Karlsruhe Institute of Technology Karlsruhe, Germany
Email: {khan, nitzsche}@fzi.de, mail@raffaela-frank.de, {lars.bauer, henkel, juergen.becker}@kit.edu

***Abstract*— The aim of this work is to enhance the side channel information that is revealed by the power consumption of a Field Programmable Gate Array (FPGA). An initial measurement setup is proposed for measuring the signal quality, and then adjustments and modifications to the hardware are done to enhance this quality. Once an acceptable signal is measurable, data is gathered and useful information in this raw data is determined using a standard leakage assessment methodology. The used methodology generates a quantitative score regarding the presence of useful information in the raw data, and can therefore indicate whether a system is vulnerable to side channel attacks or not. In this work, several modifications are presented along with their effect on the captured signal's quality and the amount of useful information in the collected raw data.**

Keywords- FPGA; Side Channel Attack; Test Vector Leakage Assessment; Advanced Encryption Standard; Power Analysis.

I. Introduction

Even though modern key-based encryption algorithms are in theory considered as mathematically secure, this assumption is not valid for their respective implementations. Sophisticated techniques like Side Channel Attacks (SCAs) can take advantage of certain implementation characteristics to reveal secret information of their inner state [1] - pp.180, which then, in turn, can be used to reconstruct the cryptographic key in use [2]. As the name states, this kind of attack is performed on side channels, information channels, which unintentionally disclose internal information of a device. Common side channels are power consumption, execution time, acoustic and ElectroMagnetic (EM) radiation [1] - pp.181. A power analysis attack for example exploits the data-dependent nature of the switching activity of a cryptographic implementation. Since these attacks can be non-invasive and only use information extracted from physical observation, it is difficult to detect them and consequently one cannot be sure if a secret key is already compromised [2].

The most common side channel analysis is power based, which is also the focus of this work. A measurement setup is presented that gathers side channel information leaked from the power consumption of an FPGA board. The board is modified in multiple stages, while collecting data on every stage and conducting analysis on it to evaluate each modification. The evaluation is performed by collecting side channel information of an Advanced Encryption Standard (AES) implementation running on an FPGA and rating it according to its impact. Contrary to other works in this field [3]-[7], this paper focuses on FPGA evaluation boards that have higher similarity with commercially available products, rather than using boards designed for physical security analysis of cryptographic modules, such as SCA Standard Evaluation Board (SASEBO) and SCA User Reference Architecture (SAKURA) board [7]. One example board designed specifically for security analysis is the SAKURA-X, which is equipped with a Xilinx Kintex-7 FPGA for cryptographic circuits and a Spartan-6 as control unit. Usually, the focus of measurement setups based on these boards is the security evaluation of an algorithm's implementation and corresponding countermeasures. Performing side channel attacks on them is considerably easier, which is also a reason why they are not used in practice [7].

This work aims to depict possible obstacles while preparing off-the-shelf FPGA boards for side channel attacks and show how to overcome them. Rather than performing a successful key extraction itself, it should support other researchers at successfully leveraging all available side channel information. The main contributions of this work are:

- a systematic modification approach for a state of the art FPGA evaluation board to enable power-based side channel attacks,
- an improvement of common measurement setups by FPGA board modifications, e.g., replacing resistors and removing capacitors,
- an improvement of common measurement setups by optimizing soft parameters, such as logic frequency,
- quantifying the quality of a measured signal for specific modifications and
- assessing the amount of useful information within captured raw data, once the signal reaches an acceptable level of quality.

The rest of the paper is organized as follows. Section II presents related work. The measurement setup is explained in Section III, while improvements of the setup are presented in Section IV. Section V presents an evaluation of the measurement data. Finally, Section VI provides a conclusion.

II. Related Work

The first published work on SCA goes back to Kocher in 1996, where it was shown that the variation in execution time of an algorithm can leak information [8]. This leakage information can be used to extract secret keys used in the algorithm. SCAs can be classified in several ways; this work will refer to the classification presented by Zhou and Feng in [9], which is based on the following three criteria.

- Control over the computation process: According to this classification, an SCA can be an active attack if the attacker influences the behavior of the system and observes the difference in the operation or information leaked. A passive attack, on the other hand, refers to SCAs where the attacker does not interfere with the operation of the target system. Fault Injection (FI) attacks are an example of the former, while power analysis attacks are of the later type.
- Way of accessing the module: This classification divides SCAs into three different types, namely invasive, semi-invasive and non-invasive attacks [10]. These types refer to the degree of tampering done to the system for acquiring information. Non-invasive, being the lowest degree equals no hardware modification. On the other hand, invasive attack means extensive modification that could include depackaging the Integrated Circuit (IC), capacitor removal or changing resistors.
- Methods used in the analysis process: This third classification is based on the process used to analyze the acquired data. The attack could be characterized as Simple SCA (SSCA) if there is a direct relation between the leakage information and the secret. However, if SSCA is not possible due to high noise, statistical methods can be used to extract the secret. Such attacks will be classified as Differential SCA (DSCA) [9].

Zhou and Feng in [9] also discussed known SCAs, which are timing, fault, power analysis, Electro-Magnetic (EM), acoustic, visible light, error message, frequency-based, cache-based and scan-based attacks. The measurement setup and modifications presented in this work are intended for power analysis. They require some modification to the board and use statistical methods for information analysis, but they do not control the algorithm's execution. Consequently, our setup can be used for passive semi-invasive differential SCA. The term "differential" in this case should not be confused with Differential Power Analysis (DPA) [13]. In power-based SCAs, Simple Power Analysis (SPA) comes under SSCA, while DPA, Correlational Power Analysis (CPA) [11] and Test Vector Leakage Assessment (TVLA) [17][18] come under the category of DSCA.

SPAs interpret the power consumption measurements directly, which means that the attacker tries to extract a key using one or few traces [12]. In practice, these attacks are not considered a major threat because they require detailed knowledge of the implementation of the cryptographic algorithm. In contrast, DPA does not require detailed knowledge of the target setup and can extract a key even if traces contain noise [12]. A trace is a set of measurement points that are measured during execution of the target algorithm, in this case AES. CPA, introduced by Brier et al. [11] and currently the most commonly used SCA, is based on the estimated correlation between the power traces of a hypothetical model and measured power traces.

In this work, evaluation of the leaked information is done using TVLA [18]. TVLA was first introduced in 2011 in Non-Invasive Attack Testing Workshop [17]. This approach requires execution of a cryptographic algorithm with pre-specified input vectors and then performs statistical tests on the measured power consumption. These tests produce scores, which can clearly show whether a cryptographic algorithm is leaking sensitive information or not. The advantage of performing TVLA analysis is that it is faster by multiple orders of magnitude in comparison to key extraction attacks, such as DPA and CPA. In addition, it is also real-time meaning the test can be performed as the measurement data is being collected. Between the two types of TVLA tests, this work utilizes general TVLA, which compares measurements from a device performing AES on fixed inputs and from a device performing AES on random inputs. According to [18], non-specific tests are most successful in leakage assessment.

For executing a successful attack, authors in [14] showed that removing decoupling capacitors and powering the device from accumulators via linear stabilizers make the environment ideal. They were able to extract the key by analyzing just 5,000 traces. The target device used in this attack was a Spartan 3E Starter Board. Moradi et al. in [16] presented a successful SCA on Virtex 4 and Virtex 5 Xilinx devices by targeting the internal bitstream decryption engine. In addition, a comparison of SASEBO and SAKURA boards, discussed earlier, is presented by Nomata et al. in [6], where it is said that one thousand to two thousand waveforms are required for obtaining all bytes of the key with SASEBO-G, SASEBO-GII and SAKURA-G boards. On SAKURA-X, additional amplification of the waveform is required to extract keys. SASEBO-G comes with a Xilinx Virtex-II, SASEBO-GII with a Xilinx Virtex-5, SAKURA-G with a Xilinx Spartan-6 and SAKURA-X with a Kintex-7 [7]. Our work is different from the rest as we are targeting a comparatively newer FPGA placed on a Xilinx Evaluation Board rather than on a FPGA board designed for side channel analysis specifically.

III. MEASUREMENT SETUP

A. *Target Cryptographic Algorithm*

In the measurement setup, the target algorithm is a hardware implementation of AES [15] with 128-bit key length. Implementation executes within 13 clock cycles, where the round keys are generated in the first two, and then a round of AES is executed during each clock. The 16 S-boxes of the Byte Substitution (BS) Layer are implemented as lookup tables and are executed in parallel in one clock that should make the attack harder in comparison to an implementation that executes one S-box per clock. AES is packaged in the Advanced Extensible Interface (AXI) and communication between AXI-wrapped AES on the FPGA and host computer is realized via a JTAG-to-AXI interface.

B. *Basics of Power Analysis*

The power consumption of FPGAs, as with all integrated circuits, is divided into dynamic and static power. Dynamic Power Consumption (DPC) is caused by changes of signal values, while static power is always present even when no signal transitions occurs [24]. DPC can be correlated with specific bits [1] - pp. 300. At a fixed point in time, an output signal of a Complementary Metal-Oxide-Semiconductor (CMOS) cell can perform one of four transitions [12] - pp. 29. The transitions $0 \rightarrow 0$ (P_{00}) and $1 \rightarrow 1$ (P_{11}) cause only static power consumption, while $0 \rightarrow 1$ (P_{01}) and $1 \rightarrow 0$ (P_{10}) consume both static and dynamic power. The exact values of P_{00}, P_{01}, P_{10} and P_{11} depend on the cell type and process technology, but generally $P_{00} \approx P_{11} << P_{01}, P_{10}$. In addition, they depend on the data being processed [12] – pp. 29.

Since registers in digital circuits are typically synchronized by a clock signal, a current flow is caused by the simultaneous switching of the logic cells at each rising edge of the clock. This current flow or the respective voltage drop can be measured using a digital oscilloscope and thus electrical signals can be recorded over a certain period. To measure characteristics such as power or current with an oscilloscope, it is necessary to generate a voltage signal that is proportional to these characteristics. In a measurement setup for power analysis attacks, there are two common ways for SCAs to generate a voltage signal that is proportional to the power consumption of the cryptographic device. It can either be generated by placing a small measurement resistor between negative (V_{SS}) or positive supply voltage (V_{DD}) of the device and the source or ground. The current flowing through this resistor causes a voltage that can then be measured.

The structure of all hardware components for doing so and their communication is shown in Figure 1. An AES implementation on the FPGA is triggered to encrypt multiple plaintexts while the attached oscilloscope measures the consumed power and transfers all captured data to a host machine.

The target device is a Xilinx Zynq-7000 All Programmable SoC ZC702 Evaluation Kit v1. This board contains a Zynq-7000 XC7Z020-1CLG484C with 85,000 logic cells.

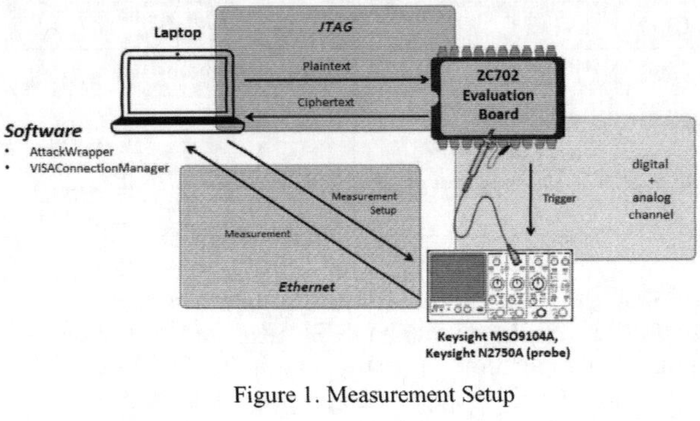

Figure 1. Measurement Setup

The Zynq-7000 series integrates an ARM Cortex-A9 based processor and a 28nm programming logic (PL). The evaluation board includes Low Pin Count - FPGA Mezzanine Card (FMC) connections to attach an FMC debug board. This is used to connect the digital channels of the oscilloscope.

Additionally, the board has three power controllers, each managing several switching regulators. The power controllers are PMBus-compliant system controllers from Texas Instruments. This allows the voltage and current levels to be set [25]. Every controller monitors different voltages. One is responsible for the core voltages, one for the auxiliary voltages and the third for the 3.3 V and 2.5 V supply voltages. The core voltage includes V_{CCINT} and V_{CCPINT} among others. V_{CCINT} is the 1V internal supply voltage for the PL [26] and therefore the target voltage for power analysis attacks on the PL. The evaluation board by default contains a $5m\Omega$ measurement resistor connected to a voltage amplifier that can be used for this purpose.

A Keysight MSO9104A oscilloscope with a resolution of 8 bits, a bandwidth of 1GHz and up to 20 GS/s sampling rate is used to perform the actual measurement. The settings of this oscilloscope are adjusted to match the target AES algorithm. The horizontal resolution is set to equal the period of one full AES round. For vertical resolution, the entire vertical range of the oscilloscope is used. The signal is sampled with a Keysight N2750A active differential probe with 1.5 GHz bandwidth. The tip of the probe is soldered to the corresponding measuring point on the board.

Test data in form of plaintexts is generated according to the TVLA specifications and sent to an AES core implementation on the programmable logic, utilizing a 128-bit symmetric key. A measurement is started at the beginning of every first AES round and all results are transferred back as raw data using Ethernet. Each measurement consists of an averaging of the same plaintext, which is performed directly on the oscilloscope. Figure 2 shows the resulting measurement plot.

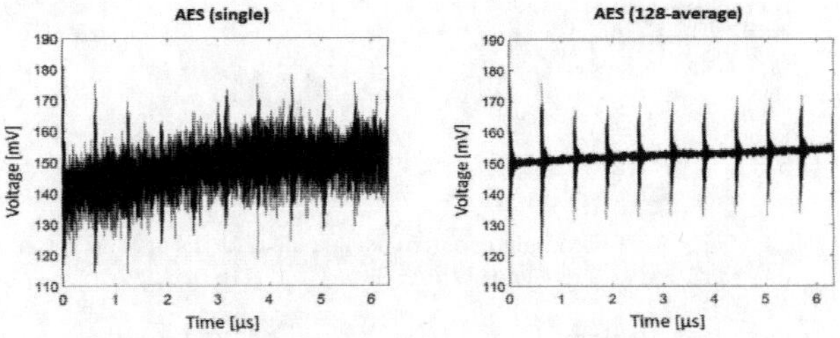

Figure 2. Measured voltage signal using the original setup for a single AES run (left) and an average of 128 AES runs (right) respectively.

IV. IMPROVING THE MEASUREMENT SETUP

In order to perform a power analysis attack, the captured data needs to meet certain quality standards. Data quality can be compared using peak-to-peak voltage (V_{P2P}) during execution of AES encryption, which should be at least 3mV according to related measurements on a SAKURA-X board [6] in order to allow successful power analysis attacks. The initial measurement, shown in Figure 2, shows ten peaks corresponding to the ten AES rounds performed. The signal quality is not sufficient to isolate intermediate computations like S-Box calculation, which are typically needed for differential power analysis, therefore no V_{P2P} can be calculated.

In order to improve data quality, multiple changes are possible. First, the internal measuring resistor can be replaced to generate a higher voltage drop and therefore a stronger signal. Secondly, the supply voltage V_{CCINT} can be stabilized by using an external power source to eliminate unrelated fluctuations [21]. Finally, fluctuations related to the actual AES execution can be amplified by removing capacitors from the board. The descriptions and results of the individual steps are discussed in the following sections.

A. Replacement of the Internal Measuring Resistor

As explained before, a measuring resistor is needed to generate an observable signal, where the exact resistance has to be chosen in a prudent manner. A higher value means higher voltage fluctuation, which is easier to measure [21]. However, the voltage drop across the resistor reduces the voltage that arrives at the cryptographic circuit. This in turn results in a lower power consumption of the cryptographic device, making it harder to measure. Therefore, a suitable trade-off has to be found for the resistance. Due to the very low resistance of the internal resistor, the resulting voltage drop is comparably low; consequently, it should be replaced. Based on experiments with other boards [19] [20], a **0.1Ω** and a **1Ω** resistor respectively is evaluated for best results. The plotted data is shown in Figure 3 and Figure 4. Even though the single AES rounds are still not visible using higher resistance, the V_{P2P} amplitude increased to roughly 1mV (0.1 Ω) or 1.5mV (1 Ω). Since the 1 Ω resistor yields better results it will be used in all subsequent experiments.

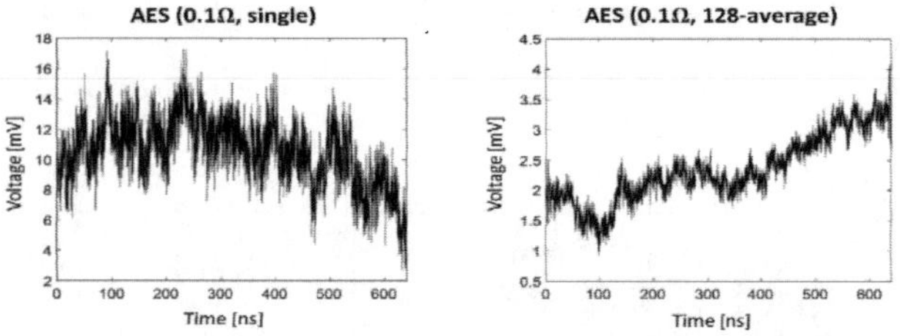

Figure 3. Measured voltage signal using a 0.1 Ω for a single AES run (left) and an average of 128 AES runs (right) respectively.

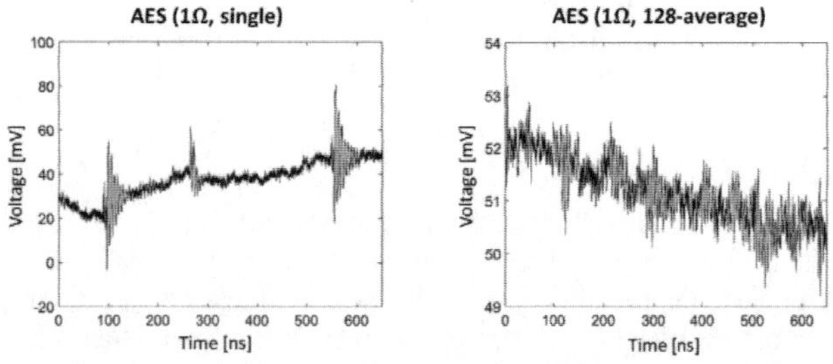

Figure 4. Measured voltage signal using a 1 Ω for a single AES run (left) and an average of 128 AES runs (right) respectively.

B. External Power Supply

Using an external power supply can further improve measurement quality by reducing noise on the voltage line, i.e., V_{CCINT} and V_{CCPINT} [22] – pp. 6. Therefore, an Agilent 66319D Power Supply Unit (PSU) is used to power the programmable logic instead of the internal power supply. This, however, interrupts the FPGA's power-on sequence; hence, it must be taken care of manually. For the programming logic, the required power-on sequence is $V_{CCINT} \rightarrow V_{CCBRAM} \rightarrow V_{CCAUX} \rightarrow V_{CCO}$, meaning the PSU has to be switched on before the FPGA board. The switch-off sequence consequently is in reverse order [26]. This change results in a voltage amplitude of up to 2.3mV, as can be seen in Figure 5 (right). Moreover, this time the single S-Box calculations are visible in the signal.

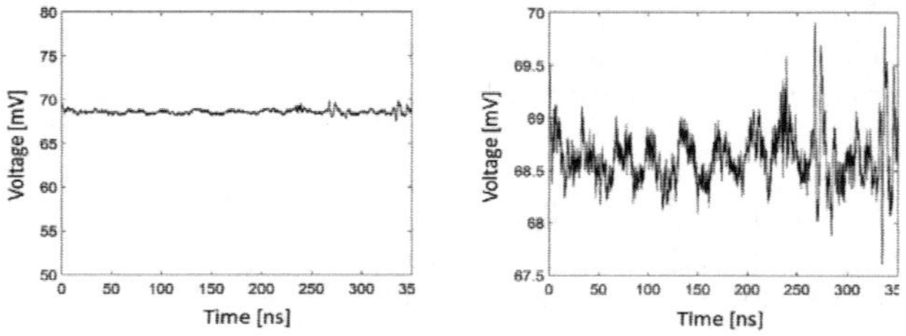

Figure 5. Average measured voltage signal using an external power supply for 128 AES runs (left) and detailed zoom of the signal (right).

C. Removing Capacitors

As can be seen in Figure 5 (left), the voltage signal is almost constant on a larger scale. This is due to multiple capacitors between V_{CCINT} and GND, which effectively prevent the power consumption from fluctuating – they smooth the signal. This causes a masking of the required power information and thus prevents power analysis attacks [23][28]. TABLE 1 provides an overview of all relevant capacitors named according to device schematic.

TABLE 1. CAPACITORS BETWEEN V_{CCINT} AND FPGA

Label	Capacity	Removed	Label	Capacity	Removed
C306	330µF		C237	4.7µF	✓
C167	100µF		C356	0.47µF	✓
C168	100µF		C357	0.47µF	✓
C169	100µF	✓	C358	0.47µF	✓
C139	47µF	✓	C359	0.47µF	✓
C233	4.7µF	✓	C360	0.47µF	✓
C234	4.7µF	✓	C361	0.47µF	✓
C235	4.7µF	✓	C362	0.47µF	✓
C236	4.7µF	✓			

To overcome this limitation, capacitors are removed if possible. Some are necessary to ensure correct operation of the FPGA. Again, the voltage is measured and plotted in Figure 6. Compared to Figure 5 the individual AES rounds are visible now. The V_{P2P} signal amplitude increases to 3mV.

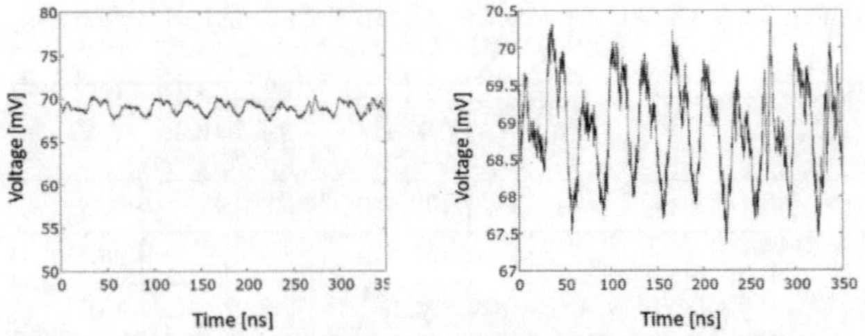

Figure 6. Average measured voltage signal using an external power supply for 128 AES runs (left) and detailed zoom of the signal (right).

D. *Reducing AES Clock Frequency*

High clock frequencies can cause the power consumption signals to overlap in successive clock cycles, resulting in noise in the measured data [12] - pp. 58. Quality of the measured traces can therefore be further improved by lowering the clock frequency of the cryptographic algorithm. Consequently, the clock frequency is reduced from 30MHz to 3.125MHz. In order to keep the scenario as realistic as possible [6][12] - pp. 58 and [1] - pp.296, the frequency is not lowered further. Average results for 128 measurement are shown in Figure 7 next to the result for a frequency of 30MHz as comparison. The signal amplitude is clearly increased, now ranging up to 4.3mV.

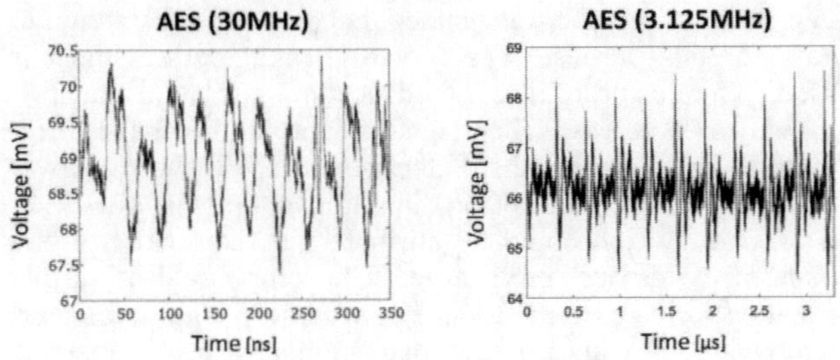

Figure 7. Average measured voltage using a frequency of 3.125 MHz for a 128AES runs (right). Results with f=30MHz for comparison (left).

This section concludes here with TABLE 2, showing results after each modification. The final value of 3.16mV shows that the quality of the captured signal is high and is comparable to the P2P value of 3mV reported in [6] using SAKURA-X Board.

TABLE 2. P2P VOLTAGE SUMMARY OF ALL MODIFICATION

Steps	P2P Voltage (mV)	P2P Moving Average[1] (mV)
R = 5mΩ, f = 30MHz	N/A	N/A
R = 100mΩ, f = 30MHz	1.01	0.66
R = 1Ω, f = 30MHz	1.57	0.95
R = 1Ω, f = 30MHz, External power supply	2.32	0.74
R = 1Ω, f = 30MHz, External power supply, Capacitors removed	3.14	1.90
R = 1Ω, f = 3.125MHz, External power supply, Capacitors removed	4.37	3.16

[1]n = 50.

V. EVALUATION OF SIDE CHANNEL INFORMATION

Until now, the paper presented several modifications and their effect on the quality of a captured signal. In this section, we will evaluate how much information is leaked by the cryptographic module after each modification.

For this, a general TVLA test is performed, which is conducted on two different sets of plaintext, i.e., random and fixed [17]. Encryption is performed on the random as well as on the fixed plaintext with the same key, and the measurement data is randomized for eliminating time dependent distortions. According to [17], if the test score is higher than 4.5 or lower than -4.5, the test is failed meaning the device is leaking enough information for a successful attack.

A. *External Power Supply and 1Ω Measuring Resistor*

Measurement data from the setup with 1Ω measuring resistor and external power supply is used to conduct a first general TVLA test. For fixed and for random input, n traces are collected. Two independent t-tests are performed; one by comparing the first half of traces from both data sets and another using the second half.

As shown in Figure 8, the maximum values of the first t-test after about 20,000 traces are briefly above the threshold of 4.5. However, because the values of the second t-test are below the limit, the test is passed. General TVLA is then applied to all measurements that is 60,000 random and 60,000 fixed inputs, which results in maximum t-value of 6.49.

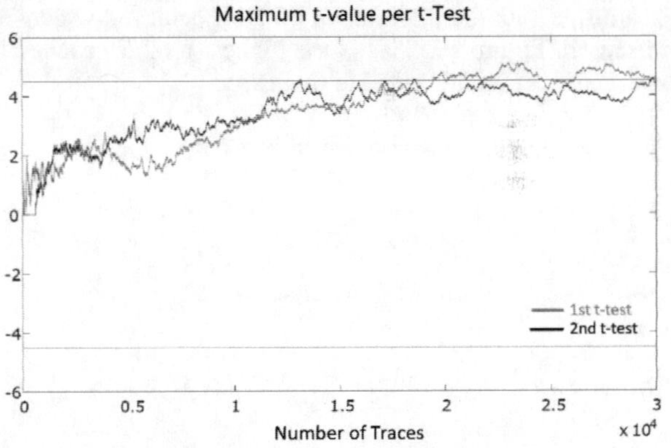

Figure 8. General TVLA test with external power supply

B. *Removing Capacitors*

Measurement data from the setup with external power supply, replaced internal resistor and removed capacitors is analyzed with TVLA as well. The test score crossed the value of 4.5 after 2,373 TVLA traces and stayed above that threshold afterwards, as can be seen in Figure 9. This corresponds to the calculation of t-tests for 9,492 measured traces (one TVLA trace is composed of four measured traces). When the test is applied to all 120,000 traces, a maximum test score of 28.45 results.

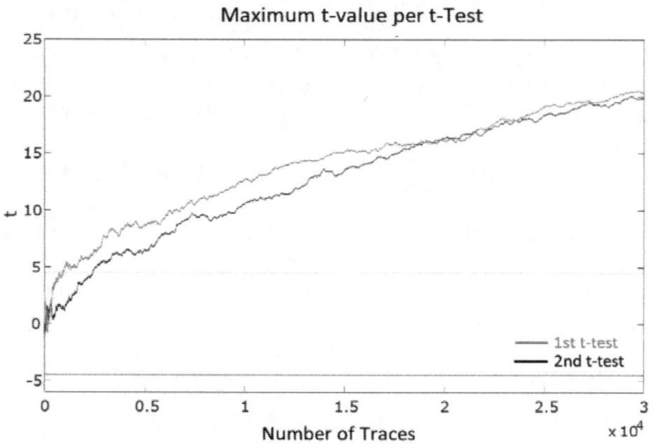

Figure 9. General TVLA test after removing the capacitors.

C. *Reduced Clock Frequency and Vertical Resolution*

Two more parameters, namely AES clock frequency and vertical resolution, are adjusted in order to get a better TVLA score. TVLA is applied on the measurement data while reducing clock frequency to 3.125MHz and setting the vertical limit to 5.9mV/div including all the previous modifications. This results in a maximum t-value of 14.23, which is lower than the 28.45 with a clock frequency of 30MHz and 5.9mV/div vertical resolution. However, when the vertical resolution is adjusted to 2.3mV/div using Zone Trigger [29][30], a maximum t-value of 60.58 is achieved which can be seen in Figure 10. This is the highest t-value reached by any modification presented in this paper.

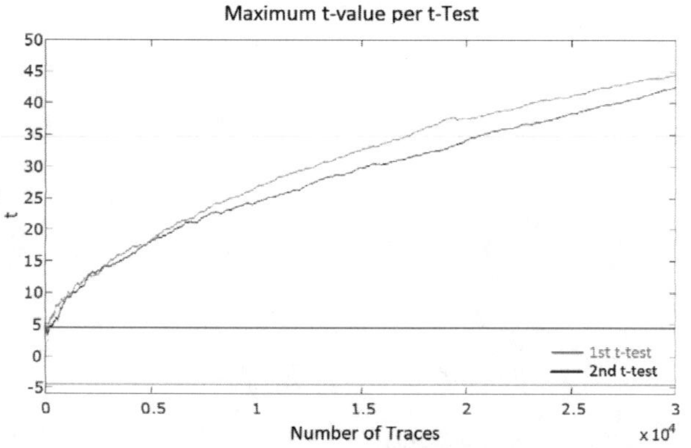

Figure 10. General TVLA test with external power supply, removed capacitors, 3.125MHz frequency.

The maximum t-values for all the modifications are summarized in TABLE 3. The t-value achieved with the final measurement setup is 60.58, which is comparably lower than 190 achieved on a SAKURA-G Board. However, the higher value could be attributed to the 65nm technology node of the Xilinx Virtex-5 used on the SASEBO-GII board [7][17].

TABLE 3. MAXIMUM T-VALUE SUMMARY FOR ALL MODIFICATIONS

Modification	**Resistor** (Ω)	**Frequency (MHz)**	**Vertical Resolution** (mV/div)	**Max. T-Value**
Ext. Power Supply	1	30	5.9	6.49
Ext. Power Supply and Cap. Removed	1	30	5.9	28.45
	1	3.125	5.9	14.23
Ext. Power Supply, Cap. Removed and Zone Trigger [29] for Vertical Resolution adjustment	1	3.125	2.3	60.58

VI. Conclusion

This work presents steps to implement a measurement setup that can capture leakage information. The target hardware, a commercial off-the-shelf board, is modified iteratively and the parameters of the setup are adjusted to acquire a higher quality signal for post processing. To compare the quality of the signal, the peak-to-peak amplitude is used. The resulting peak-to-peak voltage is 3.16mV, which is comparable to SAKURA-X Board's P2P value that is approx. 3mV. Once an acceptable quality of signal is achieved, measurement data is gathered, which is then put through a methodology to check whether the data contains useful information or not. For this purpose, Test Vector Leakage Assessment is used. The result of each modification and adjustment is shown for both cases, i.e., signal quality and leakage information. However, results of the general TVLA test show a relatively low t-value (60.58) in comparison to a SASEBO-GII board, which could be attributed to the smaller 28nm node of the device under target. The setup could be further tweaked to increase the t-value if necessary, though the current t-value already suggests that the platform is vulnerable to power analysis attacks.

Acknowledgement

This work was supported by the German Federal Ministry of Education and Research (BMBF) with funding number 16KIS0610.

References

[1] D. Mukhopadhyay and R. Subhra Chakraborty, "Hardware security: Design, threats, and safeguards," 1st edition, CRC Press Taylor & Francis Group, 2015.

[2] S. A. Huss and O. Stein, "A Novel Design Flow for a Security-Driven Synthesis of Side-Channel Hardened Cryptographic Modules," Journal of Low Power Electronics and Applications, vol. 7, issue 1, pp. 1-3, 2017.

[3] P. Sasdrich and T. Güneysu, "A grain in the silicon: SCA-protected AES in less than 30 slices," Application-specific Systems Architectures and Processors (ASAP) 2016 IEEE 27th International Conference on, pp. 25-32, 2016.

[4] M. Matsubayashi and A. Satoh, "Side-channel Attack user reference architecture board SAKURA-W for security evaluation of IC card," Consumer Electronics (GCCE) 2015 IEEE 4th Global Conference on, pp. 565-569, 2015.

[5] P. Sasdrich, A Moradi, O. Mischke, and T. Güneysu, "Achieving side-channel protection with dynamic logic reconfiguration on modern FPGAs," Hardware Oriented Security and Trust (HOST) 2015 IEEE International Symposium on, pp. 130-136, 2015.

[6] Y. Nomata, M. Matsubayashi, K. Sawada and A. Satoh, "Comparison of side-channel attack on cryptographic cirucits between old and new technology FPGAs," 2016 IEEE 5th Global Conference on Consumer Electronics, Kyoto, pp. 1-4, 2016.

[7] SAKURA Hardware Security Project. [Online]. Available: http://satoh.cs.uec.ac.jp/SAKURA/hardware.html [Accessed: 09, 2019].

[8] P. Kocher, "Timing attacks on implementations of Diffie-Hellmann, RSA, DSS, and other systems," CRYPTO 1996, LNCS 1109, pp.104-113, 1996.

[9] Y. Zhou and D. Feng, "Side-Channel Attacks: Ten Years After Its Publication and the Impacts on Cryptographic Module Security Testing," IACR Cryptology ePrint Archivet, 2005.

[10] R. Anderson, M. Bond, J. Clulow, and S. Skorobogatov, "Cryptographic Processors-A Survey," in Proceedings of the IEEE, vol. 94, no. 2, pp. 357-369, Feb. 2006.

[11] E. Brier, C. Clavier, and F. Olivier, "Correlation power analysis with a leakage model," Proc. of CHES'04, pp. 16-29, 2004.

[12] S. Mangard, E. Oswald, and T. Popp, "Power analysis attacks: Revealing the secrets of smart cards," Springer Science & Business Media, pp 29, 45, 56-58, 2007.

[13] P. Kocher, J. Jaffe, and B. Jun, "Differential Power Analysis," Proc. of CRYPTO'99, pp. 388-397, 1999.

[14] L. Mazur and M. Novotný, "Differential power analysis on FPGA board: Boundaries of success," 2017 6th Mediterranean Conference on Embedded Computing (MECO), Bar, pp.1-4, 2017.

[15] J. Daemen and V. Rijmen, "The Design of Rijndael: AES – The Advanced Encryption Standard," Springer Science & Business Media, 2002.

[16] A. Moradi, M. Kasper, and C Paar, "On the Portability of Side-Channel Attacks – An Analysis of the Xilinx Virtex 4, Virtex 5, and Spartan 6 Bitstream Encryption Mechanism," 2011.

[17] G. Goodwill, B. Jun, J. Jaffe, and P. Rohatgi, "A testing methodology for side-channel resistance," Non-Invasive Attack Testing Workshop (NIAT) 2011. [Online]. Available: https://csrc.nist.gov/CSRC/media/Events/Non-Invasive-Attack-Testing-Workshop/documents/08_Goodwill.pdf [Accessed: 09, 2019].

[18] G. Becker et al., "Test vector leakage assessment (TVLA) methodology in practice," International Cryptographic Module Conference, 2013. [Online]. Available: https://pdfs.semanticscholar.org/97b6/be2eaeebe1e13696e928e94f66b4c93719b8.pdf?_ga=2.4850867.1045323827.1568296811-418108430.1560420660 [Accessed: 09, 2019].

[19] A. Moradi, "Advances in side-channel security," Ruhr-Universität Bochum, Habilitation, 2014.

[20] N. E. Mrabet, G. Di Natale, and M. L. Flottes, "A practical Differential Power Analysis attack against the Miller algorithm," 2009 Ph.D. Research in Microelectronics and Electronics, Cork, pp. 308-311, 2009.

[21] R. Velegalati and P. Yalla, "Differential power analysis attack on FPGA implementation of AES," ECE 746 Statistical Signal Processing (2008).

[22] M. Aigner and E. Oswald, "Power analysis tutorial," 2000. [online]. Available: https://pdfs.semanticscholar.org/5ad9/fe2c8936052e9ac2a71833caa96a119218d1.pdf?_ga=2.7543858.1045323827.1568296811-418108430.1560420660 [Accessed: 09, 2019].

[23] A. Moradi, M. Kasper, and C. Paar, "Black-box side channel attacks highlight the importance of countermeasures," Topics in Cryptology CT-RSA 2012, pp. 7, 2012.

[24] I. Kuon, R. Tessier, and J. Rose, "FPGA architecture: Survey and challenges," Foundations and Trends in Electronic Design Automation, vol. 2, issue. 2, pp 162, 2008.

[25] Xilinx: ZC702 Evaluation Board for the Zynq-7000 XC7Z020 All Programmable SoC - User Guide - UG850 (v1.5). pp 58, 2015.

[26] Xilinx: Zynq-7000 All Programmable SoC (Z-7007S, Z-7012S, Z-7014S, Z-7010, Z-7015, and Z-7020): DC and AC Switching Characteristics. In: Xilinx, DS187 (v1.20), pp 2-8, 2017.

[27] M. Masoomi, M. Masoumi, and M. Ahmadian, "A practical differential power analysis attack against an FPGA implementation of AES cryptosystem," 2010 International Conference on Information Society, London, pp. 308-312, 2010.

[28] Song Sun, Zijun Yan and J. Zambreno, "Experiments in attacking FPGA-based embedded systems using differential power analysis," 2008 IEEE International Conference on Electro/Information Technology, Ames, IA, pp. 7-12, 2008.

[29] Keysight Oscilloscope Triggering. [Online]. https://www.rs-online.com/designspark/triggering [Accessed: 09, 2019]

[30] 5 Questions about Oscilloscope Zone Triggering. [Online]. https://www.electronicdesign.com/test-measurement/5-questions-about-oscilloscope-zone-triggering [Accessed: 09, 2019]

Multiple Image Fusion Encryption (MIFE) using Discrete Cosine Transformation (DCT) and Chaotic Generators

Lee Mariel Heucheun Yepdia, Alain Tiedeu
Dept. of Medical and Biomedical Engineering, Signal, Image and Systems Laboratory
Higher Teachers Technical Training College, ENSET EBOLOWA
Yaounde, Cameroon
Email: yepdiamariel26@gmail.com; alain.tiedeu@gmail.com

Zied Lachiri
Dept. of Electrical Engineering, Signal, Image and Technologies of Information Laboratory
National Engineering School, ENIT
Tunis, Tunisia
Email: ed.lachiri@enit.utm.tn

***Abstract*—This paper proposes a new multiple-image encryption algorithm based on spectral fusion of images and new chaotic generators. Logistic-May (LM), May-Gaussian (MG) and Gaussian-Gompertz (GG) were used as chaotic generators for their good properties in order to correct the flaws of 1D chaotic maps (Logistic, May, Gaussian, Gompertz) when used individually. Firstly, the Discrete Cosine Transformation (DCT) and the low-passed filter of appropriate size are used to combine the target images in the spectral domain in two different multiplex images. Secondly, each of the two images is concatenated into blocks of small size, which are mixed by changing their position following the order generated by a chaotic sequence from Logistic-May system (LM). Finally, the fusion of both scrambled images is achieved by a nonlinear mathematical expression based on Cramer's rule to obtain two hybrid encrypted images. The security analysis and experimental simulations confirmed that the proposed algorithm has a good encryption performance; it can encrypt a large number of images of different types while maintaining a reduced Mean Square Error (MSE) after decryption.**

Keywords*—*Spectral fusion; chaotic generators; image encryption.

I. Introduction

Several image encryption algorithms are being developed today to meet privacy needs in multimedia communications. With the rapid expansion of the Internet, innovative technologies and cryptanalysis, it has become necessary to build new and appropriate cryptosystems for secured data transfer, especially for digital images. Especially today, a large quantity of images is produced in various fields and exchanged through different channels, favouring the development of Multiple Images Encryption (MIE) instead of Single Image Encryption (SIE).

In literature, many encryption algorithms, such as International Data Encryption Algorithm (IDEA), Advanced Encryption Standard (AES) and Data Encryption Standard (DES) have been proposed [1]. However, these standard algorithms do not seem to be appropriate for image encryption, because of the intrinsic features of images, such as huge data capacity, high redundancy, strong correlation among adjacent pixels and low entropy [2]. Some basic properties of chaotic systems such as the sensitivity to the initial condition and control parameters, sensitivity to plain text, ergodicity and randomness behaviour, meet the requirements for a good cryptosystem. Consequently, several cryptosystems were developed by researchers, based on chaotic systems because the latter provided a good combination of speed, high security, complexity, reasonable computational overheads and computational power [3]. With these features, chaotic-based cryptosystems have excellent properties of confusion and diffusion, which are desirable in cryptography. Therefore, many techniques involving different chaotic systems have been published [2]-[12][23], and can be divided into one-dimensional (1D) chaotic maps and high-dimensional (HD) chaotic maps.

Among the chaotic encryption algorithms developed, the ones using a one-dimensional (1D) chaotic system like Logistic, Tent, and Sine map have proven to have the advantages of high-level efficiency, simplicity and high-speed encryption. 1D chaotic structures have been widely used [4] due to their simple structures, as opposed to the complex ones of higher dimensional chaotic system (which causes a relative slowness in computation). However, some schemes using the 1D map have been broken due to their weakness like non-uniform data output, small key space, periodic data output, and poor ergodicity properties for some ranges of control parameters [5][6]. To overcome this drawback, some researchers state that the 1D chaotic map should not be used alone [7][8]. Others proposed new 1D chaotic systems with better properties like Spatiotemporal chaos in [9], coupled with the 1D chaotic map [6], the

Nonlinear Chaotic map Algorithm (NCA) [10], and more recently, nonlinear combinations of two different 1D chaotic maps [3][11][12]. For example, Y. Abanda and A. Tiedeu [3] combined outputs of Duffing and Colpitts chaotic systems to encrypt grey and colour images. Y. P. Kamdeu and A. Tiedeu [11] proposed a fast and secured encryption scheme using new 1D chaotic systems obtained from Logistic, May, Gaussian and Gompertz maps. In [12], M. A. Chenaghlu et al. proposed a polynomial combination of 1D chaotic maps for image encryption using dynamic functions generation.

Recently, in order to increase the efficiency of cryptosystems for multiple images, some authors proposed algorithms integrating the concept of fusion or mixing images as a step in the encryption process. Image fusion has been proven to have potential for encryption in the spatial or frequency domain. In the last 8 years, much effort has been devoted to compressing and encrypting images at the same time [13], which is considered as a new way of decreasing the quantity of data to be transmitted and guarding the use of data against unauthorized access. In particular, the Discrete Cosine Transformation (DCT) is employed as a useful tool for spectral fusion in most of these methods. The widely used application DCT for image compression is mainly based on its energy compaction property, which means that the low-frequency coefficients are located around the top-left corner of its spectral plane. In 2018, M. Jridi and A. Alfalou [14] proposed an algorithm to enhance an existing optical Simultaneous Fusion, Compression and Encryption (SFCE) scheme [15] in terms of real-time requirements, bandwidth occupation and encryption robustness. In [16], S. Dongfeng et al. proposed a novel technique for simultaneous fusion, imaging and encryption of multiple objects using a single-pixel detector. This algorithm achieves good performance in terms of robustness as the number of images to multiplex increases, but suffered from reduced key space and good quality of images recovered. I. Mehra and N. K. Nishchal [17] proposed an image fusion encryption based on wavelets for securing multiple images through asymmetric keys. It offers a large key space, which enhances the security of the system. In 2016, Y. Qin et al. [18] proposed an Optical Multiple-Image Encryption scheme in diffractive imaging using spectral fusion and nonlinear operations.

More recently, X. Zhang and X. Wang [19][20] proposed two schemes of Multiple-Image Encryption (MIE): the first algorithm based on mixed image element and permutation, and the second MIE algorithm based on mixed image element and chaos. The cryptosystem shows good performances, but can be improved in terms of compression to reduce the size of the multiplex big image when the number of target images increases. In [21], G. L. Zhu and X. Q. Zhang proposed an encryption algorithm of mixed image element based on an elliptic curve cryptosystem. Experimental results and theoretical analysis show that the algorithm possesses a large key space and can accomplish a high level of security concerning information interaction on the network platform, but the encryption and decryption computational time is long. In 2013, A. M. Abdalla and A. A. Tamimi [22] proposed a new algorithm, which mixes two or more images of different types and sizes by using a shuffling procedure combined with S-box substitution to perform a lossless image encryption. Here, the process of mixing image combines stream cipher with block cipher, on the byte level.

After analysing most MIE algorithms operating in the spectral domain, the robustness of the cryptosystem increases with the number of input images. Consequently, the quality of decrypted images is degraded. Therefore, it is important to design cryptosystems which can keep a good compromise between a large number of images to encrypt, a small MSE after decryption and a good performance in terms of robustness and efficiency.

As a result, this paper suggests a new MIE algorithm based on the spectral fusion of different types of images of same size using Discrete Cosine Transformation (DCT) associated with a low-passed filter and chaotic maps. The proposed scheme has several strengths: it is robust, uses chaotic maps with good properties, encrypts a large number of images into two hybrid ciphered images, and the quality of the reconstructed images is good (reduced MSE). The encryption process comprises three main steps: in the first step, target images are fused into two images through DCT and low-passed filter. In the second step, the small blocks with the size of (4 X 4) images are permuted in a certain order. In the last step, which is the diffusion phase, the two scrambled images are fused by a nonlinear mathematical expression based on Cramer's rule to obtain two hybrid encrypted images. The key generation of the cryptosystem is made dependent on the plain images.

The rest of the paper is organized as follows: Section 2 presents an overview of chaotic generators used in the cryptosystem while in Section 3, spectral fusion of plain images is detailed. The proposed encryption/decryption scheme is given in Section 4. In Section 5, experimental results and algorithm analyses are presented, then compared with others in the literature. We end with a conclusion in Section 6.

II. BRIEF REVIEW ON 1D CHAOTIC SYSTEMS USED

A. 1D Logistic, May, Gaussian and Gompertz maps

The equations of 1D Logistic, May, Gaussian and Gompertz maps are described from (1) to (4), respectively.

1) 1D Logistic map

$$x_{n+1} = rx_n\left(1 - x_n\right) \qquad (1)$$

where $x_n \in [0,1]$ is the discrete state of the output chaotic sequence and r is the control parameter with values in the range [0, 4]. The chaotic behaviour of the Logistic map is observed in the range [3.5, 4].

2) May map

$$x_{n+1} = x_n \exp\left(a\left(1-x_n\right)\right) \quad (2)$$

where $x_n \in \left[0,10.9\right]$ and the control parameter a belongs to the range [0, 5].

3) Gaussian map

$$x_{n+1} = \exp\left(-\alpha x_n^2\right)+c \quad (3)$$

where $\alpha \in [4.7, 17]$, $c \in [-1, 1]$.

4) Gompertz map

$$x_{n+1} = -bx_n \ln x_n \quad (4)$$

where the control parameter $b \in [0, e\ ]$, e =2.71829… and is the exponential function.

B. Combination of new 1D chaotic maps

The chaotic properties of 1D Logistic, May, Gaussian and Gompertz maps are not suitable to build a secure cryptosystem when they are used alone. To solve this problem, Y. Zhou et al. [23] proposed to combine the different seed maps. Figure 1 shows the new map obtained from a nonlinear combination of two different 1D chaotic maps.

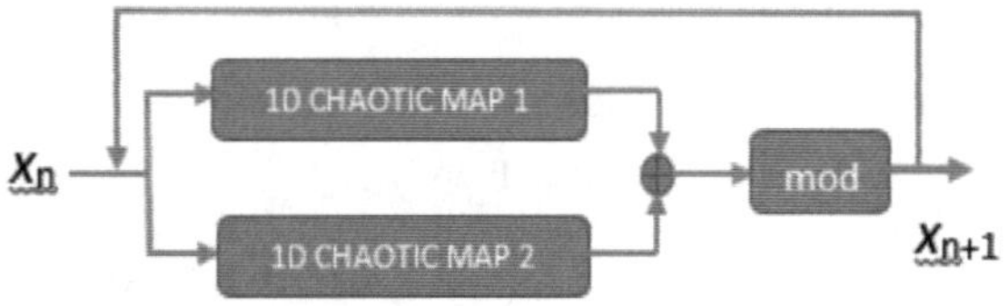

Figure 1. New chaotic scheme.

1) Logistic-May map (LM)

Its equation is defined by (5)

$$x_{n+1} = \begin{pmatrix} x_n \exp\left((r+9)(1-x_n)\right) - \\ (r+5)x_n(1-x_n) \end{pmatrix} \bmod 2 \quad (5)$$

where $x_n \in \left[0,1\right]$ and $r \in \left[0,5\right]$. From its bifurcation diagram, we can observe that chaotic properties are excellent within [0, 5], with a maximum Lyaponuv exponent equal to 8.3.

2) May-Gaussian (MG)

Equation (6) defines the May-Gaussian (MG) map

$$x_{n+1} = \begin{pmatrix} x_n \exp\left((r+10)(1-x_n)\right) + \\ \dfrac{(r+5)}{4} + \exp\left(-\alpha x_n^2\right) \end{pmatrix} \bmod 2 \quad (6)$$

where $x_n \in \left[0,1\right]$, $r \in \left[0,5\right]$, $\alpha \in \left[4.7,17\right]$. From its bifurcation diagram, the Lyaponuv exponents are positive and belong to the range [2.5, 5.6].

3) Gaussian-Gompertz

It is defined by (7)

$$x_{n+1} = \begin{pmatrix} \dfrac{(r/5+26)}{4} + \exp\left(-\alpha x_n^2\right) - \\ (r/5+26)x_n \log x_n \end{pmatrix} \bmod 2 \quad (7)$$

where $x_n \in \left[0,1\right]$, $r \in \left[0,5\right]$, $\alpha \in \left[4.7,17\right]$. It has a mean Lyaponuv exponent around 2.5

Figure 2 illustrates the bifurcation diagram and the Lyaponuv exponent graphics of these maps. Referring to Figure 2, all the previous 1D chaotic systems present a wider chaotic range and a more uniform distribution of their density functions. Furthermore, the maximum Lyaponuv exponent values obtained are respectively 8.1, 5.6 and 2.5. Then, these combined 1D systems are more suitable for secure and high-speed encryption if the encryption algorithm is built around a good algebraic structure.

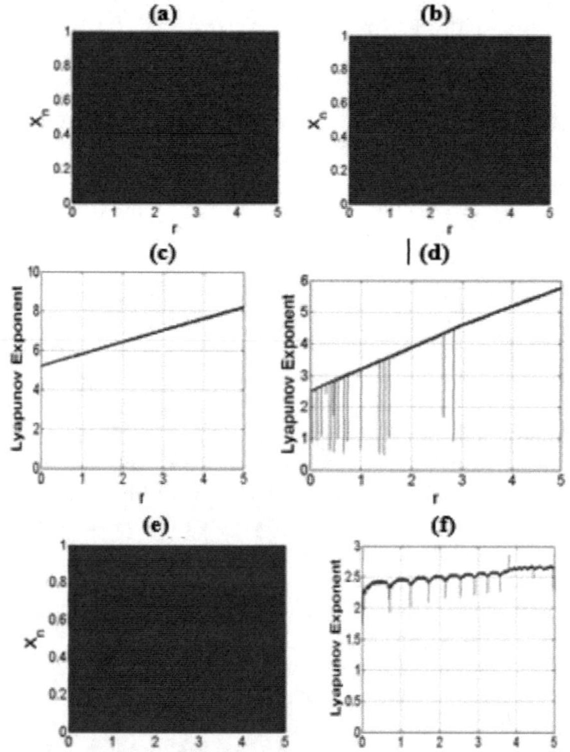

Figure 2. Bifurcation diagrams and Lyaponuv exponent graphics of combined chaotic maps, (a) and (c) Logistic-May, (b) and (d) May-Gaussian, (e) and (f) Gaussian-Gompertz.

III. SPECTRAL FUSION OF TARGET IMAGES

We consider N target images of size (M, M), which are combined with two images, each containing $\{N/2\}$ target images. As described in [24], Discrete Cosine Transformation (DCT) is first applied separately to each of the target images. Secondly, every spectrum is multiplied by a low-passed filter, of size (M', M') pixels, positioned in its upper left corner. In this way, a block containing the relevant information for reconstructing every target image is obtained. At this step, the compression rate C_r is:

C_r = 1 – *(size of multiplexed DCT spectral plane) /size of N inputs images*

$$C_r = 1 - (M^2 / N \times M^2) = 1 - (1 / N) \quad (8)$$

Then, after all of these target images are grouped together by a way of simple addition, the inverse Discrete Cosine Transform (IDCT) of the multiplex image is performed. To avoid information overlap, these blocks are shifted by a rotation before spectral multiplexing. Figure 3 illustrates the description of the process. It should be noted that the capability of multiplexing can be increased by appropriately selecting the filter size. The smaller the filter size is, the more images can be multiplexed, but the quality of recovered images may be worse. To keep a good quality of reconstructed images while maintaining a large number of target images to encrypt, we chose to group these images in two multiplex images of the same size.

IV. PROPOSED ENCRYPTION/DECRYPTION SCHEME

This section presents the proposed cryptosystem, which comprises blocks-permutation and diffusion steps using Chaotic generators. Figure 4 illustrates the entire process.

A. Blocks-Permutation

The plain image is each of the two multiplex images obtained in Section 3. The plain image is decomposed into small blocks of the same size; let us choose blocks size of (4×4) pixels. In fact, increasing the number of blocks by using smaller block size resulted in a lower correlation and higher entropy; then, the intelligible information contained in the image will be reduced.

The permutation of blocks is realised as follows:

1. Divide the plain image I of size $M \times M$ into k blocks size of (4×4), with $k = \frac{M}{4} \times \frac{M}{4}$
2. Use initial condition and control parameters x_{01}, r_{01} of Logistic-May system to generate a chaotic sequence by iterating k times (5). The values of the sequence X obtained are ranged in a row vector P of size $(1, k)$.
3. Repeat step 2 to generate a new sequence, using new initial condition and control parameters x_{02} and r_{02}. This second sequence is to permute the small blocks of the second multiplex image.
4. Sort the chaotic sequence p in ascending order, and get a new sequence $P' = \{P'_i\}_k = \{P'_{t1}, P'_{t2}, \dots, P'_{tk}\}$. Therefore, the sequence x_{01}, r_{01}, x_{02}, r_{02} is the permutation of the sequence 1, 2,…, k.
5. Number all the blocks of the plain image obtained in step 1, and adjust their positions with the previous permutation of step 3. Then, the image obtained is a block image permuted.

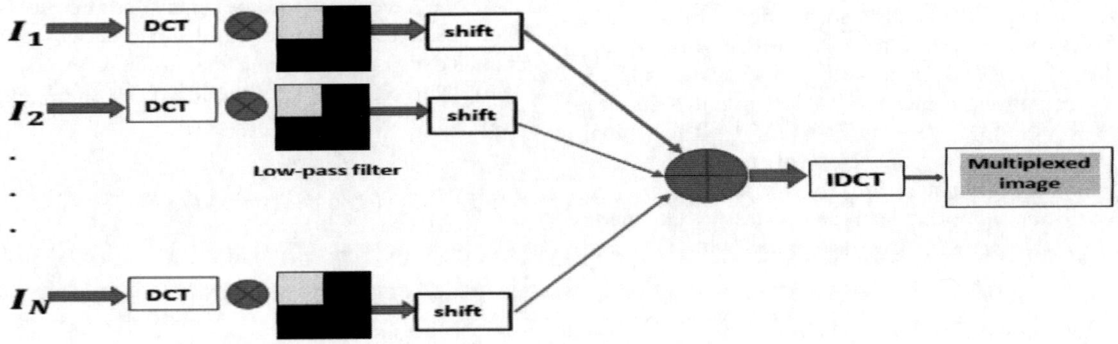

Figure 3. Spectral fusion of target images.

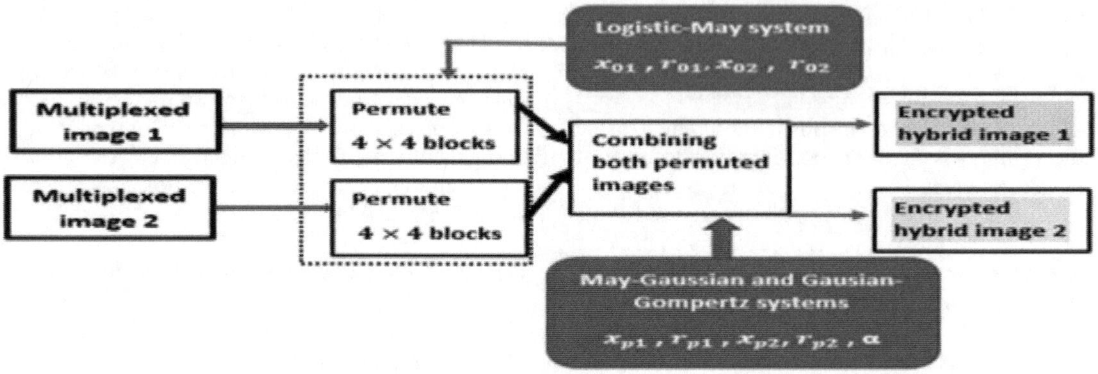

Figure 4. Encryption scheme.

The values x_{01}, r_{01}, x_{02}, r_{02} are calculated through (9) and (10). In this process, we subdivide each multiplex image I_i, ($i=1,2$) in two parts P_1 and P_2 of same size.

$$x_{0i} = (x_0 + mean\ (I_i)/255)_{\text{mod}1} \quad (9)$$

$$r_{0i}= r_0 + 0.1 \times max(S_1, S_2)/N\times M\times 2^9 \quad (10)$$

where, S_1 is the sum of pixels' intensities of the first part P_1 of the multiplex image I_i, and S_2 for P_2.
$x_0 \in [0, 0.9]$, $r \in [0, 4.9]$.

B. Diffusion of the scrambled images

1) Description of the fusion process

At this level, the two scrambled images are combined in order to create the final hybrid encrypted images that would be difficult to crack. The May-Gaussian and Gaussian-Gompertz systems (6) and (7) are used as pseudo random generators to generate two chaotic sequences after 2M*2M iterations. These values are arranged in two arrays W and T of sizes 2M*2M, respectively, where M represents the number of rows and columns of each scrambled image. W and T are converted into real values in unit 8 format; *(W=uint8(W × 255); T=uint8(T × 255))*. The initial conditions and control parameters of the two pseudo random numbers generators are x_{p1}, r_{p1} and x_{p2}, r_{p2}, α, respectively, for May-Gaussian and Gaussian-Gompertz systems. These parameters are determined with (11) and (12).

$$x_{pi} = (x_0 + 0.1 \times mean\ (I_i)/256) \quad (11)$$

$$rpi = r + 0.1\times\ [(min(I_i+1)/max(I_i+2)] \quad (12)$$

where *mean* (I_i) represents the average of the pixels' intensities values of multiplex image I_i, $(i=1,2)$; *max* (I_i) and *min* (I_i) are, respectively, maximum and minimum pixel's intensities values of I_i. $x_0 \in [0, 0.9]$, $r \in [0, 4.9]$.

The arrays W and T are divided into four sub-blocks of same size M × M.

$$W = \begin{pmatrix} w_{11} & w_{12} \\ w_{21} & w_{22} \end{pmatrix} \ ; \ T = \begin{pmatrix} t_{11} & t_{12} \\ t_{21} & t_{22} \end{pmatrix} \quad \textbf{(13)}$$

The two scrambled images $\boldsymbol{I_1}$ and $\boldsymbol{I_2}$ are linearly combined with the sub-blocks of W and T using the following equations:

$$C_1[i, j] = [(w_{11} \times I_1[i, j] + w_{12} \times I_2[i, j])_{\text{mod}256} \oplus floor(t_{11} \times t_{21}) \times 10^{15})] \quad (14)$$

$$C_2[i, j] = [(w_{21} \times I_1[i, j] + w_{22} \times I_2[i, j])_{\text{mod}256} \oplus floor(t_{12} \times t_{22}) \times 10^{15})] \quad (15)$$

where $C_1[i, j]$ and $C_2[i, j]$ are the two encrypted hybrid images of the cryptosystem, and ⊕ is the bit wise XOR operator. The mixed product $t_{ij} \times t_{ji}$ in the above relations enhances the quality of the merged images.

2) Decryption process

At the receiver end, the encrypted images are first decomposed using Cramer's rule in order to recover the scrambled images. Knowing the fusion keys (x_{p1}, r_{p1}, x_{p2}, r_{p2}, α), the receiver can get the images $\boldsymbol{I_1}$ and $\boldsymbol{I_2}$ by solving the system of equations below:

$$\begin{cases} \left(I_1[i,j] \times w_{11} + I_2[i,j] \times w_{12}\right)_{mod\,256} \\ = C_1\left(floor\left(t_{11} \times t_{21}\right) \times 10^{15}\right) \\ \left(I_1[i,j] \times w_{21} + I_2[i,j] \times w_{22}\right)_{mod\,256} \\ = C_2\left(floor\left(t_{12} \times t_{22}\right) \times 10^{15}\right) \end{cases} \quad (16)$$

Then, the two multiplex images can be obtained easily by decrypting $\boldsymbol{I_1}$ and $\boldsymbol{I_2}$ through reverse permutation operations.

V. EXPERIMENTAL RESULTS AND ALGORITHM ANALYSIS

Numerical simulation experiments have been carried out to verify the proposed encryption method using MATLAB 2016 b platform on a PC with Core (TM) i7-353U processor of 2.5GHz. We first take 8 images with 512×512 pixels and 256 grey levels as the target images to be encrypted, which are combined in two multiplex images as shown in Figure 6 (*a-h*), respectively. The compression ratio C_r is 0.75 for each multiplex image. The size of low-passed filter is (M', M') = (256,256) pixels. Results are analysed more in terms of statistical attack, differential attack, quality of decrypted images and speed. We chose the different values as keys of the proposed cryptosystem:
x_{01} = 0.351482953177765; x_{02} = 0.972970074275508; r_{01} =4.988242173292221; r_{02} = 4.909240772131021; xp_1 = 0.363606938668312; x_{p2} = 0.890363879273465; r_{p1} = 4.841585120587438; r_{p2} = 4.738149127386060; $\alpha = 6.187$.

The size of the filter *(M', M')* and the number of target images N constitute additional parameters of the key.

A. Statistical analysis

1) Histogram

The histogram of a noise-like-image must be uniform. As one can see in Figure 5, the histogram of the multiplex encrypted images is uniform.

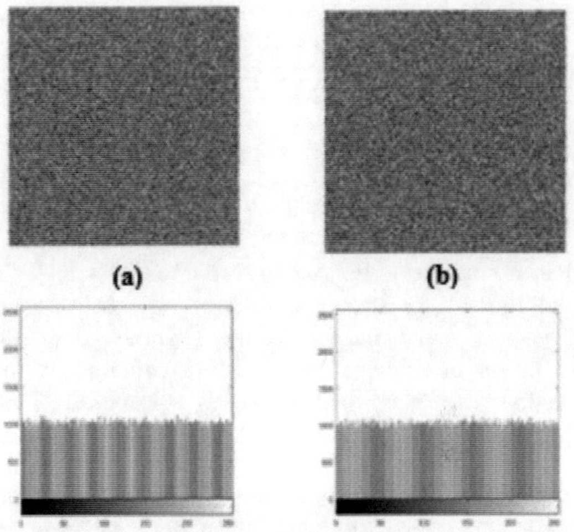

Figure 5. Encrypted images and their histograms. (a) multiplexed image 1, (b) multiplexed image 2.

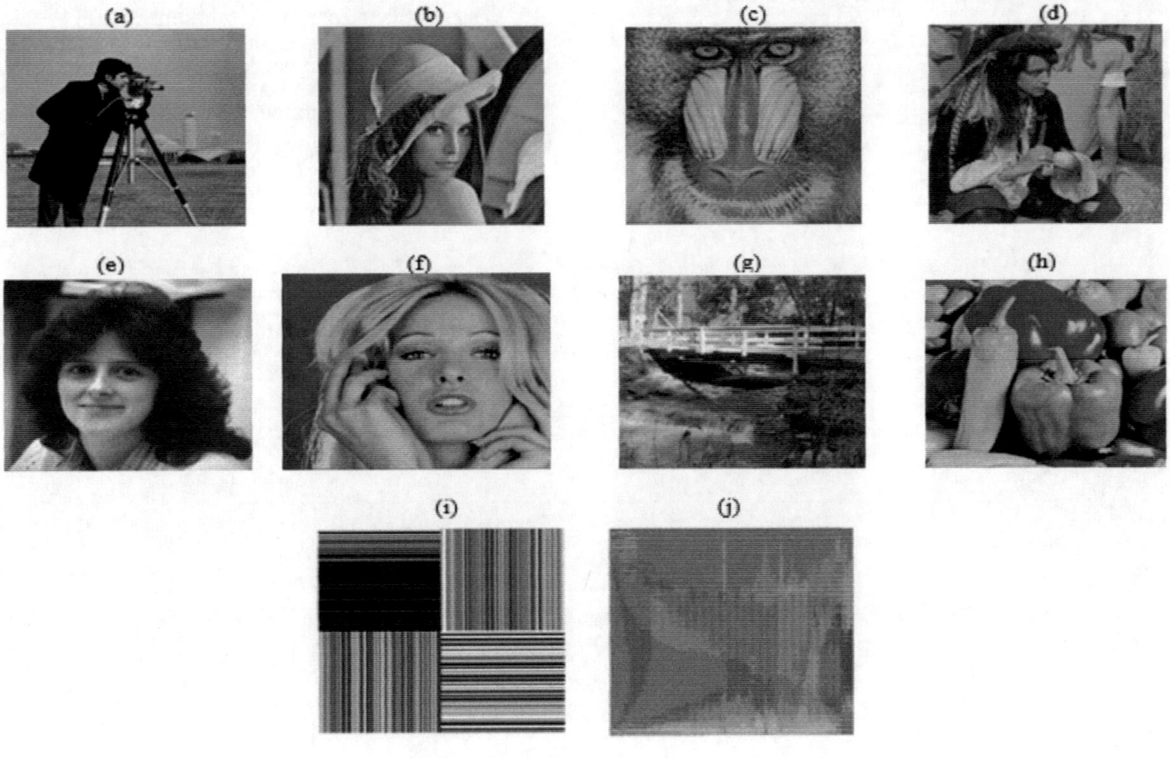

Figure 6. Plain and combined images. (a-d) images combined in multiplex image 1, (e-h) images combined in multiplex image 2 (i) Multiplex image 1 before IDCT. 2 (j) Multiplex image 1 after IDCT.

2) Correlation analysis

In the encrypted image, there must be a very poor correlation between neighbouring pixels in every direction, for this one to resist statistical attack. The common method is to calculate the correlation coefficient *Cr* of randomly chosen 5000 pairs of pixels in horizontal (HC), vertical (VC) and diagonal (DC) direction using (17).

$$Cr = \frac{K \times \sum_{i=1}^{K} X_i Y_i - \sum_{i=1}^{K} X_i^2 \times \sum_{i=1}^{K} Y_i^2}{\sqrt{\left(K \times \sum_{i=1}^{K} (X_i)^2 - \left(\sum_{i=1}^{K} X_i\right)^2\right) \times \left(N \times \sum_{i=1}^{K} (Y_i)^2 - \left(\sum_{i=1}^{K} Y_i\right)^2\right)}} \quad (17)$$

where *X* and *Y* are grey scale values of two adjacent pixels in the image, K is the number of pair of pixels. C_r is the value of correlation belonging to the range [-1, 1]. *Cr* tends to be 1 or -1 for strong correlation and tends to be 0 for every poor correlation. Table 1 shows the calculated correlation coefficient of 512×512 cameraman in every direction. A mean value of the proposed encryption algorithm is about 0.0035, which tends to be zero.

Figure 7 shows how grey values of cameraman correlated with the horizontal, vertical and diagonal direction. Statistical attack through correlation analysis between adjacent pixels cannot help to break the proposed encryption algorithm.

TABLE I. CORRELATION COEFFICIENT

Image	*Size*	*Test*	*Plain image*	*Encrypted image*
Cameraman	(512 × 512)	HC	0.9314	0.0023
		VC	0.9400	0.051
		DC	0.8931	-0.003

3) Information entropy analysis

The information entropy gives an account of the quantum of randomness present in a message (*m*) as follows:

$$H(m) = \sum_{i=0}^{2^k-1} p(m_i) \log_2 \left(\frac{1}{p(m_i)}\right) \quad (18)$$

where *p(m$_i$)* represents the probability of symbol m_i, *K* is the number of bits of the message and 2^K all possible values. For a 256-grayscale image, the pixel data has 2^8 possible values and the ideal entropy of a true random image must be 8. Table 2 shows entropy values of some images of the proposed encryption algorithm very close to 8, as expected.

TABLE II. INFORMATION ENTROPY OF SOME PLAIN IMAGES AND THEIR CIPHER IMAGE.

Gray image	Proposed algorithm	[20] (2017)	[19] (2017)
Cameraman (512 × 512)	7.9993	-	-
Lena (512 × 512)	7.9993	7.9993	7.9992
Peppers (512 × 512)	7.9994	7.9992	-

B. *Key analysis*

Key space size is the total number of different keys that can be used in an encryption algorithm. A good encryption algorithm needs to contain sufficiently large key space to make the brute-force attack infeasible. The high sensitive to initial conditions inherent to any chaotic system, i.e., exponential divergence of chaotic trajectories, ensure high security.

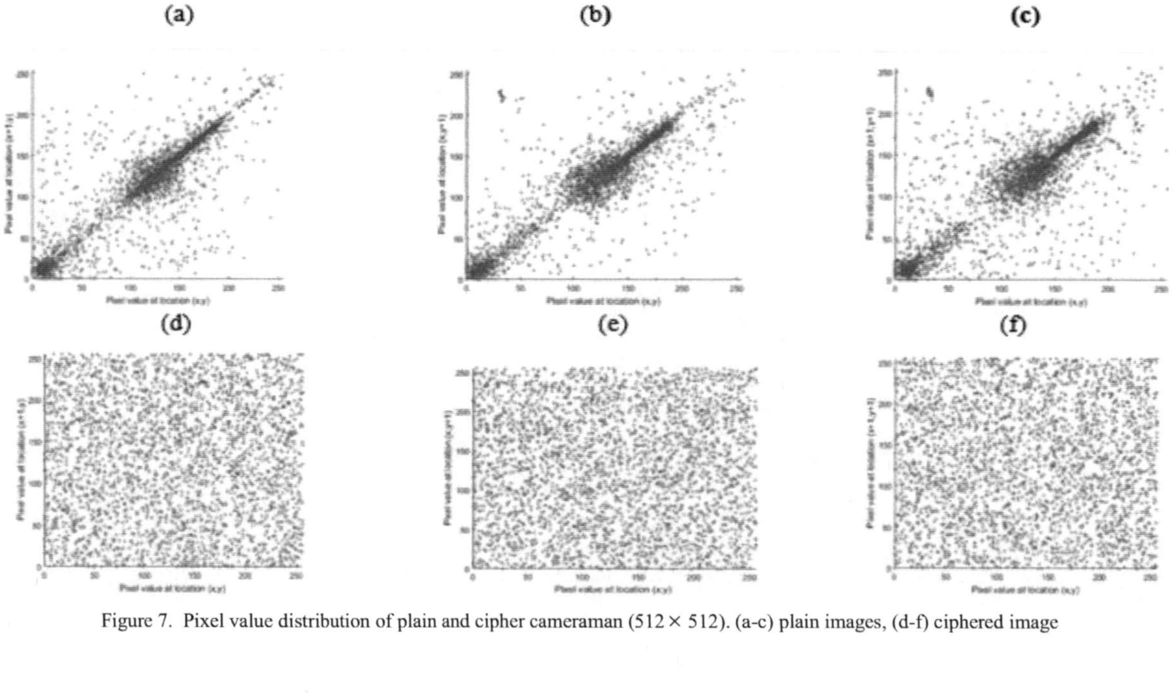

Figure 7. Pixel value distribution of plain and cipher cameraman (512 × 512). (a-c) plain images, (d-f) ciphered image

According to [19], a key size of 10^{30} is sufficient. The proposed encryption algorithm actually does have some of the following secret keys: the initial values x_{01}, x_{02}, x_{p1}, x_{p2} and control parameters r_{01}, r_{02}, r_{p1}, r_{p2} and α of the chaotic systems used; the number N of target images and the size $M' \times M'$ of the filter. We suppose that the computer precision is 10^{-15}, so the key space is greater than $10^{15 \times 9} = 10^{135}$. Therefore, this key space is large enough to resist the brute-force attack. Moreover, key sensitivity analysis has been carried out, but the results are not presented here for reasons of space. These results confirm that by changing only one bit in any parameter of the key, it is not possible to recover the plain images.

C. *Sensitivity analysis*

1) *Differential attack analysis*

An excellent encryption algorithm should have the desirable property of spreading the influence of slight change to the plain text over as much of the cipher text as possible. The sensitivity of a cryptosystem is evaluated through Number of Pixel Change Rate (NPCR) (19) and Unified Average Change Intensity (UACI) (20) criteria, which consist in testing the influence of one-pixel change of a plain image in the resulting cipher image.

$$NPCR = \frac{\sum_{i,j} D(i,j)}{W \times H} \times 100\% \tag{19}$$

$$UACI = \frac{1}{W \times H}\left[\sum_{i,j} \frac{\left|C_1(i,j) - C_2(i,j)\right|}{255}\right] \times 100\% \tag{20}$$

where C_1 and C_2 are two images with same size $W \times H$. If $C_1(i, j) \# C_2(i, j)$ then $D(i,j) = 1$, otherwise, $D(i,j) = 0$. Table 3 gives the measurement of NCPR and UACI between two cipher images of cameraman, Lena and peppers, when a Least Significant Bit (LSB) changed on grey value in the last pixel's position. We can notice that the values obtained are around the mean of 99.61 for NCPR and 33.49 for UACI. This result shows that a slight change to the original images will result in a great change in all the encrypted images. The results also imply that the proposed algorithm has an excellent ability to resist the differential attack.

TABLE III. NCPR AND UACI MEASURE AFTER A LSB CHANGE.

Image	Test	
Cameraman	NCPR	99.62
(512×512)	UACI	33.54
Lena	NCPR	99.62
(512×512)	UACI	33.46
Peppers	NCPR	99.63
(512×512)	UACI	33.47

2) *Quality of reconstructed images*

As the number of target images to encrypt increases, the quality of recovered images decreases. In order to reduce the NMSE between plain and decrypted images and enlarge the number of target images, we grouped them into two multiplexed images before encryption. To evaluate quantitatively the quality of decrypted image, we used the normalized mean square error (NMSE) between the original image and the decrypted image. The *NMSE* is defined as:

$$NMSE = \frac{\sum_{i=1}^{N}\sum_{j=1}^{M}\left[I_D(i,j) - I_E(i,j)\right]^2}{\sum_{i=1}^{N}\sum_{j=1}^{M}\left[I_E(i,j)\right]^2} \tag{21}$$

where M×N are the size of the image, $I_D(i, j)$ and $I_E(i, j)$ are the values of the decrypted image and the original image at the pixel *(i, j)*, respectively. Table 4 presents the values of NMSE of a 512×512 Lena image for different total number of target images. From this table, we can observe that for *N=16* target images combined in one multiplex image, i.e., 32 images to encrypt by the proposed cryptosystem, the NMSE is still reduced, which attests the good quality of reconstructed images and good performances of the proposed cryptosystem.

TABLE IV. NMSE OF 512×512 LENA IMAGE

Number of target image (*N*×2)	4×2	9×2	16×2
NMSE	0.00082	0.0019	0.00376

D. *Encryption/decryption time*

Table 5 reports a comparison of encryption time by the proposed algorithm with some recent works in literature for different images. The algorithm written under Matlab platform was not optimized. The computer time consumption is 0.27389 s, which is smaller than those of [19][24].

TABLE V. ENCRYPTION TIME IN SECONDS.

Number of Images	Proposed algorithm	[19] (2017)	[20] (2017)	[24] 2016
08 or 09 Size 512×512	0.27389	0.7103	0.191	11.66

VI. CONCLUSION

In this paper, an image encryption algorithm based on spectral fusion of multiple images and new chaotic generators is proposed. Logistic-May (LM), Gaussian-Gompertz (GG) and May-Gaussian (MG) systems were used as chaotic generators in the processes of confusion and diffusion. The target images were firstly combined in two multiplex images of same size through DCT and a Low-passed filter. Secondly, the previous images are scrambled by permuting the blocks size of (4×4) of each multiplex image. Finally, the later scrambled images are fused by a nonlinear mathematical expression based on Cramer's rule to obtain two hybrid encrypted images. The evaluation metrics of the proposed cryptosystem NCPR, UACI, correlation coefficient, entropy, key space and NMSE are amongst the best values in literature. More interestingly, the proposed cryptosystem can encrypt 32 target images simultaneously with a small NMSE $\approx 3.7 \times 10^{-3}$, and encrypted images are sensitive to the key. The proposed encryption algorithm can surely guarantee security and speed of all types of digital data transfer in a digital network.

ACKNOWLEDGMENTS

This work was partly supported by ERMIT, Entrepreneurship, Resources, Management, Innovation and Technologies.

REFERENCES

[1] X. Liao, S. Lai, and Q. Zhou, ''A novel image encryption algorithm based on self-adaptive wave transmission,'' J. Signal Process., vol 90, pp. 2714–2722, 2010.

[2] C. Zhu, ''A novel image encryption scheme based on improved hyperchaotic sequences,'' J. Opt. Commun., vol 285, pp. 29–37, 2012.

[3] Y. Abanda and A. Tiedeu, ''Image encryption by chaos mixing,'' IET Image Process., vol 10, pp. 742–750, 2016.

[4] X. Wang, L. Liu, and Y. Zhang, ''A Novel Chaotic block image encryption algorithm based on dynamic random growth technique,'' Optics and Lasers in Engineering, vol. 66, pp. 10-18, 2015.

[5] R. Rhouma and S. Belghith, ''Cryptanalysis of a spatiotemporal chaotic image/video cryptosystem,''J. Phys. Lett. vol. A 372, pp. 5790–5794, 2008.

[6] Y. Wang, X. Liao, T. Xiang, K. W. Wong, and D. Yang, ''Cryptanalysis and improvement on a block cryptosystem based on iteration a chaotic map,'' Physique Letters, vol. A 363, pp. 277-281, 2007.

[7] V. Patidar, N. Pareek, and K. K Sud, ''A new substitution-diffusion based image cipher using chaotic standard and logistic maps,'' Commun. Nonlinear Sci. Numer. simul., vol. 14, No. 7, pp. 3056-3075, 2009.

[8] Z. L. Zhu, W. Zhang, K. W. Wong, and H. Yu, ''A chaos-based symmetric image encryption scheme using a bit-level permutation,'' Info. Sci., vol. 181, pp. 1171-1186, 2011.

[9] C. Y. Song, Y. L. Qia, X. Z. Zhang, ''An image encryption scheme based on new spatiotemporal chaos'', Optik., vol. 124, pp. 3329-3334, 2013.

[10] H. Gao, Y. Zhang, S. Liang, D. Li, ''A new chaotic algorithm for image encryption'', Chaos Solitons Fractals, vol. 29, pp. 393-399, 2005.

[11] Y. P. Kamdeu and A. Tiedeu, ''An image encryption algorithm based on substitution technique and chaos mixing,'' Multimedia Tools and Applications, vol. 77, No. 19, 2018.

[12] M. A. Chenaghlu, M. A. Balafar, and M. R. Feizi-Derakhshi, ''A novel image encryption algorithm based on polynomial combination of chaotic maps and dynamic function generation,'' Signal Processing, 2018.

[13] A. Alfalou, C. Brosseau, and N. Abdallah, "Simultaneous compression and encryption of color video images," Opt. Commun., vol. 338, pp. 371–379, 2015.

[14] M. Jridi, A. Alfalou, '' Real-time and encryption efficiency improvements of simultaneous fusion, compression and encryption method based on chaotic generators,'' Optics and Lasers in Engineering, vol. 102, pp. 59-69, 2018.

[15] A. Alfalou, C. Brosseau, N. Abdallah, and M. Jridi, ''Simultaneous fusion, compression and encryption of multiple images'', OSA Opt. Express, 19 November, vol. 24, pp. 24023-9, 2011.

[16] S. Dongfeng, H. Jian, W. Yingjian, and Y. Kee, ''Simultaneous fusion, imaging and encryption of multiple objects using a single-pixel detector,'' Scientific Reports, pp. 18-29, 2017.

[17] I. Mehra and N. K. Nishchal, ''Wavelet-based image fusion for securing multiple images through asymmetric keys,'' Optics Communications, vol. 335, pp. 153-160, 2015.

[18] Y. Qin, Q. Gong, Z. Wang, and H. Wang, ''Optical multiple-image encryption in diffractive-imaging-based scheme using spectral fusion and nonlinear operation,'' Optics Express, Vol. 24, pp. 26877-26886, 2016.

[19] X. Zhang and X. Wang '' Multiple-image encryption algorithm based on mixed image element and permutation,'' Optics and Lasers in Engineering, vol. 92, pp. 6–16, 2017.

[20] X. Zhang and X. Wang, '' Multiple-image encryption algorithm based on mixed image element and chaos,'' Computers and Electrical Engineering, vol. 000, pp. 1-13, 2017.

[21] G. L. Zhu and X. Q. Zhang, '' Mixed image element encryption based on an elliptic curve cryptosystem,'' Journal of Electronic Imaging, vol. 17, No. 2, 023007, Apr-Jun, 2008.

[22] A. M. Abdalla and A. A. Tamimi, ''Algorithm for image mixing and encryption,'' The International Journal of Multimedia & Its Applications (IJMA) Vol. 5, No.2, April, 2013.

[23] Y. Zhou, L. Bao, and C. L. P. Chen, ''A new 1D chaotic system for image encryption,'' Signal Process., vol. 97, pp. 172-182, 2014.

[24] G. Ren, J. Han, H. Zhu, J. Fu, and M. Shan, '' High Security Multiple-image Encryption using Discrete Cosine Transform and Discrete Multiple-Parameters Fractional Fourier Transform,'' Journal of Communications, Vol. 11, No. 5, May 2016.

A Taxonomy of Metrics for Cryptographic Systems

Kimmo Halunen*, Mikko Kiviharju†, Jani Suomalainen*,
Visa Vallivaara*, Markku Kylänpää* and Outi-Marja Latvala*
*VTT Technical Research Centre of Finland Ltd
Espoo, Finland
email: firstname.lastname@vtt.fi
†Finnish Defence Research Agency
mikko.kiviharju@mil.fi

***Abstract*—Measuring the security of cryptographic systems (algorithms, protocols, software and hardware implementations etc.) is a difficult task. There does not exist one simple and easy to measure value that could be used to evaluate the relative strength of different cryptographic systems. On the other hand, there are more and more use cases where protections granted by cryptographic systems are needed. In some cases, there are certification and classification requirements for the use of cryptosystems that would benefit from good measures. Also new standards are being created for cryptography, usually based on competitions, where the proposals are evaluated based on some criteria. In this paper, we describe a taxonomy of the multiple metrics that can be associated with cryptographic systems and evaluate them based on a number of different attributes. We also reflect our taxonomy to the decisions made in several cryptographic standardisation competitions.**

Keywords–Cryptography; Security metrics; Taxonomy; Competitions; Cryptographic systems

I. Introduction

Cryptography is a key element in establishing trust in our digital society. Having reliable and correctly functioning cryptographic systems is necessary to realise many of the services that we all use in our everyday lives. Cryptography has thus become a crucial part of our critical infrastructures.

Cryptographic systems are built from different types of building blocks and designed to provide many different security goals depending on their anticipated usage. The security of the system depends on the theoretical algorithms and assumptions on their security proofs, the programming languages used to realise them, the platforms and operating systems that these programs utilise, and the hardware that runs all these. Thus, it is very difficult to give commensurate, yet simple measurements on the security of cryptographic systems.

Having such a simple metric would have great implications for developers and decision makers. A simple metric would benefit both standardisation and certification efforts that involve cryptographic systems and implementations. If an absolute metric could be devised, comparing different options would become a small exercise in comparing the values that these metrics give for different choices of cryptosystems. Alas, such a metric is not yet available and it might be nearly impossible to provide one.

However, there are many measures that are used to evaluate cryptographic protocols. The most notable one is the *key length* of a given algorithm. There are many reports, which give recommendations for key lengths for different algorithms in different contexts (e.g., [1]–[3]). These are mainly to be seen as lower limits for the key lengths of different cryptosystems and as such they offer only limited information on the security of a cryptosystem implementation. Existing efforts towards more comprehensive understanding of the traits of the cryptosystems by classifying cryptosystems from the metric perspective include metrics for algorithm security [4], and metrics from the attackers' point of view [5]. But a comprehensive metric, with commensurate components, is still not available.

In this paper, we survey the many different metrics for measuring the security of cryptographic systems and categorise them into four different categories. In Section II, we define some concepts used throughout this paper. In Section III, we discuss the properties of each measure and present an overview of our findings. For some measures, it is possible to have an ordering and for others it is not. We also study some competitions on cryptographic standards and how they have used different metrics in the decision making process in Section IV. Furthermore, in Section V, we discuss the possibilities, gaps and the necessity of having good metrics for cryptographic systems. Finally, in Section VI, we discuss the future work needed to realise better metrics for cryptographic systems and give conclusions of our research.

II. Attributes of Cryptographic Metrics

In this paper, we use the term *cryptosystem* to mean any algorithm or implementation that aims to provide cryptographic security for some defined target. Here, the cryptosystem can be a primitive, such as a hash function, or a fully-fledged file encryption software or a protocol for network security, e.g., Transport Layer Security (TLS) or something in between.

A metric is a way to measure some part or the totality of the security of a cryptosystem. A metric can have numerical values or it can be a qualitative description.

We also define some attributes that each metric can have. A metric is *measurable* if there is a standard convention on how the metric is measured and this is uniform across all applications of the metric (e.g., kilograms for weight). A metric is *semi-measurable* if there are several different conventions on how to measure the metric and some of these are not readily comparable with each other. In some cases the metric is *non-measurable*, which means that a standard for measurement does not exist or that the different values that the metric can have are not comparable in meaningful ways.

Another attribute is *practical relevance*. This measures how much the metric has practical relevance in evaluating the security of the cryptosystem. Some metrics are relevant in the theoretical frameworks and some metrics are more relevant in the practical world, where the cryptosystems are applied. An example of a very practical metric is the amount of memory required to attack a cryptosystem. A more theoretical metric is the proof framework, where a system is proven secure. In the theoretical world there is a big distinction, whether a proof is for example in the random oracle model or in the standard model, but the differences between these two do not manifest themselves as practical attacks in implementations.

We also make a distinction between *quantitative* and *qualitative* metrics. Quantitative metrics give a numerical or several numerical values to the cryptosystem and qualitative metrics give a description of the state of the cryptosystem.

III. Categories of Cryptographic Measures

This section presents our taxonomy of metrics for cryptographic systems. An overview of the taxonomy is presented in Table I.

A. *Adversarial Model Metrics*

Cryptology and especially cryptographic theory aims to formalize, how cryptographic algorithms work and withstand cryptanalysis. Due to the need for rigorous formalisms in cryptographic theory, the models used need to be very detailed, and yet general with respect to adversarial behaviour. We use the term *algorithmic metrics* to refer to metrics that involve cryptosystems independently of their realization in code or hardware. Algorithmic metrics are here divided to adversarial model metrics (Section III-A) and proof framework metrics (Section III-B).

As an example, consider the combination of the metrics in the following common concept: INDistinguishability under Chosen Ciphertext Attack or IND-CCA [6]. We observe here the following independent metrics:

- *Adversarial goal*: distinguish between random strings and actual ciphertext.
- *Adversarially available information*: a polynomial amount of information, before and after the cryptographic transformation.
- *Adversarial degrees of freedom of actions* include choosing the ciphertext-plaintext pairs adaptively (excluding the keys).

In addition to the three metrics above, we consider *adversarial resources*, which the designer of the cryptosystem expects the attackers to be able to wield. The four above metrics together are related to the *adversarial model.*

The adversarial resources consist of *computing power* and available *memory*. They are mostly well-defined and accessible metrics, with practical relevance.

Computing power is addressed here in both of its forms: exact attack complexities, and approximate or asymptotic complexities. Cryptographic theory rarely elaborates the adversarial models down to the detail of exact number of operations required to break the system. Instead, asymptotic estimates are given, and often even they are described only on the level of computational complexity classes.

In the case of exact complexities, values can be given, e.g., as the amount of floating point operations per second (FLOPS). In quantum computing, the unit can be based on, e.g., the amount of universal qubits and gates in the quantum computer. This metric is measurable and quantitative.

In the latter case, where the complexity class border is crossed, literature usually refers to different "computational models", the most common being Bounded-error Probabilistic Polynomial time (BPP), where polynomially bound, probabilistic Turing machines are expected. Other notable models include Bounded-error Quantum Polynomial-time (BQP) for quantum computers; and statistical, or unconditional security model, where the adversary is given limitless computational power. This metric is semi-measurable (as the exact relations between complexity classes are not known) and qualitative.

As the exact running time estimates can only be fixed once a cryptosystem is fully instantiated and parametrized, we consider this measure to consist of two subclasses of the whole: instantiated and non-instantiated computing power (asymptotic notations can be computed to exact metrics once the parameters, such as key size, are fixed).

Memory is the amount of memory that the attack requires. Analogously to the computing power, we divide this into two subclasses: instantiated (measurable and quantitative) and non-instantiated (semi-measurable and qualitative). Memory can also have some effect on the computing power needed for the attack. Some example memory complexity classes could be LOGSPACE and PSPACE.

Adversarially available information is the amount and type of data that the attack needs or is allowed for the adversary. We distinguish here at least six different types: *pre-crypto* (data before encryption, signing or other cryptographic transformation), *post-crypto, secret key-material* (symmetric or private asymmetric), *protocol runs, setup parameters* and *simulation environment master*. The four first ones are measured in bits, bytes or messages/keys/runs, the last two are discussed as follows:

- The access to *setup parameters* becomes relevant in cryptographic protocols, giving rise to, e.g., variants of Universal Composability (UC): Joint UC [7] and Global UC [8]. Possible value space could be {`local/global, per protocol/several runs`}.
- The control of the *master process*, which in cryptographic protocol security proofs models to what degree the adversary is able to control the (unspecified) protocol environment (resulting in yet other UC variants [9]). Possible value space could be {`Sim+Adv, Advonly, Env, *`}.

Adversarial goals need to be rigorously formalized, which usually results in case-specific definitions, and almost all values for the metric are incomparable, making it both qualitative and semi-measurable only. An example value space for typical goals is {`Semantic deduction, Information Leak, Local deduction, Global deduction, Total Break`}.

Adversarial degrees of freedom of action refer here to what the adversarial model is expecting the adversary to do. We

TABLE I. CATEGORIES AND PROPERTIES OF DIFFERENT METRICS OF CRYPTOGRAPHIC SYSTEMS.

Main category	Subcategory	Type	Measurable	Quantitative / Qualitative	Relevance
Adversarial model	Degrees of freedom		yes	Qualitative	P
		Corruption power Num. of principals	yes	Quantitative	T
		Corruption power Degree of corruption	semi	Qualitative	T
		Security game compliance	semi	Qualitative	T
	Adversarial available information	Pre-crypto	yes	Quantitative	P
		Post-crypto	yes	Quantitative	P
		Secret key material	yes	Quantitative	P
		Protocol runs	semi	Quantitative	P
		Setup parameters	semi	Qualitative	T
		Simulation environment	semi	Qualitative	T
	Adversarial goal		semi	Qualitative	P
	Adversarial resources	Computation power Instantiated	yes	Quantitative	P
		Computation power Non-instantiated	semi	Qualitative	T
		Memory Instantiated	yes	Quantitative	P
		Memory Non-instantiated	semi	Qualitative	T
Proof framework	Complexity & security assumptions		semi	Qualitative	T
	Abstraction assumptions	Type	semi	Qualitative	T
		Num. of assumptions	yes	Quantitative	T
		Maturity of assumptions	no	Qualitative	T
	Methodology	Tightness	yes	Quantitative	P
	Rigor		semi	Qualitative	T
Verification and maturity	Key length	Bits for criteria compliance	yes	Quantitative	P
	Assurance levels	Assurance standard or profile	yes	Qualitative	P
		Level, e.g. EAL	yes	Quantitative	P
	Coverage	Percentage of tests	yes	Quantitative	P
	Method efficiency	Number of detected vulnerabilities	yes	Quantitative	P
	Human efficiency	Academic research	semi	Quantitative	P
	Verification time	Time since released for evaluation	yes	Quantitative	P
		Size and efforts of eval. community	yes	Quantitative	P
	Readiness level	Technology readiness level	yes	Quantitative	T
		Integration readiness level	yes	Quantitative	T
		System readiness level	yes	Quantitative	T
		PETS maturity model	yes	Qualitative	P
Cost and performance	Time costs	Execution overhead	yes	Quantitative	P
		Communication overhead	yes	Quantitative	P
	Memory costs	Run-time	yes	Quantitative	P
		Storage	yes	Quantitative	P
		Communication	yes	Quantitative	P
	Implementation complexity	Size of software	semi	Qualitative	P
		Dedicated hardware requirements	semi	Qualitative	P
	Energy efficiency	Algorithm complexity dependent	yes	Quantitative	P
		Hardware platform dependent	yes	Quantitative	P

propose to divide the degrees of freedom into three: *General, Corruption power* and *Game compliance*.

Corruption power. In interactive protocols, the adversary is also assumed to be able to access and/or modify the private information of some of the principals. This is called corruption, and depending on the scheme, only a certain number of principals are allowed to be corrupted. Sometimes even more fine-grained "corruptive power" is allowed [10]. The example values of this metric could include a (quantitative) percentage of corrupted principals and a (qualitative) description of the degree of corruption within one principal (see [10] for subprotocol-level detail).

For the *general metrics*, cryptographic formalisms differ in the amount of principals: Single-party settings (conventional encryption and signatures) and multiparty settings (protocols). As we show below, the multi-party setting does not bring that many new metrics per sé.

In the single-party setting, only one or fixed, integral set of cryptographic transformations (a black box) are usually considered. In this case, the adversary may be able to *observe* some or all of the inputs, or to *choose* (possibly adaptively) some or all of them. Note that we consider modification of inputs and other adversarially available information to belong to the "choosing" process. Some of the possible values in the single-party setting would then be `'Observe'`, `'Choose'` and `'Choose adaptively'`, in increasing order.

In the multi-party setting, i.e., protocols, the situation with adversarial behaviour appears at first sight to be more complex, as the security models are more varied. In the Dolev-Yao model [11], the principle is that the "attacker carries the message", or that the adversary is free to read, modify, add and delete protocol messages and corrupt protocol principals (in effect stealing their private key material). However, the convention we made in the single-party setting already covers the deletion, modification and adding of protocol messages, global setup parameters modification and protocol environment control, since the ability to choose message (/parameters/environment properties) for a single party translates to all of the above. We thus conclude that we have not identified more metrics from the multi-party setting.

Game compliance. Many of the formalisms in cryptographic security can be divided into two: game-based approaches and simulation-based approaches. Game-based approaches are basically a protocol, which try to model the adversarial behaviour in some commonly thought scenarios. Simulation-based approaches try to enable showing security irrespective of the adversarial behaviour. The best the attacker can do, is to perform the idealized, non-cryptographic tasks assigned to replace crypto in the simulation (SIM) model.

In the metrics, we consider this distinction to be an adversarial degree of freedom in the sense that the adversary is either constrained to follow some security game protocol, or not. The values could be, for example {`Game-App, Game-Gen, SIM`}, making a further distinction between general security games and very application-specific games.

B. Security Proof Framework Metrics

Proof framework is the framework in which the security proof is conducted. This includes multiple assumptions (for abstractions of certain functions and for the complexity of several mathematical problems), the rigor used and the proof methodology.

A metric clearly tied to the proof methodology is *tightness* of the proof. This concept indicates, how exactly the resource needs for different phases of the proof are estimated. This metric is measurable and quantitative, as typical asymptotical $O(f(n))$ expressions are used here.

Complexity assumptions are the foundation of many types of cryptographic proofs. They are assumptions on the hardness of different mathematical problems, usually that their time-complexity is superpolynomial in the security parameter. These assumptions can have several metrics:

- Assumption's time-complexity. The metric is measurable, quantitative and practical, as it directly affects key size. The metric is expressed with the Big-Oh-notation (e.g., $O(f(n))$).
- Type, if the assumption belongs to a known sequence of implications (e.g., Decisional Diffie-Hellman (DDH) $\Leftarrow$ Computational Diffie-Hellman (CDH) $\Leftarrow$ Discrete Log (DL) problem.) A possible common labelling borrows from the general ordering for several problems, where decisional problems (DDH) are usually easier than computational problems (CDH), and finally the primitive inversion problem (DL): {`decisional, computational/search, inversion`}. This metric is semi-measurable and qualitative.

Abstraction assumptions cover, how much the proof methodology uses abstractions, what kind of type they present and their maturity. Typical abstractions give different functions as ideal oracles, the most famous probably being the Random Oracle Model (ROM, [12] with variations in [13] and [14]). Many other oracles exist as well, e.g., the Generic Group Model (GGM) [15], the Ideal Cipher Model (ICM) [16], and the Common reference string model [17]. Sometimes the oracles are implicit, such as the Dolev-Yao modelling on encryption operations (which are assumed to be secure). If no abstractions are used, the proof is said to be conducted in the Standard Model (SM).

The actual metrics are proposed as follows:

- The number of abstractions used. For a proof in SM this would be zero. Different abstractions would be weighed differently depending on their maturity and suitability for the cryptosystem
- Assumption maturity (we consider this to be in the verification category and not elaborated more here)
- Type. Not all of the abstraction are equal, as there are some known relations among them (e.g., ICM and ROM have been proven equal in some cases [18]). We then postulate, that like with the complexity assumptions, there is a common metric able to classify abstraction assumptions as well, but we leave it for future study.

Rigor refers to the level of detail of the proof, its compliance to commonly used proof techniques and the assurance in the validity of the proof. Many schemes outside the cryptologic community often rely on pure heuristics, others merely state that the scheme is essentially similar to an earlier scheme and overlook the security proof completely. Many other systems are too complex to contain fully rigorous proofs in single conference papers, making the authors only outline the proofs. Ideally, proofs should be fully detailed, and externally verified. The value space for this metric would then be {`Heuristic, Referenced, Outlined, Full, Verified`}.

C. Verification and maturity metrics

The strength and correctness of cryptographic implementations can be verified with different testing methods and tools. For instance, independent or national laboratories have product certification frameworks and programs for verifying that implementations have required functionality and behave as expected with different inputs.

As already mentioned in the introduction, *key length* is one of the most used metrics for cryptosystem security. In our taxonomy, key length considers the maturity and verification level that a cryptosystem has. It is an indicator that shows if the security parameters of a cryptosystem are up to the standards, which are defined for that cryptosystem and its use. It is a measurable, quantitative and practical metric.

Assurance Levels are measurements indicating system's security when compared against common or standard evaluation and testing requirements. For instance, Evaluation Assurance Level (EAL) is a seven point-scale metric used by the Common Criteria (CC) [19] security evaluation framework for implementations; Common Criteria's Protection Profile is simpler two point-scale (compliant/non-compliant) metric for specific product categories; Cryptographic Algorithm Validation Program (CAVP) [20] defines functional and statistical tests for algorithms with a two-point (pass-fail) scale; Cryptographic Module Validation Program (CMVP) [21] defines validation tests for hardware implementations in four point scale (i.e., FIPS 140-2 security levels); and ISO 29128 [22] Protocol Assurance Levels define requirements for the scope and automation of formal modelling and verification of cryptographic protocols. In addition to the generic frameworks, there also exist frameworks that are specific for industry field or for an area of cryptography. For instance, the Payment Card Industry [23] has defined its own test requirements for two point scale evaluation of cryptographic hardware modules and National Institute of Standards and Technology (NIST) has specified [24] a large suite for randomness testing. Verification metrics describe the coverage and effectiveness of the verification and testing actions that the cryptographic product has passed. Assurance levels are semi-measurable and quantitative metrics.

Coverage refers to the percentage of potentially vulnerable areas that are tested or verified. Coverage is complete coverage if every area with potential vulnerabilities are verified. The areas that can be tested include, e.g., functionality, interfaces and protocols, randomness, susceptibility to side-channel and fault injection attacks, life-cycle, as well as susceptibility to physical tampering and to reversing of obfuscated functionality attacks. Existing test suites, validation program requirements or common criteria profiles can be utilized when estimating whether all relevant areas are included to verification and whether all tests for the relevant areas are executed. This metric is measurable and quantitative.

Effectiveness of verification methodologies - such as requirement specifications, test patterns, statistical testing tools, formal analysis methods, and simulation tools - refers to design or implementation failures that can be detected with the given methodology. The effectiveness depends on the available software and hardware facilities, as well as on the quality of the processes in the evaluating community or laboratory. A straightforward quantitative and measurable metric of effectiveness is the amount of failures that are detected with the method. When different testing methods are available, it is also possible to estimate false positive and false negative ratios.

Effectiveness of human verification depends on the skills of human evaluators for verification and testing. These capabilities can be measured, e.g., by looking at the experience and education of evaluators, as well as past performance and reputation. Quantitative and measurable metrics for human verification include experience in years, number of performed evaluations, as well as the scientific author metrics (number of fresh related publications).

Verification time refers to the hours, months, or years that have been spend on exploring the cryptographic solution against vulnerabilities. Time accumulates from intensive product evaluations as well as from the verification and testing by scientific and user community during the system lifetime. The older and more dispersed the system is, the less unknown weaknesses it is likely to have. This is a quantitative and measurable metric.

The maturity metrics measure how ready and suitable a cryptosystem is. This can be a metric for a specific component as in Technology Readiness Levels (TRL) or a more comprehensive metric of a whole systems, such as the PETS maturity metric [25]. Some of these metrics are more complex derivations of the TRL, such as Systems Readiness Level (SRL) [26] and Integration Readiness Level (IRL) [27].

TRL measures the readiness of a single component. This metric is measurable and quantitative. *IRL* measures the readiness of components to be integrated to form a more complex system. This metric is measurable and quantitative. *SRL* measures the readiness of a complete system based on the TRLs and IRLs of the different components. The metric is measurable (if normalized) and quantitative.

PETS maturity metric is a measure for the quality and readiness of privacy enhancing technologies [25]. The measurement is carried out with both measurable indicators (such as the number of papers/patents and lines of code) and a more heuristic evaluation by experts. There is a defined procedure on how to reach consensus on possibly differing evaluations by experts. In some sense, this is similar to the jury evaluation used in some cryptographic standardisation competitions. In the PETS maturity metric, the evaluation is open and transparent, whereas in some cryptographic competitions this is not the case. The PETS maturity metric is measurable and qualitative.

D. Cost and performance metrics

The feasibility of cryptographic products depends not only of their security strength, but also other factors that are measured using cost and performance metrics. Cost and performance metrics can be calculated for the whole system or separately for an individual role (e.g., decrypter, encrypter, signer, verifier). Asymmetric cost division between roles may be beneficial, e.g., in cloud or Internet of Things scenarios where another party has more resources available for cryptographic operations.

Time costs originate from the computations, such as key generation, encryption and decryption, as well as public and private key operations, and from communications, where cryptography causes additional overhead, expands communication and negotiations. Time costs can be estimated by counting elementary operations that a cryptographic solution implies. This is a quantitative and measurable metric.

Size costs relate to the need for run-time and storage memory, as well as to the communication bandwidth. They depend on the sizes of keying material, ciphertexts, and signatures, as well as on run-time memory requirements of algorithms. This is a quantitative and measurable metric.

Implementation complexity relates to the size and costs of software or hardware implementations. A key attribute is whether the solution is suitable for standard computing platforms (e.g., Intel x86 or ARM-based) or whether it requires specialized hardware. An important attribute is also whether the performance of the algorithm can be improved with special hardware, such as parallel platforms or extended instruction sets. Complexity can be estimated either by counting lines of code or by counting required hardware resources like gate counts. This is a semi-measurable (as there are many ways to measure complexity) and qualitative metric. *Energy efficiency* depends on use of computing, memory, and communication resources and their cost in different platforms. This is a measurable and quantitative metric.

IV. Analyzing Metrics in Cryptographic Competitions

One way to evaluate our taxonomy of metrics is to take a look at the different competitions for cryptosystems. For this, we evaluated 8 different competitions and the rationales that they used to select the winning algorithm(s). The chosen competitions are Advanced Encryption Standard (AES) [28], New European Schemes for Signatures, Integrity, and Encryption (NESSIE) [29], Cryptography Research and Evaluation Committees (Cryptrec) [30], the ECRYPT Stream Cipher Project (eStream), NIST hash function competition [31], Password Hashing Competition (PHC) [32], Competition for Authenticated Encryption: Security, Applicability, and Robustness (CAESAR) [33], and Post-Quantum Cryptography Standardization (PQCS) [34].

A. AES competition

The goal of NIST's AES competition was to specify an unclassified, publicly disclosed encryption algorithm capable of protecting sensitive government information well into the next century. The algorithm would have to implement symmetric key cryptography as a block cipher and support a block size of 128 bits and key sizes of 128, 192, and 256 bits.

Competition started in January 1997 and lasted 46 months. There were 21 submissions. The winner was Rijndael which was renamed to AES, the other finalists were Serpent, Twofish, RC6 and MARS. Initial evaluation criteria were security, cost, and algorithm and implementation characteristics. Final criteria were general security, software implementations, restricted-space environments, hardware implementations, attacks on implementations, encryption versus decryption, key agility, other versatility and flexibility, and potential for instruction level parallelism [35].

NIST stated that the most emphasis in AES competition was on security. Rather than having government agencies scientists test and measure the security of each algorithm, they asked the public cryptographic community for help. Members of the cryptography community tested each algorithm's resistance to cryptoanalysis. Cryptoanalysis included testing each algorithm's security against known practical and theoretical attacks. The public also analysed the algorithms by determining the mathematical soundness. None of the finalists were statistically distinguishable from a random function. The team at NIST carefully considered the public analyses and used the results of these analyses when evaluating the algorithms. Measuring cost included licensing requirements, computational efficiency, and memory requirements. The algorithm characteristics and implementation criteria included flexibility, hardware and software suitability, and simplicity [36].

There were no known attacks on any of the five finalists at the time of the judging, so other, less palpable measures were used to determine security of the ciphers. When comparing hardware and software performance of the finalists, Rijndael and Twofish exhibited very similar results. The Rijndael implementation was clearly the simpler of two and shared close ties with an ancestor cipher, Square, that had received a significant amount of analysis, while Twofish had no such ancestor [28].

B. Cryptography standardization projects

NESSIE and Cryptrec projects were inspired by the AES competition. The goal of the NESSIE project was to identify secure cryptographic primitives. Competition started in March 2000 and lasted 36 months. There were 42 submissions and twelve algorithms were chosen for the final portfolio. Initial evaluation criteria were long-term security, market requirements, efficiency and flexibility.

The goal of the Cryptrec project was to evaluate and recommend cryptographic techniques for government and industrial use. Competition started in May 2000 and lasted 34 months. Out of 63 submissions, ten algorithms were chosen for the final portfolio. Initial criteria for evaluation were security, cost, and algorithm and implementation characteristics.

The goal of eStream project was to identify new stream ciphers suitable for widespread adoption, because in the NESSIE project all stream ciphers failed. Competition started in October 2004 and lasted 43 months. There were 34 submissions and seven algorithms were chosen in the final portfolio. Initial criteria were security, performance, simplicity and flexibility, justification and analysis, and quality of documentation.

C. Hash algorithm competitions

The goal of the NIST hash function competition was to develop a new hash function called Secure Hash Algorithm 3 (SHA-3). The competition started in November 2007 and lasted 60 months. There were 51 submissions. The winner was Keccak which was renamed to SHA-3. Other finalists were BLAKE, Grøstl, JH, and Skei. Initial criterion were security, cost, and algorithm and implementation characteristics. Final criteria were performance, security, analysis and diversity [31].

The goal of PHC was to find password hash functions that can be recognized as a recommended standard. Competition started in January 2013 and lasted 31 months. There were 24 submissions. The winner was Argon2 and the other finalists were Catena, Lyra2, Makwa, yescrypt. Initial criterion were security, efficiency, and simplicity. Final criteria were defence against GPU/FPGA/ASIC attacks, defence against time-memory tradeoffs, defence against side-channel leaks, defence against cryptanalytic attacks, elegance and simplicity of design, quality of the documentation, quality of the reference implementation, general soundness and simplicity, originality and innovation [32].

D. Recent competitions

The goal of CAESAR competition was to find new authenticated ciphers in three different categories. The competition started in January 2013 and lasted 74 months. There were 57 submissions and six were chosen for the final portfolio. The winners in the three use cases were Ascon for lightweight applications, AEGIS-128 for high-performance applications and Deoxys-II for defence in depth [33].

The goal of PQCS competition [34] is to standardize post-quantum cryptography to replace the current public key cryptosystems that can be broken with a quantum computer, e.g., [37]. The competition started in January 2017 and got 69 submissions. Initial criteria were security, cost and performance, and algorithm and implementation. The goal is to find suitable methods for digital signatures and key exchange, which are the two major use cases for public key cryptography.

E. Comparative analysis

Many of the security metrics, which were presented in the previous section, were present in the standardization competitions in different ways. As there has not been a uniform approach over the different competitions towards the metrics that our taxonomy describes, we have condensed the view especially with regards to the adversarial model and proof framework categories.

Table II summarizes our interpretation of the mapping between metrics and competitions. We looked at the metrics from three perspectives. First, we considered the main motivations to (new) standards, i.e., whether a low value for the metric in a predecessor standard (or a missing standard) was the reason for starting the competition in the first place. There were two main motivations: the development of adversarial capabilities which obsoleted earlier standards and the new security goals previously unaddressed by standards. Motivations are marked in the table with M. Secondly, we looked if competitions explicitly or implicitly expressed qualitative or quantitative requirements as their selection criteria. The existence of these metrics are marked in the table with E and I, respectively. Thirdly, we looked at publicly available measurable statistics that illustrated the verification efficiency of competitions. In particular, we evaluated the effectiveness of human verification by looking at the number of scientific articles that were published during the competition or the year after and that were returned by a Google Scholar query: "'competition name' candidate cryptography", which was performed on May 10th 2019. The relation between the amount of winners and candidates was listed as a metric of verification method; it is not an indication of failure detection rates but an indication of interest, which often leads to better results.

V. DISCUSSION

Measuring the security of systems is still a very difficult task even though the area has been researched for a long time and the interest has been increasing in recent years. Measuring the security and strength of cryptosystems seems to be even harder, because there are so many different metrics and variables involved and these also interact in many ways. Furthermore, the notion of security is very much context dependent. Even a secure cryptographic primitive used in a wrong context provides very little security. An insecure primitive in a wrong context provides even less security, e.g., [38].

Cryptographic metrics have lots of interdependencies. Some metrics directly or indirectly derive from other metrics, while other metrics are atomic responses to one particular requirement, capability, or threat. For instance, the key length is a derived metric whose value is motivated by the development of adversarial resources, limited by cost metrics, and defined by security proofs, assumptions and goals. In general, there is a trade-off between cost and performance metrics and many of the algorithmic metrics. Time and memory costs decrease directly with the corresponding adversarial resources. Higher adversarial capacities necessitates higher key lengths, complexity, stronger proofs and computation models. Each maturity metric depends directly on several of the algorithmic and verification metrics.

To illustrate the complexity of the situation, we have generated Figure 1. It depicts the different dependencies we have found in our taxonomy as arcs. The arcs are asymmetric and should be read left-to-right on the top part of the figure and right-to-left on the bottom of the figure. Bolder arcs indicate a more linear relationship, while thinner and lighter arcs indicate

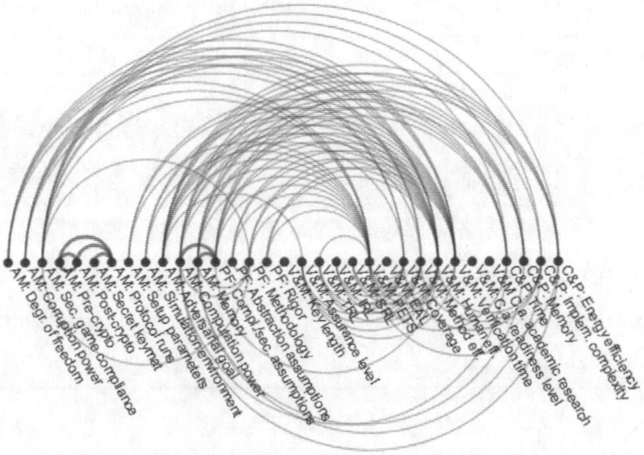

Figure 1. The complexity of the inter-metric dependencies.

that the dependency is not very linear. The abbreviations stand for Adversarial Model (AM), Proof Framework (PF), Verification and Maturity (V&M) and Cost and Performance (C&P).

Our taxonomy is open for new inter-metric derivatives. For instance, there are some measures that we have chosen, due to simplicity, not to present in our taxonomy as their own separate metrics. One is the total (monetary) cost of an attack as a resource metric. It could be argued that this is one of the most relevant metrics there is. On the other hand, it is also derivative of the attack resource metrics that have been included in our taxonomy. Another such quantity is time, which we see as a part of the computing power metrics.

Competitions must grade each candidate in order to determine the winner. This overall grade must be one-dimensional and cannot be formulated directly by counting averages, as units of measurements are not uniform and different competitions have had different valuations for their metrics. Formal means for grading exist. In particular, weighted average sum of each measurement is multiplied with a weight factor, which normalizes the scale and reflects metric's importance, and then divided with the sum of weight factors. The difficulty is in deciding which metrics get the most weight and how the qualitative metrics incorporate into the whole measurement. The decision regarding the weights of different metrics is contextual and depends on threat models and use cases. Qualitative metrics transform into numerical values with level-based grading criteria, which also depends on the context. In addition, thresholds are used in overall grading: some metrics must reach some minimal level to enable eligibility but do not affect overall grade.

One limitation of the standardisation competitions is that they usually consider only quite low level cryptosystems (block/stream ciphers, hash functions etc.) and not more complex systems or protocols. More complex cryptosystems, such as the TLS protocol, are formed through more traditional standardisation efforts. There we might expect to see different utilisation of the different metrics and perhaps more complex rationale for the decisions that are made. It seems from our results, that much of the consideration is given also to the cost

TABLE II. METRICS IN CRYPTOGRAPHIC STANDARDIZATION COMPETITIONS

Metric	AES	NESSIE	CRYPTREC	eStream	SHA-3	PHC	CAESAR	PQCS
Adversarial model	M	-	-	-	M	-	-	M
Key length	128,192,256	-	-	128, 80	-	-	-	-
Complexity				I (security analysis by community)				
Security goal	E	M,E	M,E	M,E	E	M,E	E	E
Computational model				Classical				and Quantum
Method efficiency (winners/candidates)	1/21	12/42	10/63	7/34	1/51	1/24	6/57	?/69
Human efficiency (peer-review papers)	539	179	349	46	1400	83	1400	803
Verification time	1997-2001	2000-03	2000-03	2004-09	2007-13	2013-17	2014-19	2016-
Readiness level				TRL 4 (prototype for laboratory validation)				
Time costs	E	E	E	M,E	E	E	E	E
Memory costs	E	I	E	M,E	E	I	E	E
Implementation complexity	E	E	E	E	E	E	M,E	E
Energy efficiency	I	I	I	I	I	I	I	I

and performance metrics. This is understandable because the winning algorithms are to become widely deployed standards.

In practice, none of the competitions has explicitly formulated their selection criteria or weights. Instead, all competitions have provided high-level instructions and delegated final grading to individual jurors who may have their own criteria. Typically, competitions explicitly or implicitly specify security goals, as well as adversarial models and assumed resources, but requirements related to other security and feasibility metrics are qualitative with few exceptions such as the key length targets for eStream and AES.

VI. CONCLUSION AND FUTURE WORK

This paper describes a taxonomy of different types of metrics that can be used to evaluate the security of cryptosystems. Our taxonomy has four categories: Adversarial model metrics, Proof framework metrics, Verification and maturity metrics, and Cost and performance metrics. It can be seen that different metrics have different attributes and that many of the most relevant metrics are not easy to measure and compare.

The evaluation of the competitions for cryptographic standards against our taxonomy shows that there are many commonalities between competitions, but there is no predefined set of metrics that the submissions are evaluated against. Thus, there is a need to continue research in this direction. This should lead towards a more standardised set of relevant and easy to use metrics for cryptosystems.

There is a lot of room for future work in this area. Our taxonomy provides an overview of the different metrics and their attributes, but we are still a long way from building and proposing a comprehensive metric for measuring cryptosystems. This is the major goal for future work in this area. One possible interesting direction for future research could be to utilise the TRL, IRL and SRL measures to more complex cryptosystems. The concepts have been tested in other fields, but in cryptography and cryptosystems they have not been studied yet. If this approach would be successful, we would have a potentially very general metric for measuring cryptosystems that could be used in many different contexts.

VII. ACKNOWLEDGEMENTS

This research has been funded by Defence Forces Research Program 2017 (PVTO 2017).

REFERENCES

[1] N. P. Smart, V. Rijmen, B. Gierlichs, K. Paterson, M. Stam, B. Warinschi, and G. Watson, "Algorithms, key size and parameters report," European Union Agency for Network and Information Security, 2014, pp. 0–95.

[2] BSI, "Cryptographic mechanisms: Recommendations and key lengths," https://www.bsi.bund.de/SharedDocs/Downloads/EN/BSI/Publications/TechGuidelines/TG02102/BSI-TR-02102-1.pdf, BSI TR-02102-1, Tech. Rep., 2018.

[3] E. Barker, W. Barker, W. Burr, W. Polk, and M. Smid, "NIST special publication 800-57," NIST Special Publication, vol. 800, no. 57, 2007, pp. 1–142.

[4] N. Jorstad and T. S. Landgrave, "Cryptographic algorithm metrics," 20th National Information Systems Security, 1997. [Online]. Available: http://csrc.nist.gov/nissc/1997/proceedings/128.pdf

[5] Z. Benenson, U. Kühn, and S. Lucks, "Cryptographic Attack Metrics," in Dependability Metrics. Berlin, Heidelberg: Springer Berlin Heidelberg, 2008, pp. 133–156.

[6] M. Bellare and P. Rogaway, "Optimal asymmetric encryption," in Advances in Cryptology—EUROCRYPT'94. Springer, 1995, pp. 92–111.

[7] R. Canetti and T. Rabin, "Universal composition with joint state," in Annual International Cryptology Conference. Springer, 2003, pp. 265–281.

[8] R. Canetti, Y. Dodis, R. Pass, and S. Walfish, "Universally composable security with global setup," in Theory of Cryptography Conference. Springer, 2007, pp. 61–85.

[9] A. Datta, R. Küsters, J. C. Mitchell, and A. Ramanathan, "On the relationships between notions of simulation-based security," in Theory of Cryptography Conference. Springer, 2005, pp. 476–494.

[10] R. Canetti, "Universally composable security: A new paradigm for cryptographic protocols," in Proceedings 2001 IEEE International Conference on Cluster Computing. IEEE, 2001, pp. 136–145.

[11] D. Dolev and A. Yao, "On the security of public key protocols," IEEE Transactions on information theory, vol. 29, no. 2, 1983, pp. 198–208.

[12] M. Bellare and P. Rogaway, "Random oracles are practical: A paradigm for designing efficient protocols," in Proceedings of the 1st ACM conference on Computer and communications security. ACM, 1993, pp. 62–73.

[13] P. Ananth and R. Bhaskar, "Non observability in the random oracle model," in International Conference on Provable Security. Springer, 2013, pp. 86–103.

[14] J. B. Nielsen, "Separating random oracle proofs from complexity theoretic proofs: The non-committing encryption case," in Annual International Cryptology Conference. Springer, 2002, pp. 111–126.

[15] V. Shoup, "Lower bounds for discrete logarithms and related problems," in International Conference on the Theory and Applications of Cryptographic Techniques. Springer, 1997, pp. 256–266.

[16] C. E. Shannon, "Communication theory of secrecy systems," Bell system technical journal, vol. 28, no. 4, 1949, pp. 656–715.

[17] R. Canetti and M. Fischlin, "Universally composable commitments," in Annual International Cryptology Conference. Springer, 2001, pp. 19–40.

[18] J.-S. Coron, T. Holenstein, R. Künzler, J. Patarin, Y. Seurin, and S. Tessaro, "How to build an ideal cipher: the indifferentiability of the feistel construction," Journal of cryptology, vol. 29, no. 1, 2016, pp. 61–114.

[19] Common Criteria, "Common Criteria for Information Technology Security Evaluation Part 2 : Security functional components," Security, no. April, 2017, pp. 1–323.

[20] NIST, "Cryptographic Algorithm Validation Program," 2018. [Online]. Available: https://csrc.nist.gov/Projects/Cryptographic-Algorithm-Validation-Program

[21] NIST, "Derived Test Requirements for FIPS PUB 140-2, Security Requirements for Cryptographic Modules," 2011.

[22] International Organization for Standarization, "ISO/IEC 29128:2011 - Information technology – Security techniques – Verification of cryptographic protocols," 2011.

[23] PCI Security Standards Council, "Payment card industry data security standard v3.0," 2013, https://www.pcisecuritystandards.org/security_standards/documents.php.

[24] NIST, "Special publication 800-22. a statistical test suite for random and pseudorandom number generators for cryptographic applications," 2010.

[25] M. Hansen, J. Hoepman, M. Jensen, and S. Schiffner, "Readiness analysis for the adoption and evolution of privacy enhancing technologies: Methodology, pilot assessment, and continuity plan," Tech. rep., ENISA, Tech. Rep., 2015.

[26] B. Sauser, D. Verma, J. Ramirez-Marquez, and R. Gove, "From trl to srl: The concept of systems readiness levels," in Conference on Systems Engineering Research, Los Angeles, CA, 2006, pp. 1–10.

[27] B. Sauser, R. Gove, E. Forbes, and J. E. Ramirez-Marquez, "Integration maturity metrics: Development of an integration readiness level," Information Knowledge Systems Management, vol. 9, no. 1, 2010, pp. 17–46.

[28] E. Chu, F. Liu, J. Yu, J. Sharma, P. Kim, and P. Kim, "Selection of advanced encryption standard," MIT, Tech. Rep., 2000.

[29] B. Preneel, A. Biryukov, C. De Cannière, S. Örs, E. Oswald, B. van Rompay, L. Granboulan, E. Dottax, G. Martinet, S. Murphy et al., "New european schemes for signatures, integrity, and encryption," European Project IST-1999-12324, 2004.

[30] Information Technology Promotion Agency, Telecommunications Advancement Organization of Japan, "CRYPTREC report 2002," 2003.

[31] S.-j. Chang, R. Perlner, W. Burr, M. Turan, J. Kelsey, S. Paul, and L. Bassham, "Third-round report of the sha-3 cryptographic hash algorithm competition," NIST, Tech. Rep., 2009.

[32] J. P. Aumasson, "Password hashing competition," https://password-hashing.net/, April 2019.

[33] D. J. Bernstein, "Caesar submissions," https://competitions.cr.yp.to/caesar-submissions.html, March 2019.

[34] G. Alagic et al., Status Report on the First Round of the NIST Post-Quantum Cryptography Standardization Process, NIST Internal Report 8240. US Department of Commerce, National Institute of Standards and Technology, 2019.

[35] D. J. Bernstein, "Aes: the advanced encryption standard," https://competitions.cr.yp.to/aes.html, January 2014.

[36] J. Nechvatal, E. Barker, L. Bassham, W. Burr, M. Dworkin, J. Foti, and E. Roback, "Report on the development of the advanced encryption standard," Journal of Research of the National Institute of Standards and Technology, 2001.

[37] P. W. Shor, "Polynomial-Time Algorithms for Prime Factorization and Discrete Logarithms on a Quantum Computer," SIAM Review, vol. 41, no. 2, jan 1999, pp. 303–332.

[38] F. Y. Rashid, "Adobe's hacked passwords: They are terrible!" https://uk.pcmag.com/opinion/12060/adobes-hacked-passwords-they-are-terrible, November 2013.

Comparison and Analysis of System Designs for Privacy-Preserving Genome Sequences Search

Yuki Yamada
Dept. of Information Sciences
Ochanomizu University
Tokyo, Japan
Email: yuki@ogl.is.ocha.ac.jp

Masato Oguchi
Dept. of Information Sciences
Ochanomizu University
Tokyo, Japan
Email: oguchi@is.ocha.ac.jp

***Abstract*—Genome sequences search is useful, for example, in clinical applications where a care provider needs to select a treatment option for a patient based on the exact kind of cancer the patient might have. However, privacy protection for genome analysis is one of the most important issues in the area of medical genomics. In such a situation, only homomorphic encryption is a desirable technology to be used for this application because it is non-interactive. Privacy-preserving genome sequence search using homomorphic encryption has been a practical challenge because of the scalability issues driven by the depth of computations that need to be supported for privacy-preserving genome sequence search. Comparison and analysis of system designs for such a system are important for us to put them in practical use. Therefore, in this work, we build off of earlier researches for genome sequence search to design, then implement and compare each approach. We particularly focus on the differences in the main calculation time on the server and the data transfer overhead. Our results show that each design has different trade-offs and characteristics.**

Keywords*— *Homomorphic Encryption; Genome Sequence; Secure Search; Privacy; Cloud Computing.

I. Introduction

Ever since the Human Genome Project [1] and the 1000 Genomes Project [2] have begun publishing catalogs of human variation and genotype data, genomic data analytics have found increasingly practical and important use in various fields. Privacy challenges associated with analytics on genomic data have been exacerbated by recent innovations that made it much less expensive to handle genetic information. Furthermore, it is difficult for hospitals or research institutes that have genome databases to publish the complete data because of the privacy issues, and also it is not desirable for researchers to make their work-in-progress work public. Therefore, it is needed to keep both genome database contents and the user's query in private. However, because genomic data is potentially voluminous, making scalability challenges are important when analyzing genetic data, especially when needed to be done in a privacy-preserving manner.

Of particular interest, genomic search applications look for some specific sub-strings, thus driving the need for a system that can conduct privacy-preserving string searches on vast amounts of genome data. Generic cloud computing environments are not feasible to address this need due to security and privacy concerns engendered by multi-tenancy, and the cloud may be managed by unknown and un-trusted individuals. A simple solution to the cloud-based storage of privacy-sensitive genomic information is to use encryption. If this system is built with common symmetric- or public-key encryption, the decryption key would be passed to the cloud to enable analytics, thus creating a privacy concern. Only homomorphic encryption techniques enable non-interactive computation on the data when it is encrypted. Fully Homomorphic Encryption (FHE) supports non-interactive computation on encrypted data. Hence, FHE allows a client to upload a corpus of genomic data to a high-performance off-premise computation environment and then search on that genomic data without leaking its private information to the computation host. However, search operations are considered to be "deep", meaning they are not efficient when running on homomorphically encrypted data.

Prior efforts show some methods that use FHE to protect privacy [3][4]. In these methods, encrypted data is uploaded to a cloud for privacy-preserving non-interactive computation without decryption. Although there have been attempts to accelerate these systems by introducing decentralized computing, such as in [5] as well, the calculation costs on the cloud are still too large to put into practice.

In this paper, we implement the privacy-preserving genome sequences search system in multiple designs based on the previous work [3][4] and compare their performance to explore design trade-offs. In Section II we introduce the motivating application of privacy-preserving genome sequences search. In Section III, we introduce relevant features of FHE techniques. In Section IV, we provide a broad overview of relevant prior work. In Section V, we discuss designs trade-offs and approaches that we build on and explore. In Section VI, we discuss our implementation and experimental settings and then show experimental results. In Section VII, we analyze the results of our experimentation. In Section VIII, we conclude this research and discuss future directions.

II. Genome Sequence Search Application

The goal of an application for the privacy-preserving genome sequences search is for clients to query if there are matches between a query string and the data in a genome database stored on an off-site server [6]. Genomic data are composed of sequences of 4 different kinds of nucleotides – A, G, C, and T –, therefore, we can regard this genome sequences search as a 4-kind character search [5].

A representation of this operation is seen in Figure 1.

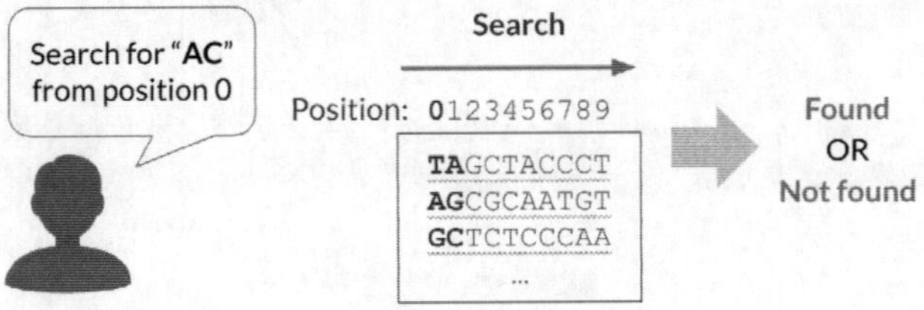

Figure 1. Genome sequences search

We assume a secure model of a privacy-preserving genome search system with a cloud environment, where the outsourcing system is implemented in the client-server style. Its representation is shown in Figure 2.

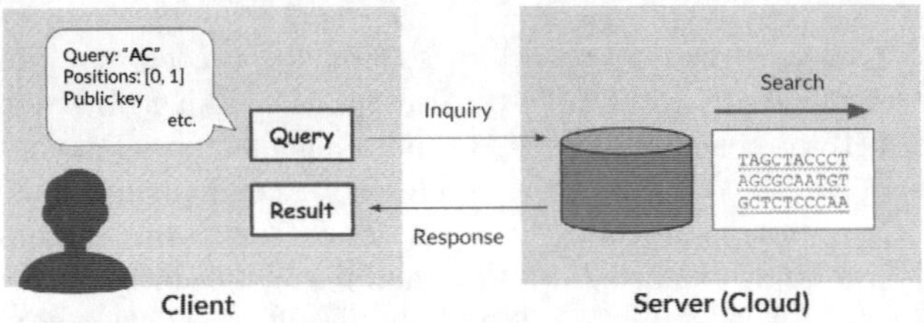

Figure 2. Application overview

A server holds a set of genome sequences data aligned by each sample in a database. This means that it is possible to search every sample in a specific position of the genome sequence. Clients send the inquiry to a server to calculate the matches between the query and the database held by the server. The query sent by the client includes not only the encrypted string that the client wants to search the genome sequence for but also some other parameters such as a public key for calculations and multiple starting points of the search for genome data strings (search positions). By designating multiple positions including dummy ones, clients can hide the actual one the clients use from the server. On receiving an inquiry from a client, the server conducts match searching on the data with FHE calculations, and then transmits the result to the client. The result transmitted by the server indicates whether there are any matches between the query string and genome sequences or not.

III. Fully Homomorphic Encryption (FHE)

As discussed in Section I, we leverage FHE to provide privacy-preserving genome sequences search. As seen respectively in (1) and (2), these homomorphisms are called the Additive Homomorphism (which supports addition over encrypted data), and the Multiplicative Homomorphism (which supports multiplication over encrypted data.)

Additive/Multiplicative Homomorphism

$$Encrypt(m) \oplus Encrypt(n) = Encrypt(m + n) \quad (1)$$

$$Encrypt(m) \otimes Encrypt(n) = Encrypt(m \times n) \quad (2)$$

FHE supports both of these homomorphism properties. By leveraging these properties, users can support the evaluation of polynomial circuits over ciphertexts analogous to how they would support similar circuits evaluated on plaintexts.

FHE was first proposed by Rivest et al. in 1987 [7] but was not known to be feasible until a candidate scheme was discovered by Gentry in 2009 [8]. This first scheme leverages polynomial rings and ideal lattices, and the encrypted text is constructed by encrypted data and random noise to guarantee its difficulty to decrypt without the appropriate secret key. This early scheme was computationally inefficient, for example, the ciphertext of this implementation would be 1 GB on encrypting 1 bit data. There have been tremendous recent strides in developing increasingly more efficient schemes and their implementations. For example, Lu et al. [9] show a scheme that supports a comparison homomorphism in addition to addition and multiplication homomorphisms.

There are still many large challenges with FHE. For example, noise accumulates in ciphertexts when computations are performed on them. As this noise grows, the ciphertexts eventually cannot be decrypted correctly after too many computations are performed. The random noise in ciphertexts grow additively with additive operations and multiplicatively with every multiplication operation. This noise growth would normally limit the size of computations that could be performed with FHE. However, there is a special method called *bootstrapping*, which reduces the noise embedded in a ciphertext, with the drawback that the bootstrapping operations are extremely computationally intensive.

Note that many practical applications of FHE schemes use a limited version of FHE without bootstrapping. The "reduced" version of FHE is called Somewhat Homomorphic Encryption (SHE or SwHE) [10]. This is the ability to conduct some simple calculations that can be derived with one-time multiplication and multiple times addition, such as the inner product of the vector, distribution, and correlation.

IV. Previous Work

A. PBWT-sec

Several previous attempts have been made to realize practical privacy-preserving genome sequences search. PBWT-sec [6] is an efficient two-party prefix much-counting protocol that combines Additive Homomorphic Encryption (AHE) and an efficient data structure for much searching called Positional-Burrows Wheeler Transform (PBWT) [11]. The server of PBWT-sec has a genome sequences database as PBWT style, that is transformed from an original aligned genome sequences database. In its searching phase, the server access to a look-up vector that is derived from PBWT recursively. This is named Recursive Oblivious Transfer (ROT) [11]. When the query string length is l, ROT consists of l times vector-lookups, which needs l rounds of communication between the client and the server. PBWT-sec also devises the idea that the client passes multiple amounts of search positions, which includes dummy ones, to a server to preserve the privacy of clients with hiding the positions that the client uses. Although AHE can be used as an encryption method, according to this work [6], it is considered that preventing genome data leakage with AHE is difficult because we cannot conduct complex calculations with it.

B. Genome sequences search with FHE

While FHE engenders a much longer computation time than that of AHE, we can extend the PBWT-sec approach to use computation methods that search with wildcards and compute statistics based on the search result by building genome sequences search with FHE.

There are two relevant prior attempts by Ishimaki et al. [3][4]. First, one [3] proposes multi-round privacy-preserving genome sequence searches with FHE based on PBWT-sec [6]. This approach replaces additive homomorphic methods in PBWT-sec with fully homomorphic methods and also introduces the packing technique proposed by Smart et al. [12]. The other [4] propose an efficient approach for one-round search with FHE by introducing bootstrapping and reducing the runtime of the system by optimizing the calculation procedure. These two work use HElib [13] and its BGV implementation as a software library for FHE calculations. The detail of the system design that is proposed by each work is discussed in Section V.

C. FHE scheme comparison for genome sequences search

There is another work we have done for privacy-preserving genome sequences search [14]. In the paper, we implemented multiple designs of genome search systems in two schemes, BFV [15] in PALISADE [16] and BGV [17] in HElib [13], and then compared their calculation time on the server. There is a myriad of options and design trade-offs associated with the application of homomorphic encryption in this domain-driven, not only design trade-offs but also scheme selection, choices in data encoding, even encryption software library.

V. Design and Trade-offs

A. Design 1

First, we introduce the Design 1, proposed by [3], shown in Figure 3 below.

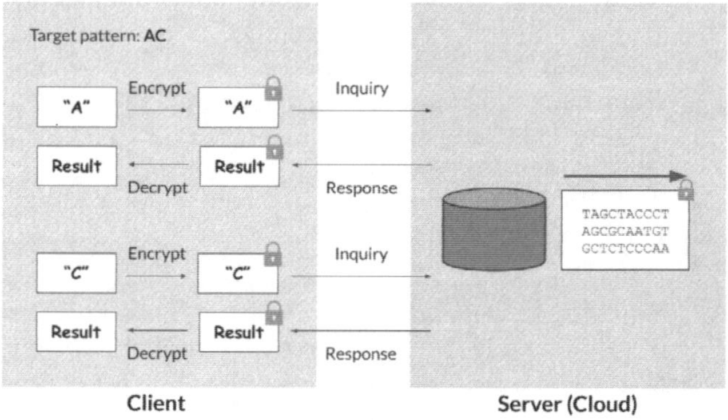

Figure 3. Application Design 1

(1) The client encrypts one character of the query string and then passes the resulting ciphertext to the server with other parameters.
(2) The server then performs FHE computations and then returns the result to the client.
(3) The client decrypts the intermediate result.
(4) The client encrypts the next character of the query using the result and sends it to the server.
(5) Repeat (2)-(4) as many times as the length of the query.

There are two approaches to support the needed depth of computation to avoid incorrect decryption: limiting the depth of FHE computations to keep the noise in ciphertexts less than noise threshold for correct decryption, or adopting bootstrap to reduce noise in ciphertexts. In this design, the server operates over a single character at a time, and thus the client gains the final result by comparing the results for all query characters. This reduces the depth of computation on the server and enables reduced noise to remove the need for bootstrapping. However, computation costs on the clients and communication costs between the client and the server increase as the length of the query increases. Since each communication involves large data transfer, this design is inappropriate for the clients with limited communication resources and requires that the clients both be available and have appropriate computation resources for repeated encryption and decryption.

B. Design 2-1 and Design 2-2

Next, we introduce Design 2-1 and Design 2-2. The server in both Design 2-1 and Design 2-2 supports the whole string search to address the issues Design 1 has. Thus Design 2-1 and Design 2-2 are more appropriate for the client with limited computation power as compared to Design 1. However, the data size of ciphertexts as welll as FHE calculation costs on the server of Design 2-1 and Design 2-2 are much greater than that of Design 1.

There are two general approaches to support the large computation depth needed on the server of Design 2. Design 2-1, proposed by [4], reduces the noise by bootstrapping as shown in Figure 4.

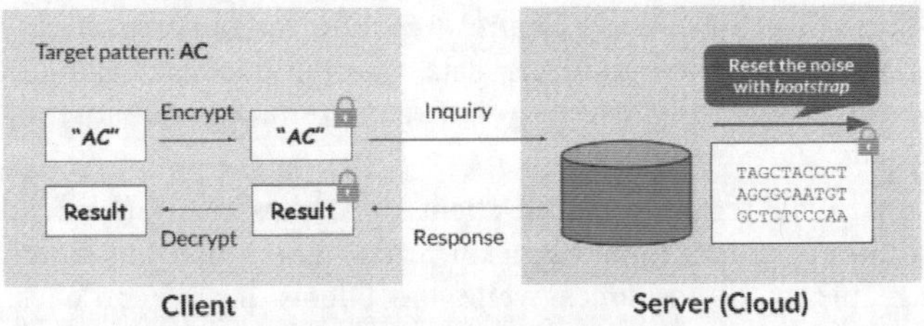

Figure 4. Application Design 2-1

(1) The client encrypts the whole query string and then passes the encrypted query string with supporting parameters to the server.
(2) The server performs FHE computations and reset noise with bootstrap accordingly.
(3) The server transmits the encrypted result to the client.
(4) The client gains a result by decrypting the received data.

The server in Design 2-1 can operate the whole string search by adopting the method called bootstrap. Bootstrap can reset the noise in the ciphertexts while each bootstrapping operation causes expensive overhead. Previous work [4] proposed the approach to minimize the number of bootstrapping with the parameters for a reduced number of calculations.

Alternatively, Design 2-2 sets sufficiently large parameters to ensure correct decryption within a limited (but large) number of operations as shown in Figure 5.

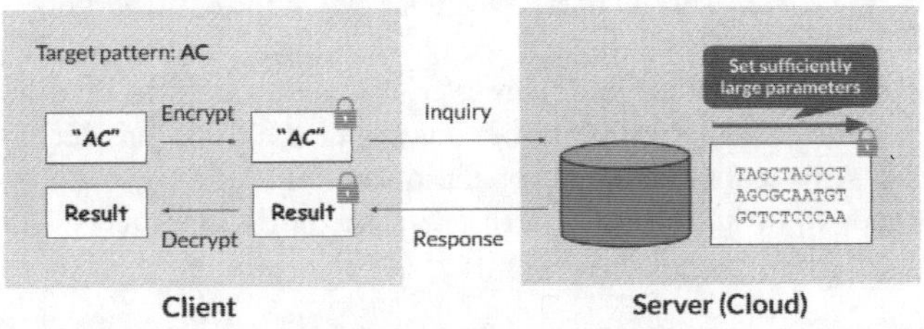

Figure 5. Applicatin Design 2-2

(1) The client encrypts the whole query string and then passes the encrypted query string with supporting parameters to the server.
(2) The server performs FHE computations with large parameters.
(3) The server transmits the encrypted result to the client.
(4) The client gains a result by decrypting the received data.

Design 2-2 is a more naive approach that sets sufficiently large parameters so that no bootstrap is needed. Using the parameters for the larger number of operations deteriorates the performance of all the arithmetic operations, while each bootstrapping operation costs expensive overhead.

VI. Experimentation

Based on previous work, we implement Design 1, Design 2-1 and Design 2-2 discussed in Section V and then compare them on real-world data.

A. *Problem settings*

The genomic data used for this experiment are Single-Nucleotide Polymorphism (SNP) [18] sequences from the 1,000 Genomes Project [2]. This data provide the representation of where variations from a reference genome are likely to appear, without showing entire genome sequences. In our experimental setting, the number of genomic data samples is 2185 and the number of characters per sample is 10,000. The range of the query length is 1–6, and clients designate just one search position.

B. *System overview*

We implemented the privacy-preserving genome sequences search system in multiple designs discussed in Section V in C++. As a software library for homomorphic encryption, we adopted HElib [13]. Both systems adopt the Chinese Reminder Theorem (CRT) packing technique by Smart et al. [12] as well. Experiments were conducted on the machines that have the specification shown in Table I and parameters used for these experiments are summarized in Table II.

TABLE I. EXPERIMENTAL ENVIRONMENT

Server	OS	CentOS 6.9
	CPU	Intel®Xeon®Processor E5-2643 v3 (3.4GHz) 6 Cores × 2 Sockets
	Main Memory	512GB
	SSD	80GB
	HDD	2TB

TABLE II. PARAMETERS FOR THE EXPERIMENTS

Design	Parameter L
Design 1	8
Design 2-1	23
Design 2-2	9 * (query length)

C. *Experimentation Results*

We ran each experiment three times and calculated the average of results.

Figures 6-7 show each graph of the average client-to-server and server-to-client data transfer overhead (volume of data) of Design 1, Design 2-1 and Design 2-2 shown in Figures 3-5, based on the length of the query. Figure 8 shows the average execution time on the server of Design 2-1 and Design 2-2 based on the length of the query.

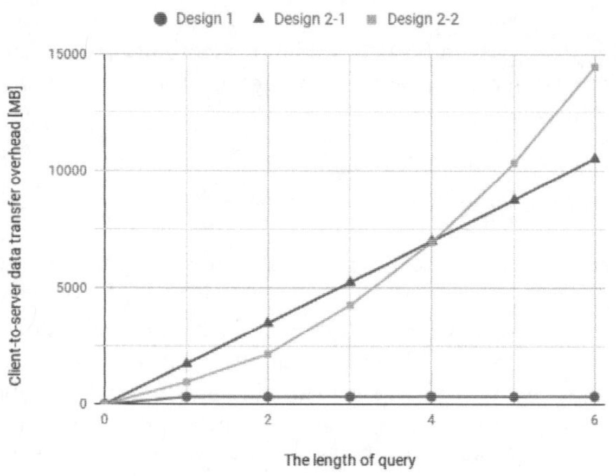

Figure 6. Client-to-server data transfer overhead

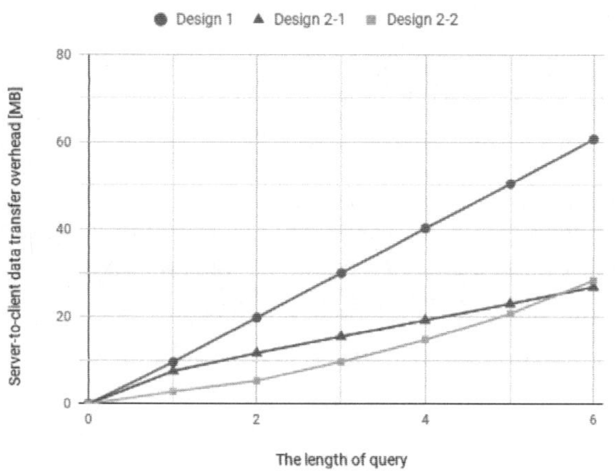

Figure 7. Server-to-client data transfer overhead

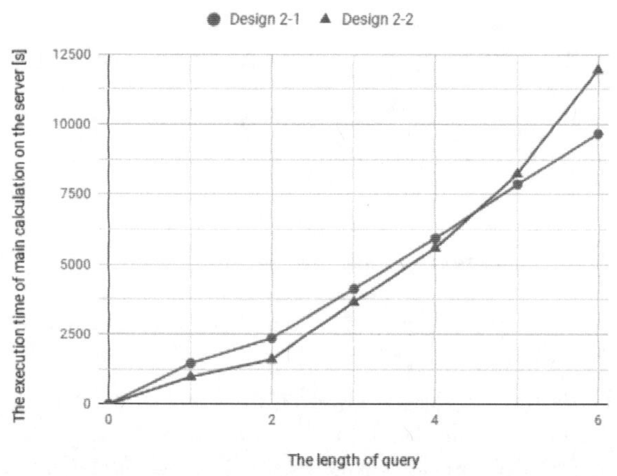

Figure 8. Average execution time of the main calculation on the server of Design 2-1 and Design 2-2 by the length of query

VII. Analysis of Experimental Results

A. *Data transfer overhead*

First, we compare client-to-server and server-to-client data transfer overhead (volume of data) by each application design. According to the result, Figures 6-7 show the opposite things: the smallest client-to-server data transfer overhead and the largest server-to-client data transfer overhead are those of Design 1.

We can regard server-to-client data transfer overhead as a more important one because it is assumed that the server has plenty of resources while the clients have poor ones, meaning that Design 2 would be more suitable for the client with less computation resource. However, it is needed to evaluate more kinds of values from more points of view to examine the best application design for the client with particular specification; we should compare not only the client-to-server and server-to-client data transfer overheads but also data transfer time between clients and server and the homomorphic calculation time on clients.

B. *Execution time*

Next, to compare Design 2-1 and Design 2-2 in detail, we compare the execution time of the main calculation on the server. Figure 8 shows the result for this comparison. It can be observed that the main calculation time on the server of Design 2-1 increases linearly while that of Design 2-2 increases in the multiplier.

This result is because of the parameters used for this experimentation shown in Table II. Although we can use the same parameters for FHE calculation in Design 2-1, the parameters for that in Design 2-2 need to get larger as the length of query increases to guarantee correct decryption without using bootstrap nor the noise in the ciphertext of FHE exceeding the threshold. However, it is also indicated that the calculation time on Design 2-2 is faster than that on Design 2-1 with a shorter length of the query. This means that it is better to switch the design to use according to the query and some other parameters.

VIII. Conclusion and Discussion

Comparison and analysis of system designs for systems is important to put them in practical use. Therefore, in this paper, we implemented and compared multiple designs for the client-server style system for privacy-preserving genome sequences search with BGV in HElib based on prior work. Our results show three things: the calculation costs on the clients in Design 1 increases more as the length of query increases, the calculation costs on the server in Design 2 increases more as the length of query increases, and it depends on the length of query and some other parameters that decide which design is the more suitable in Design 2-1 and Design 2-2. As future work, we plan to compare the execution time on the clients and data transfer time with a limited resource of clients, as well as the execution time on the server and data transfer size.

Acknowledgement

This work was partly supported by JST CREST Grant Number JPMJCR1503, Japan.

References

[1] NHGRI. (2019). The human genome project, [Online]. Available: https://www.genome.gov/human-genome-project (visited on 9–2019).

[2] EMBL-EBI. (2018). The international genome sample resource, [Online]. Available: http://www.internationalgenome.org/ (visited on 9–2019).

[3] Y. Ishimaki, K. Shimizu, K. Nuida, and H. Yamana, "Poster: Privacy-preserving string search for genome sequences using fully homomorphic encryption," in *IEEE Symposium on Security and Privacy*, 2016.

[4] Y. Ishimaki, H. Imabayashi, K. Shimizu, and H. Yamana, "Privacy-preserving string search for genome sequences with fhe bootstrapping optimization," in *2016 IEEE International Conference on Big Data (Big Data)*, IEEE, 2016, pp. 3989–3991.

[5] Y. Yamamoto and M. Oguchi, "A decentralized system of genome secret search implemented with fully homomorphic encryption," in *the 1st IEEE International Workshop on Big Data and IoT Security in Smart Computing (BITS2017)*, IEEE, 2017, pp. 1–6.

[6] K. Shimizu, K. Nuida, and G. Rätsch, "Efficient privacy-preserving string search and an application in genomics," *Bioinformatics*, vol. 32, no. 11, pp. 1652–1661, 2016.

[7] R. L. Rivest, L. Adleman, and M. L. Dertouzos, "On data banks and privacy homomorphisms," *Foundations of secure computation*, vol. 4, no. 11, pp. 169–180, 1978.

[8] C. Gentry, "Fully homomorphic encryption using ideal lattices," in *Stoc*, vol. 9, 2009, pp. 169–178.

[9] W. Lu, S. Kawasaki, and J. Sakuma, "Using fully homomorphic encryption for statistical analysis of categorical, ordinal and numerical data," *IACR Cryptology ePrint Archive*, (2016/1163).

[10] M. Naehrig, K. Lauter, and V. Vaikuntanathan, "Can homomorphic encryption be practical?" In *Proceedings of the 3rd ACM workshop on Cloud computing security workshop*, ACM, 2011, pp. 113–124.

[11] R. Durbin, "Efficient haplotype matching and storage using the positional burrows–wheeler transform (pbwt)," *Bioinformatics*, vol. 30, no. 9, pp. 1266–1272, 2014.

[12] N. P. Smart and F. Vercauteren, "Fully homomorphic simd operations," *Designs, codes and cryptography*, vol. 71, no. 1, pp. 57–81, 2014.

[13] homenc. (2019). Helib: An implementation of homomorphic encryption, [Online]. Available: https://github.com/homenc/HElib (visited on 9–2019).

[14] Y. Yamada, K. Rohloff, and M. Oguchi, "Homomorphic encryption for privacy-preserving genome sequences search," in *The 3rd IEEE International Workshop on Big Data and IoT Security in Smart Computing (BITS2019)*, 2019.

[15] J. Fan and F. Vercauteren, "Somewhat practical fully homomorphic encryption," *IACR Cryptology ePrint Archive*, vol. 2012, p. 144, 2012.

[16] PALISADE. (2019). Palisade release, [Online]. Available: https://gitlab.com/palisade/palisade-release (visited on 9–2019).

[17] Z. Brakerski, C. Gentry, and V. Vaikuntanathan, "Fully homomorphic encryption without bootstrapping," *IACR Cryptology ePrint Archive*, vol. 2011, p. 277, 2011.

[18] NIH. (2019). What are single nucleotide polymorphisms (snps)? - genetics home reference - nih, [Online]. Available: https://ghr.nlm.nih.gov/primer/genomicresearch/snp (visited on 9–2019).

Statistical Measurement of Production Environment Influence on Code Reuse Availability

Étienne Louboutin
Ecole Navale, IMT Atlantique
F-29240 Brest, France
Email: etienne.louboutin@imt-atlantique.fr

Jean-Christophe Bach, Fabien Dagnat
IMT Atlantique, Lab-STICC, UMR6285
F-29238 Brest, France
Email: {jc.bach,fabien.dagnat}@imt-atlantique.fr

***Abstract*—Return-oriented-programming is widely used for software exploits, and ten years after its academic description, little to no protection is deployed most of the time. Performance trade-offs or insufficient protection often results in no protection deployment. Address space layout randomisation is a basic protection that just increases the complexity of writing attacks but does not prevent code-reuse exploits. Its overhead is negligible enough to justify its deployment. These protections come after software development, and are implemented in the compiler or via binary modification. Usually, each binary is either critical and protected or not critical and not protected. This decision results from a usage criterion, like `gzip`, or if it exposes network interfaces, like `apache`. In this paper, we go through multiple views to expose elements that make it possible to compare binaries with respect to their available code-reuse components. We look at these elements to underline what part of the production process of a binary can increase or decrease its quantitative inclusion of code reuse components. With this evaluation, we expose certain disparities introduced by production tools, by the language used to write applications or even because of the targeted platform. We also show how hardware architectures affect this statistical measurement.**

Keywords–Return-Oriented-Programming; ROP; Code-reuse exploits.

I. INTRODUCTION

With hardware protection against code injection, software exploitation is widely based on code reuse. Starting with return-to-libc then generalised with Return Oriented Programming (ROP) [1], the class of code reuse attacks allows an intruder to recreate any arbitrary program by hijacking the control flow of a host application. To construct such an exploit, the needed instructions have to be found in the target binary. A group of instructions used during such a hijack is called a gadget. A more precise description of a gadget is provided in Section II. Address Space Layout Randomisation (ASLR) makes such a task more difficult, since it allows memory layout to be randomised when an application is started. The search of useful instructions must be done at runtime. But ASLR has been shown as not to be efficient enough for full protection, and can be bypassed, for example with blind ROP [2]. In a common playground, such as a JavaScript jail in a browser, process memory reading cannot be prevented and ASLR becomes less effective, as shown for example in the Spectre exploit [3].

For x86, solutions have been proposed [4]–[6] to protect an application against these attacks. These solutions guarantee that the execution will follow a legitimate control flow. However, they introduce more overhead in execution time than what can be accepted for general-purpose programs. Protecting only the relevant part of a program is an appealing way to reduce the induced overhead, which is done to some extents in [6]. The authors propose different selection criteria for level of protected code pointers and arbitrary jumps, giving some trade-off between performance and security.

Despite all this work, we lack a way to measure the effectiveness of these types of protection on security. It is difficult to compare two binaries, protected or not, with regard to a notion of ROP-class sensitivity. From a performance perspective, unified benchmarks are commonly used to evaluate the costs induced by the deployment of a protection. The efficiency of a given protection is more difficult to measure. Nothing exists to measure effectiveness beyond trying to write exploits, manually or with human intervention and this is hardly scalable. We develop this idea in Section III.

More generally, during the creation of an application, a lot of choices must be made. For example, we have to choose the language to write our application, the operating system it will be deployed on and, in some case, the hardware the application will support. The influence of such choices on the availability of control flow hijacks in the final binary is not known.

Brown *et al.* [7] have highlighted how debloating tools affect sensitivity to control flow hijack. They have shown that using the gadget number is not enough to define a security metric. Furthermore, they propose a binary production process that relies on a human to validate a significant security improvement. Such a process clearly does not scale and cannot be integrated in a software-automated build process.

While debloating influences the available gadgets in an application, this is probably the case as well for other steps of binary production. We want to know which tool or technology choices (compiler, language, etc.) have an effect, positive or negative, on these available gadgets. Instead of finding and exploring any combination of possible production tools for an application, we chose to select a wide range of systems. On those systems, we analyse available binaries to see if we can characterise the production process by the resulting available gadgets. We explore how different production setups affect the notion of gadget density. We investigate what is available to an attacker to craft a control flow hijack payload and what characterises a given binary with regard to code reuse exploits. The objective is to extract information from deployed binaries on living systems to provide recommendations for building applications that are more resistant to code reuse attacks. We study how the target execution environment for binaries affects the quantity and diversity of elements presented to write an exploit.

Then, the influence of environment on the quantitative measurement of code reuse availability is identified. The goal is to characterise how different steps of a process, from software creation to execution, could be leveraged to reduce the number of ROP components exposed by an application. This paper presents the method we used to define this quantitative measurement, which allows us to distinguish which binaries provide the most elements to write code reuse exploits.

This article starts by explaining how control flow hijack attacks are written in Section II, with a focus on the basic elements that compose these attacks. We then continue with the methodology used to retrieve these gadgets from binaries in Section IV. In Section V, we explore how gadgets are distributed among analysed binaries, in order to identify those that are used most often and study their diversity. Then, we analyse the disparity in binaries, given their hardware architecture or system environment (for example, the runtime Linux distribution). In Section V-D, we highlight which binary production steps influence the availability of control flow hijack components. In the end, we also show that a ROP chain crafted to target a given application built on two similar systems is unlikely to work on both.

II. Control flow hijacking

The idea behind control flow hijacking is the use of hardware processor operational behaviour to trick it out of the normal flow. One known method to hijack control flow is ROP, first described by Shacham [1]. ROP is a paradigm which allows generating a completely new application using the existing set of instructions of a given software. Exploits written with ROP need an entry point to start the attack, as detailed at the end of this section, in the threat model paragraph. Examples given in this section use the x86 family architecture but other architectures can be targeted by these attacks.

A program can be decomposed into multiple sequences of instructions linked by control flow instructions defining where the execution continues. These instructions can be function calls, system calls, jumps or returns.

During a control flow hijack, addresses used by control flow instructions are corrupted to divert the flow toward `libc` functions – for `return-to-libc` attacks. Return oriented programming uses small subsets of available code instead of full functions. These subsets are called gadgets. For example, `mov rdi, qword ptr [rbx]; call rdi` is a gadget found in some x86_64 applications.

ROP is the construction of an application by chaining gadgets together, effectively using only present and legitimate code. A ROP chain is created by corrupting the memory with a sequence of addresses pointing toward such elements. If the execution stack is corrupted, a `return` instruction is used to chain the gadgets. On hardware architecture without this `return` instruction, other instructions are used to build similar hijacks of a program execution. These constructions are shown for x86 and SPARC in [8] and for ARM in [9].

While the term ROP is used only for `return`-terminated gadgets, COP (Call-Oriented Programming) is for `call`-terminated ones and JOP (Jump-Oriented Programming) is for `jmp`-terminated ones. We also consider system call gadgets in our statistical analysis, amongst all other gadgets. Non-control data flow hijacks are out of the scope of this paper.

Threat Model: In the context of an attack following the ROP paradigm, few basic hypotheses are made on what intruders can do. The capabilities given to them are arbitrarily read in the process binary, which is not a strong hypothesis. For writing, we assume W XOR X is enforced, meaning that writing and executing are mutually exclusive. We also make the assumption that the executable part of a given program cannot be corrupted, but any write that does not violate this property is available. We also assume that a memory corruption allowing a ROP chain execution to be started is available. If the application is written in a memory-safe language, a side channel attack – either hardware or software – can be used to initiate the chain. We also make the assumption that attackers have an idea of what they attack, and have some knowledge on which gadgets they can find, expecting that hardware architecture is known.

III. Related work

In a first approach, we looked for a measurement of ROP effectiveness, apart from Turing-completeness of the set of gadgets found, which has been demonstrated if code base is sufficient enough, like the standard C library [8]. The objective here is to look at how different protections measure their results, not for performance overhead introduced but regarding ROP gadget availability.

Schwartz *et al.* proposed Q [10], a tool that hardens any ROP exploit to be resistant to ASLR. The tool effectiveness is proven by testing on which program they can construct a chain. Based on semantic analysis of gadgets without side effects, they managed to construct a chain automatically on a large set of `/usr/bin` of a given Linux system. However, the only metric that is used to measure the sensitivity of a given binary is the success of their tool to craft a chain. They also provide a statistical study on semantic gadgets available in their surveyed binaries, with just a short discussion.

Dullien *et al.* proposed another tool to look for gadgets in cross-platform environments [11]. The effectiveness of their solution is demonstrated by checking the Turing-completeness of the gadget set found in one binary on three different ARM platforms. The chosen binary is a core library linked with most applications and no other measurement is proposed.

Keromytis *et al.* published a protection against ROP [12] on a part of the binary. The published tool is evaluated in terms of both performance and security. The efficiency of the protection is tested using known software to create ROP payloads and gadgets, Q [10] and Mona [13]. They used two different results to evaluate the effectiveness of the protection. The first one is the ability to craft a chain automatically with these tools on the protected binary. The second one is the count of gadgets which were found by the two softwares and which are removed in the protected part of the binary.

In a similar way, published protections like [14], [15] or debloating techniques [16] often use either automatic crafting failure as an effectiveness measurement, with either Q [10], ROPgadget [17] or a custom tool. The default crafted chain is a shell spawning, but the failure or success of the craft on a given binary does not provide much information about its protection. Another chain, which brings as much harm, could be potentially (hand)crafted without being detected by this method of evaluation. The second method used to evaluate protections is the enumeration of available gadgets and reduction observed before and after the protection in question is applied. To do so, either Q output is used or custom processes are built. Even when a common tool is used, methods of comparison differ, implying some lack of common ground with respect to security benchmarks.

IV. GADGET DENSITY MEASUREMENT

A gadget is a sequence of instructions terminated by a jump, as defined earlier. For our analysis, a gadget is at most five instructions long, including the jump, following [8]. Furthermore Homescu *et al.* [18] have shown that one-byte instructions can be enough to achieve Turing-completeness. Therefore, all subsequences of a gadget are relevant. So for a five-instruction long gadget, all sub-gadgets of one up to five instructions are counted as different gadgets. As a result, each control flow instruction can generate up to five different gadgets. A gadget of size one is limited to a control flow instruction. For example, **call** `rdi;` can be used alone if a preceding gadget in the chain already set the content of the register `rdi` to a desired value. We also want to keep them for checking control flow instruction diversity. The basic `ret` instructions are not considered, as such gadgets are not relevant (i.e., they do nothing).

In this article, gadget classification is purely based on opcodes. Two gadgets that are similar semantically but different syntactically are considered distinct in the measurement. For example, **pop** `rax; ret` and **pop** `rbx; ret` are distinct.

The semantic analysis of gadgets is outside of the scope of this study. It has been demonstrated [10] that some arithmetic gadgets can be chained in order to create missing stores, load or any other needed gadgets. All gadgets are treated equally in the scope of this analysis whether they produce side effects or are just not usable at all.

Different metrics are used in this comparison. To fairly compare binaries of different sizes, the number of gadgets found in a binary is normalised with the size of its executable section. We define two densities with these measurements: unique gadget density, which represents the number of distinct gadgets present in a binary, and total gadget density, which includes all occurrences of each gadget in an executable file.

These metrics are used to identify how easy it is to attack a binary using control flow hijacking, given its production context. The context is composed of hardware architecture at first, completed by its target environment and its creation process. This creation process is decomposed to identify the role that each step plays in the evolution of the gadget density of a binary.

Methodology: The search for gadgets in a binary is done using a tool, ROPgadget [17], based on the library `Capstone` for assembly parsing. Even though some architectures are not supported by the highest-level tool we used, adding support for more instructions in the future is not excluded, as the library supports many more hardware platforms. On top of that, we have developed software for data aggregation and process automation, which enables an easy process to integrate more binaries for analysis, or to extract some data subsets.

V. EXPERIMENTS

This section contains an analysis of how gadgets are distributed in a binary, and of how different binaries react regarding the characteristics of gadgets exposed to an attacker.

Analysed binaries come from different Linux distributions and platforms. All binaries from `/usr/bin` are used. Most systems have various applications installed, from system utilities to window managers or web servers. We tried to have a lot of diversity in target usage of these applications to avoid any bias that may exist, for example due to applications needing more I/O accesses. All analysed binaries are the executables without their libraries, except if they are statically linked. If a program is statically compiled, we did not try to isolate what comes from the linked libraries and what is specific to the application, and we analyse it as a single binary. We excluded any standard libraries in this analysis, and other dynamically linked libraries. Given that `libc` and other libraries are so heavy, we assume that if someone wants to protect an application, they will either build without relying on such libraries, or will use static compilation. We focus on binary specific gadgets, to avoid an already known Turing-complete set.

The Linux distributions and platforms analysed – with the snapshot date when relevant – are the following: Fedora 26 (2018-01-19), Ubuntu 16.04 (2017-10-10), Debian Testing (2018-01-15), Debian 9.3 (2018-01-12), Gentoo (2017-09-07), Arch (2017-11-23), Buildroot, RISC & CISC (2018-02-05), Tar 1.30 (multiple compilation flag combinations) and Firefox (all release versions from 4.0 to 65.0b9).

Around 10 500 binaries went through this process, which was run on a dedicated platform. The dataset was created on an Intel® Xeon® CPU E5-2640 clocked at 2.4 GHz. Parsing the whole set of binaries takes around 48 hours to complete.

A. Binary Gadget Density Measurement

There is a correlation between the size of a binary and its number of gadgets. As shown in Figure 1, both unique gadgets and total gadgets increase quite linearly on a log scale with the size of the executable section (ES) of a binary. From really small binaries (less than 1 kB of ES), to large ones (more than 10 MB of ES), executable size is correlated with new gadgets, despite greater variation on small binaries. Analysed binaries present non-negligible variations in gadget count, in a window which is not correlated with ES size.

The interesting part is that while increasing in size, the number of unique gadgets keeps increasing. Intuitively, most gadgets would already be present in a binary when ES is above a certain threshold, and a slower increase or stagnation would be observed. Such behaviour is not observed, as binaries keep introducing new gadgets regularly as they grow in size. A normalised number of gadgets relative to its ES, in kB, has

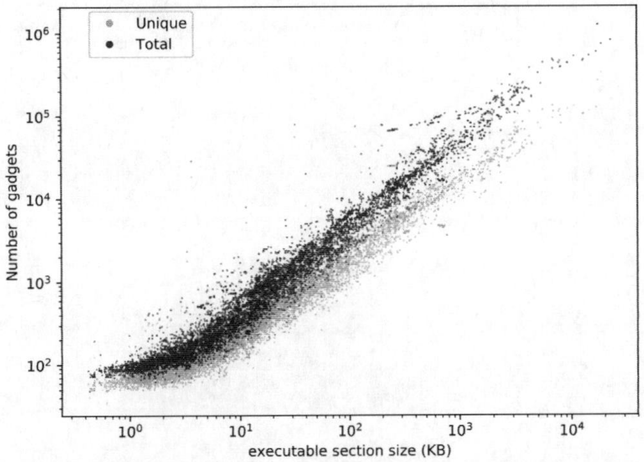

Figure 1. Gadgets found depending on the size of the executable sections

been taken as a first quantitative indicator for comparison of multiple binaries regarding ROP-class availability.

Both these total and unique gadget densities increase with size, as shown in Figure 2. Two tendencies stand out. First, a group of binaries has a ratio between the two densities around 1, meaning each gadget is rarely present more than once. Second, the binaries have a ratio that increases with their ES size. Amongst all these binaries, some have an extreme ratio, like `Quasselcore`, coming from Gentoo Linux, with a ratio of 6.2. The most impressive one is `gregorio`, from Arch Linux, which has a ratio of 8.89, around 3 times the average of the binaries with similar ES size. For example, coming from a different platform, ARM32, `grep` has a ratio of 1.17. Such a disparity in density ratio is limited to neither architecture change nor binary size. For instance, a gap is observed between `clang` (Arch Linux, x86_64), and `darcs` (Ubuntu 16.04, x86_64) with 5.2 and 2.2 for 23 MB and 19 MB of ES size, respectively.

On the code reuse availability that a binary could present, all binaries are not equal regarding what they provide to an attacker to craft an exploit. There are some extreme cases, but the global distribution shows a lot of binaries outside common trend. Moreover, an application can provide more or fewer gadgets. For example, `screen`, a binary available on all Linux systems analysed, does not have the same number of gadgets, either total or unique, and even has a changing ratio. On three architectures (SPARC v8 and leon, ARM32), the density ratio of this binary is around 1.20, 2.1 for ARM64, while it is around 2.50 on i386 & x86_64 architectures. These disparities are explored in the following sections, to observe how either system, in Section V-D, or hardware targets, in Section V-C, affect software on its control flow hijack elements.

B. Gadget representation

This section studies the diversity of gadgets amongst binaries on the x86_64 architecture. This architecture is selected because it represents 10 100 binaries out of 10 516. The goal is to determine how different a ROP chain would have to be, to execute the same attack on two distinct binaries.

Most available gadgets across all binaries are just manipulations that pop stack values into registers, *i.e.*, **pop** `r14;` **pop** `r15; ret`. Such gadgets are available in most binaries. There is only around 1 % of our binaries that do not contain these gadgets. Most gadgets are not shared amongst the binaries, with only 16 % of them in 2 or more binaries.

In our sample, some binaries expose a lot of the same gadgets. One gadget is used extensively by a few binaries, by a large margin compared to the other most popular gadgets. This gadget comes from binaries that share an interesting property, namely they are written with the Qt framework (like `Quasselcore`).

To evaluate the predominance of ROP gadgets in a binary compared to other kinds of gadgets, we isolated the ones that are terminated by any instruction except `return`. An excerpt of the results is shown in Table I. For this categorisation of gadgets, few stand out for their statistical usage. The two most used gadgets come exclusively from binaries of programs written in the programming language OCaml, with an above-average frequency. No C/C++ compiler generated these gadgets, nor did any other compiler used to produce one of the analysed binaries. We identified some but not all compilers used to generate our binaries, including `go`, `rust`, `gcc` or `clang`. This gadget can be used as a signature of OCaml binaries in our dataset.

The presence of these particular behaviours is not limited to these compilers and libraries. In a first attempt to identify software engineering choices influencing the gadget density, the production process of `tar` and a small graphical game have been modified to ensure a given compilation option set. Two compilers were used (`gcc` and `clang`) with the usual options. In this limited sample, the influence of a compilation option on gadget density does not depend on the compiled application. The effect of a given option has a similar effect on both applications. The choice of a compiler did result in different behaviour. This implies that the compilation process (the choice of the compiler and its options) cannot be neglected when designing an application to be less sensitive to code reuse, and should not depend on the application.

Since these results only concern the x86_64 architecture, it is planned to check whether such behaviour can be observed with other hardware architectures. For now, our sample size of binaries from other architectures is too small and too specific to be relevant for a comparison with x86_64 figures.

C. Hardware Influence

This section shows the impact that hardware architecture has on different measurements of gadgets in binaries. In Section V-B, we explained that x86_64 binaries were overrepresented. Therefore some bias may exist in the given results.

TABLE I. MOST USED GADGETS NOT TERMINATED BY A RETURN

Gadget	Nb of occurrence	Nb binaries	Avg Occurrence
mov rdi, **qword ptr** [rbx] ; **call** rdi	43 737	54	809.94
mov edi, **dword ptr** [rbx] ; **call** rdi	43 202	54	800.04
mov rdi, rbx ; **call** rax	22 559	698	32.32
mov edi, ebx ; **call** rax	22 536	786	28.67
add eax, edx ; **jmp** rax	16 770	1173	14.30
add rax, rdx ; **jmp** rax	16 624	1168	14.23
add edx, eax ; **jmp** rdx	15 132	455	33.26
add rdx, rax ; **jmp** rdx	15 003	398	37.70

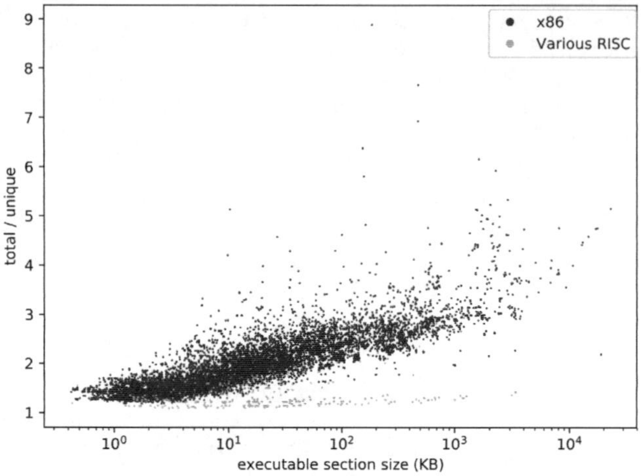

Figure 2. Ratio of total to unique gadgets by hardware architecture

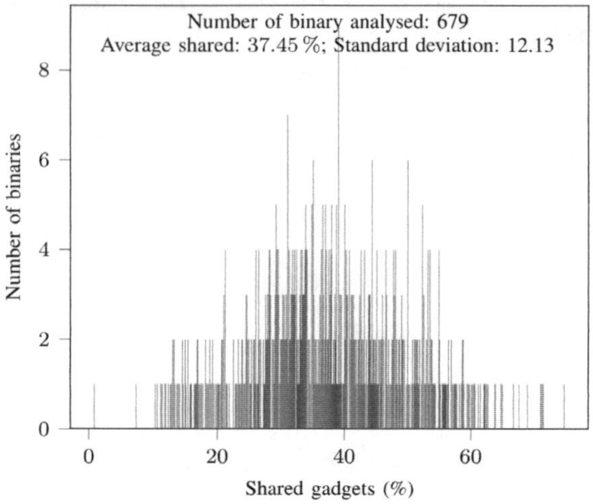

Figure 3. Percentage of shared gadgets on both Fedora and Ubuntu

Figure 2 presents the ratio between total and unique gadgets for all 10 516 binaries. It uses two colours to highlight the differences between the type of architectures, RISC –ARM (32 & 64 bits), SPARCv8– and CISC –x86 (32 & 64 bits). The main difference in behaviour between the two groups is the diversity of gadgets in RISC binaries. They rarely have a ratio above two, and the ratio does not increase with ES size. Binaries that target x86 family platform have a higher variance in gadget density ratio. The bigger the x86_64 binary ES size, the more often their gadgets appear.

`Buildroot` is a Linux distribution which targets embedded systems. A system can be built with a list of packages with a constant configuration from one hardware architecture to another. With a fixed compiler and its options, the only parameter that differs from build to build is the target architecture. Binaries are compared respectively on each architecture, to observe the differences in density.

Comparing these `Buildroot`, few differences are present between architectures. Sometimes the average of unique gadget density displayed by a system is more than twice the density on its counterpart, like between i386 and ARM32. An interesting result is that architecture family is not sufficient to classify a system with respect to its ROP availability. For example, even if there are more unique gadgets on i386 than ARM32, the comparison between their 64-bit counterpart gives an opposite result, with a lot more on ARM64. The availability of more instructions on ARM64 may be the reason for this evolution, but this is only a hypothesis that has to be explored further.

Even if what causes such behaviour is not known, it is certain that hardware architecture has a great effect on diversity and density in the quantitative measurement of ROP availability on these systems. Since gadgets cannot be compared across architectures on a syntax basis, semantics would be required to expand the discussion on hardware influence.

D. Disparities in deployment environments

In some Linux communities, security is the main focus, while in other performance or stability are privileged. This influences the choice of an application version and the production process of the binaries. For instance, in Fedora and Red Hat Enterprise [19], there are recommendations on which `gcc` compilation flags to use to publish a package. This section looks into different distributions to identify the influence that it can have on binary gadget density. We chose different types of distributions. Some use rolling release, where each application is updated with upstream updates, and others are stable or on a slow update cycle. We added some initially uninstalled packages to have better coverage for comparison.

For the purpose of comparison, only the content of `/usr/bin` is used in the five distributions. To compare two distributions, a binary is searched on both, and if it exists on only one, it is discarded from the result. If it is available on both distributions, the density of unique and total gadgets are compared. Then results are aggregated.

On average, only a small deviation can be observed between two distributions, around a few percent, and standard deviation between 25 and 30 percentage points increase or reduction in density on two distributions. Despite the majority of binaries showing little to no differences in density between two distributions, others bring up more questions, with up to three times more gadget density in one environment.

In some cases, there is only a small difference in version, like minor version or just a distribution patch that differs. On top of that, compilation flags and compilers can also vary between distributions. A lot of different behaviours are observed, since there is a huge sample of contributors involved in development and packaging. Compilation flags can be chosen for technical reasons, or due to distribution directives given to maintainers, or even users who change these themselves.

Having high average differences in density between two Linux distributions is not sufficient to evaluate the usability of a crafted chain on a similar binary from one to the other. A program available on both systems may contain different gadgets even if it exposes a similar density. Figure 3 presents the extent to which a Fedora desktop distribution and its Ubuntu counterpart share gadgets.

First, with only 37 % (around 600 gadgets) of shared gadgets on average between two distributions for a binary, the ability to create an easily distributable chain becomes compromised. An attack would probably have to use different gadgets for each target distribution. The low re-usability of a given chain is reinforced by the fact that only a few binaries between systems have up to 75 % shared gadgets, and way more than half of those analysed do not even reach 50 %. Few variations in a software production process can result in enough variations to reduce the portability of a code reuse exploit.

E. Results

These experiments have shown multiple parameters that have a significant influence on gadget density. A wide disparity of density amongst binaries is observed. Interestingly, the bigger a binary gets, the more unique gadgets it has.

We have also seen that despite gadgets being widely available on all hardware architectures, gadget availability is influenced by these architectures. Specifically, RISC architectures tend to have a gadget available only once per binary.

The results also highlighted the fact that the whole production environment has a role in the creation of gadgets. Some impactful steps are, amongst others, the choice of the source language, its compiler and the compilation options. This step can reduce or increase density, but most importantly they affect the variety and type of gadgets one can find in a binary. This fact is reinforced by the disparity in gadgets found in two binaries from the same application produced for distinct environments, shown in the last section. As a consequence, it is very unlikely to be able to port a given ROP chain at a low cost from a system to another.

VI. Conclusion and Future Work

In this paper, using a statistical analysis, we highlighted the influence of the binary production process on the number and density of gadgets. While this does not provide a direct security metric, it shows that code reuse has to be taken into account at an early stage of application design. Understanding what impacts the number of gadgets may lead to better protection, a more suitable protection, or one with less overhead.

The next step to expand this work is to consider the semantics of gadgets, to check whether each design decision has the same effect on density for gadgets with similar semantics. We have started to work on a measurement of semantic diversity, to ease the comparison of binaries. We also plan to improve the dataset of analysed programs, with more diverse source languages, and complete the dataset with more RISC binaries. We have seen limitations of our dataset with respect to hardware architecture in Section V-C, with the over-representation of x86_64. The diversity of gadgets has been inspected only with this architecture. We will expand this analysis to other available architectures. We plan to complete the study on compilation options, compilers and languages, started in Section V-B, with, for example, the addition of applications written in a memory-safe language like `rust`. The enhancement of the dataset is important to confirm what is shown on a small scale here. It would help confirm that other systems (POSIX compliant or not) behave differently than those in Section V-D. With enough information on what impacts the number of gadgets, an application could be built with guidelines to become less sensitive to code reuse exploits.

Acknowledgments

This research is supported by the Chair of Naval Cyber Defense, funded and supported by Ecole navale, ENSTA Bretagne, IMT Atlantique, Thales and Navale Group.

We also thank Pierre-Henri Horrein for his support during his work at IMT Atlantique.

References

[1] H. Shacham, "The geometry of innocent flesh on the bone: Return-into-libc without function calls (on the x86)," in Proceedings of the 14th ACM Conference on Computer and Communications Security, ser. CCS '07. New York, NY, USA: ACM, 2007, pp. 552–561.

[2] A. Bittau, A. Belay, A. Mashtizadeh, D. Mazières, and D. Boneh, "Hacking blind," in 2014 IEEE Symposium on Security and Privacy, May 2014, pp. 227–242.

[3] P. K. et al., "Spectre attacks: Exploiting speculative execution," CoRR, vol. abs/1801.01203, 2018.

[4] M. Abadi, M. Budiu, U. Erlingsson, and J. Ligatti, "Control-flow integrity," in ACM Conference on Computer and Communication Security (CCS), Alexandria, VA, November 2005, pp. 340–353.

[5] T. Coudray, A. Fontaine, and P. Chifflier, "Picon: Control flow integrity on LLVM IR," in Symposium sur la sécurité des technologies de l'information et des communications (SSTIC), 2015.

[6] V. Kuznetsov, L. Szekeres, M. Payer, G. Candea, R. Sekar, and D. Song, "Code-pointer integrity." in OSDI, vol. 14, 2014.

[7] M. D. Brown and S. Pande, "Is less really more? why reducing code reuse gadget counts via software debloating doesn't necessarily lead to better security," arXiv preprint arXiv:1902.10880, 2019.

[8] R. Roemer, E. Buchanan, H. Shacham, and S. Savage, "Return-oriented programming: Systems, languages, and applications," ACM Trans. Inf. Syst. Secur., vol. 15, no. 1, Mar. 2012, pp. 2:1–2:34.

[9] T. Kornau, "Return oriented programming for the arm architecture," Master's Thesis, Ruhr-Universität Bochum, 2010.

[10] E. J. Schwartz, T. Avgerinos, and D. Brumley, "Q: Exploit hardening made easy," in USENIX Security Symposium, 2011.

[11] T. Dullien, T. Kornau, and R.-P. Weinmann, "A framework for automated architecture-independent gadget search," in Proceedings of the 4th USENIX Conference on Offensive Technologies. Berkeley, CA, USA: USENIX Association, 2010.

[12] V. Pappas, M. Polychronakis, and A. D. Keromytis, "Smashing the gadgets: Hindering return-oriented programming using in-place code randomization," in 2012 IEEE Symposium on Security and Privacy, May 2012, pp. 601–615.

[13] Corelan team, "Mona," 2013, https://github.com/corelan/mona (last accessed on 18/09/2019).

[14] J. Hiser, A. Nguyen-Tuong, M. Co, M. Hall, and J. W. Davidson, "Ilr: Where'd my gadgets go?" in 2012 IEEE Symposium on Security and Privacy, May 2012, pp. 571–585.

[15] X. Chen, H. Bos, and C. Giuffrida, "Codearmor: Virtualizing the code space to counter disclosure attacks," in Security and Privacy (EuroS&P), IEEE European Symposium on. IEEE, 2017, pp. 514–529.

[16] G. Mururu, C. Porter, P. Barua, and S. Pande, "Binary debloating for security via demand driven loading," arXiv preprint arXiv:1902.06570, 2019.

[17] J. Salwan, "ROPgadget tool," 2012, http://shell-storm.org/project/ROPgadget (last accessed on 18/09/2019).

[18] A. Homescu, M. Stewart, P. Larsen, S. Brunthaler, and M. Franz, "Microgadgets: Size does matter in turing-complete return-oriented programming," in Proceedings of the 6th USENIX Conference on Offensive Technologies, ser. WOOT'12. Berkeley, CA, USA: USENIX Association, 2012, pp. 7–7.

[19] F. Weimer, "Recommended compiler and linker flags for gcc," https://developers.redhat.com/blog/2018/03/21/compiler-and-linker-flags-gcc (last accessed on 18/09/2019).

Zero Stars: Analysis of Cybersecurity Risk of Small COTS UAVs

Dillon Pettit
Graduate Cyber Operations
Air Force Institute of Technology
Dayton, Ohio, USA
email: Dillon.Pettit@afit.edu

Rich Dill
Dept of Computer Engineering
Air Force Institute of Technology
Dayton, Ohio, USA
email: Richard.Dill@afit.edu

Scott Graham
Dept of Computer Engineering
Air Force Institute of Technology
Dayton, Ohio, USA
email: Scott.Graham@afit.edu

***Abstract*—Commercial off the shelf small Unmanned Aerial Vehicle (UAV) market has grown immensely in popularity within the hobbyist and military inventories. The same core mission set from the hobbyists directly relates to global military strategy in the modern age, with priority on short range, low cost, real time aerial imaging and limited modular payloads. These small devices have the added perks of a small cross section, low heat signature, and a variety of transmitters to send real-time data over short distances. As with all new advances within the technological fields, security is a second-thought to reaching the market as soon as viable. New research is showing growing exploits and vulnerabilities, from individual small UAVs guidance and autopilot controls to the mobile ground station devices which may be as simple as a cellphone application. Research calls producers to fix and engineer the small UAVs to protect consumers, but consumers are left in the dark to the protections installed when buying new or used vehicles. At current date, there is no marketed or accredited risk index for small UAVs, but current research in similar realms of traditional Information Technologies, Cyber-Physical Systems, and Cyber Insurance give insight to significant factors required for future small UAV risk assessment and prioritize lessons learned. In this research, three fields of risk frameworks are analyzed to determine applicability to UAV security risk and key components that must be analyzed by a proper UAV framework. This analysis demonstrates that no adjoining field's framework can be directly applied without significant loss of fidelity and that further research is required to index risks of UAVs.**

Keywords*—*UAV; cybersecurity; quantitative; risk assessment; COTS.

I. INTRODUCTION

Cybersecurity is the Herculean task to prevent all adversarial attacks over Information Technology (IT) devices and errors that release or lose information deemed valuable to an organization or individual. As computer devices have exploded in variety and distribution around the globe, the protection task has grown and absolute security has become accepted to be a myth, though due diligence has been seen to reduce and delay incidents. IT devices have diverged into a multitude of subcategories, including Cyber-Physical Systems (CPSs) and further subsection Small Unmanned Aerial Vehicles (sUAVs). While many techniques used to map and defend IT may be extended to sUAVs, CPSs in general have significant differences in internal architecture, external networking, and overall mission sets that effect how effective and important common techniques are to cybersecurity. One aspect of cybersecurity is risk categorization of individual devices and the conglomeration on a network, which relies on common rating measures for comparison. IT devices still struggle with communication of security characteristics, though certain brands have made strides to separate themselves from the market share. As new vulnerabilities and exploitations accumulate for sUAVs, the industry will find the consumer base increasing in desire for quick and equal rating to make purchasing decisions based on their planned mission set.

Unmanned Aerial Vehicles (UAVs) have been historically built for military applications and continued by hobbyist enthusiasm. By definition, UAV includes any device that can sustain flight autonomously, which separates it from similar sub-cultures of Remotely Piloted Vehicles (RPVs) and drones [1]. UAVs are usually able to either maintain a hover or move completely via computer navigation, whereas RPVs require control instructions throughout flight and drones have limited mission and sophistication [1]. The first UAV is most likely to be considered a kite or balloon that could maintain flight when tied off and have some control input from the ground. Cameras were first attached to kites in 1887 by Douglas Archibald as a form of reconnaissance and William Eddy used the same contraption during the Spanish-American War for reconnaissance [1]. As UAV operations and innovations continued through the Vietnam War, Desert Storm, and especially the global war on Terror, the size, mission, and shape of UAVs have evolved to support military needs. Criminal uses have also grown with UAV prevalence with ingenious modifications matching latest exploits [2]. The market share of small UAVs is made up of 70% DJI brand, followed by 7% Parrot, 7% Yuneec [3], showing a strangle hold of Chinese controlled manufacturers for consumers to take note.

UAVs take a multitude of forms and designs based on mission and user base, from hand-held copters to jet-powered light aircraft. For sUAV, all follow the general component break out as seen in Figure 1, with four common components on the device and a ground station of some sort. The Basic System is a generalized term for the Operating System (OS), which is usually coded by brand per vehicle and allows near real time control. The weapon component has been seen within military operations, though the vast majority of sUAVs are used for military or hobbyist reconnaissance with the sensor component. As defined for UAV, some form of autonomous control will be built into the vehicle's navigation. The ground station is split into the Operators component and Communication links, though, with sUAVs, these are typically contained within the same device, a tablet or laptop.

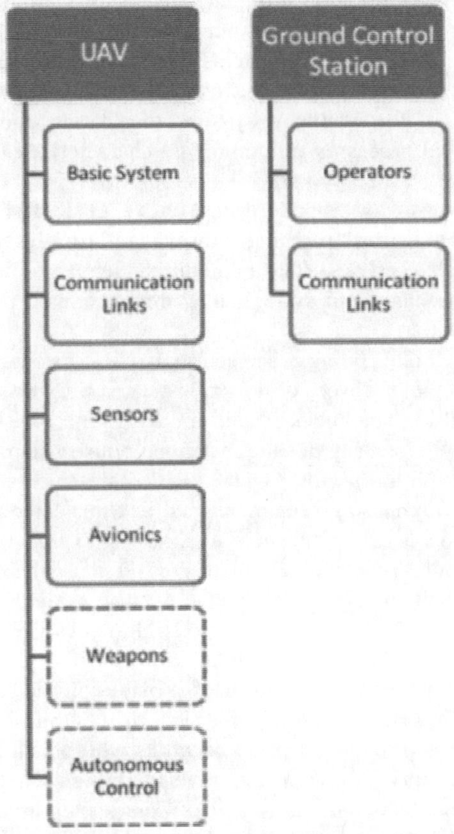

Fig. 1. Components of Typical UAV [4].

The exact definitions between sizing tiers have not been standardized between countries though, practically speaking, they consist in some format of very small, small, medium, and large. Very small UAVs exist at a miniaturization of aerodynamics that result in very low Reynolds numbers, meaning the wing interacts with the air more similarly to a fin through water due to viscosity, and are usually less than 20 inches in any dimension. Small UAVs tend to be a range of popular model aircraft used by hobbyists and have at least one dimension greater than 20 inches. While shorter in range, their size allows for access or angle of attack by altitude not normally available to individuals. Medium and Large UAVs are too large for an individual to carry and may even use full runways like light aircraft, which allows for heavier payloads and greater mission duration. sUAVs fly by the same aerodynamics as manned aircraft using lift and drag, plus control for pitch, roll, and yaw. Their internal architecture, however, differs greatly by removing the human pilot directly from the vehicle. Instead of a pilot and sensors, sUAVs are controlled by varying autonomy of their autopilot. Autopilots vary greatly by manufacturer, with the most common DJI autopilots closed-source and their specific rules hidden [2].

The rest of the paper is structured as follows. Section II explores current common rating systems for traditional IT, Supervisory Control and Data Collection (SCADA), and Insurance markets with a focus on aspects that do translate to the sUAV inventory. Section III builds out from the conglomeration of related rating indexes the important aspects that are required for a sUAV specific cybersecurity rating. Section IV analyzes each of the fields for their applicability to small UAVs risk assessment for potential adaptation. We conclude our work in Section V.

II. Related Work

No current physical or cyber security accreditation exists for UAVs. Accreditation similar to the European and American automobile safety assessments, which use a number of stars to describe and compare the intrinsic safety quality for the vehicle, would meet the demand. Since no current process exists to calculate risk, quantitative or qualitative, for sUAVs, there are no star ratings present on the market to be assigned to any sUAV, much less compare models. Adding to the issue, aerial vehicles were engineered for operational effectiveness first then marketed with minimal consideration for adversarial interference. Cyber incidents with and against UAVs have been limited with the most well-known consisting of the Iranian incident [4] and current research into hacking UAV controls. While the debate is still out on whether the United States RQ-170 was captured by Electronic Warfare (EW) or cyber means [4], the incident highlights the vulnerability of UAVs in a combat zone and the need for security in future models to maintain integrity for mission success. With 15,000 UAVs being sold in the United States every month as of 2015 [5], the availability and use of exploitations on these devices is expected to also rise as effort to reward ratio grows. Research into the vulnerability of sUAVs has also increased with a multitude of research showing specific risk in areas of Denial of Service (DoS) [6], Global Positioning System (GPS) spoofing [7], and control hijacking [8]. No security specific components have been added to UAVs in response, other than patches and more secure software or additional navigational components for the autopilot to internally cross-check location.

A. Traditional Risk Assessment

UAVs are most simply flying computer systems. Traditional risk assessments have been around since the early 2000s [9] and have almost solely focused on business devices and networks. While Network Security Risk Model (NSRM) [10] and Information Security Risk Analysis Method (ISRAM) [9] are some of the oldest quantitative risk assessment models, Common Vulnerability Scoring System V3 (CVSSv3) is the most utilized today [11].

CVSSv3 is an "open framework for communicating the characteristics and severity of software vulnerabilities [12]." The score is based on three different metrics of a Base ranging from 0.0 to 10.0, tempered by Temporal and Environmental metrics. CVSSv3 is owned and managed by FIRST Inc. and is a heavy provider to the National Vulnerability Database

(NVD). CVSS first gained large-scale usage under their version 2 score which determined only a base score through metrics for Access Vector, Access Complexity, Authentication, Confidentiality Impact, Integrity Impact, and Availability Impact. Each metric was given a rating from up to three varying responses of severity. CVSSv2 was criticized heavily for vulnerability scoring diversity compared to experimental, lack of interdependence scoring of networks, and lack of correlation between proposed mitigations and actual score improvements [11]. CVSSv3 added mandatory components for Privileges Required, User interaction, and Scope, plus the temporal and environmental metrics to influence the overall score. The current version has grown in use for vulnerability scoring, but still struggles with high false positive rates, poor predictability of future incidents, high sensitivity in regards to Availability Impact compared to all other impacts, and is heavily influenced by software type [13]. Built from CVSSv3, NVD has been found to lack in predicting mean time to next vulnerability due to the Common Vulnerability and Exploitations (CVEs) recording poor and inconsistent data by vendor and an increasing trend across vendors of zero-days [14]. CVSSv3 is the starting point for determining known vulnerabilities present within a UAV, but the embedded nature of a component, the wide brand difference within a single UAV, and unique mission sets of UAVs mean CVSSv3 is not very likely to give a good perspective at actual risk.

B. Industrial CPS and SCADA

At the other end of the spectrum for security indexing, sUAVs could be related to larger CPSs which have recently seen a surge in research to secure their unique networks. Industrial CPS and SCADA have been utilized to gradually reduce required human interaction in safety-compromised work areas and in largely distributed networks. Physical sensors that used to require eyes to read, determine system state, and adjust actuators to keep processes within safety limits and manufacturing effectiveness, now are read by network adapters, ran through Programmable Logic Controller (PLC) that determine state, then send signals to actuators to finish the feedback loop. Human-Machine Interface (HMI) screens give real-time display of system state to allow minimum human interaction to keep our modern society running smoothly. SCADA systems are owned by corporations to produce or deliver their products to consumers, and therefore the networks are not the products directly as seen by home computers or even work stations which are most commonly modelled by IT networks. As CPS stations are utilitarian and usually connected to physical sensors for input, protection schemes need to adjust for their physical process monitoring, closed control loops, attack sophistication, and legacy technology [16]. The first two categories define differences in attack vectors for cyber to cyber or cyber to physical exploitation. Regular IT exploitation follows a typical path that ends at an IT node with information or is valuable in itself, but industrial CPS exploitation usually requires exploitation to continue further to influence physical processes to either ruin or shut down systems [17]. This leads to attack sophistication differences between IT and SCADA risk, since physical process manipulation via PLCs require intense understanding of systems that are only present in the operational world. While the attack vectors require unique background, the computer systems monitoring and running the physical processes are commonly characterized by legacy equipment with many known vulnerabilities. IT cybersecurity practices push for upgrade cycles on a regular basis to keep with manufactures' patching, however industrial systems do not upgrade nearly as often and require much larger investment capital to change out systems that are considered permanent fixtures.

Research into adding cybersecurity to CPS systems skyrocketed after the discovery of the sophisticated Stuxnet virus in a nuclear plant. The nuclear plant in question has been studied, with its cybersecurity posture matching industry standards and much of the IT standards [18]. Risk assessments building from this impetus and for more than just nuclear realm have been trying to grasp the new methods to exploit processes. Most standardized methods merely cover the cyber to cyber and physical to physical exploitation, which arguably cover the easiest and most common historical attacks [19]. Stuxnet introduced publicly the possibilities of cyber to physical exploitation while little is known of possible physical to cyber vectors. To cover the cyber to physical risk, the most common technique is through Bayesian networks with attach trees and Markov chains [20]. A major drive to Bayesian networks is the complex states that physical processes may enter, which differ on Mean Time to Shut Down (MTTSD). While the probabilities to reach across the IT network to the PLCs follow well-documented methods and means through NVD or CVSSv3, detection and vectors at the PLCs require expert weighting and most likely proprietary input [19]. This method for a rating has been worked out for the nuclear industry in the form of Cyber Security Risk Index (CSRI) where all the possible physical sensor states have been propagated and the penetration testing is impossible for other methods of rating risk [21]. Detection before shut down is limited within industrial CPS to IT Intrusion Detection Systems (IDSs) that are built to overcome the unique aspects within industrial networks [16]. Even with research progressing to better characterize the risk statically and dynamically present in industrial CPS, there are no open-source rating systems in circulation, though cybersecurity companies specializing in control systems are starting to use them to better define current risk and prioritize defensive actions. While a SCADA risk index has potential for use within the UAV community, the lack of open-source index, smaller scale, and shorter lifespan of systems reduce direct applicability to sUAVs.

C. Cybersecurity Insurance

As a growing variation of quantitative cyber risk, insurance policies have been diverting some of the risk of exploitation since 1997 when the Internet use globally was only 1.7% of the population [22]. Insurance companies function on a strategy of taking premiums upfront to cover the risk of failure in the

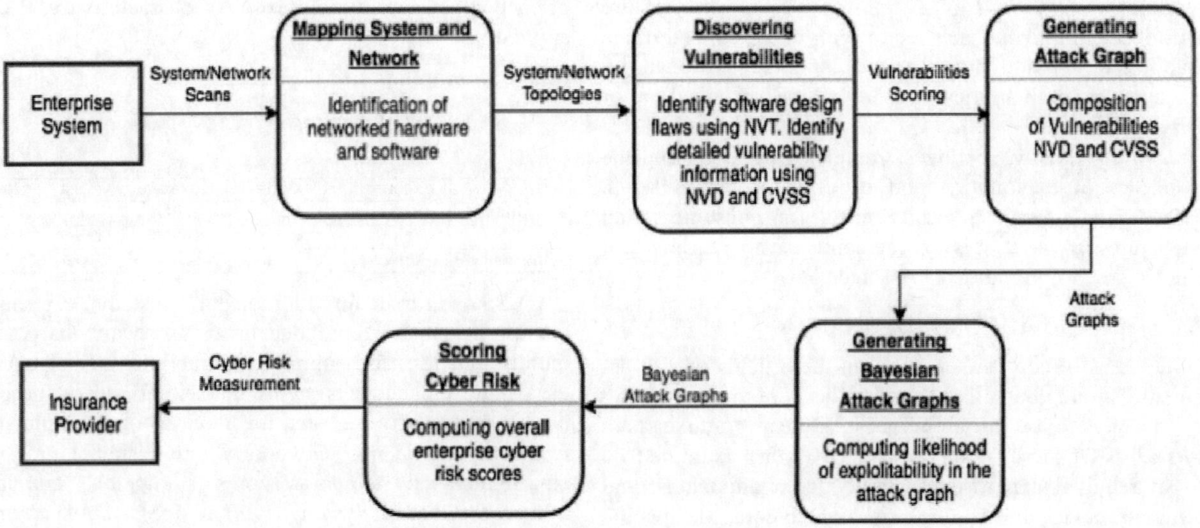

Fig. 2. Five phases of the Cyber Risk Scoring and Mitigation (CRISM) tool [15].

future and spread out the cost for the user, whether for disaster, health care, or cyber attack. The Internet has since exploded in size with the total cyber market estimated at $3 to 3.5 billion in 2017 [23], with cyber crimes costing the global economy an estimated $450 billion in 2016 [24]. The companies that issued the total cyber insurance premiums totaling $1.35 billion in 2016 [25] did so based more on an abstract perception of risk due to a lack of historical data to determine probability and actual monetary damage for previous attacks, especially when the damage is information theft or leakage [26]. The most common and simple equation for insurance is based on historical average of cost per incident times the probability of incident in the near future [15], which requires the very information that is lacking or obscured for cyber incidents. To reconcile this discrepancy in information, several research models have been developed to validate insurance investment and fewer have published methods of quantitative risk indexes. Cyber insurance is possible and good for security as long as the premiums imposed are tied directly to self-protection strategies employed by the organization [27]. For quantifying this risk versus protections, the largest issue is not previous historical data which will continue to grow over time, but mapping all possible attack vectors in the insured system which requires knowledge of all locations of valuable information and employee accesses and habits [28].

The most promising methods to grasp the state of a network are presented by the Cyber Risk Scoring and Mitigation tool (CRISM) which operates as a specially designed IDS [15]. This method used in cyber insurance is designed for IT networks where the CVSSv3 and NVD provide comprehensive insight to network vulnerabilities and usage probabilities, though was inspired by driver insurance programs where users installed a device to provide additional information to the insurance company for lower premiums. The ability to add an IDS to a Commercial Off The Shelf (COTS) UAV is most likely impossible due to size or tampering with warranty, therefore CRISM can not be directly applied to UAV risk indexing. However, their analytic model is very promising in its flexibility to include varying components. As shown in Figure 2, CRISM has five phases.

1) Mapping: The first step is static analysis of the system to determine all components and links with all currently reported vulnerabilities. This mapping phase consists of determining the data and control links (if different) at a physical and protocol layer, operating system of both ground station and UAV, avionic and embedded systems controlling the UAV, and environment that the UAV lives in for connections and external (not necessarily adversary) radio waves.

2) Vulnerabilities: With all of the mapping laid out statically, the vulnerabilities that are known across all components are then expounded. At the communication links, vulnerabilities can consist of protocol flaws, susceptibility to jamming, and leakage of information. At the OS component, vulnerabilities are better laid out via CVSSv3 and NVD such that the software and hardware vulnerabilities are better reported. The navigation vulnerabilities are based on the probability of false signals being accepted and the combination of sensors relied on reduces risk. Sensors such as Inertial Navigational System (INS) that are much more difficult to spoof than GPS reduce the cyber risk of system, but only if properly checked by the autopilot and the programmed failure state.

3) Attack Vectors: With the mapping and tabulation of known vulnerabilities, attack vectors can be determined by common methods through the entire system and the probability of attacks can be estimated. Attack vectors can be initialized only at input ports, whether on ground station or UAV. Vectors are trimmed by forward progress and ability to cause an effect on the mission.

4) Bayesian Network (BN) Graphs: Bayesian networks are then utilized to build out each vector across nodes to determine probability of forward progress and exploitation probability either through probabilities chosen by the organization or experts in the field.

5) Scoring: Lastly, scoring is completed by tabulating the probabilities of exploitation and its effect to the mission. CVSSv3 does present a usable index for consumers and manufactures, however, it is a vulnerability severity assessment and not a direct correlation to risk indexing.

III. Methodology

Three areas of comparison between these fields of risk assessment that are generally recognized as core to determining viability are as follows: usability, cost, and ease-to-understand results [29]. Of these, usability will be further examined by traits of required expertise, flexibility to modifications, and coverage of device and network risk, which compose specific UAV risk components. These criteria should provide a more detailed view into the described fields before determining applicability.

Each of the fields specifically utilize their designated risk assessments simply for the reason that they work for their devices. These tools meet an understood baseline that they are effective, but fall short when sUAVs are the subject. Any assessment that meets, but does not have the potential to exceed this baseline, is rated "Yellow" per category. Within categories, it is possible for the field's tool to fall below this baseline and miss key components for a sUAV risk assessment tool, which would then be rated "Red". In the opposite manner, some fields that properly account for sUAV characteristics and calculate risk indices on par with with that field's specific devices are to be labelled "Green". A "Green" rating is not to insinuate that all sUAV risk is completely accounted for, but that the tool reaches its own performance baseline with UAVs also.

IV. Analysis

As seen from the build out of other markets' rating systems, the validity of the rating is based on how holistic the system is examined. The layout of components and a cybersecurity risk index for sUAVs requires additional consideration for adjacent devices and networks plus the environment that the device is operating in since sUAVs are mobile. With swarm research as a far end of connectivity of a sUAV, these flying computers use wireless communications that broadcast over the open air to connect to their ground station and to other UAVs. A rating needs to include some factor of the security of these other devices and the connection protocol that allows communications, especially if another ground station or UAV can gain operational control. The environment aspect is made of the inherit radio waves that may or may not interfere with communications and control of the UAV. The data link itself may be secure, but consideration for the country, locale, or altitude may change collision rate or noise on the channel and thus effect security. Table I shows analyzed applicability of each cybersecurity field to sUAV characteristics, if directly applied.

TABLE I
Index Applicability to Small UAVs.

	Expertise	Flexibility	Coverage	Cost	Readability
Traditional	Yellow	Red	Yellow	Yellow	Green
ICS	Yellow	Red	Green	Yellow	Red
Insurance	Yellow	Green	Yellow	Red	Green

CVSSv3 is built for traditional IT systems, especially for common computer components and software that the community can test and submit vulnerabilities. The sUAV field uses more embedded systems that either run on proprietary hardware or software, and the devices operate much more frequently on ad hoc networks where a simple modifier for environment and temporal scores is imprecise and lacking. Industrial Control System (ICS) and SCADA vulnerability tests take into account the physical aspects influenced by and can effect cyber devices as seen in sUAV, however the static and unique natures of SCADA systems show an underestimation for new exploits and most quantitative indices are close held by organizations selling services. Additionally, the unique fluidity of networking and device modification would require near continuous recalculation of risk or initial calculation for every configuration. The insurance-spawned CRISM shows theoretical promise, especially within its analytic approach, though the IDS portion needs adaptation to the UAV field before the tool would be truely useful. Since the market share is dominated by proprietary minded brands, the IDS in question may need to be network only, which will reduce its effectiveness but still provide live insight into the inherit risk. Many of the holes of CVSSv3 also carry over to the insurance field since the tool borrows heavily from the same IT databases for vulnerability assessment. While CVSSv3 and SCADA indices have more operational data backing approaches, CRISM requires additional research, data comparison, and marketing before being viable main-stream, which is where a sUAV risk index will be of greatest use to the consumers.

V. Conclusion and Future Work

Small UAVs do not have a quantitative risk assessment that meets the baseline of accuracy for their unique characteristics. Current risk assessments focus on either the standard desktop configurations of hardware and software as with the traditional CVSSv3 or the network with ICS and insurance's CRISM. Of the three fields, the CRISM tool shows promise for attaining fidelity on sUAVs, but would need significant work to adapt to the ad hoc wireless networking and UAV specific protocols. Connected, CVSSv3 requires significant addition of UAV vulnerability signatures to be useful.

Future work in the field of sUAV risk assessment requires the building of a quantitative equation for the flying devices or the adaptation from a parallel assessment, as discussed at length in this research. Analytical scoring of a sampling of UAVs then would provide validity to the assessment. It is unknown at this time if an analytic only scoring would provide the best results by providing ease of use in light of highly proprietary brands defining the market. A CRISM-like adaptation needs validation through either live testing on single and networked UAVs or at least hardware in the loop simulation. Hardware in the loop is vital to simulation with UAVs due to the physical responses of the system to cyber effects. Without considering the physical response, many of the detection methods of cyber to cyber and cyber to physical attacks are lost.

Scoring, at this point, is more for internal comparison, but the future expectation is to provide a medium for the manufacture or market to convey the risks inherent in different hardware and software configurations to consumers. By providing a single metric based on mission, the buyer may be better informed based on their individual level of risk acceptance, which may be then offset by insurance premiums. Until a risk assessment becomes accredited, consumers will be reliant on manufacturer advertisement and personal expertise to compare the risk being introduced to their mission sets.

ACKNOWLEDGMENT

Disclaimer: The views expressed in this paper are those of the authors and do not necessarily reflect the official policy or position of the Air Force, the Department of Defense, or the U.S. Government. PA Case Number: 88ABW-2019-2852.

REFERENCES

[1] P. G. Fahlstrom and T. J. Gleason, "History and overview," in *Introduction to UAV Systems*, 4th ed. West Sussex, United Kingdom: John Wiley Sons, Ltd, 2012, pp. 3–31.

[2] A. Roder, K.-K. R. Choo, and N.-A. Le-Khac, "Unmanned Aerial Vehicle Forensic Investigation Process: Dji Phantom 3 Drone As A Case Study," *Digital Investigations*, pp. 1–14, 2018. [Online]. Available: http://arxiv.org/abs/1804.08649

[3] Z. Valentak, "Drone market share analysis predictions for 2018: Dji dominates, parrot and yuneec slowly catching up," *Drones Globe*, 2017, [Retrieved September 2019]. [Online]. Available: http://www. dronesglobe. com/news/drone-market-share-analysis-predictions-2018

[4] K. Hartmann and K. Giles, "UAV exploitation: A new domain for cyber power," *International Conference on Cyber Conflict, CYCON*, vol. 2016-Augus, pp. 205–221, 2016.

[5] A. Karp, "Congress to hold uav safety hearing oct. 7," 2015, [Retrieved: September 2019]. [Online]. Available: http://atwonline.com/government-affairs/congress-hold-uav-safety-hearing-oct-7

[6] T. Vuong, A. Filippoupolitis, G. Loukas, and D. Gan, "Physical indicators of cyber attacks against a rescue robot," *2014 IEEE International Conference on Pervasive Computing and Communication Workshops*, pp. 338–343, 2014.

[7] D. P. Shepard, J. A. Bhatti, T. E. Humphreys, and A. A. Fansler, "Evaluation of Smart Grid and Civilian UAV Vulnerability to GPS Spoofing Attacks," *Ion Gnss 2012*, pp. 3591–3605, 2012.

[8] T. Reed, J. Geis, and S. Dietrich, "SkyNET: a 3G-enabled mobile attack drone and stealth botmaster," *Proceedings of the 5th USENIX conference on Offensive technologies (WOOT11)*, p. 4, 2011.

[9] B. Karabacak and I. Sogukpina, "Isram: Information security risk analysis method," *Computers Security*, vol. 24.2, pp. 147–159, 2005.

[10] M. H. Henry and Y. Y. Haimes., "Comprehensive network security risk model for process control networks," *Risk Analysis: An International Journal*, vol. 29.2, pp. 223–248, 2009.

[11] K. Scarfone and P. Mell, "An analysis of CVSS version 2 vulnerability scoring," in *2009 3rd International Symposium on Empirical Software Engineering and Measurement, ESEM 2009*, 2009, pp. 516–525.

[12] FiRST, "Common Vulnerability Scoring System V3," 2015, [Retrieved: September 2019]. [Online]. Available: https://www.first.org/cvss/cvss-v30-specification-v1.8.pdf

[13] A. A. Younis and Y. K. Malaiya, "Comparing and Evaluating CVSS Base Metrics and Microsoft Rating System," in *Proceedings - 2015 IEEE International Conference on Software Quality, Reliability and Security, QRS 2015*. Institute of Electrical and Electronics Engineers Inc., 2015, pp. 252–261.

[14] S. Zhang, X. Ou, and D. Caragea, "Predicting Cyber Risks through National Vulnerability Database," *Information Security Journal*, vol. 24, no. 4-6, pp. 194–206, 2015.

[15] S. Shetty, M. McShane, L. Zhang, J. P. Kesan, C. A. Kamhoua, K. Kwiat, and L. L. Njilla, "Reducing Informational Disadvantages to Improve Cyber Risk Management," *Geneva Papers on Risk and Insurance: Issues and Practice*, 2018.

[16] R. Mitchell and I.-R. Chen, "A survey of intrusion detection techniques for cyber-physical systems," *ACM Computing Surveys*, vol. 46, no. 4, pp. 1–29, 2014.

[17] A. J. Chaves, "Increasing Cyber Resiliency of Industrial Control Systems," *Thesis and Dissertations*, vol. 1563, 2017.

[18] A. Matrosov, E. Rodionov, D. Harley, and J. Malcho, "Stuxnet under the microscope," *ESET*, 2010.

[19] K. Huang, C. Zhou, Y. C. Tian, S. Yang, and Y. Qin, "Assessing the physical impact of cyberattacks on industrial cyber-physical systems," *IEEE Transactions on Industrial Electronics*, vol. 65, no. 10, pp. 8153–8162, 2018.

[20] S. Haque, M. Keffeler, and T. Atkison, "An Evolutionary Approach of Attack Graphs and Attack Trees: A Survey of Attack Modeling," in *International Conference on Security and Management*, 2017, pp. 224–229.

[21] J. Shin, H. Son, and G. Heo, "Cyber Security Risk Evaluation of a Nuclear I&C Using BN and ET," *Nuclear Engineering and Technology*, vol. 49, no. 3, pp. 517–524, 2017.

[22] B. Brown, "The ever-evolving nature of cyber coverage," 2014, [Retrieved: September 2019]. [Online]. Available: https://www.insurancejournal.com/magazines/mag-features/2014/09/22/340633.htm

[23] C. Stanley, "Cyber market estimate," 2017, interview: 2017-06-26.

[24] L. Graham, "Cybercrime costs the global economy $450 billion: Ceo," 2017, [Retrieved: September 2019]. [Online]. Available: https://www.cnbc.com/2017/02/07/cybercrime-costs-the-global-economy-450-billion-ceo.html

[25] InsuranceJournal.com, "Cyber insurance premium volume grew 35% to $1.3 billion in 2016," 2017, [Retrieved: September 2019]. [Online]. Available: https://www.insurancejournal.com/news/national/2017/06/23/455508.htm

[26] J. Yin, "Cyber insurance: Why is the market still largely untapped?" 2015, [Retrieved: September 2019]. [Online]. Available: http://www.aei.org/publication/cyber-insurance-why-is-the-market-still-largely-untapped

[27] J. Bolot and M. Lelarge, "Cyber Insurance as an Incentive for Internet Security," Tech. Rep.

[28] A. Panou, C. Xenakis, and C. Ntantogian, "RiSKi: A Framework for Modeling Cyber Threats to Estimate Risk for Data Breach Insurance," *Association for Computing Machinery*, 2017.

[29] I. Stine, M. Rice, S. Dunlap, and J. Pecarina, "A cyber risk scoring system for medical devices," *International Journal of Critical Infrastructure Protection*, vol. 19, pp. 32–46, 2017. [Online]. Available: https://doi.org/10.1016/j.ijcip.2017.04.001

A Study about FP-growth on a Distributed System Using Homomorphic Encryption

Mayuko Tanemura

Master School of Computer Science
Ochanomizu University
Tokyo, Japan
Email: mtanemura@is.ocha.ac.jp

Masato Oguchi

Ochanomizu University
Tokyo, Japan
Email: oguchi@is.ocha.ac.jp

***Abstract*—Large data collections, such as big data, are utilized and analyzed in business.Because large-scale data calculations require a computer system with high processing power, it is practical to outsource the processing to an external server. However, especially when consigning confidential data, such as personal information, it is important to take measures against information leakage. There are various methods, such as data anonymization processing for privacy protection, but in this research, as a method of data confidentiality protection, a Fully Homomorphic Encryption (FHE) that can be calculated in an encrypted state is used. As in a previous study, P3CC (Privacy Preserving Protocol for Counting Candidates) is used, which applies FHE to a client-server type system that performs frequent pattern mining with the Apriori algorithm. To implement this system, the Apriori algorithm is changed to the FP-growth (frequent pattern growth) algorithm in our research work, and the results are compared with those of the existing method using the Apriori algorithm.**

Keywords–Fully Homomorphic Encryption; Data Mining; Distributed System.

I. INTRODUCTION

Big data and large-scale data have been utilized in various fields of business. To perform calculations that deal with large-size data, a computer system with a high processing power is required. When it is difficult to provide such a system, external computing resources, such as the cloud can be used. In that case, it is necessary to take sufficient measures to prevent the leakage of the information to be transmitted during the consignment processing of data, such as personal information and medical data, for which it is necessary to ensure confidentiality. When the processing of confidential information is outsourced, it is possible to perform addition and multiplication calculation processing without showing plaintext data to the consignee server by using fully homomorphic encryption (FHE). Therefore, there is an expectation that data can be entrusted even if transmitted by a server that is not reliable. As an application example of FHE, Liu et al.'s P3CC [1] performed the frequent pattern mining of transaction data by the Apriori algorithm; studies on speeding up the approach have also been conducted [2] [3], in addition to distributed processing using the FUP (Fast Update) algorithm [4], as described in Section IV. In this research, we implement the system of frequent pattern mining but with the part processed by the FP-growth algorithm instead of by Apriori, and we compare the results with those of previous studies. The remainder of this paper is organized as follows. Sections II and III introduce related technologies. In Section IV, some of the previous researches are shown. Sections VI and VII-A are about the experiment conducted in this research. Finally, in Section VIII, the conclusion and future plans are stated.

II. FULLY HOMOMORPHIC ENCRYPTION

A. Overview

Privacy homomorphism was firstly proposed by Rivest et al. [5]. They proposed privacy homomorphism as the property of being able to perform operations while being encrypted. FHE is an encryption method that combines the features of additive homomorphism and multiplicative homomorphism.

This approach has the function of a public key cryptosystem, and capabilities for the addition and multiplication of ciphertexts in an encrypted state are established. In other words, it is possible to manipulate the plaintext before it is decrypted by computing the ciphertexts. Therefore, by using FHE, there is an expectation that calculation processing can be outsourced without showing plaintext data to the outsourced server.

For FHE, Gentry proposed a lattice-based implementation method in 2009 [6]. In each ciphertext, random noise is added to increase the indecipherability of the encryption.

The problem is that the computational complexity of the process can be massive because of the large data size of the ciphertext and key, and the value of the noise increases each time the ciphertext is calculated. If the noise exceeds the threshold, the decryption becomes impossible. The noise value increases significantly, especially when performing multiplication. By performing a bootstrapping process, it is possible to refresh the noise of the ciphertext, but this process also requires a large amount of calculation.

B. Leveled FHE

Leveled FHE is an implementation of FHE that does not use bootstrapping, and it was proposed by Brakerski et al. [7]. Leveled FHE is a structure of perfect homomorphic cryptography that can evaluate the result of a logic circuit of fixed depth L. If the calculation logic circuit depth is small enough for the level given in advance, there is no need to do bootstrapping. This study uses Leveled FHE, so it does not use bootstrapping.

III. FREQUENT PATTERN MINING

Frequent pattern mining is a method aimed at extracting correlation rules from a large quantity of data. This study deals with transaction data.

In the frequent pattern mining used in this research, which item is included in each transaction is represented as a binary matrix. Frequent item sets are extracted based on whether the support value is greater than or equal to the given minimum support value. The support value of each item set is the ratio of the number of transactions including the item set to the total number of transactions. Apriori and FP-growth are typical algorithms for frequent pattern mining. The outline of each algorithm is provided below.

A. Apriori

Apriori algorithm was proposed by Agrawal et al. in 1993 [8]. Apriori is a breadth-first search algorithm that compares the support value III with the given minimum support value in order to acquire the list of frequent item set from size of 1. Apriori is used in the previous research described in Section IV. Even if there are few types of items, the number of possible combinations of items can be massive. To reduce the calculation amount, pruning is adopted. For example, if the support value of an item set of item length n is less than the minimum support value, it is determined that the pattern of item length $n + 1$ including the item set is not frequent anymore. The implementation of Apriori is relatively easy.

B. FP-growth

FP-growth is another algorithm used to extract frequent item sets. In contrast to Apriori, FP-growth is a depth-first search. The results of these two algorithms, the list of frequent itemsets, will correspond to each other. The process of FP-growth is different from Apriori in terms of the data structure; it uses tree-structured data to search for frequent itemsets. First, the database is scanned, and the transaction data are stored in the tree structure of a prefix tree called FP-tree. Then, frequent patterns are found by scanning the tree. It is different from Apriori in that it does not enumerate the frequent item set candidates. Depending on the data size and data characteristics, there is an expectation that the search can be made more efficient than Apriori, in which the enumeration of frequent items becomes a bottleneck. The implementation is also more complex than that of Apriori. FP-tree is defined as follows [9]:

1) It consists of one root labeled as "null", a set of item prefix subtrees as the children of the root, and a frequent-item header table.
2) Each node in the item prefix subtree consists of three fields: item-name, count, and nodelink, where item-name registers which item this node represents, count registers the number of transactions represented by the portion of the path reaching this node, and node-link links to the next node in the FP-tree carrying the same item-name, or null if there is none.
3) Each entry in the frequent-item header table consists of two fields, (1) item-name and (2) head of node-link, which points to the first node in the FP-tree carrying the item-name.

To construct an FP-tree, transaction data and minimum support values are needed as input data. To pick the frequent item sets, scan the constructed FP-tree recursively.

IV. PREVIOUS RESEARCH

An outline of the previous research on secure data mining using FHE is provided below. The algorithm for frequent pattern mining adopted in all of the previous research mentioned in this section is Apriori.

A. P3CC

P3CC is a secure method for a frequent pattern mining consignment system using FHE proposed by Liu et al. [1]. Comparing operations between ciphertexts are difficult when FHE is used. Therefore, when the values of ciphertexts need to be compared, they are sent back to the client machine. To reduce the data size of the ciphertext, the numbers of items and transactions are not encrypted, and only a binary matrix that represents which items each transaction includes is encrypted. Furthermore, adding dummy data on the client side prevents the guessing of plaintext data from the server.

B. Speedup of P3CC with Cipher Text Packing and Cipher Text Caching

Imabayashi et al. [2] proposed a method to speed up P3CC by introducing a packing scheme by Smart and Vercauteren [10]. The method reduced the amount of ciphertext and the multiplication of ciphertexts using ciphertext packing by encrypting multiple integers as a vector. As a result, the process achieved a 10-fold speedup compared to the case without packing. This method can be applied not only to Apriori, but also to secure search and other data mining algorithms. Then, they proposed a method of caching a ciphertext to reduce the space-time complexity of frequent pattern mining with FHE. It is shown that the proposed method can greatly reduce the execution time and memory usage of Apriori by P3CC, and the effect is larger when the data set is large or when a dummy set is added. In particular, when the number of transactions is 10,000, a 430-fold faster speed and 94.7 % memory usage reduction are realized compared to P3CC [3].

C. Implementation of P3CC in a distributed environment and speeding up update with FUP algorithm

Yamamoto et al. [4] implemented a secure data mining system using the FUP algorithm to speed up Apriori algorithm when the database is updated [4]. They also applied a master/worker-type distributed processing to speed up the system. Item set division was applied to the distributed processing method. As a result, the execution time of the recalculation when the FUP algorithm is introduced at the time of the database update can be shortened by approximately 3- to 4-fold compared with recalculation by the Apriori algorithm. Additionally, due to the decentralized processing, the calculation time on the master side is reduced according to the number of distributed machines.

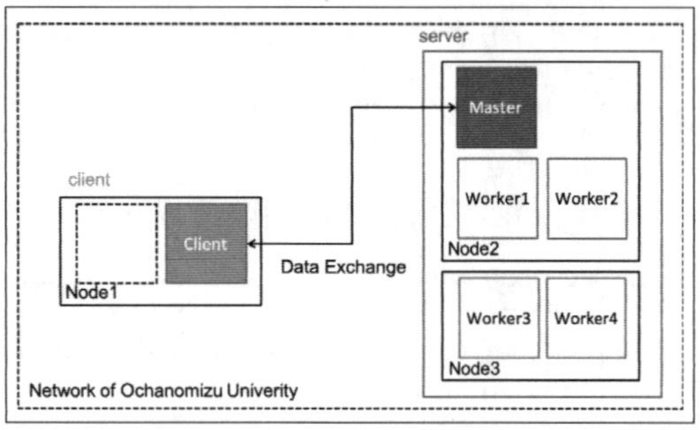

Figure 1. execution time when FP-growth was used (Client)

V. Implementation of Secure Frequent Pattern Mining

In this research, a system like the one presented Figure 1 is used. In this study, a master-worker (master-slave) distributed system is adopted for processing on the server. The number of workers is set from 1 to 4. Two algorithms of frequent pattern mining are used in this system: FP-growth and Apriori (from previous research). For both programs, we used ciphertext packing based on previous research [2] by Imabayashi et al. [2]. The program using Apriori is the one produced by Yamamoto et al. [4]. This system was implemented in C++, the library of the FHE is Helib [11], and the distributed/parallel processing library is MPI [12].

The following shows the processing for each system using the two types of algorithms.

A. Outline of processing using Apriori

The process is partially delegated to the server, as indicated in Section IV. The procedure is shown below.

1) Preparing data on the client
   a) Encrypt transaction data with FHE.
   b) Create candidate items and send them to the server.
2) Consigned processing on the server
   a) Receive encrypted data from client and calculate support value of item without decryption. Then, send the result back to the client. In this process, master-worker type distributed processing is performed.
3) Comparison with minimum support value on the client
   a) Receive file from the server
   b) Retrieve items whose support value is equal to or greater than the minimum support value.
   c) Return to procedure 1b and send the candidate whose item set size is one larger. Repeat until the number of candidates is 0.

B. Outline of processing using FP-growth

When using FP-growth, the procedure is similar to the process with Apriori in the first step. In this program, the calculation of the support value of the item, which is the first step of the construction of FP-tree, is consigned to the server, while the construction and scanning of the FP-tree are done on the client machine. Because it is necessary to perform many comparison operations to construct and scan an FP-tree, in this research, these processes were performed on the client. Even if the process on the client is not finished, the server ends the program after sending the support value calculation result to the client. The procedure FP-tree construction and scanning is shown below.

1) Preparing data on the client
   a) Encrypt transaction data with FHE.
   b) Create candidate items and send them to the server.
2) Consigned processing on the server
   a) Receive encrypted data from client and calculate support value of item without decryption. Then, send the result back to the client. In this process, master-worker type distributed processing is performed.
3) FP-tree construction on client
   a) Receive file from the server.
   b) Retrieve items whose support value is equal to or greater than the minimum support value.
   c) Sort the items in the order of occurrence and recreate the transaction excluding the items that are not frequent.
   d) Construct an FP-tree.
4) FP-tree scanning on the client
   a) Scan the constructed FP-tree and output the result.

VI. Experiment

A. Experiment outline

The client program and server program were run on each computer using two computers in the same network. We confirm the execution time by changing the minimum support value and the number of transactions.

B. Experiment environment

The performance of the computer used in the experiment is shown in Table I.

TABLE I. DETAILS OF THE MACHINE USED IN THE EXPERIMENT

OS	CentOS 6.9
CPU	Intel® Xeon® Processor E5-2643 v3 3.6 GHz 6 core 12 threads
Memory	512 GB

One machine of the type shown in the Table I was used as a client and a server. On the server side, as shown in Section V, master-worker type distributed processing is performed, but in this experiment, it is fixed to one. Additionally, the worker runs on the same machine as the master.

C. Experiment method

1) Investigation of the lowest possible level for experimental data: For each transaction data, when minimum support value is 0.01, an experiment was conducted with the possible lowest level. In this case, the lowest level represents the lowest one that the cyphertext can be normally decoded until the end of the calculation. The level was specified by trial. In all experiments in this study, the level is set to 17 in Apriori and 3 in FP-growth. These values of the level are the lowest that can be applied to each method. If the levels are lower than these values, execution will be end with a decode error.

2) Measurement of Execution time: The execution time was measured for each combination of input data and minimum support value.

3) Measurement of Resource Usage: CPU and memory usage are measured by dstat command.

D. Input data

The input data in this experiment were artificially created. Data generation was performed using IBM Quest Synthetic Data Generator, and the parameters were generated by specifying the average item length, the maximum pattern size, the number of item types, and the number of transactions.

TABLE II. PARAMETERS OF INPUT DATA

Average transaction length	5
Maximum pattern size	5
Number of item types	30
Number of transactions	9900

The value of each parameter is specified as shown in Table II.

VII. RESULTS AND DISCUSSION

A. Results

The execution time shown is the average of three trials for each parameter. Figure 2 shows the execution time on the client when FP-growth is used.

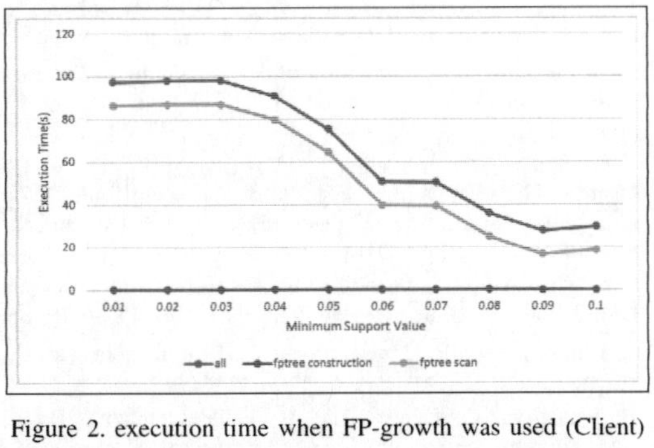

Figure 2. execution time when FP-growth was used (Client)

The execution time on the client side decreases almost monotonically as the support value increases. It is the FP-tree scan that is most affected by the computation time, and this changes with the size of the tree created. The creation time of the tree itself ends in linear time, but the scanning requires recursive processing, so when the minimum support value is small, the calculation time tends to jump. In the current implementation, the calculation time on the server side is approximately 10 seconds and hardly changes because the process is the same if the data are the same.

Second, the execution time when FP-growth was distributed is shown in Figure 3.

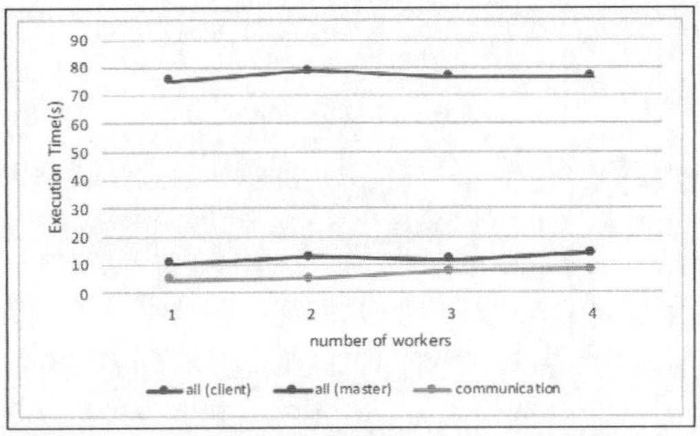

Figure 3. execution time when FP-growth was used (distributed)

The communication time increases as the number of workers increases. However, since there were few parts of the processing that were entrusted to the servers, the overhead was large and the distribution effect was not so great.

A comparison between two programs with the two different algorithms is shown in Figure 4.

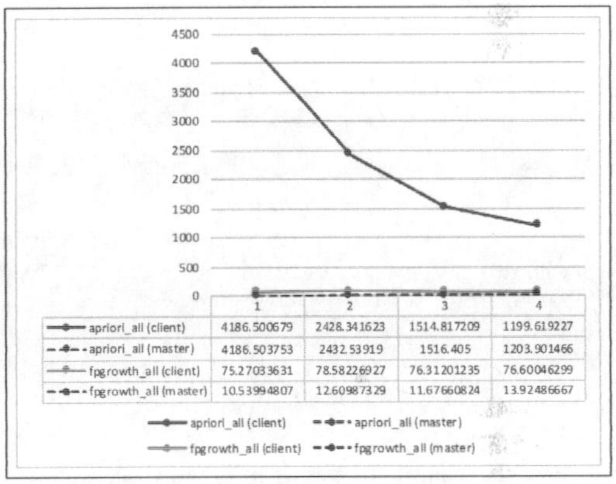

Figure 4. comparison of execution time between the programs using Apriori and FP-growth

The minimum value of the required level differs significantly between the systems using the two algorithms. This difference directly affects the size of the ciphertext and the execution time.

Figure 5 and Figure 6 show a comparison of the resources used by the client's machine. The data is measured when it is run with four workers and minimum support value is 0.05. In the system by Apriori, the CPU utilization peaked at the timing of receiving data. In FP-growth, after receiving data, FP-tree scan is performed in the part where the value is continuously 10%. In addition, the memory usage rate continued to be high during entrustment processing in both programs.

B. Discussion

When Apriori is used, once the transaction data are encrypted, re-decryption is not performed every time when data is exchanged with the server. Therefore, as the number of loops of the calculation increases, in other words, as the maximum value of the frequent item set length increases, the amount of noise in the ciphertext increases. To prevent decryption error, it

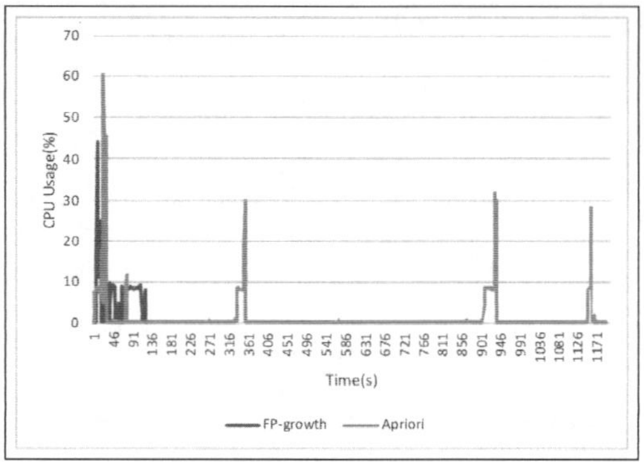

Figure 5. comparison of cpu usage between the programs using Apriori and FP-growth

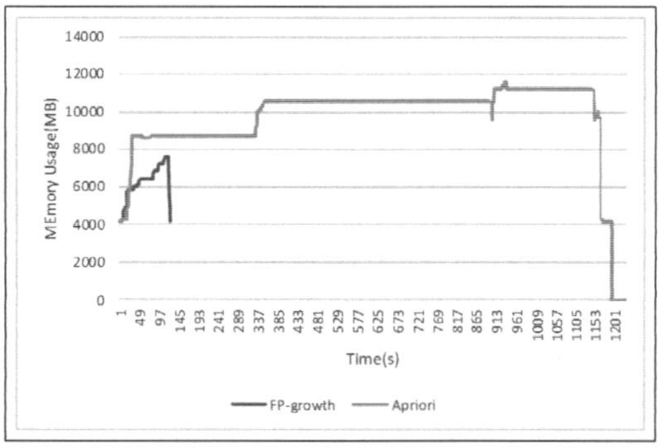

Figure 6. comparison of memory usage amount between the programs using Apriori and FP-growth

is necessary to set the value of the ciphertext level sufficiently large in advance.

On the other hand, in this implemetation, transaction data exchange with the server is performed only once in FP-growth; the initial value of the level needs to be able to calculate the support value only one time, so the required level compared with Apriori is smaller.

In addition, it can be seen that the increase in the number of candidate item sets more strongly affects the required level than the number of transactions due to the change in the support value. It can be confirmed that the execution time of FP-growth is approximately 100-fold smaller than the execution time of Apriori at maximum. The execution time is longer in Apriori's system. The higher the level is, the larger the size of the ciphertext, and the amount of processing could also be large. In FP-growth, although the amount of computation in scanning of the FP-tree is also large, it was found that it is extremely small when compared with the processing of the ciphertext in this experiment.

In the experiment, it is confirmed that the difference in the results between the two different systems was not only due to the difference in the algorithm itself but the difference in implementation also had a relatively large effect. In the current implementation using FP-growth, although the system using Apriori exchanges with the server multiple times, the portion of the processing entrusted to the server is small. The amount of the process dealing with cyphertext is generally large, so when the number of processes used to manipulate the ciphertext is reduced, a large difference is observed in the execution time.

VIII. Conclusion and Future Plans

A system doing frequent pattern mining by the FP-growth algorithm using a FHE was implemented. Then, the execution time and the amount of resource usage of this system were measured, and they were compared with previous system using the Apriori algorithm. In the comparison of the execution time, the system using FP-growth was approximately 100-fold faster than the system of the previous research. This result is considered to be the reason for much of the difference between the implementation of the system, rather than the algorithm itself. In the future, to improve the FP-growth system, it is considered necessary to reduce the number of times of the transmission and reception of the ciphertext data between the client and the server when increasing the ratio of processing on the server.

Acknowledgment

This research could not have been done without considerable support and advice from Professor Hayato Yamana as well as the professors and other researchers who belong to the research group. This research is supported by JST CREST JPMJCR1503.

References

[1] J. Liu, J. Li, S. Xu, and B. C. Fung, "Secure outsourced frequent pattern mining by fully homomorphic encryption," in International Conference on Big Data Analytics and Knowledge Discovery. Springer, 2015, pp. 70–81.

[2] H. Imabayashi, Y. Ishimaki, A. Umayabara, H. Sato, and H. Yamana, "Secure Frequent Pattern Mining by Fully Homomorphic Encryption with Ciphertext Packing," in Data Privacy Management and Security Assurance, G. Livraga, V. Torra, A. Aldini, F. Martinelli, and N. Suri, Eds. Cham: Springer International Publishing, 2016, pp. 181–195.

[3] ——, "Streamline Computation of Secure Frequent Pattern Mining by Fully Homomorphic Encryption," IPSJ TOD, vol. 10, no. 1, mar 2017, pp. 1–12.

[4] Y. Yamamoto and M. Oguchi, "Distributed System for Secret Data Mining while Updating Large Itemsets using Fully Homomorphic Encryption," in Multimedia, Distributed, Cooperative, and Mobile Symposium, vol. 2018, jun 2018, pp. 992–998.

[5] R. L. Rivest et al., "On data banks and privacy homomorphisms," Foundations of secure computation, vol. 4, no. 11, 1978, pp. 169–180.

[6] C. Gentry, "A Fully Homomorphic Encryption Scheme," Ph.D. dissertation, Stanford, CA, USA, 2009, aAI3382729.

[7] Z. Brakerski, C. Gentry, and V. Vaikuntanathan, "(Leveled) Fully Homomorphic Encryption Without Bootstrapping," ACM Trans. Comput. Theory, vol. 6, no. 3, Jul. 2014, pp. 13:1–13:36. [Online]. Available: http://doi.acm.org/10.1145/2633600

[8] R. Agrawal, T. Imieliński, and A. Swami, "Mining association rules between sets of items in large databases," in Acm sigmod record, vol. 22, no. 2. ACM, 1993, pp. 207–216.

[9] J. Han, J. Pei, and Y. Yin, "Mining Frequent Patterns Without Candidate Generation," in Proceedings of the 2000 ACM SIGMOD International Conference on Management of Data, ser. SIGMOD '00. New York, NY, USA: ACM, 2000, pp. 1–12. [Online]. Available: http://doi.acm.org/10.1145/342009.335372

[10] N. P. Smart and F. Vercauteren, "Fully homomorphic SIMD operations," Designs, codes and cryptography, vol. 71, no. 1, 2014, pp. 57–81.

[11] HElib. https://github.com/homenc/HElib (visited on 18/09/2019).

[12] Open MPI. https://www.open-mpi.org/ (visited on 18/09/2019).

IoTAMU: Protecting Smart Home Networks via Obfuscation and Encryption

Youngjun Park
School of Electrical and Computer Engineering
Air Force Institute of Technology
Wright-Patterson AFB, USA
Email: youngjun.park@afit.edu

Richard Dill
School of Electrical and Computer Engineering
Air Force Institute of Technology
Wright-Patterson AFB, USA
Email: richard.dill@afit.edu

Barry E. Mullins
School of Electrical and Computer Engineering
Air Force Institute of Technology
Wright-Patterson AFB, USA
Email: barry.mullins@afit.edu

Abstract—**In the changing landscape where an increasing number of organizations deploy smart devices to their networks, one of the greatest challenges they face is security. While the use of Internet of Things (IoT) has enabled new capabilities, such as ease of access, remote control, and interoperability, it has also introduced new attack vectors. For example, due to the limited hardware capacity, IoT devices lack the additional computational resources required for security, such as data encryption. As a result, gaining access to the data associated with the IoT devices becomes almost trivial assuming the adversary has physical access to the device or logical access to the network. Unfortunately, the production of the IoT devices cannot be effectively regulated without a governing policy, leaving the burden to secure the devices to the end users. To help mitigate the vulnerabilities stemming from the hardware limitations of IoT devices, we present Internet of Things Active Management Unit (IoTAMU), a defensive model to obscure the sensitive data sent over Wi-Fi. As a proof of concept, we first show that the video stream created by one of the most popular IoT cameras being sold on Amazon can be recreated via passive sniffing. Then, we present an automated tool to extract the video stream from network traffic. In 100 percent of test cases, the tool was able to extract a recognizable video stream from captured network traffic. Finally, we propose IoTAMU, a central management agent which acts as the network proxy for the vulnerable IoT devices to both obfuscate the network traffic by mimicking real devices, and to serve as an encryption agent for the devices with limited computational capacity. The model requires minimum set up for the users, and is compatible with any device that is configurable over Wi-Fi. IoTAMU will help pioneer easily deployable user-end security agents to protect the confidentiality in smart home networks.**

Keywords–Internet of Things (IoT); data security; network obfuscation; Wi-Fi camera.

I. INTRODUCTION

The term Internet of Things (IoT) represents a wave of embedded technologies with the added functionality of connectivity. Since its inception, IoT has infiltrated numerous public sectors in Industrial Control Systems (ICS), cities, healthcare, and government [1]; according to the International Data Corporation, the IoT industry is projected to reach 1.2 trillion dollars by the year 2022 [2]. However, the rapid growth of the industry is rivaled by the increasing number of vulnerabilities that are discovered in the devices. As the devices continue to be deployed in critical infrastructures and national institutions, investigating secure policies for the use of IoT becomes one of the priorities for organizations such as the U.S. Department of Defense [3].

Embedded systems found in automotives, Supervisory Control and Data Acquisition (SCADA) systems, among others, were originally designed to function as closed systems. By connecting those systems to the Internet, the devices presented numerous vulnerabilities that cannot be easily defended. The dangers of these design deficiencies were highlighted in a 2015 study on the infotainment system found in modern vehicles, which discovered a vulnerability that allowed an adversary to gain remote control of the vehicle [4]. Security experts have recognized the security flaws in IoT devices and have investigated potential attack surfaces to help the manufacturers and the users to mitigate them, including the effort by the Open Web Application Security Project (OWASP) [5]. However, the hardware limitations of the devices often become the bottleneck for meaningful security measures such as encryption, which requires large computational power. Security is therefore left in large part to the end users.

Currently, one of the most common modes of communication for IoT devices is Wi-Fi [1]. While the security of Wi-Fi has improved after transitioning from the Wired Equivalent Privacy (WEP) standard to Wireless Protected Access 2 (WPA2) [6], there still exists vulnerabilities that allow an adversary to gain access to the network through publicly available password cracking tools such as Aircrack-ng [7] and Cain [9]. One of the vulnerabilities of many IoT devices is that they send and receive data in the clear, allowing an attacker with Wi-Fi access to passively sniff the network traffic.

In this study, we reverse engineer one of the most popular wireless cameras on Amazon to illustrate its vulnerability to eavesdropping. Numerous studies, including those of [10]-[12], have demonstrated vulnerabilities that exist in network cameras. In particular, Ostrom and Sambamoorthy [11] showcase a series of attacks that can be launched against IoT cameras via Address Resolution Protocol (ARP) cache poisoning, a common technique to eavesdrop on network traffic between hosts [13]. This study highlights the pervasiveness of eavesdropping via passive network scans 10 years after the DEFCON talk.

Over the years, researchers have sought out ways to mitigate the inherent security threats present in IoT networks. These approaches include Local Area Network (LAN) management schemes via Software Defined Networks (SDN) [14][15], deployment of encryption gateways [16][17], and obfuscating network traffic by sending crafted traffic [18]. While the SDN approach prevents a compromised device or a malicious host from further attacks, it does not prevent a bystander from passively eavesdropping on the network traffic. Using encryption gateways prevents an adversary from eavesdropping on sensitive data such as those of IoT cameras. However, the proposed methods of [16] utilize a cloud architecture, which does not provide an end-to-end protection of the communication. The recently proposed edge computing approach of [17] implements security agents with greater computational capacity on edge devices such as a wireless router. But the framework requires the modification of the IoT device's existing protocols. Lastly, the authors of [18] demonstrate the feasibility of IoT device fingerprinting from encrypted Wi-Fi traffic; they are able to infer the duration and time in which a user is present in a smart home. They defeat device fingerprinting and information leakage in a smart home by spoofing Wi-Fi traffic to mimic the IoT devices using a Raspberry Pi. This study presents IoTAMU, a defense a model that couples encryption agents and network traffic spoofing to enhance the confidentiality of an IoT network.

This research provides the following contributions:

- We exploit an eavesdrop vulnerability in a popular IoT camera
- We present an automated tool to extract the H.264 video stream from network traffic
- We introduce Internet of Things Active Management Unit (IoTAMU): a data confidentiality model for IoT networks that performs network traffic obfuscation and application level encryption

The rest of the paper is structured as follows: Section 2 describes the threat model in which the experiment was designed, and Section 3 presents the vulnerabilities found in an IoT camera and the results of reverse engineering its proprietary protocol. Section 4 presents the design of IoTAMU. Finally, Section 5 concludes the paper and discusses future work.

II. Threat Model

The threat model of this study consists of the following:

- A smart home network set up by a user which consists of a central router acting as the Access Point (AP) [19] to connect different IoT devices via Wi-Fi secured with WPA2
- A user accessing the video feed from an IoT camera at a remote location via an application provided by the vendor
- An adversary in proximity to the smart home who has gained access to the network by cracking the WPA2 preshared key and passively sniffing the network [20][21]

Other modes of wireless communications for IoT such as Zigbee [22], and Bluetooth [23] exist, but they are out of scope of this study.

After gaining access to the network, the adversary passively sniffs the network traffic and analyzes the data without detection with Wireshark [24]. Because many IoT devices send unencrypted data over the network [5], the adversary collects sensitive information without authorized access to the device. As highlighted in [25], there are numerous attacks that an adversary can perform after gaining access to a target network. However, this study focuses on compromise of data confidentiality as a result of eavesdropping in an unprotected network.

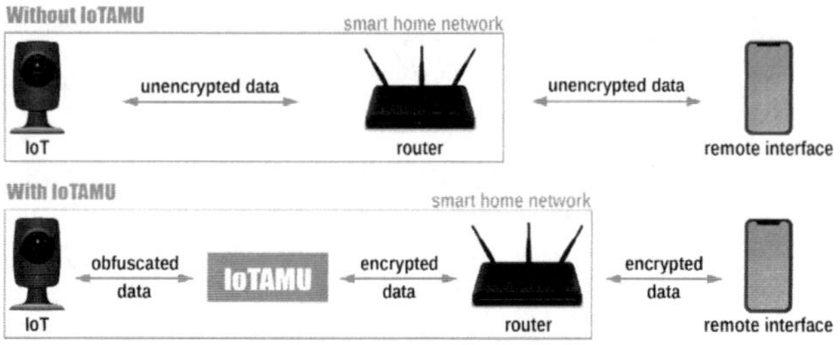

Figure 1. Communication in smart home networks with and without IoTAMU.

The primary goal of IoTAMU is to protect sensitive data in transit to and from an IoT device. Figure 1 depicts a smart home network with and without the use of IoTAMU. As previously mentioned, a typical smart home network is vulnerable to eavesdropping as it exchanges unencrypted data. IoTAMU is a security agent located between the devices and the router, encrypting their communication. It is paired with a decryption agent on the other end of the communication that sits on the device the user uses to interact with the IoT devices. The IoTAMU also performs periodic spoofing to deter device fingerprinting and obfuscate the network data from sniffers.

III. Investigating the Vulnerabilities of an IoT Camera

As a proof of concept, we investigate the vulnerability of the network protocol for Wansview Wireless 1080P Security Camera model Q3 being sold on Amazon [26]. As of September 18, 2019 it holds the Amazons Choice label on the website for the keywords "wi-fi baby monitor" with more than 3,000 customer reviews of average 4.1 out of 5-star rating scale. A comprehensive list of tools used in this work is summarized in Table 1.

A. Experimental Setup

As shown in Figure 2, the IoT camera is connected to the router via Wi-Fi and communicates with the vendor application (Wansview) running on an Android device (Samsung Galaxy S8) over the 4G network provided by the cellular provider (T-Mobile in this case). In proximity to the smart home is an adversary on a laptop (Lenovo Thinkpad) running Kali as its operating system. An Alfa wireless card is connected to the laptop to capture the network traffic in the smart home. The captured data is then passed into Wireshark for decoding and analysis. There are methods publicly available to gain root access to the camera with its admin credentials [27], which has been verified by the authors. However, this study focuses on passive network sniffing which does not require direct interaction with the device.

B. Sniffing the Network Traffic from IoT

To sniff the network traffic, the Alfa card connected to the laptop was first set to monitor mode via Airmon-ng [7]. Then, Airodump-ng was used to identify the Internet Protocol (IP)

TABLE I. LIST OF TOOLS USED

Name	Version	Description
Motorola Router	MG7540	Router that connects the IoT camera to the Internet via Wi-Fi
Lenovo Thinkpad	W541 I7-4910MQ (Kali 2018.4)	Laptop used for sniffing network traffic
Wansview Wireless Camera	Q3S (X Series)	IoT camera
Samsung Galaxy S8	SM-G950U1 (Android version 9)	Smartphone to remotely control the camera
Alfa Card	AWUS036NHA	Wireless network interface controller to send and receive 802.11 traffic
Wireshark	2.6.8	Software used for packet analysis
Airodump-ng	1.5.2	Software used to capture network traffic
Aireplay-ng	1.5.2	Software used to inject network traffic
Airmon-ng	1.5.2	Software used to configure the wireless card for network sniffing
Wansview	1.0.16	Mobile application to interact with IoT Camera
Python	3.5.2	Programming language used for automated H.264 video extraction

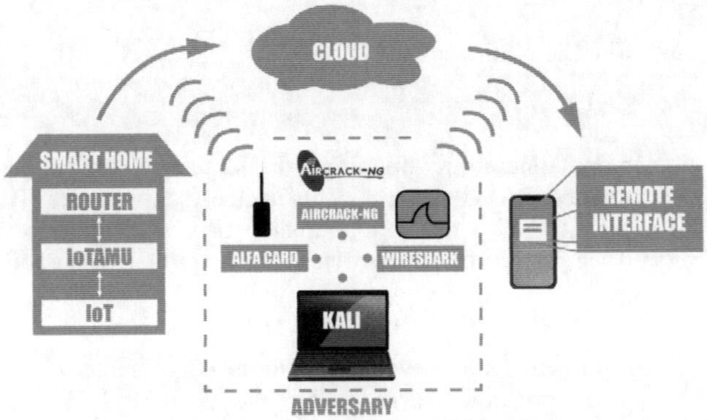

Figure 2. An overview of the experimental setup.

[8] address of the router acting as the AP. Next, Airodump-ng is used again to record network traffic associated with the target router, and Aireplay-ng was used to send spoofed deauthentication messages to the IoT camera to capture the WPA 4-way handshake between the router and the camera. The messages in the handshake are used by Wireshark along with the WPA2 preshared key to decode the encrypted Wi-Fi messages. For the purpose of this experiment, it is assumed that the adversary has gained access to the WPA2 preshared key. While gathering network data, the user in a remote location accessed the camera feed through the mobile application. After a period of time, the sniffer was stopped and the recorded data was viewed in Wireshark for analysis. In order to view the encrypted Wi-Fi data in Wireshark, the preshared key for WPA2 was input under the IEEE 802.11 decryption key setting.

C. Decoding the Video Stream Protocol

When the video stream was initiated from the remote user, the camera first performed a Domain Name System (DNS) [28] lookup of its cloud server followed by a series of network discovery protocols including Simple Service Discovery Protocol (SSDP) [29]. Its primary transport protocol was User Datagram Protocol (UDP), which is often used for transportation of time-sensitive data like video streams [19].

Determining the initial start time of video stream was clear within Wireshark, highlighted by the jump in the length of payload from mostly sub-100 range to 1,032 bytes. At first glance, Wireshark was unable to determine the type of data being transmitted. However, exporting one of the 1,032 payload and analyzing its entropy showed a steep downward slope suggesting that the payload was not encrypted (Figure 3). Upon further inspection, the first packet of the stream contained the file signature of a JPEG image, which can be recognized by the characters "JFIF". The subsequent packets showed that the video was transferred as an H.264 [30] stream, suggesting that the initial JPEG image corresponds to the thumbnail image shown in the Android application.

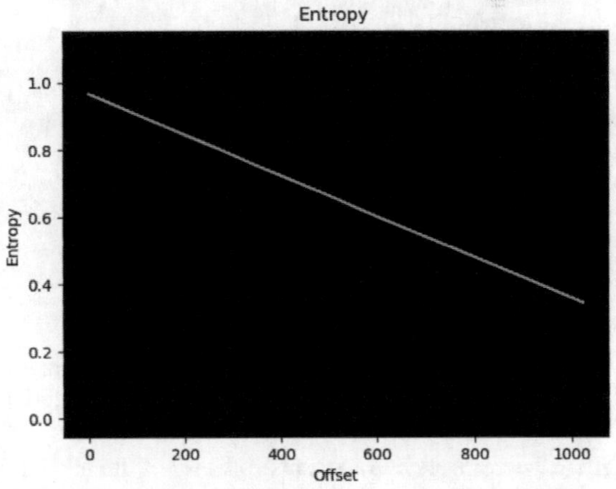

Figure 3. Entropy of a sample payload during video stream.

Once the video stream began, on top of the stream data, the UDP payloads also contained various control information consisting of a 4-to-8-byte block header and an optional block that varied from 0 to 40 bytes. Figure 4 illustrates the breakdown of the proprietary protocol in all packets. The first byte of the payload was a fixed value of `0xf1`, which was followed by either `0xd0`, `0xd1`, `0xe0`, `0xe1`. The control byte `0xd0` was used in payloads with stream data, whereas `0xd1` served as acknowledgement packets analogous to the Transmission Control Protocol (TCP) [19] counterpart. `0xe0`, and `0xe1` were sent out by both the server and the client, always followed by a 2-byte zero padding, representing a keep alive signal to leave the stream open to prevent replay attacks. The next two varying bytes represented the length of the payload following the two bytes (i.e., length of UDP payload in bytes - 4 bytes). They were followed by a `0xd100` for any data part of the JPEG image, `0xd101` for H.264 video stream, and `0xd102` for MPEG Audio Data Transport Stream (ADTS) [31] data. The final two bytes in the 8-byte header represented

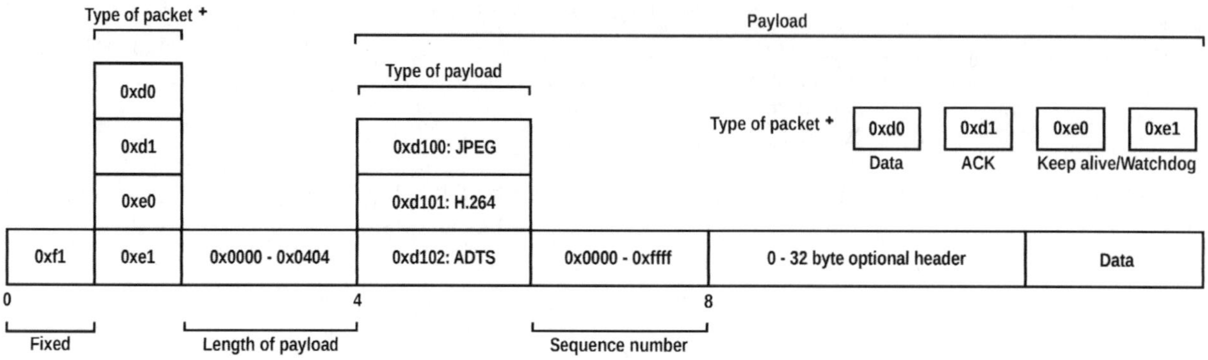

Figure 4. Breakdown of a UDP packet payload during camera stream.

Figure 5. A snapshot of the reconstructed video stream.

the sequence number of the data to follow in a data stream packet, or the number of packets being acknowledged in an ACK packet.

There were a few variations of the optional overhead following the 8-byte header depending on the type of packet. However, for the purpose of extracting the video feed, we were only required to determine that the optional header for the packet containing the JPEG header was 8 bytes, and the optional header for the packet containing the H.264 and the audio header was 32 bytes. Any stream data directly following the initial headers did not contain optional headers. There were, however, optional 32-byte headers for H.264 packets that were not the first in the series of packets. These headers could be distinguished by the `0x55aa` sequence following the first 8-byte header, and pertinent data could be correctly extracted by filtering for the specific sequence.

The aforementioned header information was used to build an automated H.264 videos stream extraction tool written in Python [32] to recreate the video stream (Figure 5) from a pcap capture file without having physical access to the camera or its credentials. The tool was able to extract a recognizable video stream from the pcap file in 100 percent of the test cases.

Due to the inconsistent nature of Wi-Fi traffic and the unreliability of UDP, the reconstructed video feed was not a perfect replication of the video data stream sniffed en route to the mobile application. As previously identified in [5], the eavesdrop vulnerability found in this research showcases its pervasiveness in IoT devices. This security flaw can easily be taken advantage by a malicious insider or a determined adversary; it warrants further research to mitigate this vulnerability.

IV. IoTAMU Design

To mitigate the eavesdrop vulnerability created by unencrypted application-level traffic, we propose IoTAMU, a central network gateway for IoT. Its setup in a typical smart home is depicted in Figure 6. In an end-to-end communication involving a smart home, as shown in Figure 2, there are two ends of traffic an adversary can capture: data exchanged between the IoT device and the cloud, and those between the remote interface and the cloud. However, the easier of the two end hosts is the smart home end of the communication, because the IoT devices are often stationary, and remain static in the network.

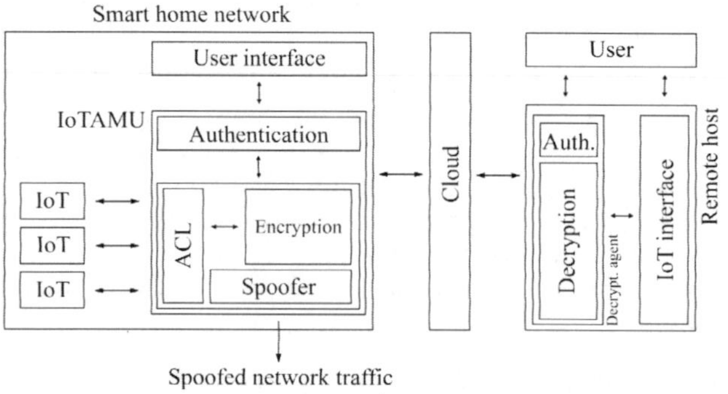

Figure 6. An overview of the IoTAMU model in a smart home network.

IoTAMU will protect this vulnerable end of the communication by serving as the network proxy to all IoT devices present in the network to encrypt their application level traffic before forwarding it to the router. The proxy can be easily set up in the network by designating it as the default gateway for the IoT devices through the Dynamic Host Configuration Protocol (DHCP) [33] in the LAN. The encryption agent within IoTAMU will be paired with a decryption agent living on the other host as a background process, often with enough computational capacity to perform encryption and decryption (e.g., computer, smartphone) by itself. IoTMU will consist of the following capabilities: (1) Authentication, (2) Access control list (3) Encryption, and finally (4) Spoofing.

The encryption agents will be accessed and configured (i.e., add or remove devices) through an authentication mechanism via username and password set by the user. In addition, to ensure only the intended devices are communicating with it, IoTAMU will store an access control list based on the network signatures of the IoT devices such as Media Access Control (MAC) address [34], IP address, etc. This does not in fact prevent an adversary from spoofing one of the IoT devices to communicate with the gateway. But since the intention of the gateway is data confidentiality, its vulnerability to spoofing will not affect its functionality.

Similar to the approach taken by [16], the encryption can be performed through Public Key Encryption (PKI). This requires the exchange of keys between IoTAMU in the smart home network and each of the encryption agents residing in the other end host. The encryption agents for the end hosts can take the form of a smart phone application that runs in the background or an executable on a computer. Initially, each participating hosts will exchange their public keys in a certificate signed by a common entity whose public key will be preinstalled on the agents. All subsequent traffic will be encrypted and decrypted using the private key and the public key of the end hosts. The use of PKI will prevent a bystander from intercepting a common key to decrypt the messages. Although taking an approach like SSL, which uses PKI to exchange session keys and using symmetric keys for later exchanges may lessen the computational demand, it is vulnerable to man-in-the-middle attacks [13], which defeats the purpose of IoTAMU.

Finally, the IoTAMU will periodically send out spoofed Wi-Fi traffic to mimic certain device types. Spoofing network traffic substantiated by the research in [18] will help fortify the network against fingerprinting and information leakage in a smart home. It will also protect the unencrypted data being exchanged between IoTAMU and the IoT devices by concealing the actual communication among spoofed traffic. Creation of spoofed packets can be variations on the following criteria:

- Length of the payload in the network
- Frequency and timing of the packets sent
- Spoofing unused IP address in the network
- Spoofing a plausible MAC addresses of certain vendors to mimic device types

Using the aforementioned criteria, a central IoT gateway design will help secure a smart home network without changing any existing protocols or relying on the vendors for security. The latency and the packet overhead imposed by encryption and the effect of periodic spoofing on network congestion is left for future investigation.

V. CONCLUSION

This paper discusses the vulnerabilities of IoT devices in a smart home network. We demonstrated the eavesdrop vulnerability in the Wansview IoT camera by reverse engineering its proprietary communication protocol, and by creating an automated tool to extract the H.264 stream created by the camera. The proposed design of IoTAMU mitigates this vulnerability for the IoT devices in smart homes through encryption and spoofing. As it does not rely on any existing protocols, IoTAMU can be implemented for the varying protocols utilized by the IoT devices to easily deploy in smart home networks. Development of a Wireshark dissector for the proprietary protocol, the implementation of IoTAMU, and the analysis of its performance is left as future work.

ACKNOWLEDGMENT

The views expressed are those of the authors and do not necessarily reflect the official policy or position of the Air Force, the Department of Defense, or the U.S. Government.

REFERENCES

[1] P. P. Ray, "A Survey on Internet of Things Architectures," J. King Saud Univ. - Comput. Inf. Sci., vol. 30, no. 3, pp. 291-319, 2018.

[2] M. Torchia and M. Shirer, "IDC Forecasts Worldwide Technology Spending on the Internet of Things to Reach $1.2 Trillion in 2022," International Data Corporation, 2018, URL: https://www.idc.com/getdoc.jsp?containerId=prUS43994118 [accessed: 2019-09-18].

[3] United States Government Accountability Office, "INTERNET OF THINGS Enhanced Assessments and Guidance Are Needed to Address Security Risks in DOD," 2017, URL: https://www.gao.gov/assets/690/686203.pdf [accessed: 2019-10-21]

[4] C. Valasek and C. Miller, "Remote Exploitation of an Unaltered Passenger Vehicle," Black Hat USA, pp. 1-91, 2015.

[5] Open Web Application Security Project, "IoT Attack Surface Areas," 2015, URL: https://www.owasp.org/index.php/IoT_Attack_Surface_Areas [accessed: 2019-09-18].

[6] A. Sari and M. Karay, "Comparative Analysis of Wireless Security Protocols: WEP vs WPA," Int. J. Commun. Netw. Syst. Sci., vol. 08, no. 12, pp. 483-491, Dec. 2015.

[7] "Aircrack-ng," 2018, URL: https://www.aircrack-ng.org [accessed: 2019-09-18]

[8] J. Postel "Internet Protocol," RFC 791, 1981, URL: https://tools.ietf.org/html/rfc791 [accessed: 2019-09-18]

[9] "Cain and Abel," 2014 [Online]. Available from: https://www.oxid.it/cain.html [accessed: 2019-09-18]

[10] C. Heffner, "Exploiting Surveillance Cameras Like a Hollywood Hacker," no. February, p. 1-30, 2013.

[11] J. Ostrom and A. Sambamoorthy, "DEFCON 17: Advancing Video Application Attacks with Video Interception, Recording, and Replay," 2009, URL: https://www.youtube.com/watch?v=QcsQ6UzMJiU [accessed: 2019-09-18]

[12] N. Kalbo, "I Got My EyeOn You - Security Vulnerabilities in D-Links Baby Monitor," 2018, URL: https://dojo.bullguard.com/dojo-by-bullguard/blog/i-got-my-eyeon-you-security-vulnerabilities-in-baby-monitor/ [accessed: 2019-09-18]

[13] E. Skoudis and T. Liston, Counter hack reloaded: a step-by-step guide to computer attacks and effective defenses, Prentice Hall Press, 2005.

[14] M. Miettinen et al., "IoT Sentinel Demo: Automated Device-Type Identification for Security Enforcement in IoT," Proc. - Int. Conf. Distrib. Comput. Syst., pp. 2511-2514, 2017.

[15] D. Soteris et al., "SDN-driven protection of smart home WiFi devices from malicious mobile apps," Proc. 10th ACM Conf. Secur. Priv. Wirel. Mob. Networks, pp. 122-133, 2017.

[16] C. Doukas, I. Maglogiannis, V. Koufi, F. Malamateniou, and G. Vassilacopoulos, "Enabling data protection through PKI encryption in IoT m-Health devices," IEEE 12th Int. Conf. Bioinforma. Bioeng., pp. 25-29, 2012.

[17] R. Hsu, J. Lee, T. Q. S. Quek, and J. Chen, "Reconfigurable Security: Edge Computing-based Framework for IoT," IEEE Network., vol. 32, no. 5, pp. 92-99, 2018.

[18] S. M. Beyer, B. E. Mullins, S. R. Graham, and J. M. Bindewald, "Pattern-of-Life Modeling in Smart Homes," IEEE Internet Things J., vol. 5, no. 6, pp. 5317-5325, Dec. 2018.

[19] J. F. Kurose and K. W. Ross, Computer networking: a top-down approach, 7th ed. New Jersey: Pearson, 2017.

[20] O. Nakhila and C. Zou, "Parallel Active Dictionary Attack on IEEE 802.11 Enterprise Networks," in MILCOM IEEE Military Communications Conference, 2016, pp. 265-270.

[21] A. Abdelrahman, H. Khaled, E. Shaaban, and W. S. Elkilani, "WPA-WPA2 PSK Cracking Implementation on Parallel Platforms," in 2018 13th International Conference on Computer Engineering and Systems (ICCES), 2018, pp. 448-453.

[22] Zigbee Alliance, "What is Zigbee?," 2018, URL: https://www.zigbee.org/what-is-zigbee/ [accessed: 2019-09-18]

[23] Bluetooth SIG, "Protocol Specifications," 2019, URL: https://www.bluetooth.com/specifications/protocol-specifications/ [accessed: 2019-09-18]

[24] "Wireshark," 2019, URL: https://www.wireshark.org/ [accessed: 2019-09-18]

[25] M. Nawir, A. Amir, N. Yaakob, and O. B. Lynn, "Internet of Things (IoT): Taxonomy of security attacks," in 2016 3rd International Conference on Electronic Design, 2016, pp. 321-326.

[26] "Wansview Wireless 1080P Security Camera, WiFi Home Surveillance IP Camra for Baby/Elder/Pet/Nanny Monitor, Pan/Tilt, Two-Way Audio & Night Vision Q3-S," Amazon, 2019, URL: https://www.amazon.com/Wansview-Wireless-Security-Surveillance-Monitor/dp/B075K89NTR/ref=sr_1_14?keywords=wi-fi+baby+monitor&qid=1568920347&s=gateway&sr=8-14 [accessed: 2019-09-18]

[27] J. Wedell, "Rooting a cheap IP camera (Wansview K2)," Ramblin Wedells, 2017, URL: https://jonwedell.com/rooting-a-cheap-ip-camera/ [accessed: 2019-09-18]

[28] P. Mockapetris, "Domain names - implementation aqnd Specification," RFC 1035, 1987, URL: https://www.ietf.org/rfc/rfc1035.txt [accessed: 2019-09-18]

[29] A. Donoho et al., "UPnP Device Architecture," UPnP Forum, 2015, URL: http://upnp.org/specs/arch/UPnP-arch-DeviceArchitecture-v2.0.pdf [accessed: 2019-09-18]

[30] "H.264: Advanced video coding for generic audiocisual services," International Telecommunication Union, 2019. [Online]. Available: https://www.itu.int/rec/T-REC-H.264 [accessed: 2019-09-18]

[31] "White Paper on AAC Transport Formats" International Organisation for Standardisation, 2014, URL: https://mpeg.chiariglione.org/white-papers [accessed: 2019-09-18]

[32] "Python," Python, 2019, URL: https://www.python.org/ [accessed: 2019-09-18]

[33] R. Droms "Dynamic Host Configuration Protocol," RFC 2131, 1997, URL: https://tools.ietf.org/html/rfc2131 [accessed: 2019-09-18]

[34] "Standard Group MAC Addresses: A Tutorial Guide," IEEE Standards Association, 2019, URL: https://standards.ieee.org/content/dam/ieee-standards/standards/web/documents/tutorials/macgrp.pdf [accessed: 2019-09-18]

IoTAG: An Open Standard for *IoT* Device Identific*A*tion and Reco*G*nition

Sebastian Fischer
Secure Systems Engineering
Fraunhofer AISEC
Berlin, Germany
email:
sebastian.fischer@aisec.fraunhofer.de

Katrin Neubauer* and Rudolf Hackenberg†
Dept. Computer Science and Mathematics
Ostbayerische Technische Hochschule
Regensburg, Germany
email:
katrin1.neubauer@oth-regensburg.de*
rudolf.hackenberg@oth-regensburg.de†

Lukas Hinterberger‡ and Bernhard Weber§
Dept. Electrical Engineering and Information Technology
Ostbayerische Technische Hochschule
Regensburg, Germany
email:
lukas.hinterberger@st.oth-regensburg.de‡
bernhard1.weber@st.oth-regensburg.de§

***Abstract*—With the increasing amount of Internet of Things (IoT) devices in smart homes, insecure and old devices are leading to big security issues. A private network can be attacked over an insecure IoT device, to use it in a botnet or infect it with ransomware and compromise the whole network. Non-technical users do not know which devices in their homes are secure and how to keep track of all the old and new ones. We have built a typical smart home as a test environment to evaluate a scoring system for the security of the whole network. First, all devices are discovered with nmap and then all the possible information, like the open ports or the Wi-Fi technology, are retrieved. In the next step, all the information leads to an overall score for each device. Combined together, the final score for the whole network is created. A non-technical user can now determine, if the network is secure or not. We show the proof of concept of the scoring system with our test environment. However, some challenges exist. Not all information can be retrieved by just scanning the devices over the network. Some devices just return hostnames like "ESP_6A786B". It is nearly impossible to tell the kind of device and the manufacturer. Additionally, no information about the running firmware is provided. To calculate a meaningful score, much more information has to be collected. To collect the missing data, we introduce the first version of a new, open standard for *IoT* Device Identific*A*tion and Reco*G*nition (IoTAG). This JSON based model provides all the important information about the device. Besides the device name, type and the manufacturer, it shows a list of the services, the firmware version and the supported encryption. IoTAG allows to create an overview of the whole IoT network and the development of an automated scoring system. In the future, additional information about security vulnerabilities can be collected from the Internet, to warn the user about insecure devices.**

Keywords*—*Internet of Things; device identification; open standard; IoTAG; security rating.

I. Introduction

Internet of Things (IoT) is an ongoing innovation and trend in nearly all industries and smart homes. The development is extremely fast and most of the time, the security risks of IoT networks are underestimated or not even taken into account at all. This leads to insecure devices, e.g., with missing encryption or authentication. Overall, a large number of IoT devices in general, are critical to operate. Some risks are comparable harmless attacks, which just destroy the device, but others can lead to hijacking of complete company networks [1] [2].

To avoid these problems, the user should be able to tell which devices are in the network and if they are running with the latest software. Currently, there are no existing systems for automated device scanning. It is possible to obtain parts of the required information in single steps. For example, the network scanners Nmap [3] or Fing [4] can be used for finding addressable network ports. But the results of this scans will not be analyzed or evaluated. To help a non-technical user, an easy to use scoring system for IoT devices is necessary.

The first scan of a network detects all the containing IoT devices. Each detected device gets a security rank based on the provided meta data, information collected by the scanner itself and a database of known vulnerabilities, which are collected from multiple publicly available sources. All the ranks together will provide an overall network rank. The scanner should be able to show the rank, a list of all known vulnerabilities and general risks of the IoT setup to the user.

The goal of this project is to identify requirements for the development of a standard, which provides the needed metadata and also checks the authenticity of the received information. In this paper, we present the first version of IoTAG. The paper is structured as follows. Section II describes the related work. Section III introduces our hardware setup and device scanning, while Section IV defines the security criteria. Section V shows the device rating and Section VI the results. The standard IoTAG is presented in Section VII, followed by a conclusion in Section VIII.

II. Related Work

One possible solution for IoT device identification uses device fingerprints. Miettinen et al. [5] are categorizing and classifying (secure and insecure) IoT devices by device fingerprint. Another research project [6] is developing a system for anomaly recognition (smart home networks). There are several publications [7]–[10] covering the subject device identification with device fingerprints and similar approaches. These publications are demonstrating working approaches for the detection of IoT devices in a network. However, it is not possible to identify detailed information such as the current firmware version or a device ID for further recognition.

Some researchers provide mechanisms to evaluate the security and privacy for IoT devices with different security ratings. One very similar approach [11] uses protocols, open ports and the encryption to create the rating. But it is not very flexible and user-friendly because of the missing weighting of each criteria and the missing overall score of the network. Park et al. [12] and Ali et al. [13] are offering a very good approach for the focus of the risk, which can be used to evaluate the weighting. Both papers do not provide a rating, but a list of security requirements in IoT services. Another approach uses vulnerabilities and known exploits to generate a metric value for the security of an IoT device [14].

With the Device Description Language for the T in IoT from Khaled et al. [15] and the Thing Description as Enabler of Semantic Interoperability on the Web of Things from Kaebisch et al. [16], there are some publications, proposing a machine readable description for IoT devices. These descriptions are only for the functionality of a device and cover information like the turn off command. With IoTAG, we do not want to get the functions of a device, instead we want to get the security characteristics. It is possible to extend these descriptions with our IoTAG information.

This paper extends the initial work of Hinterberger, introducing the evaluation criteria and scanning methods for the device rating [17], with further research and the new IoTAG standard.

III. Hardware Setup and Device Scanning

We have built a small smart home environment with ten devices, as seen in Table I and started a network scan to detect all the connected devices. Some devices reply with their hostname, but, in most cases, the response contains something like "ESP" or it is totally missing. In the next step, a deeper scan with "nmap -p 1-65535 192.168.0.0/24" is performed. Additional information about the devices on port 80 HTTP and a list of all open TCP (Transmission Control Protocol) and UDP (User Datagram Protocol) ports are shown in Table II. With this information, we can give more details about the running services and the device communication. For example, with an open port 80, an unencrypted connection is likely.

However, with all the given information, it is still impossible to detect the exact devices. The iPhone and Google Home mini are detectable with their hostname, but only if the hostname is not changed.

IV. Security Criteria

In order to define a test scheme that can be applied individually to any device, it is necessary to develop a procedure that allows the security risks to be assessed separately for each device. Afterwards, the individual assessments can be offset against each other in order to obtain the overall assessment of a device.

TABLE I. HARDWARE OVERVIEW

device	hostname
Amazon Echo 2	amazon-183e3c119
Apple iPhone 5	Kluges-iPhone
Floureon M32B	
Google Home mini	Google-Home-Mini
Grandstream GXP1610	
Raspberry Pi 3 Model B	raspberrypi
Sonoff Wi-Fi Smart Switch	ESP_6A768B
Wi-Fi Smart Bulb	ESP_4C3210
Wi-Fi Smart Plug	ESP_3D1EB6
Wi-Fi Touch Switch	ESP_469ACF

TABLE II. OVERVIEW OF OPEN AND RESTRICTED PORTS

Raspberry Pi 3 Model B				
port		**state**	**service**	**reason**
22	TCP	open	ssh	syn-ack
53	TCP	open	domain	syn-ack
Sonoff Wi-Fi Smart Switch				
port		**state**	**service**	**reason**
		restricted		
Wi-Fi Touch Switch				
port		**state**	**service**	**reason**
8081	TCP	open	blackice-icecap	syn-ack
Wi-Fi Smart Plug				
port		**state**	**service**	**reason**
10000	TCP	open	snet-sensor-mgmt	syn-ack
Grandstream GXP1610				
port		**state**	**service**	**reason**
22	TCP	open	ssh	syn-ack
80	TCP	open	http	syn-ack

For the evaluation scheme, a three-level point system is defined as the basis for evaluation. If a security criterion is completely violated, the equipment in question is assessed zero points in that category. For non-critical violations one point and for no violations two points are awarded. Several individual evaluations are offset against each other by calculating an average value. It should be noted that individual categories can be weighted differently. The used security criteria are listed in Table III and described as follows in detail.

A. Wi-Fi technology

As the encryption technology for wireless networks, the WPA2 (Wi-Fi Protected Access) and WPA3 standards are rated with the highest score. Networks based on the WPA or WEP (Wired Equivalent Privacy) standard cannot be classified as secure because the "RC4" encryption method used, is no longer state of the art and considered as broken [18].

B. Services

This evaluation criterion deals with the services provided at network level and can be used to communicate with the respective device. In particular, it checks whether the communication procedures offered are based on encryption. The assessment is based on a presorting of known services and

TABLE III. SECURITY CRITERIA

audit criteria			score
radio technology			
WPA/WEP or no encryption			0
WPA2/WPA3			2
Bluetooth version			0-2
ZigBee version			0-2
manufacturer			
unknown manufacturer			0
usual patch time			0-2
experience			0-2
known unpatched devices			0-2
bug bounty program			0/2
services			
service	**default port**	**comment**	
HTTP	80	unencrypted login details	0
MQTT	1883	unencrypted control data	0
UPnP	49152/1900	firewall manipulation	0
rtsp	554	unencrypted video data	0
SIP	5060	unencrypted	0
service	**default port**	**comment**	
HTTPS	443	encrypted	2
MQTTS	8883	encrypted	2
SCP	10001	encrypted	2
SIPS	5061	encrypted	2
SSH	22	encrypted	2
LAN and WAN communication			
service	**default port**	**comment**	
HTTP	80	unencrypted login details	0
MQTT	1883	unencrypted control data	0
UPnP	49152/1900	firewall manipulation	0
rtsp	554	unencrypted video data	0
SIP	5060	unencrypted	0
service	**default port**	**comment**	
HTTPS	443	encrypted	2
MQTTS	8883	encrypted	2
SCP	10001	encrypted	2
SIPS	5061	encrypted	2
SSH	22	encrypted	2
other			
vulnerable to replay attacks			0
create own Wi-Fi			0
data retrieval without authentication			0
vulnerable to jamming			0-2
vulnerable to Denial of Service (DoS)			0-2
insecure configuration			0
continuous device number			0-2
known vulnerabilities			0
support lifetime			0-2
insecure / default password			0/2
software version			0-2
technical guidelines			0-2
certification			0-2

protocols in black and white lists. Services on the black-list are rated with zero points, services on the white-list with two points and unknown services with one point.

C. Communication

As with device services, device communication is tested for the use of encryption methods. Since the used protocols cannot be queried by scanning the devices, the current communication must be analyzed. In addition to the encryption technology, it is also possible to check the number of external resources a device communicates with and where they are located. Predefined protocol lists are also used for this evaluation criterion. The communication is separated in LAN (local area network) and WAN (Wide area network), to cover the different security requirements. In Table III, both are displayed in the same section.

D. Default passwords

The use of standard passwords assigned by device manufacturers, that can be applied to multiple devices, is a major problem with the safety of IoT devices. It is important to check whether authentication on a device is possible using known passwords. In this case, the device is considered to be at risk and should therefore be evaluated with zero points.

E. Firmware version

Known security vulnerabilities are often stored in public accessible databases and can be accessed by potential attackers. A known outdated software version of a device can be used for systematic attacks. It must be possible to check which software version is running on a device and whether updates are available for it. If no updates are available and security gaps are known for the existing software, the device must be classified as severely endangered. If updates are available but not installed, they are considered to be at risk, otherwise they are considered to be safe.

V. Device Rating

In this section, we describe the proceeding to receive the information for all the security criteria and how they are rated in detail.

A. Wi-Fi technology

The encryption technology of the wireless network can be queried in the router configuration. In the case of our experimental environment, the task of the router is taken over by a Raspberry Pi as Wi-Fi access point. The setup query is made via the configuration file of the access point software "hostapd". Thus, the configuration is done in the file "/etc/hostapd". The entry "wpa=2" indicates the exclusive use of the WPA2 standard. This leads to a score of two points for each device. If an unsafe technology is used, this will also affect the evaluation of each individual device, as the entire network will be endangered. In this case, all devices have to be rated with zero points in this category.

B. Services

The running services are checked by scanning the network components. For this purpose, Nmap is used for both TCP and UDP connections [19]. The scan might produce the output shown in Table IV.

TABLE IV. PORT SCAN

port	protocol
22	ssh
80	http
5060	sip

Based on these results, the device can be rated. The already mentioned categorization lists are used. The example in Table IV leads to a rating with 0.66 points, because http and sip are rated with zero and ssh with two points.

C. Communication

The communication of the devices to external resources is analyzed by recording and analyzing the network traffic. Existing technologies, like the tshark [20] software, are used. From the communication packets, the MAC address of the local resource, source and destination port, as well as the used protocols, are extracted. Incoming and outgoing traffic are handled separately. Analogous to the evaluation of the services, the evaluation of the communication is also based on predefined protocol lists. With the scan results in the output shown in Table V, the device will be rated with zero points in this category.

TABLE V. COMMUNICATION SCAN

source device	**destination port**	**protocol**
00:11:22:33:44:55	5060	sip

D. Default passwords

In order to check whether an insecure password has been configured for a device, a dictionary attack against the corresponding device is carried out with the aid of the THC-Hydra [21] software. Both the user name and the password are attacked with known and frequently used terms. The required specification for which type of service a login should be performed, is taken from the previous service scan. The software tests all possible combinations with a brute force attack. If a device turns out to be vulnerable, it is highly vulnerable. Otherwise, it will be classified as harmless. If we consider an ssh login with "root" as the user and a well-known default password like "admin" as possible, this would lead to an rating with zero points.

An undefined handling of nonstandard, manufacturer-specific login procedures can lead to a problem with this kind of password check. For each specific procedure, a separate test algorithm must be developed, which may require adaptation after a software update by the device manufacturer. As an example of a manufacturer-specific login procedure, the challenge-response-mechanism that AVM uses for the Web interface of their Fritz!Box Routers can be mentioned [22].

E. Firmware

It was not possible to develop an automated procedure for checking the firmware version, because of the lack of a standardized interface for querying information about the device software. The use of Nmap makes rough assumptions about the operating system of a device possible. But these are not sufficient for a valid risk assessment due to the gross inaccuracies. Furthermore, Nmap is only able to identify systems where an identification has already taken place [23]. It would be possible to create a Nmap fingerprint for each network device and include it in the database for system identification, but this procedure is not relevant in practice, as it requires specific knowledge of the software. Also, it is not guaranteed that the detection characteristics will not change after a software update, making it impossible to clearly determine the version. The same applies to independent test procedures, developed outside Nmap.

F. Overall rating

After all ratings have been performed, an overall rating for a device can be calculated, by determining the average score. This score describes the vulnerability of a device based on Table VI. A ports score of 0.66 points, a communication score of 0.00 points and a password score of 0.00 points will lead to an overall device rating of 0.22 points and indicates a highly vulnerable device. The average score is used to compare the different devices. If we used the minimum score, each device would get zero points. Normally, the weakest point is attacked, but every missing or insecure security criteria does not necessary lead to a vulnerability.

TABLE VI. VULNERABILITY CATEGORIES

score	**category**
0.00 to 0.80	high vulnerability
0.81 to 1.80	moderate vulnerability
1.81 to 2.00	small vulnerability

VI. RESULTS

To validate the concept of the rating system, the following devices have been evaluated: Amazon Echo 2 (1), Apple iPhone 5 (2), Floureon M32B (3), Google Home mini (4), Renkforce RenkCast (5), Sonoff Wi-Fi Smart Switch (6), Wi-Fi Smart Bulb (7), Wi-Fi Smart Plug (8) and Wi-Fi Touch Switch (9). Exemplary (not final) results can be found in Table VII (a dash indicates the parameter was not determined on that device). Afterwards, the devices were manually tested regarding their security. The evaluation has been compared with the previous determined scores. The conclusion is an overall success: the scoring fits the manual evaluation most of the time. This proves that the scoring system fulfills its purpose and can be used as a time saving way to rate the security of IoT devices. The process of scoring can be automated once the information is collected, which helps speeding up the security rating of an IoT network.

TABLE VII. EXAMPLE RESULTS

parameter	**1**	**2**	**3**	**4**	**5**	**6**	**7**	**8**	**9**
Wi-Fi encryption	2.00	2.00	2.00	2.00	2.00	2.00	2.00	2.00	2.00
services	1.00	2.00	0.33	1.00	2.00	2.00	1.00	2.00	2.00
LAN communication	2.00	2.00	2.00	2.00	2.00	2.00	2.00	2.00	2.00
WAN communication	2.00	2.00	2.00	2.00	2.00	2.00	2.00	2.00	2.00
wired connection	1.00	1.00	2.00	1.00	1.00	1.00	1.00	1.00	1.00
cloud only	1.00	-	2.00	1.00	2.00	-	-	-	-
default password	2.00	2.00	1.00	2.00	2.00	2.00	2.00	2.00	2.00
overall score	**1.57**	**1.83**	**1.62**	**1.57**	**1.86**	**1.83**	**1.67**	**1.83**	**1.83**

With all the device scores, an overall network score can be achieved by taking the lowest single device score. The weakness of a network is always defined by its weakest device.

After we evaluated the scoring system, we tried to find a solution for an automated process to gather all the necessary information. As stated in Section III, a completely automated scan without any additional information is not reliable. Therefore, we introduce an Open Standard for IoT Device Identification and Recognition (IoTAG), which will allow an automated and secure way to identify and index all IoT devices in a certain network.

VII. IoTAG

Every IoT device should provide detailed information about itself and the current running software and firmware version. This enables an easy overview of the network and the security level with the previously shown device rating. We suggest to use a Transport Layer Security (TLS) 1.3 request to get the device information from the device. The response should use the JavaScript Object Notation (JSON) as standardized in ECMA-404 [24] and RFC 8259 [25]. JSON is faster to progress and uses less storage than for instance XML [26]. This benefits low powered IoT devices with restricted hardware.

The following information should be provided by the device:

- device ID
- device name
- device type
- manufacturer
- connectivity (e.g., Ethernet, Wi-Fi, Bluetooth, ...)
- firmware version
- firmware update URL
- software version (client)
- software update URL (client)
- auto updates enabled
- services and associated ports
- supported encryption

The device ID should be unique for each device, to allow a recognition. The device name can be extended with a revision number to ensure an exact assignment through multiple device versions.

Some possible device types are:

- sensor
- control
- camera
- smart TV
- smart speaker
- entertainment
- gaming
- household
- lightning

The device types are not exhaustive and can be extended. The manufacturer should allow a clear assignment to the responsible company. With a list of all the connectivity, the security rating can be extended and new threads in transmission technologies can be reported in a timely manner.

The firmware and possible existing client software version is very important for the scoring and to keep the whole network up to date. Additional to the version, a Uniform Resource Locator (URL), should be given. This URL must provide the current version and a secondary link to the new software version. This enables a third device to check the software version. In addition, the current auto update setting should be provided. In case this function is disabled, a security warning can be displayed.

As described in Section V, services and associated ports are a big part of the scoring system. The information about all running services improves the score and enables the possibility to check the proper configuration of the device. The protocol version can be used to identify outdated versions.

To check if the device can be used in a secure network, information about the supported encryption is necessary. This can be used to detect old devices with insecure encryption algorithms or exclude devices with no encryption at all.

The following data provides an example for the Google Home mini:


```
{
  "ID": "af0eb0335f952132b4e65999a373ce20",
  "name": "Home Mini revX",
  "type": "smart speaker",
  "manufacturer": "Google LLC",
  "connectivity": {
    "Wi-Fi": {
      "802.11": {
        "b": true,
        "g": true,
        "n": true,
        "ac": true
      },
      "frequencies": {
        "2.4": true,
        "5": true
      }
    },
    "bluetooth": "4.1"
  },
  "firmwareVersion": "1.27.090",
  "firmwareURL": "https://support.google.com/
     googlehome/answer/7365257?hl=en",
  "softwareVersion": "",
  "softwareURL": "",
  "autoUpdatesEnabled": true,
  "services": [
    {
      "name": "http",
      "port": "8008",
      "protocol": "tcp",
      "protocolVersion": "",
      "softwareVersion": ""
    },
    {
      "name": "ajp13",
      "port": "8009",
      "protocol": "tcp",
      "protocolVersion": "",
      "softwareVersion": ""
    },
    {
      "name": "https-alt",
      "port": "8443",
      "protocol": "tcp",
      "protocolVersion": "",
```

```
      "softwareVersion": ""
    },
    {
      "name": "cslistener",
      "port": "9000",
      "protocol": "tcp",
      "protocolVersion": "",
      "softwareVersion": ""
    },
    {
      "name": "scp-config",
      "port": "10001",
      "protocol": "tcp",
      "protocolVersion": "",
      "softwareVersion": ""
    }
  ],
  "encryption" : {
      ...
  }
}
```


These information provides no authenticity. Every device can send false IoTAG data and an attacker can impersonate a harmless device. Because of this, it is strongly recommended to sign this information with a private key, which can be trusted and verified over a public key infrastructure.

If an attacker has access to the network and uses the provided information from IoTAG to scan for insecure or unpatched devices, it brings out the importance for software and firmware updates. If all the devices use IoTAG, a central gateway (e.g., the router) can periodical check all devices. In case of a new vulnerability or missing software updates, the gateway can send a security warning or temporary disable the communication with the insecure device.

VIII. Conclusion and Future Work

The operation of a secure IoT network in the context of a smart home is currently not possible for non-technical users. One solution can be the reoccurring scoring of the network. First, the complete network is scanned and all devices are rated with different criteria. With this device scoring, an overall score for the network is calculated, which is easy to read by a non-technical user. These ratings can be used to improve the security by updating old firmware or software versions, as well as replacing old, insecure devices with new ones. By performing this scan and rating on a daily basis, a quick response to new threads is possible. In the future, we plan to improve this approach by scanning vulnerability databases. If a new vulnerability emerges for a device in the network, the user can be warned immediately.

For an accurate and detailed device identification and recognition, the new standard IoTAG must be implemented by every manufacturer. State of the art network scans can not provide enough information to rate the security of a device. For example, with nmap it is possible to guess the running services but not their software version.

We are currently working on a test environment and application to demonstrate the benefits of IoTAG. However, for this tool to be widely used, we need the feedback and cooperation of IoT manufacturers. Also, we are planning to improve the network scoring system by testing it on further networks.

References

[1] D. Goodin, Rash of in-the-wild attacks permanently destroys poorly secured IoT devices, Ars Technica, 2017. [Online]. Available from: https://arstechnica.com/information-technology/2017/04/rash-of-in-the-wild-attacks-permanently-detroys-poorly-secured-iot-devices/ [retrieved: 05, 2019].

[2] J. Wallen, Five nightmarish attacks that show the risks of IoT security, ZDNet, 2017. [Online]. Available from: https://www.zdnet.com/article/5-nightmarish-attacks-that-show-the-risks-of-iot-security/ [retrieved: 09, 2019].

[3] G. Lyon, Nmap: the Network Mapper - Free Security Scanner. [Online]. Available from: https://nmap.org [retrieved: 10, 2019].

[4] Fing Limited, Fing - IoT device intelligence for the connected world. [Online]. Available from: https://www.fing.com [retrieved: 10, 2019].

[5] M. Miettinen et al., "IOT SENTINEL Demo: Automated Device-Type Identification for Security Enforcement in IoT", IEEE 37th International Conference on Distributed Computing Systems (ICDCS), pp. 2511-2514, 2017.

[6] T. D. Nguyen et al., "DOT: A Federated Self-learning Anomaly Detection System for IoT", CoRR, pp. 756-767, 2019.

[7] T. Kohno, A. Broido, and K. C. Claffy, "Remote physical device fingerprinting", IEEE Trans. Dependable Secure Comput., vol. 2, no. 2, pp. 93108, April 2005.

[8] J. Cache, Fingerprinting 802.11 implementations via statistical analysis of the duration field, Uninformed, org 5, 2006.

[9] J. Franklin, D. McCoy, P. Tabriz, V. Neagoe, J. Van Randwyk, and D. Sicker, "Passive data link layer 802.11 wireless device driver fingerprinting", in USENIX Security Symposium, USENIX, pp. 167-178, 2006.

[10] V. Brik, S. Banerjee, M. Gruteser, and S. Oh, "Wireless device identification with radiometric signatures", International Conference on Mobile Computing and Networking, ACM, pp. 116127, 2008.

[11] F. Loiy, A. Sivanathany, H. H. Gharakheiliy, A. Radford, and V. Sivaraman, "Systematically Evaluating Security and Privacy for Consumer IoT Devices", IoT S&P 2017, pp. 1-6, 2017.

[12] K. C. Park and D. Shin, "Security assessment framework for IoT service", Telecommun Syst, pp. 193209, 2017.

[13] B. Ali and A. I. Awad, "Cyber and Physical Security Vulnerability Assessment for IoT-Based Smart Homes", sensors journal, vol 18(3), pp. 817, 2018.

[14] R. I. Bonilla, J. Crow, L. Basantes, and L. Cruz, "A Metric for Measuring IoT Devices Security Levels", IEEE 15th Intl Conf on Dependable, Autonomic and Secure Computing, pp. 704-709, 2017.

[15] A. E. Khaled, H. Abdelsalam, L. Wyatt, and L. Choonhwa, "IoT-DDL device description language for the T in IoT", IEEE Access 6, pp. 24048-24063, 2018.

[16] S. Kaebisch and A. Darko, "Thing description as enabler of semantic interoperability on the Web of Things", IoT Semantic Interoperability Workshop, pp. 1-3, 2016.

[17] L. Hinterberger, "Automated Risk Analysis of IoT-Infrastructures", Applied Research Conference, pp. 586-588, 2019.

[18] J. Schmidt, Cryptography in IT - recommendations on encryption and procedures, Kryptographie in der IT - Empfehlungen zu Verschluesselung und Verfahren, 2017. [Online]. Available from: https://www.heise.de/security/artikel/Kryptographie-in-der-IT-Empfehlungen-zu-Verschluesselung-und-Verfahren-3221002.html [retrieved: 09, 2019].

[19] G. Lyon, Service and version detection, Dienst- und Versionserkennung. [Online]. Available from: https://nmap.org/man/de/man-version-detection.html [retrieved: 09, 2019].

[20] Wireshark Foundation, tshark - Dump and analyze network traffic. [Online]. Available from: https://www.wireshark.org/docs/man-pages/tshark.html [retrieved: 10, 2019].

[21] The Hacker's Choice, thc-hydra. [Online]. Available from: https://github.com/vanhauser-thc/thc-hydra [retrieved: 10, 2019].

[22] AVM GmbH, Login to the FRITZ!Box Web Interface, 2018. [Online]. Available from: https://avm.de/fileadmin/user_upload/Global/Service/Schnittstellen/ Session-ID_english_13Nov18.pdf [retrieved: 07, 2019].

[23] G. Lyon, OS Detection - Nmap Network Scanning. [Online]. Available from: https://nmap.org/book/man-os-detection.html [retrieved: 09, 2019].

[24] Ecma International, ECMA-404: The JSON Data Interchange Syntax, 2017.
[25] Internet Engineering Task Force (IETF), The JavaScript Object Notation (JSON) Data Interchange Format, https://tools.ietf.org/html/rfc8259, 2017.
[26] N. Nurseitov, M. Paulson, R. Reynolds, and C. Izurieta, Comparison of JSON and XML Data Interchange Formats: A Case Study, CAINE, 2009.

Automotive Network Protocol Detection for Supporting Penetration Testing

Florian Sommer*, Jürgen Dürrwang†, Marius Wolf‡, Hendrik Juraschek§, Richard Ranert¶ and Reiner Kriesten‖
Institute of Energy Efficient Mobility (IEEM)
Karlsruhe University of Applied Sciences
Karlsruhe, Germany
email:{*florian.sommer, †juergen.duerrwang, ‡woma1029, §juhe1012, ¶rari1012, ‖reiner.kriesten}@hs-karlsruhe.de

***Abstract*—Currently, the automotive industry aims to integrate security into the vehicle development process. In this process, a vehicle is analyzed for possible security threats in order to develop security concepts or security measures. Another important aspect in vehicle security development is security testing. Penetration testing is often used for this purpose. In penetration testing, a tester acts from the perspective of an attacker and tries to violate security properties of a vehicle through attacks (tests) in order to uncover possible vulnerabilities. Since this task is usually performed as a black box test with little knowledge about the system, penetration testing is a highly experience-based activity. Due to this, an automation of this process is hard to achieve. In this paper, we want to support the penetration testing process and its automation by introducing an extension of our automotive portscanner tool. This scanner was developed to scan vehicle networks, which are different from typical Information Technology (IT) networks, in order to extract information about the vehicle. Our tool is able to gather Electronic Control Units (ECUs) installed in a vehicle, as well as diagnostic services and subfunctions they provide. This functionality is extended by an automatic detection of transport and diagnostic protocols used in vehicles. With this knowledge, new use cases and functionalities like fuzzing or an automated generation of penetration test cases can be realized.**

***Keywords*–Automotive Security; Penetration Testing; Automation; Network Protocols.**

I. INTRODUCTION

A trend towards autonomous driving is currently pursued in the automotive industry [1]. This increases the number of sensors and actuators installed in vehicles, as well as the complexity of internal and external communication of vehicle components. The required communication with the outside world for autonomous driving results in an increased risk of security attacks. This has already been demonstrated by various research groups [2]–[8]. Attacks were carried out on vehicles in which it was possible to manipulate actuators, which had an influence on driving physics, such as steering and braking systems. Since only a few methods have been established in the automotive sector to protect against such attacks, a high effort is currently being invested in research and development of security measures, standards and processes. The development partnership AUTomotive Open System ARchitecture (AUTOSAR) presented a measure to secure internal vehicle networks with Secure Onboard Communication (SecOC) [9], which enables authenticated communication of the vehicle's internal bus systems. In January 2016, Society of Automotive Engineers (SAE) International published SAE J3061 (Cybersecurity Guidebook for Cyber-Physical Vehicle Systems) [10], a guideline in which security was integrated into the vehicle development process. In this process, a vehicle is analyzed for possible security threats in order to develop security concepts or security measures. Another important aspect in vehicle security development is security testing. In addition to the verification of implemented security measures, this also includes testing the vehicle for vulnerabilities. Penetration testing [11] is often used for this purpose. In penetration testing, a tester acts from the perspective of an attacker. The tester tries to violate security properties of a vehicle through attacks (tests) in order to uncover possible vulnerabilities. Penetration tests can be carried out as black box tests, without any information about the internal function of a system, or as white box tests in case of knowledge about the internal function. Especially in case of black box tests, the success of a penetration test depends on the experience of a tester, since there is limited knowledge about the system.

Problem: Penetration testing can be time consuming and potential vulnerabilities could be missed, depending on available system information. It is an explorative test method which highly depends on a tester's experience. As a result, an automation of this process is hard to achieve.

Approach: We present a way to support the process of penetration testing through a tool-based solution. Our automotive portscanner, which was introduced in the past [12], serves as a basis. This scanner was developed in order to scan vehicle networks, since they differ from IT networks by used communication technologies, protocols and operating systems. Our tool is used to support the information gathering process and it is able to gather ECUs installed in a vehicle, as well as their diagnostic services and subfunctions.

Contribution: We extend the functionality of our portscanner by an automatic detection of transport and diagnostic protocols which delivers additional information about a vehicle and its internal structure. This leads to a greater coverage when extracting vehicle data. We show how this can contribute to an automation of penetration testing subprocesses by presenting use cases which are possible with the knowledge about a vehicle's transport and diagnostic protocols. As a result, new functionalities like automated testing of attacks or fuzzing [13] based on these transport and diagnostic protocols can be realized.

This work is structured as follows: In Section II, we discuss existing vehicle network communication systems and relevant transport and diagnostic protocols. Furthermore, we present basic penetration testing processes and automotive related adaptions. In Section III, we present our automotive portscanner, as well as its extension for automatic protocol detection and resulting use cases. We also illustrate, how ECUs, transport protocols and diagnostic protocols are automatically detected. To point out how this can contribute to support automated penetration tests, we present different functionalities in Section IV, which can be realized by our automatic protocol detection. Finally, we summarize our results in Section V and present planned future work.

II. Background

In this section, we want to give a short overview of a vehicle's network and its communication systems, as well as the process of penetration testing and how it is performed in the automotive domain.

A. Vehicle Network Protocols

The Open Systems Interconnection (OSI) layer model [14] is used for a structured description of communication systems. It describes seven different layers which include specific tasks of message transmission. Since we focus on transport and diagnostic protocols for automotive communication systems, the relevant layers for our purposes are: physical layer (1), data link layer (2), transport layer (4) and application layer (7). The layers 1 and 2 are represented by the used communication systems. There are different communication systems in a vehicle, like FlexRay [15], Controller Area Network (CAN) [16], Local Interconnect Network (LIN) [17], Ethernet [18] and Media Oriented System Transport (MOST) [19]. These systems are used for various applications and have different properties. FlexRay is a cyclic network communication system which is used for applications requiring high data rates (10 Mbit/s). MOST and Ethernet are mainly applied for multimedia purposes with even higher data rates. LIN is a serial network protocol which connects components like sensors and ECUs. For the automotive sector, CAN [16] is one of the most important and commonly used bus systems. It is a bitstream-oriented bus system, using twisted pair wires as physical medium. CAN is a broadcast system in which each message is uniquely characterized by an identifier. Since it is currently the most used bus system in the automotive domain, we first focus on CAN for the automated protocol detection. To explain the functionality of that mechanism, this paper is focused on CAN-based transport and diagnostic protocols. Transport protocols represent the fourth layer of the OSI layer model. They are required to transfer data larger than the maximum message length. This is particularly necessary for diagnostic applications and flash programming of ECUs. A further task of the transport protocols is to control time intervals between individual data packages. Transport protocols are also used to forward messages via gateways to networks with a different address space. The widespread protocols are International Organization for Standardization Transport Protocol (ISOTP) [20] and SAE J1939 [21], which are standardized, and Transport Protocol (TP) 2.0 [22], which is a proprietary protocol of vehicle manufacturer Volkswagen. ISOTP and TP 2.0 come into operation for passenger cars, whereas the SAE J1939 protocol is used for commercial vehicles. The application layer is represented by diagnostic protocols. Diagnostic protocols use a so-called Service Identifier (SID) [23] to select different diagnostic services an ECU offers. To understand their functionality, the communication principle is shown in Figure 1. An external diagnostic testing device runs as a client, whereas the ECU runs as a server. To start a diagnostic communication, the diagnostic testing device has to send a diagnostic request message to an ECU. This request contains a SID and a subfunction which is necessary to address diagnostic services like reading the error memory. The addressed ECU can answer with a positive or negative response. A positive response is characterized by the addition of value 0x40 to the SID. A negative response is characterized by an Error-ID (0x7F), the original SID and a Response Code that contains the reason for the negative reponse.

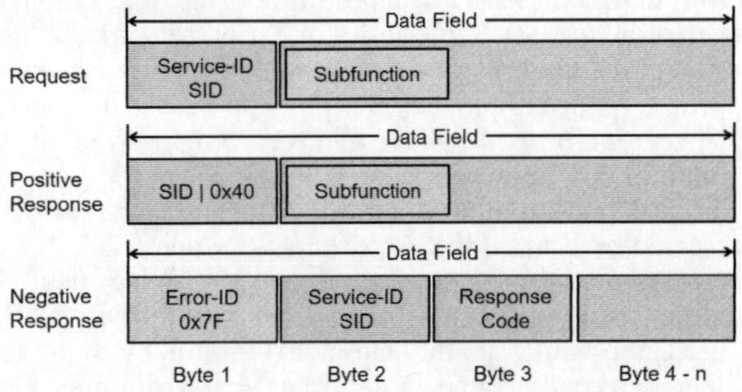

Figure 1. Request and response scheme of automotive diagnostic protocols.

The following three diagnostic protocols are relevant: Keyword Protocol (KWP) 2000 [24], Unified Diagnostic Services (UDS) [23] and On-Board Diagnostics (OBD) [25]. These protocols are standardized and similar to each other, since all of them follow the communication principle in Figure 1. To sum up, there are three relevant components in vehicle networks: the communication systems, tranport protocols and diagnostic protocols. The transport protocol is embedded into the data field of the communication system message and the diagnostic protocol is embedded into the transport protocol.

B. Penetration Testing

Penetration tests are carried out on running systems and take place in the late phases of the development cycle. Usually, these tests are black box tests, since the tester has no knowledge of the internal functionality of the system. Thus, the tester acts from the attacker's point of view. Several standards and guidelines have been published for conducting penetration tests. Pure penetration testing standards can be seen as a part of security assessment methods, whereas security assessment methods describe a comprehensive assessment of the security of a system or company. Examples for security assessment guides are National Institute of Standards and Technology (NIST) SP 800-115 (Technical Guide to Information Security Testing and Assessment) [26], Open Source Security Testing Methodology Manual (OSSTMM) 3 [27], Information Systems Security Assessment Framework (ISSAF) [28] and Open Web Application Security Project (OWASP) Testing Guide [29]. An example of a pure penetration testing standard is the Penetration Testing Execution Standard (PTES) [30], which is intended to support companies and security service providers in conducting penetration tests. A methodology for security testing in the automotive sector is presented in the dissertation [31] with Automotive Security Testing Methodology (ASTM), which is divided into five areas: planning phase, detection phase, safe state analysis, moving vehicle analysis, documentation and review. The methodology covers the typical phases of the aforementioned methods and transfers them to the automotive sector, especially the vehicle networking of the control units. Our portscanner is used as an examplary tool for the information gathering phase (detection phase). Vehicle penetration testing has also been addressed in other works. Bayer et al. [32] address penetration testing as a part of practical automotive security testing. In [33], they classify penetration testing as a parallel test method to functional testing, fuzz testing and vulnerability testing, distinguishing between hardware, software, backend and network penetration testing and also considering organizational aspects. In [34], Bayer et al. present an approach for the realization of a penetration testing framework for CAN networks which is based on the work mentioned above and enables a systematic approach for penetration testers. This approach is demonstrated by two examples in which a reverse engineering of CAN identifiers and an exploitation of UDS diagnostic commands is carried out. Another approach to penetration testing was presented by Smith [35]. An overview of possible CAN tools was presented by Pozzobon et al. [36] and Sintsov [37]. Additionally, Dürrwang et al. [38] emphasise the benefits of penetration testing in the automotive sector by exploiting a vulnerability they found in an airbag ECU with a systematic penetration testing process.

III. APPROACH

In this section, our automotive portscanner and its extension for an automated detection of a vehicle's network protocols is introduced.

A. *Automotive Portscanner*

The portscanner's purpose is to detect ECUs in a vehicle and to search for offered diagnostic services and subservices, as well as specific data from an ECU. The tool operates without the knowledge of any manufacturer specific information by the user and can be connected to the OBD connector, as shown in Figure 2, and also directly to a bus system.

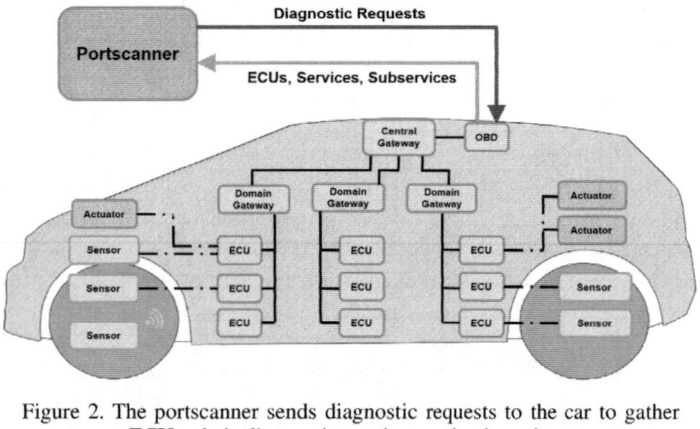

Figure 2. The portscanner sends diagnostic requests to the car to gather ECUs, their diagnostic services and subservices.

In the first step, the portscanner uses an exhaustive search method to detect all ECUs inside a vehicle network. Therefore, standard diagnostic requests, as defined in International Organization for Standardisation (ISO) 14229, are sequencially sent to every possible CAN Identifier (ID). If a response to a request is received (positive or negative), an ECU is identified. In the next step, supported diagnostic services are identified. Similar to the ECU identification process before, every possible SID is checked by sending diagnostic requests to every detected ECU. A service is supported if there is a positive or negative response to a request. As a last step, subservices of all found diagnostic services are identified by sending diagnostic requests to every possible subservice for all supported services of each ECU. A challenge with the portscanner is the variation of transport protocols that can be used in vehicle networks. ISOTP in combination with OBD is required by law for diagnostic purposes. However, specific areas are reserved for vehicle manufacturers in diagnostic standards. For example, transport protocols, such as TP 2.0 are used for these diagnostic requests in vehicles of Volkswagen AG. An example of current capabilities of the portscanner is given in [31], where the tool was applied on two vehicles. On the first vehicle, our portscanner could find 47 ECUs, 380 diagnostic services and 1,924 subservices within 48 minutes and 27 seconds. On the second vehicle, it could find 43 ECUs, 282 diagnostic services and 2,538 subservices within 36 minutes and 5 seconds. A further evaluation across several vehicle types and manufacturers will have to be carried out in the future. The portscanner functionality is extended by an automatic protocol detection in order to achieve a greater coverage during the extraction of vehicle data.

B. *Automatic Protocol Detection*

To operate the portscanner in an automated way, it is necessary to know the used transport protocol and type of CAN identifiers. Unfortunately, this information is unknown by default. Because of that, we decided to develop an automatic protocol detection to extend the functionality of our portscanner. At first, a differentiation between 11-bit and 29-bit CAN bus systems is necessary. The 11-bit CAN system is refered to as CAN 2.0A, while a 29-bit system is refered to as CAN 2.0B. Both formats are specified in [16]. A differentiation between these formats can be made by the Identifier Extension (IDE) bit, which is a part of the control field of a CAN message. On this account, the tool monitors the CAN bus and checks if the IDE bit is dominant (value 0) or recessive (value 1). A dominant bit signals the usage of the standard 11-bit format. After the ID format is known, transport and diagnostic protocols can be identified. As mentioned in Section II, relevant diagnostic protocols (UDS, OBD, KWP 2000) follow the same scheme, which is illustrated in Figure 1. The main difference between these protocols are the services they address. This results in different SID areas that can be called. In order to identify supported diagnostic protocols, requests have to be sent to vehicle ECUs in which potential SIDs are addressed. In case of a response to a SID, the service and its related diagnostic protocol is supported. Since diagnostic protocols are embedded in a transport protocol format, the identification of these protocols can be executed at the same time. In order to identify a transport protocol, the exhaustive search attempt of the portscanner is extended. The method starts by sending diagnostic requests embedded in every possible transport protocol (ISOTP, TP 2.0, SAE J1939). If there is a response (positive or negative) to one of the combinations, the used transport protocol is supported. In Figure 3, this process is illustrated for 11-bit CAN IDs. If the CAN ID is in range 0x7E0 to 0x7EF, it concerns OBD, since that range is reserved for this diagnostic protocol combined with ISOTP. If the CAN ID is not in that range, we have to check for the transport protocol by checking the CAN frame for ISOTP and TP 2.0 formats. After the transport protocol is recognized, the diganostic protocol support for UDS and KWP 2000 is checked. After the diagnostic protocol is recognized, the next CAN frame with the next CAN ID can be evaluated until all IDs are checked. It should be mentioned that more than one transport protocol can be used within a communication system. For example, even if CAN uses ISOTP, it can additionally use

TP 2.0. The same applies for diagnostic protocols.

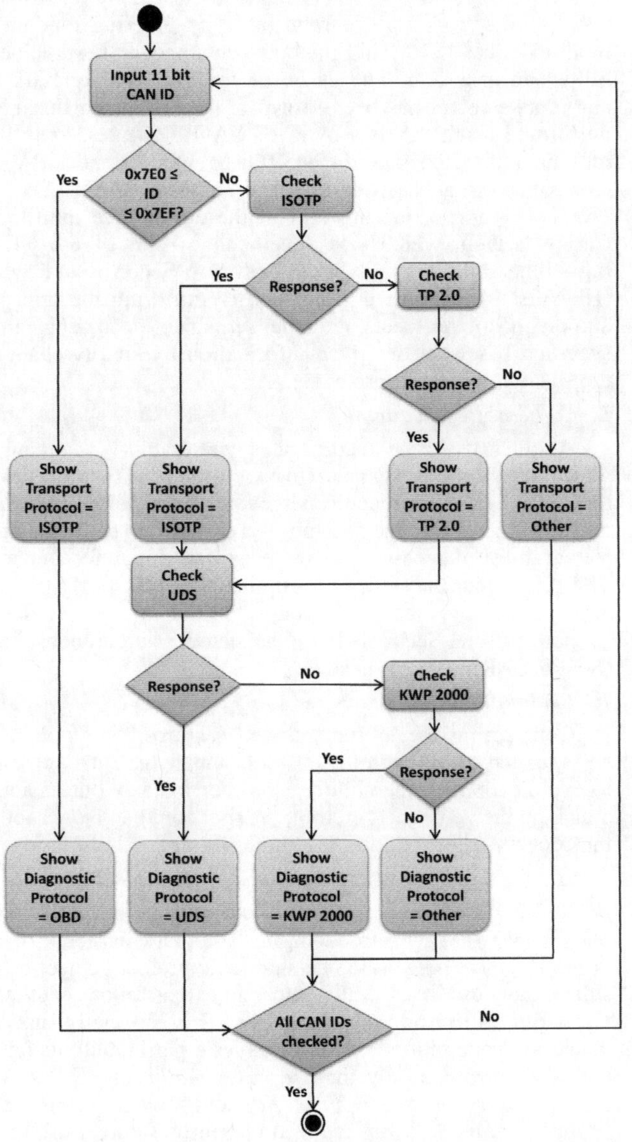

Figure 3. Protocol detection procedure for 11-bit CAN IDs.

This possibility is not shown in Figure 3 due to clearness of the process illustration. Based on the CAN ID, it is possible to reduce the number of potential protocol combinations. For example, since SAE J1939 is only defined for 29-bit systems, it has not to be considered for 11-bit CAN systems. Another reduction can be made for 29-bit CAN IDs. In theory, there are 2^{29} possible IDs for these systems, so an exhaustive search on a 29-bit identifier is not feasible in practice. In order to bypass this problem, the specifications of diagnostic protocols are used. For diagnostic purposes, 29-bit CAN IDs have a specified structure. For ISO 15765, the ID structure is illustrated in Figure 4. As can be seen, there is a differentiation between Source and Destination Address. Source Address is the testers (portscanners) address, which is usually set to 0xF1. Destination Address is the address of an ECU. Since a Destination Address only consists of 11 bit, the number of possible identifiers is reduced to 2^{11}, which is equal to CAN 2.0A 11-bit IDs. The SAE J1939 protocol has a similar structure in which the Destination Address only consists of 8 bit, so there are just 2^8 possible identifiers. These two specifications lead to a significant reduction of the original 2^{29} possible CAN IDs.

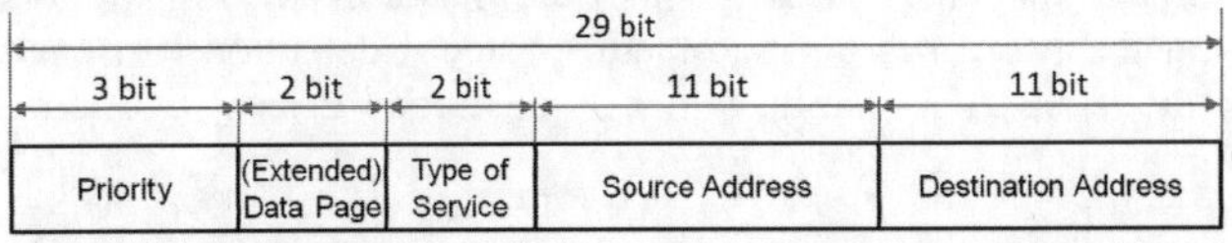

Figure 4. 29-bit CAN identifier in ISO 15765.

C. Example

To illustrate how the protocol detection works, its functionality is described with an example of a 11-bit CAN system, which is shown in Table I. This example follows the control flow shown in Figure 3 and distinguishes three iterations. In the first iteration (line 1 in Table I) of the example, the protocol detection for ISOTP in combination with OBD is explained. The second iteration (line 2) explains the protocol detection for ISOTP in combination with UDS. The last iteration (line 3) shows the detection for ISOTP in combination with KWP 2000. For conciseness reasons, we decided not to show an example of the protocol detection for TP 2.0 or ISOTP in case of a message segmentation (more than 8 data bytes), since the structure of these transport protocols is far more complex and would go beyond the scope of this publication.

TABLE I. EXAMPLE OF THE AUTOMATIC PROTOCOL DETECTION BY SENDING DIFFERENT REQUESTS AS DESCRIBED IN FIGURE 3 (NUMBERS ARE IN HEXADECIMAL FORMAT).

Message	ID	Data	Identified
ISOTP OBD Request	7E0	02 01 05 00 00 00 00 00	ISOTP,
ISOTP OBD Response	7E8	06 41 05 22 AA 00 D5 00	OBD
ISOTP UDS Request	602	02 10 03 00 00 00 00 00	ISOTP,
ISOTP UDS Response	630	04 40 03 00 CD 00 00 00	UDS
ISOTP KWP 2000 Request	604	02 1A 01 00 00 00 00 00	ISOTP,
ISOTP KWP 2000 Response	6A0	06 5A 01 00 89 23 41 00	KWP 2000

In the first iteration (line 1), a diagnostic request based on ISOTP and OBD is sent on CAN. Since there is a response to this request and the CAN ID is in range 0x7E0 to 0x7EF, the transport protocol ISOTP and the diagnostic protocol OBD is supported. The second iteration (line 2) is similar to the first one. The difference is the diagnostic protocol used for the request, which is UDS now. The CAN ID of the reponse is not in the OBD ID range, so according to Figure 3 the response is checked for ISOTP, which is supported, since the reponse has the format of this transport protocol. After that, the diagnostic protocol has to be recognized. The requested service (SID = 0x10) and its subservice (0x03) is a UDS specific service, so the diagnostic protocol is UDS. The last iteration (line 3) contains a diagnostic request based on ISOTP and KWP 2000. The detection works similar to the former two iterations. Since the requested service (SID = 0x1A) is a KWP 2000 specific service, the diagnostic protocol is KWP 2000. It should be mentioned that presented transport and diagnostic protocols are relatively complex, so the example in Table I and detection process in Figure 3 can differ for some protocol combinations or detection functions. UDS, for example, is a replacement for KWP 2000 and many services between those protocols have the same SID, so in this case a differentiation has to be made at the level of subservices. Another difference could be more physical when considering the baudrate of the bus system. For example, UDS does not prescribe a baudrate, in contrast to OBD. We do not want to go into too much detail of the special protocol properties. Instead, we want to focus on the use cases our automatic protocol detection can enable for penetration testing, which is described in next Section.

IV. Use Cases

In this section, use cases of the portscanner and its automatic protocol detection for penetration testing purposes are presented.

A. Gathering ECUs, Services, Subservices and Vehicle Data

The possibility to extract information about existing ECUs, its diagnostic services and subservices has been described before and is part of the portscanner functionality. Another feature facilitates the extraction of vehicle data like fault memory, chassis number, or ECU firmware versions. This can be done by requesting diagnostic services. Further, the extension to support an automatic protocol detection enables our tool to achieve a greater coverage by gathering even more vehicle information including prescribed and manufacturer-specific diagnostic functions. This is an advantage for penetration testing, as it enables the tester to obtain far more information about the vehicle which is particularly relevant for black box penetration tests.

B. Reverse Engineering of the Routing Table

Normally, a diagnostic tester is connected to the OBD connector of a vehicle. For vehicles, which usually have several bus systems, these bus systems are separated via gateways, whereas each gateway is responsible for mapping the message format of one bus system to the message format of another bus system (for example CAN to LIN). If a diagnostic request is sent to a control unit that is connected to the OBD connector via several gateways and bus systems, diagnostic messages have to be routed via these connections to the target ECU. This routing is determined during the development of the vehicle in form of a routing table, which is not known to testers. From a penetration testing point of view, reverse engineering of that table can be accomplished with the automatic protocol detection by sending a diagnostic request to observe the message routing on the bus systems between OBD connector, gateways and target ECUs. However, it should be mentioned that this requires a physical connection to these bus systems.

C. Automatic Test Case Generation

Based on recognized vehicle network protocols, it is possible to automatically derive test cases. This can be done on the basis of known vulnerabilities which can be used for an exploitation of diagnostic services that were attacked in the past. Many of the attacks mentioned in Section I are based on exploited diagnostic services [2]–[4]. Therefore, this information can be used as data input for the automatic generation of test cases. Another possible data input could be our own collection [39] of vulnerabilities and attacks on vehicles, which was classified in form of a taxonomy [40], to support penetration testing.

D. Fuzzing

In fuzzing, an attempt is made to test a system for its susceptibility to errors or robustness by entering random or modified data [13]. This method can uncover new vulnerabilities in a system. The usage of fuzzing techniques in the automotive sector has been shown in [41] in which fuzzing is performed using the data bytes of CAN messages, or in [42] in which the fuzzing tool beSTORM was extended by the Controller Area Network Flexible Datarate (CAN FD) [43] protocol. Another fuzzing tool in the automotive industry is CaringCaribou, which was developed as part of the HEAling Vulnerabilities to ENhance Software Security and Safety (HEAVENS) research project [44]. By knowing the transport and diagnostic protocols, the input sequence for fuzzing can be specified based on the given information by simply changing the data within these protocols.

E. Vulnerability Scanning

Another use case incorporates vulnerability scanning in which a system is scanned for known security vulnerabilities. Through an automatic detection of supported vehicular network protocols, the scanning process can be automated. Vulnerability databases can serve as data input for our tool. The Karlsruhe University of Applied Sciences [45] currently aims to develop such a database for the automotive sector as part of the Security For Connected, Autonomous caRs (SecForCARs) [46] project.

F. Exploitation Tool

Considering the aforementioned features, our tool could be extended to an exploitation tool, with which it is possible to exploit found vulnerabilities, in order to carry out an actual attack on the vehicle. Therefore, the tool could actively support the process of penetration testing and its partial automation.

V. Conclusion and Future Work

In this paper, we presented an extension of our automotive portscanner [12] by introducing an automatic protocol detection for vehicle networks. The automatic protocol detection results in new use cases, which allow an extension of penetration test activities by additional functions. This especially supports black box penetration tests and enables a partial automation of the process. Since only the use cases *Gathering ECUs, Services, Subservices and Vehicle Data* and *Reverse Engineering of the Routing Table* are realized currently, future work could include the extension of our tool by further use cases. To put the aforementioned use cases into practice, an incorporation of further bus systems into our tool is required. Examples are LIN, Ethernet, CAN FD and FlexRay. These bus systems partially use different protocols like User Datagram Protocol (UDP) [47] and Transmission Control Protocol (TCP) [48] for the transport layer or Diagnostics over IP (DoIP) [49] for the application layer of Ethernet. An extension of our tool by these protocols could be conceivable. Since there have been several remote attacks on vehicles, another extension could include an implementation of wireless technologies to our tool, so the risk for this type of attack can be assessed. In this way, the portscanner can be extended to a useful penetration testing tool for vehicle networks.

Acknowledgements

This work has been developed in the project SAFE ME ASAP (reference number: 03FH011IX5) that is partly funded by the German ministry of education and research (BMBF).

REFERENCES

[1] M. Maurer, J. C. Gerdes, B. Lenz, and H. Winner, "Autonomes Fahren: technische, rechtliche und gesellschaftliche Aspekte [Autonomous Driving: Technical, Legal and Social Aspects]". Springer-Verlag, 2015.

[2] C. Miller and C. Valasek, "Adventures in automotive networks and control units," Def Con, vol. 21, 2013, pp. 260–264.

[3] ——, "A survey of remote automotive attack surfaces," Black Hat USA, vol. 2014, 2014.

[4] ——, "Remote exploitation of an unaltered passenger vehicle," Black Hat USA, vol. 2015, 2015.

[5] Keen Lab, "Experimental Security Assessment of BMW Cars: A Summary Report," 2017.

[6] K. Mahaffey, "Hacking a Tesla Model S: What we found and what we learned," 2015, https://blog.lookout.com/hacking-a-tesla. [accessed: 2019-09-03].

[7] K. Koscher et al., "Experimental Security Analysis of a Modern Automobile," in 2010 IEEE Symposium on Security and Privacy. IEEE, 5/16/2010 - 5/19/2010, pp. 447–462.

[8] S. Checkoway et al., "Comprehensive Experimental Analyses of Automotive Attack Surfaces," in USENIX Security Symposium, 2011.

[9] AUTOSAR, "Specification of Secure Onboard Communication," 2018, https://www.autosar.org/fileadmin/user_upload/standards/classic/4-3/AUTOSAR_SWS_SecureOnboardCommunication.pdf. [accessed: 2019-09-03].

[10] SAE Vehicle Electrical System Security Committee, "SAE J3061-Cybersecurity Guidebook for Cyber-Physical Vehicle Systems," SAE-Society of Automotive Engineers, 2016.

[11] B. Arkin, S. Stender, and G. McGraw, "Software penetration testing," IEEE Security & Privacy, vol. 3, no. 1, 2005, pp. 84–87.

[12] M. Ring, J. Dürrwang, F. Sommer, and R. Kriesten, "Survey on Vehicular Attacks - Building a Vulnerability Database," in 2015 IEEE International Conference on Vehicular Electronics and Safety (ICVES). IEEE, 11/5/2015 - 11/7/2015, pp. 208–212.

[13] B. P. Miller, L. Fredriksen, and B. So, "An empirical study of the reliability of UNIX utilities," Communications of the ACM, vol. 33, no. 12, 1990, pp. 32–44.

[14] ISO/IEC 7498-1:1994, "Information technology - Open Systems Interconnection - Basic Reference Model: The Basic Model," 1994.

[15] ISO 17458-1:2013, "Road vehicles–FlexRay communications system–Part 1: General information and use case definition," International Organization for Standardization, 2013.

[16] ISO 11898-1:2015, "Road vehicles – Controller area network (CAN) – Part 1: Data link layer and physical signalling," 1993.

[17] L. Consortium, "LIN: Specification Package. Revision 2.2 A, 2010."

[18] IEEE 802.3bw-2015, "IEEE Standard for Ethernet Amendment 1: Physical Layer Specifications and Management Parameters for 100 Mb/s Operation over a Single Balanced Twisted Pair Cable (100BASE-T1)," 2015.

[19] M. Cooperation, "MOST Specification Rev 3.0," 2008.

[20] ISO 15765-2:2016, "Road vehicles – Diagnostic communication over Controller Area Network (DoCAN) – Part 2: Transport protocol and network layer services," 2016.

[21] SAE J1939_201206, "Serial Control and Communications Heavy Duty Vehicle Network - Top Level Document," 2012.

[22] W. Zimmermann and R. Schmidgall, "Bussysteme in der Fahrzeugtechnik: Protokolle, Standards und Softwarearchitektur [Bus Systems in Automotive Engineering: Protocols, Standards and Software Architecture]", 5th ed. Wiesbaden: Springer Vieweg, 2014.

[23] ISO 14229:2006, "Road vehicles — Unified diagnostic services (UDS) — Specification and requirements," 2006.

[24] ISO 14230-3:1999, "Road vehicles – Diagnostic systems – Keyword Protocol 2000 – Part 3: Application layer," 1999.

[25] ISO 15031-3:2016, "Road vehicles – Communication between vehicle and external equipment for emissions-related diagnostics – Part 3: Diagnostic connector and related electrical circuits: Specification and use," 2016.

[26] K. A. Scarfone, M. P. Souppaya, A. Cody, and A. D. Orebaugh, "SP 800-115. Technical Guide to Information Security Testing and Assessment," 2008.

[27] P. Herzog, "Open-Source Security Testing Methodology Manual," Institute for Security and Open Methodologies (ISECOM), 2003.

[28] B. Rathore et al., "ISSAF-Information System Security Assesment Framework-30.04," 2006.

[29] M. Meucci, E. Keary, and D. Cuthbert, "OWASP Testing Guide, v3," OWASP Foundation, vol. 16, 2008.

[30] C. Nickerson et al., "The Penetration Testing Execution Standard," 2017.

[31] M. Ring, "Systematische Security-Tests von Kraftfahrzeugen [Systematic Security Tests of Motor Vehicles]," Dissertation, Universität Ulm, Ulm, 2019.

[32] S. Bayer, T. Enderle, D. Oka, and M. Wolf, "Automotive Security Testing—The Digital Crash Test," in Energy Consumption and Autonomous Driving. Springer, 2016, pp. 13–22.

[33] S. Bayer, "Practical Security Evaluations of Automotive Onboard IT Components," 2015.

[34] S. Bayer, K. Hirata, and D. Oka, "Towards a Systematic Pentesting Framework for In-Vehicular CAN," 2016.

[35] C. Smith, The Car Hacker's Handbook: A Guide for the Penetration Tester. No Starch Press, 2016.

[36] E. Pozzobon, N. Weiss, S. Renner, and R. Hackenberg, "A Survey on Media Access Solutions for CAN Penetration Testing," 2018.

[37] A. Sintsov, "Pentesting Vehicles with CANToolz: YACHT - Yet Another Car Hacking Tool," 2016.

[38] J. Dürrwang, J. Braun, M. Rumez, R. Kriesten, and A. Pretschner, "Enhancement of Automotive Penetration Testing with Threat Analyses Results," SAE International Journal of Transportation Cybersecurity and Privacy, vol. 1, no. 11-01-02-0005, 2018, pp. 91–112.

[39] F. Sommer and J. Dürrwang, "Automotive Attack Database (AAD)," 2019, https://github.com/IEEM-HsKA/AAD [accessed: 2019-09-03].

[40] F. Sommer, J. Dürrwang, and R. Kriesten, "Survey and Classification of Automotive Security Attacks," Information, vol. 10, no. 4, 2019, p. 148.

[41] H. Lee, K. Choi, K. Chung, J. Kim, and K. Yim, "Fuzzing CAN Packets into Automobiles," in 2015 IEEE 29th International Conference on Advanced Information Networking and Applications, 2015, pp. 817–821.

[42] R. Nishimura et al., "Implementation of the CAN-FD protocol in the fuzzing tool beSTORM," in 2016 IEEE International Conference on Vehicular Electronics and Safety (ICVES), 2016, pp. 1–6.

[43] F. Hartwich, "CAN with flexible data-rate," in Proc. iCC. Citeseer, 2012, pp. 1–9.

[44] The HEAVENS project, "CaringCaribou: A friendly car security exploration tool," https://github.com/CaringCaribou/caringcaribou, 2019, https://github.com/CaringCaribou/caringcaribou [accessed: 2019-09-03].

[45] Karlsruhe University of Applied Sciences, "Sichere Datenverarbeitung beim autonomen Fahren: Starke IT-Sicherheit für das Auto der Zukunft – Forschungsverbund entwickelt neue Ansätze [Secure Data Processing during Autonomous Driving: Strong IT Security for the Car of the Future – Research Consortium develops new Approaches]," 2019, https://www.hs-karlsruhe.de/presse/secforcars/. [accessed: 2019-09-03].

[46] Federal Ministry of Education and Research, "SecForCARs: Security For Connected, Autonomous Cars," 2019, https://www.forschung-it-sicherheit-kommunikationssysteme.de/projekte/sicherheit-fuer-vernetzte-autonome-fahrzeuge. [accessed: 2019-09-03].

[47] J. Postel, "RFC 768: User datagram protocol," Tech. Rep., 1980.

[48] ——, "RFC 793: Transmission control protocol," 1981.

[49] ISO 13400-2:20126, "Road vehicles - Diagnostic communication over Internet Protocol (DoIP) – Part 2: Transport protocol and network layer services," 2012.

Aggregation-Based Certificate Transparency Gossip

Rasmus Dahlberg, Tobias Pulls, Jonathan Vestin, Toke Høiland-Jørgensen and Andreas Kassler

Karlstad University
Universitetsgatan 2, 651 88 Karlstad, Sweden
email: `first.last@kau.se`

***Abstract*—Certificate Transparency (CT) requires that every certificate which is issued by a certificate authority must be publicly logged. While a CT log can be untrusted in theory, it relies on the assumption that every client observes and cryptographically verifies the same log. As such, some form of gossip mechanism is needed in practice. Despite CT being adopted by several major browser vendors, no gossip mechanism is widely deployed. We suggest an aggregation-based gossip mechanism that passively observes cryptographic material that CT logs emit in plaintext, aggregating at packet processors (such as routers and switches) to periodically verify log consistency off-path. In other words, gossip is provided as-a-service by the network. Our proposal can be implemented for a variety of programmable packet processors at line-speed without aggregation distinguishers (throughput), and, based on 20 days of RIPE Atlas measurements that represent clients from 3500 autonomous systems, we show that significant protection against split-viewing CT logs can be achieved with a realistic threat model and an incremental deployment scenario.**

Keywords–Certificate Transparency; Gossip; P4; XDP.

I. Introduction

The HyperText Transfer Protocol Secure (HTTPS) ecosystem is going through a paradigm shift. As opposed to blindly trusting that Certificate Authorities (CAs) only issue certificates to the rightful domain owners—a model known for its weakest-link security [1]—transparency into the set of issued certificates is incrementally being required by major browser vendors [2][3]. This transparency is forced and takes the form of Certificate Transparency (CT) logs: the idea is to reject any Transport Layer Security (TLS) certificate that have yet to be publicly logged, such that domain owners can monitor the logs for client-accepted certificates to *detect* certificate mis-issuance *after the fact* [4]. While the requirement of certificate logging is a significant improvement to the HTTPS ecosystem, the underlying problem of trusting CAs cannot be solved by the status quo of trusted CT logs (described further in Section II-A). Therefore, it is paramount that nobody needs to trust these logs once incremental deployments are matured.

CT is formalized and cryptographically verifiable [5], supporting inclusion and consistency proofs. This means that a client can verify whether a log is operated correctly: said certificates are included in the log, and nothing is being removed or modified. Despite the ability to cryptographically verify these two properties, there are no assurances that everybody observes *the same log* [4][6]. For example, certificate mis-issuance would not be detected by a domain owner that monitors the logs if fraudulently issued certificates are shown to the clients selectively. A log that serves different versions of itself is said to present a *split view* [7]. Unless such log misbehaviour can be detected, we must trust it not to happen.

The solution to the split viewing problem is a gossip mechanism which ensures that everybody observes *the same* consistent log [4]. This assumption is simple in theory but remarkably hard in practice due to client privacy, varying threat models, and deployment challenges [7][8]. While Google started on a package that supports minimal gossip [9] and the mechanisms of Nordberg *et al.* [7], there is "next to no deployment in the wild" [10]. To this end, we propose a gossip mechanism that helps detecting split-view attacks retroactively based on the idea of packet processors, such as routers and middleboxes, that *aggregate* Signed Tree Heads (STHs)—succinct representations of the logs' states—that are exposed to the network *in plaintext*. The aggregated STHs are then used to challenge the logs to prove consistency via an off-path, such that the logs cannot distinguish between challenges that come from different aggregators. Given this indistinguishability assumption, it is non-trivial to serve a consistent split-view to an unknown location [11]. Thus, all aggregators must be on the same view, and accordingly all clients that are covered by these aggregators must also be on the same view *despite not doing any explicit gossip themselves* because gossip is provided as-a-service by the network. An isolated client (i.e., untrusted network path to the aggregator) is notably beyond reach of any retroactive gossip [8].

The premise of having STHs in plaintext is controversial given current trends to encrypt transport protocols, which is otherwise an approach that combats inspection of network traffic and protocol ossification [12][13]. We argue that keeping gossip related material in plaintext to support aggregation-based gossip comes with few downsides though: it is easy to implement, there are no major negative privacy impacts, and it would offer significant protection for a large portion of the Internet with a realistic threat model *despite relatively small deployment efforts*. The three main limitations are no protection against isolated clients, reliance on clients that fetch STHs from the logs in plaintext, and possible concerns surrounding protocol ossification [13]. Our contributions are:

- Design and security considerations for a network-based gossip mechanism that passively aggregates STHs to verify log consistency off-path (Section III).
- Generic implementations of the aggregation step using Programming Protocol independent Packet Processors (P4) [14] and eXpress Data Path (XDP) [15] for plaintext STHs, supporting line-speed packet processing on systems that range from switches, routers, network interface cards, and Linux (Section IV).
- A simulation based on RIPE Atlas measurements that evaluate the impact of deploying aggregation-based

gossip at Autonomous Systems (ASes) and Internet Exchange Points (IXPs). Our evaluation shows that incremental roll-out at well-connected locations would protect a significant portion of all Internet clients from undetected split views (Section V).

Besides the sections referenced above, the paper introduces necessary background in Section II and provides discussion, conclusion, and future work in Sections VI–VIII. A full version with additional implementation details is available online [16].

II. Background

First, additional prerequisites are provided on CT and the status quo, then the techniques which allow us to program custom packet processors are introduced.

A. Certificate Transparency

The main motivation of CT is that the CA ecosystem is error-prone [17]: a CA can normally issue certificates for *any* domain name, and given that there are hundreds of trusted CAs an attacker only needs to target the weakest link [1]. While the requirement of CT logging all certificates cannot prevent mis-issuance proactively, it allows anyone to detect it retroactively by monitoring the logs [4]. After a log promises to include a certificate by issuing a Signed Certificate Timestamp (SCT), a new STH including the appended certificate must be issued within a Maximum Merge Delay (MMD). Typically, logs use 24 hour MMDs. Should non-included SCTs and/or inconsistent STHs be found, binding evidence of misbehaviour exists because these statements are digitally signed by the logs. Other than MMD a log's policy defines parameters such as STH frequency: the number of STHs that can be issued during an MMD, making it harder to track clients [7].

CT is being deployed across Apple's platform [2] and Google's Chrome [3]. The status quo is to trust a CA-signed certificate if it is accompanied by two or more SCTs, thereby relying on at least one log to append each certificate so that mis-issuance can be detected by monitors that inspect the logs. The next step of this incremental deployment is to *verify* that these certificates are logged by querying for inclusion [18], and that the log's append-only property is respected by challenging the log to prove STH consistency. Finally, to fully distrust CT logs we need mechanisms that detect split-views. One such mechanism which is based on programmable packet processors (introduced next) is presented in Section III, and it is compared to related work on CT gossip in Section VI.

B. Programmable Data Planes

Packet processors such as switches, routers, and network interface cards are typically integrated tightly using customized hardware and application-specific integrated circuits. This inflexible design limits the potential for innovation and leads to long product upgrade cycles, where it takes *years* to introduce new processing capabilities and support for different protocols and header fields (mostly following lengthy standardization cycles). The recent shift towards flexible *match+action* packet-processing pipelines—including Reconfigurable Match Tables (RMT) [19], Intel FlexPipe [20], Cavium XPliant packet Architecture (XPA) [21], and Barefoot Tofino [22]—now have the potential to change the way in which packet processing hardware is implemented: it enables programmability using high-level languages, such as P4, while at the same time maintaining performance comparable to fixed-function chips.

1) P4: The main goal of P4 is to simplify programming of protocol-independent packet processors by providing an abstract programming model for the network data plane [14]. In this setting, the functionality of a packet processing device is specified without assuming any hardwired protocols and headers. Consequently, a P4 program must parse headers and connect the values of those protocol fields to the actions that should be executed based on a pipeline of reconfigurable match+action tables. Based on the specified P4 code, a front-end compiler generates a high-level intermediate representation that a back-end compiler uses to create a target-dependent program representation. Compilers are available for several platforms, including the software-based simple switch architecture [23], SDNet for Xilinx's NetFPGA (Field-Programmable Gate Array) boards [24], and Netronome's smart network interfaces [25]. It is also possible to compile basic P4 programs into eBPF byte code [26].

2) XDP: The Berkeley Packet Filter (BPF) is a Linux-based packet filtering mechanism [27]. Verified bytecode is injected from user space, and executed for each received packet in kernel space by a just-in-time compiler. Extended BPF (eBPF) enhances the original BPF concept, enabling faster runtime and many new features. For example, an eBPF program can be attached to the Linux traffic control tool `tc`, and additional hooks were defined for XDP [15]. In contrast to the Intel Data Plane Development Kit (DPDK), which runs in user space and completely controls a given network interface that supports a DPDK driver, XDP cooperates with the Linux stack to achieve fast, programmable, and reconfigurable packet processing using C-like programs.

III. Design

An overview of aggregation-based gossip is shown in Figure 1. The setting consists of logs that send plaintext STHs to clients over a network, and, as part of the network, inline *packet processors* passively aggregate observed STHs to their own off-path *challengers* which challenge the logs to prove consistency. A log cannot present split views to different clients that share an aggregating vantage point because it would trivially be detected by that vantage point's challenger. A log also cannot present a persistent split view to different challengers because they are off-path in the sense that they are indistinguishable from one another. This means that every client that is covered by an aggregator must be on the same view because at least one challenger will otherwise detect an inconsistency and report it. A client that is not directly covered by an aggregator may receive indirect protection in the form of herd immunity. This is discussed in Section VII-D.

A. Threat Model and Security Notion

The overarching threat is undetectable domain impersonation (ex-post) by an attacker that is capable of compromising at least one CA and a sufficient number of CT logs to convince a client into accepting a forged certificate. We assume that any illegitimately issued certificate would be detected by the legitimate domain owner through self or delegated third-party monitoring. This means that an attacker must either provide a split view towards the victim or the monitoring entity. We also assume that clients query the logs for certificate inclusion based on STHs that they acquire from the logs via plaintext mechanisms that packet processors can observe, and that some

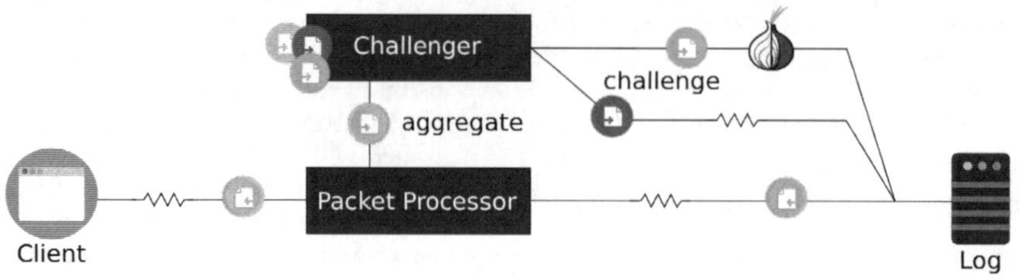

Figure 1. Packet processor that aggregates plaintext STHs for off-path verification.

other entities than challengers process STHs using the chosen off-paths (SectionVII-A). We do not account for the fact that CA compromises may be detected by other means, focusing solely on split-viewing CT logs.

1) Limitations: Our gossip mechanism is limited to STHs that packet processors can observe. As such, a client isolated by an attacker is not protected. We limit ourselves to attackers that act over a network some distance (in the sense of network path length) from a client in plaintext so that aggregation can take place. Our limitations and assumptions are further discussed in Section VII-A.

2) Attackers: Exceptionally powerful attackers can isolate clients, *but clients are not necessarily easy to isolate* for a significant number of relevant attackers. Isolation may require physical control over a device [28], clients may be using anonymity networks like Tor where path selection is inherently unpredictable [29], or sufficiently large parts of the network cannot be controlled to ensure that no aggregation takes place. This may be the case if we consider a nation state actor attacking another nation state actor, the prevalence of edge security middleboxes, and that home routers or network interfaces nearby the clients could aggregate. Any attacker that cannot account for these considerations is within our threat model.

3) Security Notion: To bypass our approach towards gossip, an adaptive attacker may attempt to actively probe the network for aggregating packet processors. This leads us to the key security notion: *aggregation indistinguishability*. An attacker should not be able to determine if a packet processor is aggregating STHs. The importance of aggregation indistinguishability motivates the design of our gossip mechanism into two distinct components: aggregation that takes place inline at packet processors, and periodic off-path log challenging that checks whether the observed STHs are consistent.

B. Packet Processor Aggregation

An aggregating packet-processor determines for each packet if it is STH-related. If so, the packet is cloned and sent to a challenging component for off-path verification. The exact definition of *STH-related* depends on the plaintext source, but it is ultimately the process of inspecting multiple packet headers such as transport protocol and port number. It should be noted that the original packet must not be dropped or modified. For example, an aggregator would have a trivial aggregation distinguisher if it dropped any malformed STH.

For each aggregating packet processor, we have to take IP fragmentation into consideration. Recall that IP fragmentation usually occurs when a packet is larger than the Maximum Transmission Unit (MTU), splitting it into multiple smaller IP packets that are reassembled at the destination host. Normally, an STH should not be fragmented because it is much smaller than the de-facto minimum MTU of (at least) 576 bytes [30][31], but an attacker could use fragmentation to *intentionally* spread expected headers across multiple packets. Assuming stateless packet processing, an aggregator cannot identify such fragmented packets as STH-related because some header would be absent (cf. stateless firewalls). All tiny fragments should therefore be aggregated to account for intentional IP fragmentation, which appears to have little or no impact on normal traffic because tiny fragments are anomalies [32]. The threat of multi-path fragmentation is discussed in Section VII-A.

Large traffic loads must also be taken into account. If an aggregating packet processor degrades in performance as the portion of STH-related traffic increases, a distant attacker may probe for such behaviour to determine if a path contains an aggregator. Each *implementation* must therefore be evaluated individually for such behaviour, and, if trivial aggregation distinguishers exist, this needs to be solved. For example, STH-related traffic could be aggregated probabilistically to reduce the amount of work. Another option is to load-balance the traffic before aggregation, i.e., avoid worst-case loads that cannot be handled.

C. Off-Path Log Challenging

A challenger is setup to listen for aggregated traffic, reassembling IP fragments and storing the aggregated STHs for periodic off-path verification. Periodic off-path verification means that the challenger challenges the log based on its own (off-path fetched) STHs and the observed (aggregated) STHs to verify log consistency periodically, e.g., every day. The definition of *off-path* is that the challenger must not be linkable to its aggregating packet processor(s) or any other challenger (including itself). Without an off-path, there is no gossip step amongst aggregator-challenger instances that are operated by different actors, and our approach towards gossip would only assert that clients behind the same vantage point observe the same logs. If a log cannot distinguish between different challengers due to the use of off-paths, however, it is non-trivial to maintain a targeted split-view towards an unknown location. Therefore, we get a form of *implicit gossip* [11] because at least one challenger would detect an inconsistency unless everybody observes the same log. If every challenger observes the same log, so does every client that is covered by an aggregating packet processor. Notably, the challenger component *does not run inline* to avoid timing distinguishers. Note that there are other important considerations when implementing a challenger, as discussed in Section VII-A.

IV. Distinguishability Experiments

There are many different ways to implement the aggregation step. We decided to use P4 and XDP because a large variety of programmable packet processors support these languages (Section II-B). The aggregated plaintext source is assumed to be CT-over-DNS [33], which means that a client obtains STHs by fetching IN TXT resource records. Since languages for programmable packet processors are somewhat restricted, we facilitated packet processing by requiring that at most one STH is sent per UDP packet. This is reasonable because logs should only have one *most recent* STH. A DNS STH is roughly 170 bytes without any packet headers and should normally not be fragmented, but to ensure that we do not miss any intentionally fragmented STHs we aggregate every tiny fragment. We did not implement the challenging component because it is relatively easy given an existing off-path. Should any scalability issue arise for the challenger there is nothing that prevents a distributed front-end that processes the aggregated material before storage. Storage is not an issue because there are only a limited amount of unique STHs per day and log (one new STH per hour is a common policy, and browsers recognize ≈ 40 logs). Further implementation details can be found online [16][34].

A. Setup

We used a test-bed consisting of a traffic generator, a traffic receiver, and an aggregating target in between. The first target is a P4-enabled NetFPGA SUME board that runs an adapted version of our P4 reference implementation. The second target is a net-next kernel v4.17.0-rc6 Linux machine that runs XDP on one core with a 10 Gb SFP+ X520 82599ES Intel card, a 3.6 GHz Intel Core i7-4790 CPU, and 16 GB of RAM at 1600 MHz (Hynix/Hyundai). We would like to determine whether there are any aggregation distinguishers as the fraction of STHs (experiment 1) and tiny fragments (experiment 2) in the traffic is increased from 0–100%, i.e., does performance degrade as a function of STH-related rate? Non-fragmented STH packets are 411 bytes (we used excessively large DNS headers to maximize the packet parsing overhead), and tiny fragments are 64 bytes. All background traffic has the same packet sizes but is not deemed STH-related.

B. Results

Figure 2a shows throughput as a function of STH-related rate for the P4-enabled NetFPGA. While we were unable to observe any distinguisher between normal routing and the edge case of 100% aggregation for non-fragmented STH packets, there is a small constant throughput difference for tiny fragments (7.5 Kbps). This is a non-negligible *program distinguisher* if a packet processor is physically isolated as in our benchmark, i.e., something other than a routing program is running but it is not necessarily an aggregator because performance does not degrade as a function of increased STH-related rate. However, we found such degradation behaviour for the single-core XDP case (Figure 2b). If line-speed is higher than 2 Gbps, STHs could be aggregated probabilistically or traffic could be load-balanced to *overcome* this issue.

C. Lessons learned

P4-NetFPGA provides aggregation indistinguishability regardless of STH load. For XDP, it depends on the scenario: what is the line-rate criteria and how many cores are available. For example, five cores support 10 Gbps aggregation indistinguishability without probabilistic filtering or load balancing.

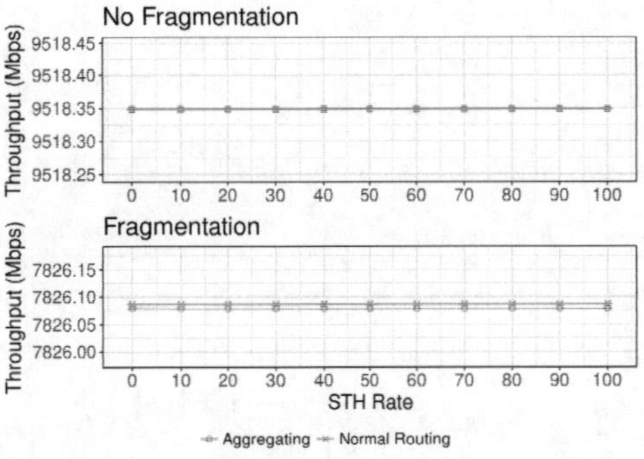

(a) P4 NetFPGA

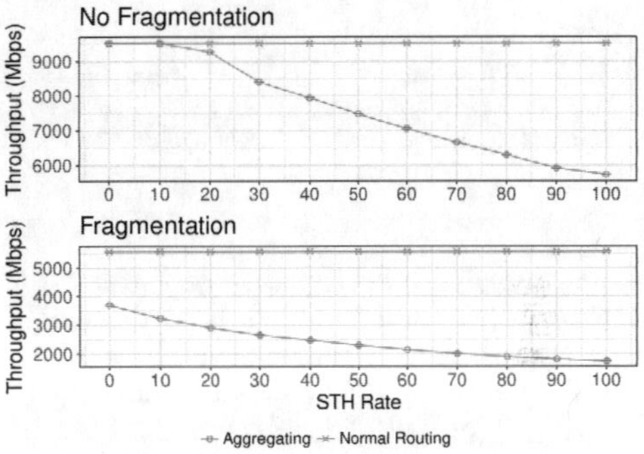

(b) XDP on a single core

Figure 2. Throughput as a function of STH-related traffic that is aggregated.

V. Estimated Impact of Deployment

We conducted 20 daily traceroute measurements during the spring of 2018 on the RIPE Atlas platform to evaluate the effectiveness of aggregation-based gossip. The basic idea is to look at client coverage as central ASes and IXPs aggregate STHs. If any significant client coverage can be achieved, the likelihood of pulling off an undetected split-view will be small.

A. Setup

We scheduled RIPE Atlas measurements from roughly 3500 unique ASes that represent 40% of the IPv4 space, trace-routing Google's authoritative CT-over-DNS server and NORDUnet's CT log to simulate clients that fetch DNS STHs in plaintext. Each traceroute result is a list of traversed IPs, and it can be translated into the corresponding ASes and IXPs using public data sets [35][36]. In other words, traversed ASes and IXPs can be determined for each probe. Since we are interested in client coverage as ASes and IXPs aggregate, each probe is weighted by the IPv4 space of its AS. While an IP address is an imperfect representation of a client, e.g., an IP may be unused or reused, it gives a decent idea of how significant it is to cover a given probe.

B. Results

Figure 3 shows AS/IXP path length and stability from the probes to the targets. If the AS path length is one, a single

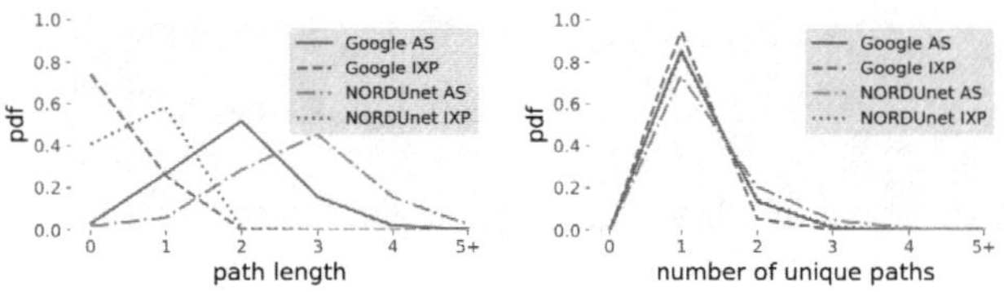

Figure 3. Path length and stability towards Google and NORDUnet.

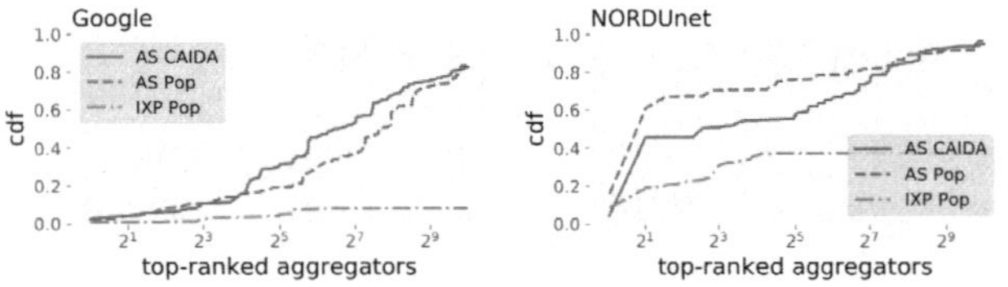

Figure 4. Coverage as a function of aggregation opt-in.

AS is traversed *before reaching the target*. It is evident that an AS path tends to be one hop longer towards NORDUnet than Google because there is a rough off-by-one offset on the x-axis. A similar trend of greater path length towards NORDUnet can be observed for IXPs. For example, 74.0% of all paths traversed no IXP towards Google, but 58.5% of all paths traversed a single IXP towards NORDUnet. These results can be explained by infrastructural differences of our targets: since Google is a worldwide actor an average path should be shorter than compared to a region-restricted actor like NORDUnet. We also observed that AS and IXP paths tend to be quite stable over 20 days (the duration of our measurements). In other words, if AS a and b are traversed it is unlikely to suddenly be routed via AS c.

Figure 4 shows coverage of the RIPE Atlas network as $1 \ldots n$ actors aggregate STHs. For example, 100% and 50% coverage means that at least 40% and 20% of the full IPv4 space is covered. The aggregating ASes and IXPs were selected based on the most commonly traversed vantage points in our measurements (Pop), as well as CAIDA's largest AS ranking [37]. We found that more coverage is achieved when targeting NORDUnet than Google. This is expected given that the paths tend to be longer. Further, if CAIDA's top-32 enabled aggregation the coverage would be significant towards Google (31.6%) and NORDUnet (58.1%).

C. Lessons learned

A vast majority of all clients traverse *at least* one AS that could aggregate. It is relatively rare to traverse IXPs towards Google but not NORDUnet. We also learned that paths tends to be stable, which means that the time until split view detection would be at least 20 days *if* it is possible to find an unprotected client. This increases the importance of aggregation indistinguishability. Finally, we identified vantage points that are commonly traversed using Pop, and these vantage points are represented well by CAIDA's independent AS ranking. Little opt-in from ASes and IXPs provides significant coverage against an attacker that is relatively close to a client (cf. world-wide infrastructure of Google). Although we got better coverage for NORDUnet, any weak attacker would approach Google's coverage by renting infrastructure nearby. Any weak attacker could also circumvent IXP aggregation by detecting the IXP itself [38]. As such, top-ranked AS aggregation should give the best split-view protection.

VI. Related Work

Earlier approaches towards CT gossip are categorized as *proactive* or *retroactive* in Figure 5. We consider an approach proactive if gossip takes place *before* SCTs and/or STHs reach the broader audience of clients. Syta *et al.* proposed proactive witness cosigning, in which an STH is collectively signed by a *large* number of witnesses and at most a fraction of those can be faulty to ensure that a benevolent witness observed an STH [8]. STH cross-logging [9][39][40] is similar in that an STH must be proactively disclosed in another transparency log to be trusted, avoiding any additional cosigning infrastructure at the cost of reducing the size and diversity of the witnessing group. Tomescu and Devadas [41] suggested a similar cross-logging scheme, but split-view detection is instead reduced to the difficulty of forking the Bitcoin blockchain (big-O cost of downloading all block headers as a TLS client). The final proactive approach is STH pushing, where a trusted third-party pushes the same verified STH history to a base of clients [18].

We consider a gossip mechanism retroactive if gossip takes place *after* SCTs and/or STHs reach the broader audience of clients. Chuat *et al.* proposed that TLS clients and TLS servers be modified to pool exchanged STHs and relevant consistency proofs [6]. Nordberg *et al.* continued this line of work, suggesting privacy-preserving client-server pollination of fresh STHs [7]. Nordberg *et al.* also proposed that clients feedback SCTs and certificate chains on every server revisit, and that trusted auditor relationships could be engaged if privacy need not be protected. The latter is somewhat similar to the formalized client-monitor gossip of Chase and Meiklejohn [43], as well as the CT honey bee project where a client process fetches and submits STHs to a pre-compiled list of auditors [42]. Laurie suggested that a client can resolve privacy-sensitive SCTs to privacy-insensitive STHs via DNS (which are easier to gossip) [33]. Private information retrievals could likely achieve something similar [44]. Assuming that TLS clients are indistinguishable from one another, split-view detection could also be implicit as proposed by Gunn *et al.* for the verifiable key-value store CONIKS [11][45].

Given that aggregation-based gossip takes place after an STH is issued, it is a retroactive approach. As such, we cannot protect an isolated client from split-views [8]. Similar to STH pooling and STH pollination, we rely on client-driven communication and an existing infrastructure of packet processors to aggregate. Our off-path verification is based on the same multi-path probing and indistinguishability assumptions as Gunn *et al.* [11][46][47]. Further, given that aggregation is application neutral and deployable on hosts, it could provide gossip *for* the CT honey bee project (assuming plaintext STHs) and any other transparency application like Trillian [48]. Another benefit when compared to browsing-centric and vendor-specific approaches is that a plethora of HTTPS clients are covered, ranging from niche web browsers to command line tools and embedded libraries that are vital to protect but yet lack the resources of major browser vendors [49][50].

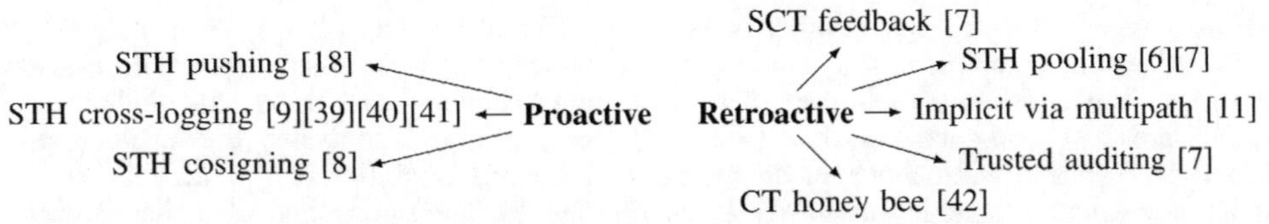

Figure 5. A categorization of approaches towards CT gossip.

Our approach coexists well with witness cosigning and cross-logging due to different threat models, but not necessarily STH pushing if the secure channel is encrypted (no need to fetch what a trusted party provides).

VII. Discussion

Next, we discuss assumptions, limitations and deployment, showing that our approach towards retroactive gossip can be deployed to detect split-views by many relevant attackers with relatively little effort. The main drawback is reliance on clients fetching STHs in plaintext, e.g., using CT-over-DNS [33].

A. Assumptions and Limitations

Aggregation-based gossip is limited to network traffic that packet processors can observe. The strongest type of attacker in this setting—who can completely isolate a client—trivially defeats our gossip mechanism and other retroactive approaches in the literature (see Section VI). A weaker attacker cannot isolate a client, but is located nearby in a network path length sense. This limits the opportunity for packet processor aggregation, but an attacker cannot rule it out given aggregation indistinguishability. Section IV showed based on performance that it is non-trivial to distinguish between (non-)aggregating packet processors on two different targets using P4 and XDP. Off-path challengers must also be indistinguishable from one another to achieve *implicit gossip*. While we suggested the use of anonymity networks like Tor, a prerequisite is that this is in and of itself not an aggregation distinguisher. Therefore, we assume that other entities also use off-paths to fetch and verify STHs. The fact that a unique STH *is not audited* from an off-path could also be an aggregation distinguisher. To avoid this we could rely on a verifiable STH history [51] and wait until the next MMD to audit or simply monitor the full log so that consistency proofs are unnecessary.

The existence of multiple network paths are fundamental to the structure and functioning of the Internet. A weak attacker may use IP fragmentation such that each individual STH fragment is injected from a different location to make aggregation harder, approaching the capabilities of a stronger attacker that is located closer to the client. This is further exacerbated by the deployment of multi-path transport protocols like MPTCP (which can also be fragmented). Looking back at our RIPE Atlas measurements in Section V, the results towards Google's world-wide infrastructure better represent an active attacker that takes *some* measures to circumvent aggregation by approaching a client nearby the edge. Given that the likelihood of aggregation is high if *any* IXP is present (Figure 4), aggregation at well-connected IXPs are most likely to be circumvented.

B. Deployment

Besides aggregating at strategic locations in the Internet's backbone, Internet Service Providers (ISPs) and enterprise networks have the opportunity to protect all of their clients with relatively little effort. Deployment of special-purpose middleboxes are already prevalent in these environments, and then the inconvenience of fragmentation tends to go away due to features such as packet reassembly. Further, an attacker cannot trivially circumvent the edge of a network topology—especially not if aggregation takes place on an end-system: all fragments are needed to reassemble a packet, which means that multi-path fragmentation is no longer a threat. If aggregation-based gossip is deployed on an end-system, STHs could be hooked using other approaches than P4/XDP. For example, shim-layers that intercept TLS certificates higher up in the networking stack were already proposed by Bates *et al.* [52] and O'Neill *et al.* [53]. In this setting, an end-system is viewed as the aggregating packet processor, and it reports back to an off-path challenger that may be a local process running on the same system or a remote entity, e.g., a TelCo could host challengers that collect aggregated STHs from smartphones.

While we looked at programming physical packet processors like routers, STH aggregation could be approached in hypervisors and software switches [54] to protect many virtual hosts. If CT-over-DNS is used to fetch STHs, it would be promising to output DNS server caches to implement the aggregation step. Similar to DNS servers, so called Tor exist relays also operate DNS caches. In other words, P4 and XDP are only examples of how to *instantiate* the aggregation step. Depending on the used plaintext source, packet processor, and network topology other approaches may be more suitable, e.g., C for vendor-specific middleboxes.

C. Retroactive Gossip Benefits From Plaintext

As opposed to an Internet core that only forwards IP packets, extra functionality is often embedded which causes complex processing dependencies and protocol ossification [13]. Many security and protocol issues were found for middleboxes that provides extra functionality [12][55], resulting in the mindset that *everything* should be encrypted [55]. Our work is controversial because it goes against this mindset and advocates that STHs should be communicated in plaintext. We argue that this makes sense in the context of STHs due to the absence of privacy concerns and because the entire point of gossip is to make STHs *available* (rather than end-to-end). The idea of intentionally exposing information to the network is not new, e.g., MPQUIC is designed to support traffic shaping [56].

While we used CT-over-DNS as a plaintext source, there is a push towards DNS-over-TLS [57] and DNS-over-HTTPS [58]. Wide use of these approaches could undermine our gossip mechanism, but ironically the security of TLS could be jeopardized unless gossip is deployed. In other words, long term gossip is an essential component of CT and other transparency logs to avoid becoming yet another class of trusted third-parties. If proactive approaches such as witness cosigning are rejected in favour of retroactive mechanisms, then ensuring that STHs are widely spread and easily accessible is vital. An STH needs no secrecy if the appropriate measures are taken to make it privacy-insensitive [7]. While secure channels also provide integrity and replay protection, an STH is already signed by logs and freshness is covered by MMDs, as well as issue frequency to protect privacy. A valid argument against exposing any plaintext to the network is protocol ossification. We emphasize that our design motivates why packet processors should fail open: otherwise there is no aggregation indistinguishability. Note that there are other plaintext sources than CT-over-DNS that could be aggregated. However, if these sources require stream-reassembly it is generally hard to process in languages such as P4 and XDP [59].

D. Indistinguishability and Herd Immunity

An attacker that gains control over a CT log is bound to be more risk averse than an attacker that compromises a CA. There is an order of magnitude fewer logs than CAs, and client vendors are likely going to be exceptionally picky when it comes to accepted and rejected logs. We have already seen examples of this, including Google Chrome disqualifying logs that made mistakes: Izenpe used the same key for production and testing [60], and Venafi suffered from an unfortunate power outage [61]. Risk averse attackers combined with packet processors that are aggregation indistinguishable may lead to *herd immunity*: despite a significant fraction of clients that lack aggregators, indirect protection may be provided because the risk of eventual detection is unacceptable to many attackers. Hof and Carle [40] and Nordberg *et al.* [7] discussed herd immunity briefly before us. While herd immunity is promising, it should be noted that aggregation distinguishable packet processors at *the edge of a network topology* may be acceptable for some. In other words, if an aggregator cannot be circumvented but it is detectable split-views would still be deterred against covered clients if the challenger is off-path.

VIII. Conclusion and Future Work

Wide spread modifications of TLS clients are inevitable to support CT gossip. We propose that these modifications include challenging the logs to prove certificate inclusion based on STHs *fetched in plaintext*, thereby enabling the traversed packet processors to assist in split view detection retroactively by aggregating STHs for periodic off-path verification. Our results show that the aggregation-step can be implemented without throughput-based distinguishers for a distant attacker, and that our approach offers rapid incremental deployment with high impact on a significant fraction of Internet users. Beyond being an application neutral approach that is complementary to proactive gossip, a compelling aspect is that core packet processors are used (rather than clients) as a key building block: should a consistency issue arise, it is already in the hands of an actor that is better equipped to investigate the cause manually. Further, considering that far from all TLS clients are backed by big browser vendors (not to mention other use-cases of transparency logs in general) it is likely a long-term win to avoid pushing complex retroactive gossip logic into all the different types of clients when there are orders of magnitudes fewer packet processors that could aggregate to their own off-path challengers. Future work includes different instantiations of the aggregation step and evaluating whether aggregation indistinguishability is provided based on throughput and/or latency. The setting may also change in some scenarios, e.g., if DNS caches are aggregated the transport need not be plaintext.

Acknowledgment

We would like to thank Stefan Alfredsson and Philipp Winter for their RIPE Atlas credits, as well as Jonas Karlsson and Ricardo Santos for helping with the NetFPGA setup. We also received funding from the HITS research profile which is funded by the Swedish Knowledge Foundation.

References

[1] Z. Durumeric, J. Kasten, M. Bailey, and J. A. Halderman, "Analysis of the HTTPS certificate ecosystem," in ICM, 2013, pp. 291–304.

[2] "Apple's certificate transparency policy," 2018, URL: https://web.archive.org/web/20190401135231/https://support.apple.com/en-us/HT205280 [accessed 2019-09-04].

[3] D. O'Brien, "Certificate transparency enforcement in Google Chrome," 2018, URL: https://groups.google.com/a/chromium.org/forum/\#!msg/ct-policy/wHILiYf31DE/iMFmpMEkAQAJ [accessed 2019-09-04].

[4] B. Laurie, A. Langley, and E. Kasper, "Certificate transparency," RFC 6962, 2013.

[5] B. Dowling, F. Günther, U. Herath, and D. Stebila, "Secure logging schemes and certificate transparency," in ESORICS, 2016, pp. 140–158.

[6] L. Chuat, P. Szalachowski, A. Perrig, B. Laurie, and E. Messeri, "Efficient gossip protocols for verifying the consistency of certificate logs," in CNS, 2015, pp. 415–423.

[7] L. Nordberg, D. K. Gillmor, and T. Ritter, "Gossiping in CT," Internet-draft draft-ietf-trans-gossip-05, 2018.

[8] E. Syta *et al.*, "Keeping authorities "honest or bust" with decentralized witness cosigning," in IEEE SP, 2016, pp. 526–545.

[9] D. Drysdale, "Minimal gossip," 2018, URL: https://github.com/google/certificate-transparency-go/blob/master/gossip/minimal [accessed 2019-09-04].

[10] O. Gasser, B. Hof, M. Helm, M. Korczynski, R. Holz, and G. Carle, "In log we trust: Revealing poor security practices with certificate transparency logs and Internet measurements," in PAM, 2018, pp. 173–185.

[11] L. J. Gunn, A. Allison, and D. Abbott, "Safety in numbers: Anonymization makes keyservers trustworthy," in HotPETs, 2017, pp. 1–2.

[12] Z. Durumeric *et al.*, "The security impact of HTTPS interception," in NDSS, 2017.

[13] M. Honda, Y. Nishida, C. Raiciu, A. Greenhalgh, M. Handley, and H. Tokuda, "Is it still possible to extend TCP?" in ICM, 2011, pp. 181–194.

[14] P. Bosshart *et al.*, "P4: Programming protocol-independent packet processors," CCR, vol. 44, no. 3, 2014, pp. 87–95.

[15] T. Høiland-Jørgensen *et al.*, "The express data path: Fast programmable packet processing in the operating system kernel," in CoNEXT, 2018, pp. 54–66.

[16] R. Dahlberg, T. Pulls, J. Vestin, T. Høiland-Jørgensen, and A. Kassler, "Aggregation-based gossip for certificate transparency," CoRR, vol. abs/1806.08817, 2019, pp. 1–20.

[17] B. Laurie, "Certificate transparency," ACM Queue, vol. 12, no. 8, 2014, pp. 10–19.

[18] R. Sleevi and E. Messeri, "Certificate transparency in Chrome: Monitoring CT logs consistency," 2017, URL: https://docs.google.com/document/d/1FP5J5Sfsg0OR9P4YT0q1dM02iavhi8ix1mZlZe_z-ls/edit?pref=2&pli=1 [accessed 2019-09-04].

[19] P. Bosshart *et al.*, "Forwarding metamorphosis: Fast programmable match-action processing in hardware for SDN," in ACM SIGCOMM, 2013, pp. 99–110.

[20] "Intel ethernet switch FM600 series: 10/40 GbE low latency switching silicon," URL: https://www.intel.com/content/dam/www/public/us/en/documents/product-briefs/ethernet-switch-fm6000-series-brief.pdf [accessed 2019-09-04].

[21] "Cavium and XPliant introduce a fully programmable switch silicon family scaling to 3.2 terabits per second," URL: https://cavium.com/newsevents-cavium-and-xpliant-introduce-a-fully-programmable-switch-silicon-family.html [accessed 2019-09-04].

[22] "Tofino: World's fastest P4-programmable ethernet switch ASICs," URL: https://barefootnetworks.com/products/brief-tofino/ [accessed 2019-09-04].

[23] "Behavioral model repository," URL: https://github.com/p4lang/behavioral-model [accessed 2019-09-04].

[24] G. Brebner, "P4 for an FPGA target," in P4 Workshop, 2015, URL: \fullversion{https://web.archive.org/web/20190418085926/https://p4workshop2015.sched.com/event/3ZQA/p4-for-an-fpga-target}{https://p4workshop2015.sched.com/event/3ZQA/p4-for-an-fpga-targe} [accessed 2019-09-04].

[25] "Programming NFP with P4 and C," URL: https://www.netronome.com/media/redactor_files/WP_Programming_with_P4_and_C.pdf [accessed 2019-09-04].

[26] M. Budiu, "Compiling P4 to eBPF," URL: https://github.com/iovisor/bcc/tree/master/src/cc/frontends/p4 [accessed 2019-09-04].

[27] S. McCanne and V. Jacobson, "The BSD packet filter: A new architecture for user-level packet capture," in Usenix Winter Technical Conference, 1993, pp. 259–270.

[28] "Apple challenges FBI: All writs act order (CA)," URL: https://www.eff.org/cases/apple-challenges-fbi-all-writs-act-order [accessed 2019-09-04].

[29] R. Dingledine, N. Mathewson, and P. F. Syverson, "Tor: The second-generation onion router," in USENIX Security, 2004, pp. 303–320.

[30] R. Braden, "Requirements for Internet hosts—communication layers," RFC 1122.

[31] S. Deering and R. Hinden, "Internet protocol version 6 (IPv6) specification," RFC 8200.

[32] C. Shannon, D. Moore, and K. C. Claffy, "Beyond folklore: Observations on fragmented traffic," IEEE/ACM Trans. Netw., vol. 10, no. 6, 2002, pp. 709–720.

[33] B. Laurie, "Certificate transparency over DNS," 2016, URL: https://github.com/google/certificate-transparency-rfcs/blob/master/dns [accessed 2019-09-04].

[34] "Aggregation-based gossip for certificate transparency logs," 2018, URL: https://github.com/rgdd/ctga [acessed 2019-09-04].

[35] "The CAIDA UCSD IXPs dataset," February 2018, URL: https://www.caida.org/data/ixps/ [accessed 2019-09-04].

[36] "The Routeviews MRT format RIBs and UPDATEs dataset," March 2018, URL: http://archive.routeviews.org/bgpdata/2018.03/RIBS/ [accessed 2019-09-04].

[37] "ARank," URL: http://as-rank.caida.org/ [accessed 2019-09-04].

[38] G. Nomikos and X. A. Dimitropoulos, "traIXroute: Detecting IXPs in traceroute paths," in PAM, 2016, pp. 346–358.

[39] B. Hof, "STH cross logging," Internet-draft draft-hof-trans-cross-00, 2017.

[40] B. Hof and G. Carle, "Software distribution transparency and auditability," CoRR, vol. abs/1711.07278, 2017, pp. 1–14.

[41] A. Tomescu and S. Devadas, "Catena: Efficient non-equivocation via Bitcoin," in IEEE SP, 2017, pp. 393–409.

[42] A. Ayer, "Lightweight program that pollinates STHs between certificate transparency logs and auditors," 2018, URL: https://github.com/SSLMate/ct-honeybee [accessed 2019-09-04].

[43] M. Chase and S. Meiklejohn, "Transparency overlays and applications," in CCS, 2016, pp. 168–179.

[44] W. Lueks and I. Goldberg, "Sublinear scaling for multi-client private information retrieval," in FC, 2015, pp. 168–186.

[45] M. S. Melara, A. Blankstein, J. Bonneau, E. W. Felten, and M. J. Freedman, "CONIKS: Bringing key transparency to end users," in USENIX Security, 2015, pp. 383–398.

[46] M. Alicherry and A. D. Keromytis, "DoubleCheck: Multi-path verification against man-in-the-middle attacks," in ISCC, 2009, pp. 557–563.

[47] D. Wendlandt, D. G. Andersen, and A. Perrig, "Perspectives: Improving SSH-style host authentication with multi-path probing," in USENIX ATC, 2008, pp. 321–334.

[48] A. Eijdenberg, B. Laurie, and A. Cutter, "Verifiable data structures," 2015, URL: https://github.com/google/trillian/blob/master/docs/papers [accessed 2019-09-04].

[49] M. Backes, S. Bugiel, and E. Derr, "Reliable third-party library detection in Android and its security applications," in CCS, 2016, pp. 356–367.

[50] E. Derr, S. Bugiel, S. Fahl, Y. Acar, and M. Backes, "Keep me updated: An empirical study of third-party library updatability on Android," in CCS, 2017, pp. 2187–2200.

[51] L. Nordberg, "Re: [Trans] providing the history of STHs a log has issued (in 6962-bis)," URL: https://mailarchive.ietf.org/arch/msg/trans/JbFiwO90PjcYzXrEgh-Y7bFG5Fw [accessed 2019-09-04].

[52] A. M. Bates *et al.*, "Securing SSL certificate verification through dynamic linking," in CCS, 2014, pp. 394–405.

[53] M. O'Neill *et al.*, "TrustBase: An architecture to repair and strengthen certificate-based authentication," in USENIX Security, 2017, pp. 609–624.

[54] M. Shahbaz *et al.*, "PISCES: a programmable, protocol-independent software switch," in ACM SIGCOMM, 2016, pp. 525–538.

[55] A. Langley *et al.*, "The QUIC transport protocol: Design and Internet-scale deployment," in SIGCOMM, 2017, pp. 183–196.

[56] Q. D. Coninck and O. Bonaventure, "Multipath QUIC: Design and evaluation," in CoNEXT, 2017, pp. 160–166.

[57] S. Dickinson, D. Gillmor, and T. Reddy, "Usage profiles for DNS over TLS and DNS over DTLS," RFC 8310, 2016.

[58] P. Hoffman and P. McManus, "DNS queries over HTTPS (DoH)," RFC 8484, 2018.

[59] R. Dahlberg, "Aggregating certificate transparency gossip using programmable packet processors," Master Thesis, Karlstad University, 2018.

[60] R. Sleevi, "Upcoming CT log removal: Izenpe," 2018, URL: https://groups.google.com/a/chromium.org/forum/#!topic/ct-policy/qOorKuhL1vA [accessed 2019-09-04].

[61] ——, "Upcoming log removal: Venafi ct log server," 2017, URL: https://groups.google.com/a/chromium.org/forum/#!topic/ct-policy/KMAcNT3asTQ [accessed 2019-09-04].

Surveying the Incorporation of IoT Devices into Cybersecurity Risk Management Frameworks

Aaron J. Pendleton
Graduate Cyber Operations
Air Force Institute of Technology
Dayton, United States
email: Aaron.Pendleton@afit.edu

Richard Dill
Assistant Professor
Dept of Electrical & Computer Engineering
Air Force Institute of Technology
Dayton, United States
email: Richard.Dill@afit.edu

Dillon Pettit
Graduate Cyber Operations
Air Force Institute of Technology
Dayton, United States
email: Dillon.Pettit@afit.edu

***Abstract*—This paper reviews the state of the art for incorporating Mobile Devices, Industrial Control Systems, and Internet of Things systems into present risk analysis framework models. Internet of Things devices present unique risks to a network due to their highly connective and physically interactive nature. This physical influence can be leveraged to access peripherals beyond the immediate scope of the network, or to gain unauthorized access to systems which would not otherwise be accessible. A 2017 Government Accountability Office report on the current state of Internet of Things device security noted a lack of dedicated policy and guidance within the United States government cybersecurity risk assessment construct and similar private sector equivalents. Surveyed in this paper are 28 original frameworks designed to be implemented in enterprise networks. In this research the comparison of frameworks is analyzed to assess each system's ability to provide risk analysis for Internet of Things devices. The research categories are level of implementation, quantitative or qualitative scoring matrix, and support for future development. This survey demonstrates there are few risk management frameworks currently available which attempt to incorporate both cyber-physical systems and enterprise architecture in a large scale network.**

Keywords*— *IoT; RMF; cybersecurity; risk; ICS.

I. Introduction

Industrial Control Systems (ICS) and Internet of Things (IoT) devices have infiltrated most networks that would traditionally be classified as enterprise networks. Their unprecedented rise in popularity has made it challenging for companies to assess and mitigate the additional risk.

IoT devices present unique risks to a network due to their highly connective and often cyber-physical nature. This physical influence can be leveraged to gain unauthorized access to systems which would not otherwise be accessible.

The United States (U.S.) Government Accountability Office (GAO), an independent and nonpartisan U.S. Congressional watchdog organization, provides objective and reliable information to the government regarding work and spending practices. GAO focuses on identifying problems and proposes solutions [32]. In July 2017, GAO released a report titled *Internet of Things: Enhanced Assessments and Guidance Are Needed to Address Security Risks in DOD* in order to highlight shortcomings in most current operational risk assessment frameworks to include those implemented by the U.S. Department of Defense (DOD). The report includes security concerns with Mobile Devices, Supervisory Control and Data Acquisition (SCADA), Programmable Logic Controllers (PLC), and Remote Terminal Units (RTU) in the U.S. DOD [32].

GAO noted a lack of dedicated policy and guidance within the U.S. government cybersecurity risk assessment construct and similar private sector equivalents. In the report, GAO defines IoT devices as any personal wearable fitness device, portable electronic device, smartphone, or infrastructure device related to industrial control systems [32].

Present DOD Instructional Guidance does not address IoT devices sufficiently [32]. Furthermore, no single DOD entity is responsible for the security of IoT systems, and the primary guidance on IoT security is the strategic directive to establish an operations security program. This paper furthers the research done by GAO in order to expand the scope of analysis beyond the U.S. DOD and into the greater field of published cyber risk solutions.

A risk analysis methodology must account for more than just traditional enterprise network components in order to mitigate the risks presented by an unregulated or loosely defined set of devices on an otherwise secure network. The purpose of this survey is to analyze the pace of development and compare the strengths and weaknesses of each analyzed framework with regard to IoT and ICS devices. 27 original cyber risk assessment and management models will be compared based on their method of risk scoring, level of implementation, and future development plans. These metrics will be used to gauge the effectiveness of a framework when accounting for devices which may not be consistently part of the secure baseline, or may not be commonly patched and secured. The ability of a risk analysis model to incorporate these common, but otherwise difficult to attribute systems will be compared in order to determine the state of the art. Frameworks published from as early as 2002 were identified and assessed for their ability to adapt to IoT devices. This paper analyzes the extent that network risk analysis and management frameworks have adapted to this evolving threat terrain. Section II outlines the risk framework models and their attributes, Section III presents the methods used to analyze and evaluate the frameworks in order to make appropriate comparisons, and Section IV provides an assessment of the current state of the art in order to then make recommendations for future research. We conclude this work in Section V.

II. Related Work

A. Risk Management Framework (RMF)

The primary risk assessment and management framework used by the U.S. Military and DOD to conduct mission assurance is the cybersecurity Risk Management Framework (RMF) developed by the National Institute of Standards and Technology (NIST). NIST RMF is a 6 step qualitative analysis method for assessing risk. It establishes a secure baseline through identifying controls that are to be updated as changes are detected [1]. Common NIST RMF implementation policy requires end users to disable the impertinent network components of most IoT devices, but this can encourage subversion of the RMF process for personal and government devices by dis-associating some capabilities from the network and the secure baseline. This presents heightened risk levels that are left unaccounted for in the overall assessment [32]. Qualitative frameworks such as RMF rely on scanning tools and strict Information Assurance (IA) policy to prevent unauthorized activity. These security measures can be subverted by IoT devices because they often have limited up-time, minimal support, a notable lack of associated scanning tools, and a smaller footprint for vulnerability testing [32]. Note: The NIST Cybersecurity Framework (CSF) and RMF are different, and CSF is directed at a higher level of protection specific to Critical Infrastructure (CI) not analyzed in this paper.

B. Control Objectives for Information and related Technology (COBIT) 5

COBIT 5 is the latest COBIT version analyzed. It was developed by the Information Systems Audit and Control Association (ISACA) and is a qualitative framework designed to provide top-down security of a business sized network. It relies on control objectives to build out the security requirements, and the level of security is assessed by maturity models. COBIT follows a purpose built model which is intended to allow for only necessary systems to be on the network in order to minimize risk [2] [34] . COBIT 2019 has been announced and is expected to address IoT more directly [22].

C. ISO27K Series

Published the International Organization for Standardization (ISO) and the International Electrotechnical Commission (IEC), the ISO/IEC 27000 series is a large framework of best practices. It provides a security control based qualitative framework with significant modularity for varying levels of implementation similar to the NIST RMF and COBIT. The strength of this model is its inherent ability to scale to the needs of the network, but allows for weaknesses where the framework is not fully implemented. It is currently in extensive use [3] [19].

D. Information Security Maturity Model (ISMM) (2011)

The ISMM model was created by analyzing eight existing models: NIST, Information Security Management Maturity Model (ISM3), Generic Security Maturity Model (GSMM), Gartner's Information Security Awarness Maturity Model (GISMM), SUNY's Information Security Initiatives (ISI), IBM Security Framework, Citigroup's Information Security Evaluation Maturity Model (ISEM), and Information Security Management System (ISMS) Maturity Capability Model. ISMM assesses the security requirements of an organization and then assigns a maturity level that will provide the correct balance of security and accessibility. They propose a method of quantifying risk at a very abstracted level, but the model itself is primarily a qualitative system to initiate compulsory levels of security [21].

E. Information Security Maturity Model (ISMM) (2017)

This ISMM model was also created following a comparison of several current implementations of risk modeling frameworks to include NIST RMF, COBIT, and ISO 27001. ISMM attempts to directly map each capability provided by current models to determine the most mature framework. The findings discovered weaknesses in all frameworks, and a single composite framework was introduced as a solution which provides all capabilities of currently implementations in one system. The framework is still at a theoretical stage of implementation, but has the potential to create a more complete qualitative solution [1].

F. Operationally Critical Threat, Asset, and Vulnerability Evaluation (OCTAVE)

1) OCTAVE (original): OCTAVE is a self directed risk management solution for large enterprises. It relies on the network staff's knowledge of critical systems and components to create a secure baseline. The weakness of this system is it is outdated (2003) and reliant on having an expert team with significant resources. There have not been significant updates to OCTAVE following the release of OCTAVE-Allegro and it could now be considered a legacy framework [4].

2) OCTAVE-S: OCTAVE-S is designed as a smaller scale implementation of OCTAVE, but suffers from several similar pitfalls. A manually created baseline that is updated as changes are observed cannot be easily adapted. OCTAVE-S provides additional structure for a less experienced team, but at the expense of significant system constraints as the implementation matures [4].

3) OCTAVE-Allegro: Allegro attempts to make risk management system more approachable than the original models. The complexity level of OCTAVE Allegro is lowered and the system is shifted to a more information-centric container based approach. Allegro is one of the first qualitative systems to incorporate an abstracted level of quantitative analysis using the containers as network elements. Due to the still largely qualitative nature of Allegro, it can have issues with implementation consistency. This can be especially challenging when accounting for IoT devices [10].

G. Holistic Cyber Security Implementation Framework (HCS-IF)

Atoum introduces HCS-IF in an attempt to create a more complete approach to risk management that avoids the fragmented stovepipe nature that developed over several iterations of abstracted quantification in many risk management frameworks. The HCS-IF has not yet been tested, but has potential value to be assessed in future studies [6].

H. IoT/M2M

Cisco introduces the IoT/M2M framework in order to address the rising challenge of securing networks saturated with relatively insecure IoT devices. The downside to this otherwise very effective model is the cost and difficulty in building a network from essentially the ground up as opposed to introducing new security measures to an existing network. It is a qualitative zero trust approach to security that attempts to limit the access of IoT devices in order to prevent them from being leveraged to influence otherwise secure devices. Live network evaluation has not yet been published [14].

I. Mobius

Mobius creates a quantifiable model which allows for risk calculations to be made using custom designed profiles for each device. The weakness is in the scaling and implementation relative to more modern tools. It requires extensive expertise to properly employ, and additional development to account for IoT devices [12].

J. Online Services Security Framework (OSSF)

The OSSF framework is designed to manage risk in an enterprise network offering online services. It provides the structure to create a secure baseline for both the provider and the consumer, but inherently must be configured by the end user. It accounts for broadly connected devices like IoT well, but it is limited in its application until it can be expanded to more diverse networks [24].

K. The CORAS Method

The CORAS approach is an 8 step model-based solution which allows a great deal of flexibility in implementation. A risk evaluation matrix is populated using CORAS that provides both high and low level analysis, but at the cost of significant labor as the baseline is constantly redefined when IoT devices are introduced [23].

L. Threat Agent Risk Assessment (TARA) (2009)

TARA was created by Intel and uses a calculation matrix to predict which agents pose the highest risk to the network. The output is then cross-referenced with known vulnerabilities and controls to mitigate risk. A meaningful published application of the TARA system has not been identified during this survey [26].

M. Threat Assessment & Remediation Analysis (TARA)(2011)

The MITRE Corporation created the TARA system to secure specific networks known to be of interest to potential actors. TARA uses a scoring model to identify probability of attack and potential attack vectors. It is difficult to scale, but can provide very sophisticated assessments if the cybersecurity budget is sufficiently large [35].

N. CCTA Risk Analysis and Management Method (CRAMM)

CRAMM is a framework designed by the United Kingdom (UK) Central Computer and Telecommunications Agency (CCTA). It is a relatively outdated method of providing qualitative analysis across multiple asset groups and requires them to be built out on a per-network basis. This makes the modular construction useful, but at the cost of significant overhead to implement. It has been implemented in many countries, but has not been updated since CRAMM 5 in 2003 [36].

O. Cyber Assessment Framework (CAF) 2.0

Created by the UK National Cyber Security Centre (NCSC), the CAF is a model based risk assessment system similar to NIST RMF which provides extensibility across many devices and network types including SCADA [33]. The framework is very new without published academic assessment, but has been adopted at an international level with a particular focus on SCADA and business IT systems [31].

P. Cyber Risk Scoring and Mitigation (CRISM)

CRISM uses Bayesian graphs to build an end-to-end automated capability which can provide security scores and prioritized mitigation plans. A high level of automation is achieved which makes implementation much simpler for small teams. Additional testing and development has the potential to create a powerful tool [29].

Q. Network Security Risk Model (NSRM)

NSRM relies on establishing a secure baseline and comparing risk levels after the introduction of each new device. This method is relatively outdated and labor intensive, but can provide good results if it is effectively implemented. It is targeted at Process Control Networks (PCN) which have less variance, and is not suitable for a large enterprise network [18].

R. Cyber Physical Systems Security (CPSS)

DiMase identified the need for a Cyber-Physical System (CPS) centric risk framework to account for the rise in CPS devices across enterprise networks. It relies on a heuristics based approach rather than a secure baseline to provide an initial level of security, and over time creates an operational baseline. Extensive future development is required before fielding on a large network [13].

S. Harmonized Threat & Risk Assessment (HTRA)

Published by the Canadian Government, HTRA provides a risk management framework which expounds rapid adjustments to account for quickly evolving threat terrain, but still implements a traditional secure baseline structure. HTRA suffers from the same pitfalls of most large frameworks in that the size of the network often determines how effectively the model is implemented [17].

T. System-Fault Risk (SFR)

The qualitative framework created by Ye accounts for several layers of interconnection by creating multiple attack origin classification models. It is modular and capable of extension into nearly any device that operates on a network, but at extreme cost. It is not primarily intended to be used as a full enterprise solution [37].

U. Hierarchical Model Based Risk Assessment

Baiardi introduces a framework based on security dependency hypergraphs which have the capability to identify attack paths which an analyst may miss in a qualitative assessment. Tools for basic implementation were developed but not widely tested in a live network [7].

V. Patel & Ziveri Model

The model is a quantitative system which depends on predetermined types of attacks and devices. Additional research would be required in order to account for anything outside of the current scope of the model. It is presently designed for implementation in SCADA networks, and does not account well for IoT or any attack that is not within the matrix [25].

W. IBM Security Framework

The IBM security blueprint stovepipes security into domains which are broken down further into distinct objectives and services. Each sub-domain is then to be implemented according to industry best practices [8]. An update in 2014 showed successful results in several live networks [9].

X. Information Security Risk Analysis Method (ISRAM)

ISRAM is an attempt to bridge the gap between the overwhelming challenge of implementing a quantitative model on a complex network and the inconsistencies of a qualitative model. While sound in theory, the product still suffers from the extensibility issues faces by quantitative models [20].

Y. Amin Cyber-Physical Security (CPS) Model

Amin attempts to create a quantitative framework to address the risks presented by cyber-phsyical systems on a network, but struggles to account for all components simultaneously in a large composite model [5].

Z. Cybernomics

Cybernomics is an attempt to incorporate cyber risk management and economic modeling to build a quantifiable framework which can be scaled to a larger enterprise network. It provides a more network centric portfolio, and in turn may be capable of providing sound IoT accountability. Live network testing is anticipated in a future publication [28].

III. METHODOLOGY

Four primary elements common to each framework are evaluated. This establishes a basic standard used to make comparisons, and highlights several key differences between otherwise similar methods. These attributes are mapped and graded to determine the level of efficacy provided. It is challenging to conduct a full pairwise comparison between any two models due to their inability to target IoT devices at all. Nearly all models surveyed neglected to take special measures towards securing IoT devices versus other enterprise components. This led to a largely qualitative analysis of the merits of each model, with models that have a particularly outstanding system being highlighted in Section IV.

A. Quantitative vs. Qualitative

Each framework surveyed was classified as either primarily qualitative, or quantitative. The constraints of the quantitative model are similar to the strengths of a qualitative model, and vice versa. Quantitative models often provide unparalleled modeling at the expense of scalability. In order to classify a framework as quantitative, it needed to exhibit device based calculations. Any framework which used only abstractions for a quantitative analysis was relegated to the qualitative category.

B. Level of Implementation

Models are assigned an implementation score of high, low, or N/A in order to account for the broad range of real-world testing frameworks have received. A framework with hundreds of implementations and years of feedback will have more data points to evaluate than a network which is conceptual or in its first live network test. Many surveyed frameworks that are recently published have not yet been employed in a significant capacity on a live network.

C. Age and Support Level

Risk assessment frameworks which no longer have a robust implementation or supporting entity may no longer be viable. It is important to consider that legacy models may no longer provide adequate security.

D. Overall Rating

The current standard for a risk assessment framework is a qualitative model which relies on robust security policy and patching processes alongside vulnerability scanning and security controls. These methods are suitable for securing a traditional enterprise network, but fall short when IoT devices are introduced. Any framework that meets, but does not have the potential to exceed this baseline is rated "Yellow". Yellow rated models are relatively good assessments of cyber risk, but do not manage IoT devices well. Any framework which is unable to achieve the same level of network protection as the current generation of frameworks are rated "Red". Models which have made a meaningful step towards properly accounting for IoT devices within enterprise networks will be rated "Green". The rating of green does not mean that they have fully accounted for IoT devices, but that it is an advancement over most currently implemented models.

IV. Analysis of Risk Assessment Frameworks

TABLE 1. RISK FRAMEWORK COMPARISON

Reviewed Framework	Framework Analysis		
	Rating	*Implementation*	*Year*
*Amin CPS Model [5]	Red	N/A	2013
†CAF [33]	Yellow	High	2018
†COBIT 5 [3] [34]	Yellow	High	2012
†CORAS [30]	Red	Low	2003
†CPSS [13]	Red	N/A	2015
*CRAMM [36]	Red	Low	2003
*CRISM [29]	Green	N/A	2018
*Cybernomics [28]	Green	N/A	2017
†HCS-IF [6]	Green	N/A	2014
†*Hierarchical Model [7]	Red	N/A	2009
†HTRA [17]	Yellow	High	2007
†IBM Framework [8]	Yellow	Low	2010
†IoT/M2M [14]	Green	N/A	2016
†ISO27K [3] [19]	Yellow	High	2005
*ISRAM [20]	Red	N/A	2005
†ISSM [1]	Green	N/A	2017
†ISSM [21]	Yellow	Low	2011
*Mobius [12]	Red	N/A	2002
†NIST [27]	Yellow	High	2015
*NSRM [18]	Red	N/A	2009
†OCTAVE [4]	Red	Low	2003
†OCTAVE-S [4]	Red	Low	2003
†OCTAVE-Allegro [10]	Red	Low	2007
†OSSF [24]	Green	N/A	2017
*Patel & Ziveri Model [25]	Red	N/A	2010
†SFR [37]	Red	N/A	2005
†*TARA (Intel) [26]	Yellow	Low	2009
†*TARA (MITRE) [35]	Yellow	Low	2011

†Indicates Qualitative *Indicates Quantitative

A. Common Framework Pitfalls

No surveyed model rated "green" for IoT advancement has been implemented in a live network. Similarly, all models rated "high" for implementation scored "yellow" in IoT advancement. This overwhelmingly indicates that the state of the art has not yet accounted for IoT properly, and no single framework can be recommended as an immediate solution to the IoT problem. The current model of a qualitative risk assessment may no longer be viable as IoT devices continue to become more critically integrated into networks. Each qualitative model surveyed attempts to use only existing resources to secure the IoT threat vector. In order to continue using existing risk models, it is necessary to either invest in new architecture to account for the largely unknown vulnerabilities presented by current off the shelf IoT systems, or incorporate only IoT systems which have been subjected to a much higher degree of security analysis. The current model of minimal support and small device marketshare footprint is unlikely to result in a solution to the IoT problem.

B. IoT Advancements

It is imperative that security development be proactive due to the increasingly vital role that IoT devices have in enterprise networks. Among the most promising proposed models is the zero trust approach in the IoT/M2M framework. Rather than attempt to impose enterprise security methods on IoT devices, it attempts to section them off as much as possible into other network segments. This is not a full solution, but it may prove more effective than current implementations. The frameworks that have the ability to accurately model risks to ICS and IoT systems primarily have implemented a quantitative risk assessment approach, but no solution has been able to provide cost-effective coverage to a larger network. The primary weakness to this solution is some devices will eventually have to have a trusted relationship, and this will lead to inevitable vulnerabilities. This method is at best a technique to shrink the attack surface of a network, and does not fully mitigate the risk of IoT devices.

C. Proposed Solutions

Two courses of action for securing IoT devices based on the analysis of the 28 frameworks surveyed are:

1) Short Term: Use network segmentation and a zero trust model: IoT devices cannot be considered trusted or secure by a risk analysis model until a more robust vulnerability assessment process can be developed. Designing network architecture to create the smallest foothold possible for compromised IoT devices may be an effective short term solution. Potential examples of this would be creating an IoT device Virtual Local Area Network (VLAN), De-Militarized Zone (DMZ), or using bastions as IoT interface servers. Similarly, isolating IoT devices from domain credentials and trust settings is also vital to ensuring that a vulnerable IoT device does minimized damage if exploited.

2) Long Term: Increase viability of quantifiable risk assessment frameworks with Machine Learning: Quantitative frameworks have demonstrated the highest level of potential risk analysis, but are not capable of modeling large networks in their present state. The next iteration of quantitative framework must solve this problem in order for them to become viable. This could be accomplished by using machine learning to implement their risk algorithm, and to develop the individual device profiles. This direction would require substantial resources to establish, but potentially yield lower operating costs. The threat profile and logical/physical location of a device would be inputted, and the risk profile of the network could be automatically adjusted to compensate for the addition. This system would also allow for very accurate projections of security level in proposed architecture developments, as well as software migrations and patching.

V. Conclusion and Future Work

The breakdown of findings shows significant shortcomings in all state of the art risk assessment frameworks. No developmental model was identified that could be considered deployment ready with capabilities clearly exceeding those of the current generation of qualitative system. Several proposed frameworks with the ability to incorporate both cyber-physical systems and enterprise architecture in a large scale network were reviewed, but none have been tested in a live environment. At this time, there is still a significant need for research on methods to incorporate IoT devices into enterprise networks without losing either accessibility or security. The scale and diversity of IoT has been insurmountable for qualitative models, but future research developing Proposed Solution 1). may yield significant advancements. A significant change in funding or ease of implementation will be necessary in order to drastically alter the current risk assessment terrain away from qualitative models. Minimal published research on the application of machine learning to cyber risk assessment was identified, but this avenue of research outlined in Proposed Solution 2). is one of the primary methods of making the quantitative model viable again.

ACKNOWLEDGMENT

Disclaimer: The views expressed in this paper are those of the author and do not necessarily reflect the official policy or position of the Air Force, the Department of Defense, or the U.S. Government.

REFERENCES

[1] S. Almuhammadi and M. Alsaleh, "Information Security Maturity Model for NIST Cyber Security Framework." Computer Science & Information Technology 51 2017.

[2] M. Ahlmeyer and A. M. Chircu, "Securing the Internet of Things: A review." Issues in Information Systems, vol. 17, no. 4, 2016.

[3] W. Al-Ahmad and B. Mohammad, "Can a Single Security Framework Address Information Security Risks Adequately." International Journal of Digital Information and Wireless Communications, vol. 2, no. 3, pp. 222-230, 2012.

[4] C. Alberts, A. Dorofee, and J. Stevens, "Introduction to the OCTAVE Approach." Carnegie-Mellon Univ. Software Engineering Inst, 2003.

[5] S. Amin, G. A. Schwartz, and A. Hussain, "In Quest of Benchmarking Security Risks to Cyber-Physical Systems." IEEE Network, vol. 27, no. 1, pp. 19-24, 2013.

[6] I. Atoum, A. Otoom, and A. A. Ali, "A Holistic Cyber Security Implementation framework." Information Management & Computer Security, vol. 22, no. 3, pp. 251-264, 2014.

[7] F. Baiardi, C. Telmon, and D. Sgandurra, Hierarchical, Model-Based Risk Management of Critical Infrastructures, Reliability Engineering & System Safety, vol. 94, no. 9, pp. 1403-1415, 2009.

[8] A. Buecker, M. Borrett, C. Lorenz, and C. Powers, "Introducing the IBM security Framework and IBM Security Blueprint to Realize Business-Driven Security." IBM Redpaper 4528, no. 1, pp. 1-96, 2010.

[9] A. Buecker, S. Arunkumar, B. Blackshaw, M. Borrett, P. Brittenham, J. Flegr, and J. Jacobs, "Using the IBM Security Framework and IBM Security Blueprint to Realize Business-Driven Security." IBM Redbooks, 2014.

[10] R. Caralli, J. Stevens, L. Young, and W. R. Wilson, "Introducing Octave Allegro: Improving the Information Security Risk Assessment Process. No. CMU/SEI-2007-TR-012. Carnegie-Mellon Univ. Pittsburgh PA Software Engineering Inst, 2007.

[11] J. Cebula and L. R. Young, "A Taxonomy of Operational Cyber Security Risks." Carnegie-Mellon Univ. Pittsburgh PA Software Engineering Inst, No. CMU/SEI-2010-TN-028, 2010.

[12] D. D. Deavours, G. Clark, T. Courtney, and D. Daly, "The Mobius framework and its Implementation." IEEE Transactions on Software Engineering, vol. 28, no. 10, pp. 956-969, 2002.

[13] D. DiMase, Z. A. Collier, K. Heffner, and I. Linkov, "Systems Engineering Framework for Cyber Physical Security and Resilience." Environment Systems and Decisions, vol. 35, no. 2, pp. 291-300, 2015.

[14] J. Frahim, "Cisco: Securing the Internet of Things: A Proposed Framework." 2016.

[15] C. Fruhwirth and T. Mannisto. "Improving CVSS-Based Vulnerability Prioritization and Response with Context Information." Proceedings of the 2009 3rd international Symposium on Empirical Software Engineering and Measurement, IEEE Computer Society, 2009.

[16] G. Giannopoulos, R. Filippini, and M. Schimmer, "Risk Assessment Methodologies for Critical Infrastructure Protection. Part I: A state of the art." JRC Technical Notes, 2012

[17] Government of Canada, "Harmonized Threat and Risk Assessment Methodology" Ottawa, 2007. Accessed Sep. 11, 2019

[18] M. H. Henry and Y. Y. Haimes. "A Comprehensive Network Security Risk Model for Process Control Networks." Risk Analysis: An International Journal, vol. 29, no. 2, pp. 223-248, 2009.

[19] T. Humphreys, "State-of-the-Art Information Security Management Systems with ISO/IEC 27001: 2005." ISO Management Systems, vol. 6, no. 1, 2006.

[20] B. Karabacak and I. Sogukpinar, "ISRAM: Information Security Risk Analysis Method." Computers & Security, vol. 24, no. 2, pp. 147-159, 2005.

[21] G. Karokola, S. Kowalski, and L. Yngstrm, "Towards An Information Security Maturity Model for Secure e-Government Services: A Stakeholders View." In HAISA, pp. 58-73, 2011.

[22] J. Lainhart, "Introducing COBIT 2019: The Motivation for the Update?" ISACA Webinar Blog Post, 2018. Accessed Sep. 9, 2019.

[23] M. S. Lund, B. Solhaug, and K. Stlen. "A Guided Tour of the CORAS Method. In Model-Driven Risk Analysis" Springer, Berlin, pp. 23-43, 2011.

[24] J. Meszaros and A. Buchalcevova. "Introducing OSSF: A Framework for Online Service Cybersecurity Risk Management." Computers & Security, vol. 65, pp. 300-313, 2017.

[25] S. Patel and J. Zaveri. "A Risk-Assessment Model for Cyber Attacks on Information Systems." Journal of Computers, vol. 5, no. 3, pp. 352-359, 2010.

[26] M. Rosenquist, Prioritizing Information Security Risks with Threat Agent Risk Assessment Intel, 2009.

[27] R. Ross, "Guide for Applying the Risk Management Framework to Federal Information Systems" NIST, SP 800-37, Revision 1, 2010.

[28] K. Ruan, "Introducing Cybernomics: A Unifying Economic Framework for Measuring Cyber Risk." Computers & Security, vol. 65, pp. 77-89, 2017.

[29] S. Shetty, M. McShane, L. Zhang, and J.P. Kesan, "Reducing Informational Disadvantages to Improve Cyber Risk Management." The Geneva Papers on Risk and Insurance-Issues and Practice, vol. 43, no. 2, pp. 224-238, 2018.

[30] K. Stolen, F. den Braber, T. Dimitrakos, and R. Fredriksen, "Model-Based Risk Assessment: The CORAS Approach." iTrust Workshop, 2002.

[31] T. Kevin. "Introducing the Cyber Assessment Framework v2.0" NSCS Blog Post, 2018. Accessed Sep. 9, 2019.

[32] U.S. Government Accountability Office INTERNET OF THINGS: Enhanced Assessments and Guidance Are Needed to Address Security Risks in DOD Publication No. GAO-17-668, 2017.

[33] U.K. National Cyber Security Centre "Cyber Assessment Framework" Accessed sep. 9, 2019.

[34] K. V. Wal, J. Lainhart, and P. Tessin, "A COBIT 5 overview." ISACA Webinar Program, 2012.

[35] J. Wynn, J. Whitmore, G. Upton, L. Spriggs, and D. McKinnon, "Threat assessment & Remediation Analysis (TARA): Methodology" MITRE CORP BEDFORD MA, ver. 1.0, No. MTR110176, 2011.

[36] Z. Yazar, "A Qualitative Risk Analysis & Management Tool: CRAMM." SANS InfoSec Reading Room, White Paper 11, 2002.

[37] N. Ye, C. Newman, and T. Farley. "A System-Fault-Risk Framework for Cyber Attack Classification." Information Knowledge Systems Management, vol. 5, no. 2, pp. 135-151, 2005.